DATE DUE

Diasporas in conflict

D0732769

Diasporas in conflict: Peace-makers or peace-wreckers?

Edited by Hazel Smith and Paul Stares

United Nations
University Press

TOKYO · NEW YORK · PARIS

© United Nations University, 2007

The views expressed in this publication are those of the authors and do not necessarily reflect the views of the United Nations University.

United Nations University Press
United Nations University, 53-70, Jingumae 5-chome,
Shibuya-ku, Tokyo 150-8925, Japan
Tel: +81-3-3499-2811   Fax: +81-3-3406-7345
E-mail: sales@hq.unu.edu   general enquiries: press@hq.unu.edu
http://www.unu.edu

United Nations University Office at the United Nations, New York
2 United Nations Plaza, Room DC2-2062, New York, NY 10017, USA
Tel: +1-212-963-6387   Fax: +1-212-371-9454
E-mail: unuona@ony.unu.edu

United Nations University Press is the publishing division of the United Nations University.

Cover design by Mea Rhee

Printed in Hong Kong

ISBN 978-92-808-1140-7

Library of Congress Cataloging-in-Publication Data

Diasporas in conflict : peace-makers or peace-wreckers? / edited by Hazel Smith and Paul Stares.
     p.   cm.
  Includes bibliographical references and index.
  ISBN 978-9280811407 (pbk.)
  1. Emigration and immigration—Political aspects—Case studies.
2. Immigrants—Political activity—Case studies. 3. Conflict management—
Case studies. 4. World politics—Case studies. I. Smith, Hazel, 1954–
II. Stares, Paul B.
JV6255.D53   2007
304.8—dc22   2007002607

Contents

Figures and tables

Preface

Diasporas matter in international conflict. That is the premise of this book and the basis upon which the research project that resulted in this book was conceived. The work was jointly undertaken by the United Nations University and the United States Institute of Peace after both institutions had independently begun to identify this under-studied topic as a potentially fruitful area of empirical and policy-relevant research.

Our contributors, all distinguished scholars of diasporas, were each asked, not to produce new research on the diaspora per se, but to use their knowledge to think about diaspora intervention in international conflict. Our aim was to use case-study comparison to offer some tentative conclusions about the role, function and potential of diasporas in future conflicts. Contributors were therefore asked to write a case study that considered how a specific diaspora intervened in a specific international conflict. Crudely speaking, the question asked of our contributors was: "Was the particular diaspora you studied a peace-wrecker or a peace-maker?"

The majority of the contributors met, most for the first time, in a research workshop in Macau in September 2004, to discuss their draft chapters. After a two-day vigorous exchange of views, contributors returned home to re-write their chapters. The outcome is this book, which argues that diasporas can be both peace-wreckers and peace-makers, sometimes at one and the same time. The question for policy-makers is, then, how to channel the positive contributions of diasporas so as to support conflict resolution and also how to mitigate the impact of negative interventions by diasporas in conflict.

We would like to thank all at United Nations University (UNU) in Tokyo and Macau and the United States Institute of Peace (USIP) in Washington, DC, who contributed to the project. We are particularly grateful to Yoshie Sawada in Tokyo and to Elise Murphy at USIP who between them organized the vast majority of the administrative work without which this book would not have been possible. We also thank our contributors, who gave their time, energy and intellectual efforts to make this volume possible.

Hazel Smith and Paul Stares

List of contributors

Nadje S. Al-Ali is Senior Lecturer in Social Anthropology at the Institute of Arab & Islamic Studies at the University of Exeter, UK. She is specialized in gendered aspects of transnational migration and diaspora mobilization. Her publications include *Secularism, Gender and the State in the Middle East* (Cambridge University Press, 2000) and, as editor, *New Approaches to Migration* (Routledge, 2002).

Mohammed A. Bamyeh is currently the Hubert Humphrey Professor of International Studies at Macalester College in Minnesota, USA. He is a former SSRC-MacArthur Fellow in International Peace and Security, and has previously taught at Georgetown University, New York University, SUNY-Buffalo, and the University of Massachusetts, USA. He received his PhD in sociology from the University of Wisconsin-Madison in 1990. He has written many scholarly articles and his books include *The Ends of Globalization* (University of Minnesota Press, 2000), *The Social Origins of Islam* (University of Minnesota Press, 1999), and the edited special issue *Palestine America* (*South Atlantic Quarterly*, 2003).

Jacob Bercovitch is Professor of International Relations at the University of Canterbury in Christchurch, New Zealand. His current research interests include conflict resolution and international mediation. He is the author and editor of 10 books and numerous scientific papers, which have appeared in all the main journals.

Virginia M. Bouvier is Senior Program Officer at the United States Institute of Peace, Washington, DC, USA. She is editor of *The Globalization of U.S.-Latin American Relations* (Praeger Publishers, 2002), was previously on the faculty at the University of Maryland, USA, and holds her PhD in Latin American Studies from the University of California at Berkeley, USA.

C. Christine Fair is Senior Research Associate at the United States Institute of Peace, Washington, DC, USA, specializing in South Asian political and military affairs. Prior to joining USIP, she was a political scientist at RAND. Fair has an MA in Public Policy and a PhD in South Asian Languages and Civilizations, both from the University of Chicago, USA.

Jean Grugel is Professor in the Department of Politics, University of Sheffield, UK. She has written widely on Latin American political economy and processes of democratization. She is currently working on global governance, transnational activism and children's rights and the comparative political economy of governance after economic crisis.

Henry Kippin is a postgraduate student in the Department of Politics, University of Sheffield, UK. He is working on the political economy of development.

Khalid Koser is Deputy Director of the Brookings-Bern Project on Internal Displacement, The Brookings Institution, Washington, DC, USA. Previously he was Senior Policy Analyst at the Global Commission on International Migration and Lecturer in Human Geography at University College London, UK.

Denise Natali is Honorary Fellow at the Institute for Arab and Islamic Studies, Exeter University, UK. She is currently teaching at the Department of Politics, University of Kurdistan, Arbil, Kurdistan Region of Iraq, and is a fellowship recipient of the American Academic Research Institute in Iraq (TAARI). Natali is the author of numerous publications on Kurdish nationalism and politics, including *The Kurds and the State: Evolving National Identity in Iraq, Turkey, and Iran* (Syracuse University Press, 2005) and *The Kurdish Quasi-State: Development and Dependency in Post-Gulf War Iraq* (Syracuse University Press, forthcoming).

Gabriel (Gabi) Sheffer is Professor in the Political Science department, the Hebrew University of Jerusalem, Israel, and Senior Fellow at the Jerusalem Van Leer Institute. Sheffer was previously Director of the Jerusalem Group for National Planning, the Jerusalem Van Leer Institute; Director of the Leonard Davis Institute for International Relations, the Hebrew University of Jerusalem; editor of *The Jerusalem Journal for International Relations*; Visiting Professor at Cornell University, University of Wisconsin-Madison, University of California, Berkeley, New South Wales University, Australia, University of Pittsburgh and University of Maryland; and Fellow of the Woodrow Wilson Institute, Washington, DC.

Zlatko Skrbiš is Senior Lecturer in Sociology and Director of Postgraduate Studies in the School of Social Science, University of Queensland, Australia. Prior to this appointment he was Lecturer at the

Queensland University of Technology. His publications include *Long-Distance Nationalism* (Ashgate Publishing, 1999) and *Constructing Singapore* (with Michael Barr, NIAS Press, forthcoming 2006).

Hazel Smith is Professor of International Relations at the University of Warwick, UK. Smith's recent books include *Hungry for Peace: International Security, Humanitarian Assistance and Social Change in North Korea* (United States Institute of Peace Press, 2005) and the edited volume (with Larry Minear) *Humanitarian Diplomacy: Practitioners and Their Craft* (United Nations University Press, 2007).

Paul Stares is Vice President of the United States Institute of Peace, Washington, DC, USA, and Director of its Center for Conflict Analysis and Prevention. Prior to joining USIP in 2002, Stares was Associate Director and Senior Research Scholar at the Center for International Security and Cooperation at Stanford University, USA.

Khachig Tölölyan is Professor of Humanities at the Department of English and the College of Letters at Wesleyan University in Middletown, CT, USA. He founded and edits *Diaspora: A Journal of Transnational Studies*. He writes in English and Armenian on theories of diaspora and on the Armenian diaspora. His earlier work dealt with terrorism, the modern novel and cultural theory.

Khatharya Um is a political scientist and Associate Professor and Chair of Asian American Studies at the University of California, Berkeley, USA. Her research interests include international migration, diaspora studies and human security. She has written extensively on politics and developments in Southeast Asia and refugee communities.

Part I

The analytical and conceptual framework

1

Diasporas in international conflict

Hazel Smith

The study of diasporas in conflict reflects an urgent international social problem. The capacity of some diasporas to secure tangible and intangible resources in support of armed conflicts, the often opaque institutional and network structures that can allow for transnational transfers of arms and money to state and non-state actors, including terrorist groups, as well as to more deserving causes (for instance as humanitarian assistance), along with rapid transnational communication, mean that, in the era of globalization, diasporas have been reconstructed as new and potentially powerful actors in international politics.

A large body of excellent scholarship has investigated the notion of diaspora, not least that by many contributors to this book, including Nadje Al-Ali, Khalid Koser, Gabriel Sheffer, Zlatko Skrbiš and Khachig Tölölyan.[1] Others who have made seminal contributions include, for instance, Avtar Brah, Robin Cohen and William Safran.[2] There is less research explicitly on the role of diasporas in conflict, with major exceptions being the work of Yossi Shain and of Paul Collier and his colleagues at the World Bank.[3] This book is intended to supplement this latter literature by offering a comparative study of diasporas in international conflict, informed by an explicit analytical and conceptual framework, which is set out in Chapters 2 and 3, and based on detailed empirical case studies.

Theoretically, the book invades the discipline of political science and international relations and establishes a conflict resolution analytical framework. Conceptually, the book supports the view that it is dif-

Diasporas in conflict: Peace-makers or peace-wreckers?, Smith and Stares
(eds), United Nations University Press, 2007, ISBN 978-92-808-1140-7

ficult to offer an unproblematic shared understanding of the concept of diaspora but also takes as a premise that there is enough commonality of understanding of the concept that a comparative investigation of patterns of diaspora interventions in conflicts makes sense. The key empirical research question that contributors were asked to respond to was: "In the case of a specific conflict, how did the diaspora respond? Were they peace-wreckers or peace-makers?"

This volume has three core objectives. These are normative, empirical and policy related. The normative objective is to find ways to encourage peaceful resolution to conflicts through the active and positive intervention of diasporas and to discourage intervention that fuels conflicts. The empirical objective is to chart and analyse diaspora interventions in conflict and to see if any cautious generalizations may be made about such interventions. The policy objective is to identify leverage points in the different stages of conflict such that constructive interventions by diasporas may be encouraged and destructive interventions discouraged.

The theoretical framework

This book investigates the diverse roles of diasporas in different phases of what conflict resolution theorists sometimes call the "conflict cycle", as outlined by Jacob Bercovitch in Chapter 2 of this book.[4] The book therefore starts with an explicit conflict cycle framework that incorporates analytically separate but practically related normative, conceptual, empirical and policy lenses.

Contributors to the volume also attempt definitional tasks to allow for taxonomies of diasporas and diasporic activity in conflict. Sheffer, for instance, whose work is cited by a number of our contributors and who also writes in this volume in Chapter 4 on the Jewish Diaspora, refers to a fundamental difference between state-linked and stateless diasporas. He identifies the development of diasporas as historical phenomena – arguing for three historical waves of diasporic formation. These are the "historical" diasporas, formed in pre-modern times; the "new" diasporas, formed since the industrial revolution; and, lastly, the "incipient ethnonational" diasporas – those of very recent origin. Sheffer further argues that a fruitful way to frame the analysis of diaspora activity "at home abroad" is to conceive of the "diaspora profile". This includes identification patterns, strategies towards host counties, organizational activities and transnational activities.

The conceptual framework

The conceptual foundation more or less assumes that diasporas are social groups that (i) settle and establish themselves in another country and (ii) are internally heterogeneous. Different parts of the same diaspora can and do have different interests, defined among other things by class, gender, generation, occupation or religion. Diasporas are rarely constituted by a single factor other than the broadest of connections to a specific homeland. Diasporas are not, for instance, defined by their religion. The Palestinian diaspora provides a good example of where one marker of difference is that between Christian and Muslim.

Diasporas involve a complex of always shifting power relations. Change in relations of power within diasporas, and the way these changes intersect with external configurations of power, provide much of the conceptual framework for this book. Although this book is multidisciplinary, it nevertheless adopts a political science perspective, which is essentially concerned with "who gets what, where, when and how and who is advantaged and disadvantaged in this process" – the classic questions of political analysis. We assume that the outcomes of shifting power relations are consequential in answering these questions.

We also assume that the nature of diaspora intervention in conflict is a result of the respective power relations within diasporas and between diaspora, home and host country. Diasporas intervene in conflict because they can. Diasporas without access to power of some sort, whether direct or surrogate, do not intervene in conflicts.

The gender dimension

Given that our approach views diaspora as non-homogeneous and as constituted by unequal relations of power within and between itself and other social groups, and that significant axes of power inequality can be class, gender, ethnicity and religion, the next research question must be when and why these differential power relations matter in conflict. Our generic response is that they all matter at different times in different conflicts. More specifically, however, the book draws on the growing body of scholarly research and empirical evidence from humanitarian organizations that women suffer disproportionately in conflict because of the gendered nature of social relations that universally allocate caring or nurturing responsibilities and roles to women.

None of our contributors takes the simplistic view that women suffer more than men in all circumstances in all conflicts. Instead our approach is that men and women, boys and girls experience conflict differently owing to the pervasive nature and strength of socially constructed gendered roles in any society. In Chapter 3 of this book, Nadje Al-Ali, following the conflict cycle framework established by Bercovitch in Chapter 2, shows that gender matters at every stage of conflict – whether this be pre-conflict and pre-escalatory phases, acute conflict and war, or peacemaking and post-conflict reconstruction.[5] All women and men directly experience conflict through a gendered prism. This gendered patterning of human and social behaviour in conflict affects women's and men's lives.

Al-Ali emphasizes, however, that gendered patterns of social relations do not result in a "uni-dimensional" experience of conflict for women and men. Women are not always victims; sometimes they are perpetrators of violence and sometimes agents of peace. Women may be relatively more vulnerable in times of war but, conversely, the rupture to societal norms, which is often caused by war, may also open up new possibilities for women to participate in public and political life. Nor does gender ever matter on its own. Al-Ali insists that gender is only one aspect of power hierarchies within social relations, "and does not necessarily constitute the most significant factor". Social relations are also built around, for instance, "economic class, ethnic and religious differentiation, sexual orientation and political affiliation".

Paying attention to the diverse social constitution of diasporas, including the gendered differentiations, does more than remind us of the differing experiences of women and men in conflict. As Al-Ali points out, it is also a powerful reminder that diasporas are heterogeneous entities. Politically this has the significant consequence of forcing a rethink of who should represent diasporas, perhaps helping, Al-Ali argues, "to shift away from the tendency to portray elder male political leaders as representative of the communities' views, politics and aspirations".

The 10 case studies that comprise the remainder of the book build on the theoretical and conceptual framework established in the preceding chapters to investigate the central research question – are diasporas peacewreckers or peace-makers?

Space precludes an investigation of each and every diaspora and all activities in every conflict, although some attempt is made to provide a representative range of cases from Africa, Asia, Europe and the Middle East. Similarly, the case studies address diasporic activity at varying stages of the conflict cycle, depending on the diaspora input to the particular conflict.

Diaspora involvement in enduring or long-lasting conflicts as well as in conflicts of more recent origin is evaluated. In Chapter 4, Gabriel Sheffer examines what for some is the paradigmatic diaspora, that of the Jews, in the context of the Arab–Palestinian–Israeli conflict. In Chapter 6, Khachig Tölölyan also analyses an "old" diaspora – that of the Armenians, in the context of the Karabagh conflict between Armenians and the state of Azerbaijan. By contrast, in Chapter 5, Mohammed Bamyeh evaluates the relatively "new" Palestinian diaspora, formed in the wake of the 1948 refugee movements of Palestinians from what is now the state of Israel, in the context of the continuing Palestinian–Israeli conflict.

The remaining case studies, of Colombians, Cubans, Sri Lankan Tamils, Kurds, Croats, Eritreans and Cambodians, are of diasporic intervention in conflicts that began well before the post–Cold War period. The major exception is the Colombian conflict, in which the violence has developed exponentially in the post–Cold War period. Nevertheless, Virginia Bouvier points out in Chapter 7 that the roots of the conflict, which engages the government, the military, left-wing military groups and right-wing paramilitaries, lie in the guerrilla warfare against the state that began in the 1960s.

The Cold War origins of conflict between Fidel Castro's Communist, pro-Soviet Cuba and the United States, the leader of the capitalist and democratic world camp, are evaluated by Jean Grugel and Henry Kippin. They argue in Chapter 8 that relations between the two and, by extension, the Cuban diaspora in the United States have been frozen "in an outmoded Cold War mould". By contrast, C. Christine Fair, analysing the Sri Lankan Tamil diaspora in Chapter 9, explicitly claims that the "origins and continuation" of the Sri Lankan conflict are "exogenous to the dynamics of the Cold War and its demise". Fair goes on to argue that, if any international event shaped Sri Lankan Tamil diaspora involvement in the conflict, it was the terrorist attacks on New York's Twin Towers on 11 September 2001. The diaspora did not want to be associated with anything that could be called "terrorist" and thus began to dissociate itself from Tamil Tiger activity in Sri Lanka. In other words, the international "political opportunity structure" changed in 2001, and the separation of the diaspora from the insurgents became more likely and more feasible.[6]

Denise Natali in Chapter 10 also makes use of the idea of "political opportunity structure" as an analytical framework to investigate the involvement of the Kurdish diaspora in the Iraq conflict from 1998 onwards.[7] Natali points to the Kurdish diaspora's differentiated opportunities arising from its different states and political systems – Iraq, Turkey, Iran and Syria – and from its dispersal in Europe, the United States, Canada, Australia, Israel and Greece. The Kurdish diaspora, Natali finds, was both peace-maker and peace-wrecker. Natali shows that here were "varying diasporic roles during different periods of the conflict cycle, some of which supported peace-making and some of which encouraged conflict".

The Kurdish diaspora came tantalizingly close to achieving, at least partially, its goal of a political community, if not a state, that it could call its own in northern Iraq in the aftermath of the 1990/1991 Gulf war. The Croatian diaspora, in contrast, achieved what many of its members had previously only dreamt about – the establishment of a fully fledged, internationally recognized sovereign state in the early 1990s. Zlatko Skrbiš evaluates the Croat experience in Chapter 11, demonstrating among other things that, although not as "old" a diaspora as the Kurdish one, Croatian aspirations for statehood were of long duration. Again similarly to the Kurdish experience, it was the international political opportunity structure that provided the possibilities for diaspora intervention in support of those aspirations. In the case of the Kurds, the two wars in Iraq, in 1991 and in 2003, provided the opening for the diaspora to intervene in support of the struggle to achieve an independent sovereign state; in the case of Croatia, it was the end of the Cold War that provided this opening.

Natali and Skrbiš argue respectively that Kurds and Croats were both peace-wreckers and, at different times, contributors to peace-building. Both also argue that the type of diaspora intervention was shaped by the political opportunity structure, including, more particularly (according to Skrbiš), the way in which the diaspora itself had been constituted through historical experience. Understanding the historical interests, aspirations and efforts of the diaspora and its organizational structures helps in understanding whether and in what circumstances diasporas might enter into conflicts as either peace-wreckers or peace-makers or as neither.

Khalid Koser, in his discussion of the Eritrean diaspora in Chapter 12, reiterates the point that diasporas can be both peace-wreckers and peace-makers but argues strongly that the positive side of diaspora intervention in conflict has been little told.[8] To this end his chapter seeks to redress the balance. Koser shows that the Eritrean diaspora made positive contributions to reconstruction after conflict, "not once but twice", in the aftermath of independence and of the conflict with Ethiopia. Koser charts these contributions schematically in terms of economic, political, social and cultural activities, which have both a home and a host country focus. This useful schema could well be used to analyse diaspora involvement in other post-war reconstruction efforts and thus extend our analytical capacities for understanding what diasporas may or may not do in the aftermath of conflict.

In our final chapter, Khatharya Um evaluates the activities of a comparatively very recent diaspora, the Cambodians, which was largely generated out of the most savage of conflicts in the 1970s when over 1 million people died in Cambodia and half a million became refugees. Um reinforces the message of all the contributors to this volume that diasporic intervention in the "home" country and the form that it takes are constrained and shaped by the opportunities available in host countries and in the transnational spaces in which they operate. Um insists that the "ability of diasporas to engage in homeland politics thus depends not only on their desire and intrinsic capabilities but also on the *opportunity* to do so" (emphasis in the original). Um, like Natali and Skrbiš among others, discusses the phenomenon of diasporic involvement in post-conflict governments. Incidentally, Um points out the high-profile role of diaspora women in the Cambodian government. Um's conclusions echo those of all the case-study contributors. Diasporic involvement in conflict still needs to be studied but what can be said is that diasporas play "significant and varied roles" in the whole range of activities in the conflict cycle.

Peace-wreckers, peace-makers or neither?

The case-study contributors have produced a number of rich empirical and analytical findings. Some of these are case-study specific but, perhaps somewhat surprisingly, many of the analytical and conceptual conclusions are shared. Some of these findings have already been alluded to above, but perhaps the most significant, and worth reiterating, is that diasporas play varied roles in conflict; and different groups and individuals within the same diaspora may have different approaches, organizations, interests and objectives within the same conflict. Even where a diaspora is more united on objectives, it may play a positive role in peace-making but also may play a negative role in terms of a contribution to continued conflict. Whether a diaspora will play either or none of those roles can best be understood, according to our contributors, by tracing not just the capacities of the diaspora (agency) but also the transnational opportunities available to it (structure).

In the rest of this section I summarize the findings of this research in a more schematic manner and look at the policy implications. The chapter closes by identifying areas that could be fruitful for further research.

The findings

- Perhaps the first finding of all the contributors to this volume is that "history counts". From Cambodia to Croatia, Palestine to Israel, and Eritrea to Armenia, evaluating the historical context enables both analyst and policy-maker to understand the interests, aspirations, institutions and objectives of diasporic communities as actors in international conflict.

- C. Christine Fair, Denise Natali and Khatharya Um, in their studies of, respectively, the Tamils in the Sri Lankan conflict, the Kurds in the Iraq conflict and the Cambodians in conflict and post-conflict reconstruction, explicitly remind us that history certainly counts – but it counts in very specific ways. Diasporas are agents but specific and empirically observable "political opportunity structures" provide both constraints and opportunities that shape what diasporas can and cannot do in each stage of the conflict cycle.
- Diasporas can be both peace-makers and peace-wreckers in conflict and, significantly, can choose to play neither role. Khalid Koser, for instance, argues strongly that the Eritrean diaspora plays a positive role in the conflict cycle. Given its ongoing substantial contributions to the reconstruction of its homeland, it is a peace-maker. In fact, it is hard to find from this research an example of a diaspora in conflict that has been a thorough-going peace-wrecker. All arguably want peace – the major question is, on what terms. The radical Croatian independence movement located in the diaspora may come nearest to the crude conceptualization of "peace-wrecker" if the criterion used is that of acting as fund-raiser for the purchase of arms on international illegal markets. As Zlatko Skrbiš points out, however, even the radical elements wanted peace – but peace with independence, not peace per se. By contrast, Virginia Bouvier finds that members of the Colombian diaspora in the United States by and large do not want to be associated with the Colombian conflict – believing that such an association threatens the stability of the life they are building in the United States and as transnational agents between Colombia and the United States.
- Owing partly to the very opportunity structures identified in our second finding, a diaspora can be both peace-maker and peace-wrecker in the same conflict at different periods. In other words, diaspora involvement can be both positive and negative in the same conflict.
- Because of the heterogeneity of diasporas, diaspora individuals and organizations can play contradictory roles, some contributing to conflict and others contributing to peace. Jean Grugel and Henry Kippin, for example, find that, whereas the dominant factions in the Cuban diaspora in the United States have maintained a highly conflictual approach to Castro's Cuba, there are indications that a younger generation would welcome a more pragmatic approach to the conflict.
- A surprise finding was that diasporic activity was not significantly influenced by whether or not Cold War or post–Cold War conditions applied – except as the most distant of background factors. The demise of the Soviet Union and the change in the international landscape from bipolarity, characterized by rivalry between the former Soviet Union and the United States, to a unipolar international system, led by the

United States, no doubt did allow for the emergence of "hot" conflicts in Croatia and Karabagh and for greater opportunities for the achievement of objectives in terms of the Kurdish diaspora. These case studies nevertheless indicate that the process and outcome of diasporic activity in post–Cold War conflict provided only one of a number of salient factors in the structure/agency matrix within which the activities of diasporas in conflict can be explained.

- We did not discover strong patterns of correlation of diasporic activity across the different stages of the conflict cycle. In other words, diasporas did not all participate in the same way in each specific phase of the conflict. In periods of hot conflict, for instance, the Sri Lankan Tamil diaspora, especially in the aftermath of the bombing of the Twin Towers in New York on 11 September 2001, and the Colombian diaspora were, broadly speaking, not supportive of armed struggles, whereas the Croatian diaspora actively raised funds for weapons and occasionally donated combat personnel.

- There are no predetermined patterns of diasporic activity in conflict. Those looking for a predictive theory of diasporic involvement in international conflict could be pointed in the direction of the transnational political opportunity structures identified by a number of our contributors as affecting the transnational political organization of the diaspora. Analysis of the political opportunities available in the "host" country and the international normative environment that supports or condemns diasporic activity in a particular conflict could help build a model of diasporic opportunity in conflict. Whether this would be a predictive model awaits further research.

- This research has conceptual implications. Drawing on her case study, Virginia Bouvier calls into question the presumption that diaspora Colombians in the United States primarily conceive of themselves in relation to Colombia as the "homeland". Bouvier goes on to raise doubts about whether the concept of "homeland" can withstand empirical evidence that indicates that the Colombian diaspora, and possibly other diasporas, can best be understood as primarily transnational, as opposed to national, subjects of international politics. Bouvier argues that, if this is the case, then the old frame of reference of sending/receiving countries also becomes questionable, perhaps even redundant and unhelpful for analysis.

Khatharya Um's research reinforces Bouvier's findings that the way in which the terms "host" and "home" country are used in the majority of scholarship evaluating transnational migration is unsatisfactory, in that it fails "fully to capture the nuances and complexity of the transnational experience" and can thus be misleading. "Home", she argues, is not a single fixed place for the Cambodian diasporic individual and neither is the "host" country a transitory place for most. Um criticizes the vantage point of the home/host dichotomy which connotes "a defined linearity ... from the point of exit to the point of re-incorporation".

Zlatko Skrbiš tackles the concept of peace itself. Skrbiš shows that for the Croatian diaspora the pursuit of peace was compatible with the purchase of illegal arms abroad to support Croatian belligerents in the Balkan wars of the 1990s. This is because peace, for diaspora Croats, meant peace with independence. Peace without independence was not conceived of as peace at all. For outside observers therefore, the Croatian diaspora could have been seen as a peace-wrecker, because of its fund-raising for illegal arms shipments. For the diaspora, such fund-raising meant support for a final peace, which was "achievable only through military victory"; it was "interested in victory that would bring peace rather than in peace per se".

- Finally, our contributors demonstrate that targeted policy interventions can make a difference to whether, and to what extent, diasporas play a positive or a negative role in conflict. Outcomes are not all accidental, despite the powerful shaping abilities of the political opportunity structures that both constrain and enable. Agency matters.

The right policy at the right time "both in origin and in destination countries", as Khalid Koser argues in his discussion of the Eritrean diaspora, is important. Natali's work on Kurdish involvement in the conflicts in Iraq supports the conclusion that host country policy matters in terms of diasporic propensity to contribute to peace or to become involved in aggravating tensions in order to perpetuate conflict. Natali's study builds a carefully substantiated argument that is worth reporting in its entirety because of its detailed analysis and its potentially useful foundation for host country policy guidelines towards diasporas involved in international conflict.

Stateless diasporic communities linked to legitimized leaders and organizations are more likely to pursue strategies based on negotiation than are diasporas de-legitimized in the international arena. Legitimate networks can serve the peaceful interests of their diasporas and homelands, whereas illegitimate ones can discourage peace-making. Second, diasporas are likely to act as peace-makers if engagement in homeland politics is perceived as identity-reinforcing and legitimate. The more inclusive the political system or proposed system, the more are diasporic activities channelled into that system and shaped accordingly, rather than taking place outside the system in more confrontational forms. Third, the higher the stakes for achieving nationalist claims in the war's outcome (nationalism legalized, statehood or autonomy), the more likely it is that interventions will support conflict resolution. Similarly, the lower the stakes (continuation of the status quo, loss of territorial sovereignty), the more likely it is that diasporas will refrain from negotiation or will engage in hostility.

Policy implications

The first policy recommendation is that specific analysis of specific diasporas at specific stages in specific conflicts needs to take place and that over-generalizations about what diasporas may or may not contribute to international conflicts are rarely helpful. Not all diasporas have the same capacities, opportunities or motivation to intervene in conflict and diasporas rarely are monolithic entities in terms of interests and objectives. Moreover, a diaspora may have different objectives at different stages of the conflict. For instance, the Croatian diaspora both funded armed conflict and, in the later stages of conflict, was active in support for peace-building once national independence had been achieved.

A second policy recommendation is that host states can change the opportunity structures available for diaspora contributions in such a way as to channel positive contributions to peace-making and to dissuade the negative contributions of peace-wreckers. Diaspora organizations and leadership that promote peace should be included in policy-making processes and those that support military activities should be penalized.

It can be argued that some diaspora organizations may be supporting military activities "in a good cause", perhaps with the objective of over-throwing dictatorships in their home countries. This is not a satisfactory reason to ignore fund-raising or propaganda activities by diasporas that support military actions abroad, however, because in well-ordered and democratic states it is the government's responsibility and prerogative alone to decide on military activities abroad. If a diaspora wishes to influence the policy choices of its host government in support of military activities in the homeland, the only acceptable avenue of influence should be through lobbying within the normal domestic process.

It would equally be a mistake to underestimate or to overestimate the potential contribution of diasporas in international conflict. Global policy-makers can be greatly assisted by diaspora communities in particular crucial phases of conflict, for instance in providing remittances in post-conflict reconstruction. Koser shows in his chapter on Eritrea for example that the Eritrean diaspora contributed substantially to nation-building after conflict. Each diaspora is different, however, and some diaspora individuals may simply wish to be allowed to carry on their new lives in the host country, away from the conflict from which they have escaped, as for instance Bouvier shows in the chapter on Colombia.

Another lesson is that in most cases the home country will need to exercise leadership and certainly coordination of diasporic activities. This would help avoid resentment by local populations of diasporic leaders "parachuting in" to tell those who have endured the suffering of war what to do from the safe confines of Western capitals. Home country governments will also wish to exert control over powerful diasporic groups with access to external resources, including access to governments in major capitals, in order to maintain the prerogatives of sovereign governments.

On the other hand, if diasporas are to contribute to peace processes, they will need passive or active support from host and home countries. If major powers want to encourage diasporas to engage productively in peace processes, they need to create the legislative framework to make that possible. This could be as simple as giving tax breaks on remittances for post-conflict reconstruction or facilitating access to relevant policy-makers in host countries.

A final lesson for global policy-makers is that major powers and international organizations cannot abrogate their own responsibilities to seek peace in long-lasting and intractable conflicts. Even the most dynamic diaspora is not equipped to resolve major conflicts on its own. Israeli and Palestinian diasporas are unlikely, for instance, to have much impact on the promotion of peace in the Middle East unless substantial intervention by the major powers provides some realistic hope that peace might be possible. In the meantime, these diasporas can contribute only marginally to positive initiatives, leaving a wide space for more negative contributions by sections of the diaspora that do not see room for compromise. For global policy-makers, the additional lesson therefore is that diasporas do not solve conflict on their own.

Further research

There is clearly more room for research on how, why, when and to what effect diasporas become involved in international conflict. This book investigates just 10 case studies but attempts to draw some qualified generalizations by using an analytical prism offered by Jacob Bercovitch's conflict cycle schema. This proved useful both to the contributors – as an organizing framework – and to the editors – helping to provide the foundation for some comparative analyses – but could certainly be developed to offer more systematic analysis of a larger number of cases. Future development of the schema could perhaps include Khalid Koser's taxonomic categorization of diasporic input in conflict. Such a schema would also benefit from having a specific analytical frame devoted to the differential activities of diasporic women and men in conflict.

On its own, however, the further development of schemata will not be enough to answer more fully the research questions in which we are interested. The non-glamorous, pedestrian but, it is hoped, rewarding task of more and better empirical work is still necessary to start building the foundations for more sophisticated inductive *and* deductive theories of diasporas in conflict. Induction may need facts on which to build its theoretical edifices but, equally importantly, deductivists need better facts so that their initial speculative hypotheses are bound by some level of "reality check".

This book has less to say on the "ethics" of diasporic involvement in conflict and the question of responsibility for conflict than on the empirics and the explanatory analysis of diasporic interventions. Mohammed Bamyeh in his discussion of the Palestinian diaspora in Chapter 5 is an important exception. Bamyeh raises some very difficult ethical issues concerning the allocation of responsibility for conflict as part of the process that is necessary to create sustainable peace. Bamyeh's contention is that South Africa's Truth and Reconciliation Commission is a useful example of opposing sides in the aftermath of a violent and divisive conflict being able to develop a common narrative of responsibility for historic injustice in order to provide the foundations for peace.

Ethical issues are also touched on to a certain extent by Skrbiš in his discussion of what sort of peace, and on what terms, is acceptable to diaspora groups. Although our volume does not come to large conclusions on these important and sensitive ethical issues, it does identify a role for further research to tackle the ethical imperatives of diasporas in peacemaking and peace-building. These include the ethical questions raised by a number of contributors in this book of whether or not diasporas should be engaged in conflicts in the "home" state at all. This is not simply a question for the host state government, which may discourage such involvement. Diasporic involvement in conflict sometimes causes irritation, even anger, back in the "home" country, especially if a diasporic community is wealthier and has access to international political connections that the homeland leaders do not.

Meeting normative, empirical and policy objectives

The normative objective of the book is to try to discover patterns of diasporic activity in conflict such as to support positive and discourage negative activities. In charting the empirical case studies and thus meeting our second objective, our contributors demonstrate that, although transnational political opportunity structures do indeed "shape and shove" diasporic activities, it is also true to say that diasporas are not powerless victims of circumstances. Diasporas have agency, however limited. This means that policy interventions can be designed to discourage peace-wrecking and encourage diasporic peace-making initiatives. These chapters show where that has been possible and also demonstrate to policy-makers of the future that it is worth paying attention to diasporas in conflict. They can be an enemy of efforts to end conflict – but they can also be a powerful ally in conflict resolution and sustainable peace-building.

Notes

1. Nadje Al-Ali and Khalid Koser, eds, *New Approaches to Migration: Transnational Communities and the Transformation of Home*, London: Routledge, 2002; Khalid Koser, ed., *New African Diasporas*, London: Routledge, 2003; Gabriel Sheffer, *Diaspora Politics: At Home Abroad*, Cambridge: Cambridge University Press, 2003; Zlatko Skrbiš, *Long-Distance Nationalism: Diasporas, Homelands and Identities*, Aldershot: Ashgate Publishing, 1999; Khachig Tölölyan, "Rethinking Diasporas: Stateless Power in the Transnational Moment", *Diaspora: A Journal of Transnational Studies*, 1996, 5(1): 3–36.
2. See, for example, Avtar Brah, *Cartographies of Diaspora, Contesting Identities*, London and New York: Routledge, 1996; Robin Cohen, *Global Diasporas: An Introduction*, Seattle: University of Washington Press, 1997; William Safran, "Comparing Diasporas: A Review Essay", *Diaspora*, 1999, 8(3): 255–292.
3. See, for example, Yossi Shain, "Marketing the American Creed Abroad: Diasporas in the Age of Multiculturalism", *Diaspora: A Journal of Transnational Studies*, 1994, 4(1): 85–111; Yossi Shain, "The Role of Diasporas in Conflict Perpetuation or Resolution", *SAIS Review*, 2002, 22(2): 116; Paul Collier and Anke Hoeffler, *Greed and Grievance in Civil War*, Washington, DC: World Bank, 2000.
4. See also Jacob Bercovitch, *Social Conflicts and Third Parties*, Boulder, CO: Westview Press, 1984.
5. For related work, see Al-Ali and Koser, eds, *New Approaches to Migration*.
6. Fair uses the concept of political opportunity structure to explain change in diaspora activity in conflict, as do a number of contributors to this volume. Fair cites Sarah Wayland's work as the inspiration for this approach. See Sarah Wayland, "Ethnonationalist Networks and Transnational Opportunities: The Sri Lankan Tamil Diaspora", *Review of International Studies*, 2004, 30: 405–426.
7. See also Denise Natali, *Manufacturing Identity and Managing Kurds in Iraq, Turkey, and Iran*, Syracuse: Syracuse University Press, 2005.
8. For other work by Khalid Koser on this subject, see Koser, ed., *New African Diasporas*.

2

A neglected relationship: Diasporas and conflict resolution

Jacob Bercovitch

Introduction

Conflicts have been part of our lives for as long as human beings have gathered together to pursue goals or resources they could not gain by themselves. There is nothing unusual or extraordinary about actors in conflict. It is normal for all political and social actors to experience conflict. Often conflicts help to transform relations or inappropriate structures into more receptive ones, but at times there is a tendency for conflict to escalate and become violent and destructive. Hence the interest in managing and resolving conflicts is really related to the desire to reduce or minimize the violent aspects of a conflict. Since the 1950s this interest has produced a veritable avalanche of books all seeking to understand and prescribe ways of how best to deal with conflicts. What all these studies had in common was the emphasis on the spatial and dyadic nature of conflict. Here I want to challenge this perspective and suggest that one of the major shifts in international relations in the past two decades or so has been the interpenetration of conflicts and spatiality by numerous outsiders, such as international organizations, refugees, non-governmental organizations (NGOs) and, most prominently, diasporas. Diasporas have become involved in numerous conflicts, in all parts of the world. At times their involvement contributes to conflict resolution, at other times their activities may well exacerbate an existing conflict.

This chapter aims to contribute to our understanding of the relationship between diasporas and conflict by looking at how conflict structure

Diasporas in conflict: Peace-makers or peace-wreckers?, Smith and Stares (eds), United Nations University Press, 2007, ISBN 978-92-808-1140-7

and conflict behaviour are affected by the presence or absence of diasporas. Little attention has been paid to diasporas – how they maintain their sense of identity and belonging while away from home and how they impact on the structure and behaviour of a conflict. My purpose here is to redress this anomaly and present diasporas as important political actors in their own right, with a decided impact on politics in general and on conflict behaviour in particular.

One of the main points to emphasize is that conflicts, in our globalized era, are rarely, if ever, a contest between two states or communal groups only.[1] Regional and international organizations, as well as diasporas and other organized communities, all have an interest in a given conflict and a strong desire to influence its course and possible resolution. The influence of these political entities on a conflict has been all but neglected in the scholarly literature. Thus, I propose to develop a conceptual framework to understand the nature of diasporas and how their identification with a home country may affect a conflict. In particular, I examine the various channels and mechanisms through which diasporas may influence the continuation or termination of a conflict. Subsequent chapters will look at specific cases where diasporas were involved in conflicts directly or indirectly; they will assess how exactly diasporas operated, and with what effects, and what conclusions may be drawn from their efforts. This, we hope, will provide us with a few relevant policy guidelines that may prove useful to decision-makers in conflict.

Diasporas

The term "diaspora" derives from the Greek word *diaspeirein*, meaning the dispersal or scattering of seeds.[2] The concept was originally used to refer to the dispersal of the Jews from their historical homeland. Today we speak of Koreans, Palestinians, Chinese, Kurds, Armenians, Mexicans, Tamils and numerous other groups as constituting the new diasporas. Indicative of the semantic malleability of the label "diaspora" is its appropriation by and application to a variety of vastly different ethno-cultural groups, many of which may bear little similarity to archetypal dispersed peoples, such as the Jews. Because the meaning and concept of diaspora may vary greatly, the issue of defining diaspora has been the subject of continual debate. A definition or a label confers status, and a group of people defined as a diaspora is a community of people embedded, through psychological and physical links, in a larger context or environment. What all diasporic communities have in common is that they settled outside their original or imagined territories, and they acknowledge that the old country has some claim on their loyalty, emotions and level of possible support. Here we define diasporic communities as transnational communities created as a result of the movement of peoples, living in one or more host countries, organized on the basis of solidarity, shared ideas and collective identities, and showing loyalty to, and affinity with, their host country as well as their original homeland.

A feature common to all diasporas is the attempt to maintain multiple levels of identity. This is usually accomplished through the establishment of "intricate support organisations" in the host country.[3] There are continual contacts and exchanges (financial, political, cultural and even military) with their homeland and their fellow diasporic groups in other host countries. Whereas "immigrant" connotes individuals who are trying to come to terms with a new society, "diaspora" acknowledges that communities settled outside their original territories maintain some level of ties with their place of origin. The conceptualization of diaspora used here entails three levels of relations: diaspora groups, their host states, and their original homeland states. Each of these relationships may unfold in different forms and give rise to different problems. Diasporas are not homogeneous groups. Each has its own pattern of relations and forms of identity with the host country and its original homeland, and each displays many generational, ideological and social differences.

Globalizing diasporas

One of the central forces in the modern world is the movement of people, either voluntarily or involuntarily. Approximately 175 million people – 2.9 per cent of the world population – live outside their birth country, and this number is increasing.[4] Globalization and the ease of transportation of people, movements and ideas have encouraged transnational systems and the diaspora phenomenon. Transnationalism is defined by Basch et al. as "the processes by which immigrants forge and sustain multi-stranded social relations that link together their societies of origin and settlement. We call these processes trans-nationalism to emphasize that many immigrants today build social fields that cross geographic, cultural and political borders."[5] It is arguable that the "processes of globalization have, among other things, led to the emergence of de-territorialized ethnicities". Accordingly, "ethnicity, once a genie contained in the bottle of some sort of locality (however large) has now become a global force, forever slipping in and through the cracks between states and borders".[6]

Globalization increases the opportunities for diaspora formation and has dramatically affected the potential influence of diasporas. The changes in technology, communication, modes of travel, the movement of ideas or the synchronization of cultures now make it easy for diasporas to build, nurture and sustain strong links with their homeland communities. Diasporas can utilize these changes to their best advantage. In its cultural dimension, globalization, driven by a technological revolution that has made communication instantaneous over large distances, breaks down the barriers of territorial identity, facilitating the development of new kinds of "imagined community". Diaspora communities challenge the socio-spatial/territorial assumptions of community and politics by transcending physical space, reaching across international borders and incorporating members based on ethno-national identities. Such identities can create, exacerbate or ameliorate a conflict.

Globalization expedites the extent and the influence of diasporas as political agents in several ways. First, advances in communications, transport and finance mean that diasporas are able to act internationally without the consent of the states in which they reside. Policy-makers in the host state face increasing limits on their ability to pressure immigrants and their descendants to sever ties with their homelands and become fully acculturated in their new environment. Members of an ethno-national diaspora group dispersed throughout the world are able to maintain ties through publications, websites and chat groups on the Internet. Second, these same globalizing factors enable migrants to retain an interest in homeland politics. Events in the country of origin seem closer than ever before. Developments resulting from globalization have brought conflicts closer to the diaspora and simultaneously brought the diaspora closer to the conflict. Being able to view the conflict on television or read about it can incite diasporic communities to action. Third, diasporas can generate the original impetus for ethnic mobilization and, eventually, secession. For example, Sikh mobilization for an independent Khalistan in India originated in the diaspora community rather than from within the Punjab itself.

The overall effect has been the creation of communities with multiple loyalties, whose attentions focus simultaneously on their situation in their country of settlement and transnationally on their homeland, as well as on kindred ethnic groups in other countries. The involvement of migrants and exiles in the politics of their homeland is not a new phenomenon. However, characteristic of the increasing change in the pace and scale of globalization in recent years is the change in the location of political, economic and social developments, which are taking place more and more outside the sovereign territory of the nation-state. Sassen argues that although "sovereignty remains a feature of the system ... it is now located in a multiplicity of institutional arenas" and that this "reconfiguration of space may signal a more fundamental transformation in the matter of sovereignty".[7] In addition, new arenas for political expression are opened, particularly for ethnic communities that did not enjoy freedom of expression in the homeland. They can take advantage of freedoms of assembly, the press and other forms of expression, and lobby the host state to implement desired foreign policies toward the homeland.

It should be recognized at the outset that the study of diasporas in general, and of diasporas in conflict in particular, is a new area of scholarship. For too long diasporas have been largely excluded from the theories and discourses on international relations. Boundaries and sovereignty defined all international phenomena. All international problems were seen as territorial in nature, and groups or issues that could not be defined in territorial terms hardly figured in our discussions. With increased globalization, migration and overall mobility of people, goods and ideas, this position was no longer tenable. The growth in ethnic and civil conflicts since 1989 has also focused our attention on sub-groups and other non-state actors. Diasporas have come to be seen as politically active actors who can influence events within their territory (e.g. elections) or outside it (e.g. a foreign policy action or a vote in the United Nations). Diasporas are communities of individuals who may possess resources and have access to international organizations, international media and powerful host governments. This means that diasporas may now act on the international stage and have an influence on events well beyond one territory, ranging from economic cooperation to conflict duration.

Diasporas in politics

Globalization and the rise of ethnic conflicts have allowed diasporas to become important international political forces. Globalization has also intensified diasporic groups' ties with their homeland and increased their ability to influence a conflict in their homeland. Many diasporas (for example, the Kurdish, Armenian, Palestinian or Jewish) seek an active role in the resolution or continuation of their homeland conflict. Their ability to do so is affected, *inter alia*, by their social or political status, the views of their host society and government of the conflict, and the political and social character of their kin state. The effect of homeland conflicts on diasporas economically, socially or in terms of their self-image, and how that affects their identity or how they are viewed by their host society, ensures high stakes for diasporas in either the continuation or the resolution of the conflict.[8]

Diasporas function on four levels in politics: the domestic level in a host country; the regional level; the trans-state level; and the level of the entire dispersed group in other countries. At each of these levels, a diaspora's functions fall into three broad activities, namely, the maintenance, defence and promotion of its interests. Maintenance functions include activities to maintain cohesion and a sense of separate identity in a host country (e.g. fund-raising or the routine administration of cultural, economic and social functions such as schools, churches, synagogues or research institutions). Defence includes activities designed to offer actual physical protection for diaspora members where the conditions in a host country are either adverse or restrictive (e.g. self-defence, community housing schemes, legal challenges of discriminatory practices). And promotion includes activities where a diaspora works actively through the political and economic channels in its host country to promote the concerns and interests of its homeland. All of the diasporic communities in the world today engage in one or more of these functions.

Diasporas and conflict

Diasporas can influence patterns of politics within their host country, they can even affect the politics of their homeland country, but can diasporas really exert any influence on a conflict in which they have a strong emotional investment? The argument I wish to advance is that diasporas can indeed have a profound impact on a conflict, and that this impact can affect any phase of a conflict and any kind of conflict. To appreciate how this is done, we need to say something about conflict and how best to conceive of it.

Conflict is one of those social processes that evoke different meanings and associations. Etymologically, the word "conflict" is made up of two Latin words that literally mean "to strike together". The way in which modern scholars use the term implies that conflict encompasses a wide range of situations in which two or more parties have incompatible interests and behave accordingly.[9] In the minds of many, conflict tends to have negative associations. Some, therefore, see conflicts as essentially destructive and intractable processes that result in high costs in human and material terms. There is no doubt that the human and social costs of preparing for and waging conflicts are simply staggering, as evidenced by the millions of people who have died in the past 50 years or so and the vastness of the scale of destruction.[10] Conflict, however, can also denote opportunities for change, growth and creativity. Whether or not conflict will manifest negative or positive features depends primarily on the way in which it is managed. Conflicts can be managed constructively and result in better social relations, or they can be managed destructively and entail violence and death.[11]

Knowledge of the factors affecting conflict and its management can contribute to a more constructive expression of a conflict, be it between individuals, groups or states. Such knowledge is predicated upon an understanding of the nature of conflict, the issues in contention, the features of the parties involved and, above all, how different factors, dimensions and actors may influence the structure of a conflict or its dynamics. In what follows, therefore, I propose to analyse the essential features of a conflict, understand how these manifest themselves and look more specifically at how a diasporic community can have an impact on some of the characteristics of a conflict or the way it unfolds.

Conflict parties

At the most basic level, conflicts occur when two or more actors have incompatible interests, values or positions.[12] One of the key issues in the analysis of any conflict concerns the identity of the parties in conflict. When we speak of parties in conflict we mean individuals, groups, organizations or nations in conflict. A party is an analytical construct referring to the actors who initiate a conflict, pursue it and determine its outcome. If we want to understand conflict situations, we have to know something about the nature of the parties. Identifying parties in the abstract may be self-evident, but it is not always so in the real world. Parties in conflict normally entail sub-systems or are themselves sub-systems of a larger unit. Parties in conflict may experience intra-party strife, or they may be manipulated by a stronger and much wealthier party. Some parties are autonomous units, others are not. Some parties act rationally, others do not. Some parties are democratic polities and responsive to their citizens, others are not.

Groups, nations or communities who engage in conflict directly are the primary parties in any analysis. Other groups, organizations or nations with an interest in the outcome are secondary parties. Often, it is impossible to draw precise distinctions between primary and secondary parties, but we can safely say that, the larger the number of primary and secondary parties, the more difficult it will be to resolve a conflict.[13] Clearly, a conflict in which primary parties, secondary parties and diaspora communities are all involved would pose very serious challenges for any would-be conflict manager.

Conflict issues

Issues in conflict define the nature and extent of incompatibility, and basically tell us what a conflict is about. Issues can be described in terms of interests, where the basic incompatibility is perceived as a difference over the preferred distribution of something tangible (e.g. food, territory). Or they may be described in terms of intangible resources or values, where the basic incompatibility is perceived in terms of a difference over religious beliefs, ideologies or cognitive structure. How issues are perceived and defined has important consequences for the dynamics and termination of a conflict.

One of the interesting features about the conflicts in which diasporic communities tend to get involved is that these conflicts usually touch on identity, beliefs, values, cultural norms or a way of life. Such conflicts are over issues that are quite intangible, and are often referred to as zero-sum conflicts. Intangible issues tend to make a conflict more violent, less amenable to compromise and resolution, and more prolonged and intractable. The involvement of a diaspora in such conflicts can only make matters worse.

Conflict environment

All conflicts occur within a specific social context or environment. This context affects conflict, and is in turn affected by it. A conflict may take place in a structured environment, where it is largely institutionalized and where the parties' behaviour and the manner in which resources are allocated are specified or prescribed by norms – for example, family conflict or conflict between labour and management. A structured environment provides the parties with various instruments of conflict management, and determines acceptable and legitimate kinds of behaviour. Conflict in a structured environment usually takes place between parties who have a shared understanding and commitment to non-coercive strategies.

When a conflict occurs in an unstructured environment, for example a civil war, rebellion or terrorism, the belief that parties are in a zero-sum situation may well increase. Here the parties lack formal and informal norms that could provide some sense of community, so, when a conflict becomes manifest, each party's behaviour may be limited only by its own capacity and disposition. In an unstructured environment, each party may consider the other as a threat, and each is prepared to act violently against the other, even if it means injuring or eliminating the other. It stands to reason that the involvement of a diaspora in such a conflict will hardly be productive and may well exacerbate it even further.

Conflict dynamics

Conflicts are dynamic social processes with their own life cycle: they have a beginning, they evolve and at some stage they may come to an end. There is nothing predetermined about the evolution, course or termina-

tion of a conflict. Each phase of a conflict denotes different types of behaviour, different potential for conflict management and different possibilities for intervention by a diasporic community.

Normally, we think of a conflict as having a first latent phase. This is
a phase in which, although conflict differences may be present, no party
wants to pursue these any further. This phase exists whenever individuals, groups, organizations or nations have different issues, but these are
not great enough to change a stable situation into a conflict situation. In
the second phase, issue differences between the parties are articulated
and given concrete expression. At this stage a conflict is said to have
emerged. Once a conflict emerges and parties become fully aware of the
differences between them, resources are mobilized and an escalation of
conflict takes place. Here the parties are prepared to use violence against
each other. This is the phase of a conflict that normally attracts media attention because it involves direct acts of violent behaviour. An escalating
conflict may go on until the parties have reached a point of mutual exhaustion, a point where they have lost too many people and resources.
This is the point where violence is at its most intense and losses are at
their highest. We refer to this phase as the "hurting stalemate" phase.[14]
However intense and violent a conflict is, it does eventually de-escalate
to a point where the parties are prepared to engage in negotiation or
some other non-violent methods of dealing with their conflict. The shift
to de-escalation constitutes a dramatic transformation in the course of a
conflict, which is usually accompanied by internal changes within each
party (e.g. changes in leadership or ideology) and a mutual desire to explore less costly alternatives. This phase may, if successful, culminate in
an agreement to cease fire and a formal termination of the conflict (the
conflict may, and often does, recur later on). The final phase of a conflict
is the one where the parties in conflict and, more importantly, regional
and international actors become engaged in a series of post-conflict
peace-building measures to ensure conflict does not take place again
(here we are thinking of measures such as economic aid, fair electoral
systems and monitoring of human rights abuse).[15]

The various phases of a conflict's evolution and transition from stable
peace to war, and then back to some peace, provide useful signposts for
the most appropriate approach to a conflict and the contribution that outside parties, such as diasporas, may make at each phase. Thus, preventive
diplomacy measures, akin to sounding the alarm, are most relevant at the
early stages when a conflict is latent or of very low intensity. They are
designed to prevent conflict from becoming violent or spreading further
afield, and include such steps as preventive deployment, early mediation
and any other proactive measures.[16] If preventive measures fail, the parties will, in the next phase, engage in crisis management, where they will

attempt to stop their slippery slide toward mutual violence. Here, direct negotiations or indirect channels will be utilized to encourage leaders not to escalate a conflict. If crisis management talks are not successful and a conflict does escalate, there may be a need for regional or international peace-keeping forces to interpose themselves between the combatants to stop further killings and to provide some breathing space to allow peace-making activities (e.g. mediation, UN fact-finding commissions) to take place. Finally, when a conflict is ended, NGOs and humanitarian development agencies, as well as the United Nations and other concerned parties (e.g. diasporas), can all come in to help rebuild the disaster-stricken areas of a conflict and to create some structures on the ground that may stop the conflict from recurring.[17]

The various phases of a conflict, and the strategies that may be used in each phase, can be depicted graphically, as in Figure 2.1. Progress from one phase to the next is rarely smooth and conflicts may go through phases several times. In reality, conflicts usually do not follow a linear path – they emerge, escalate, become quiescent and escalate again, or they may emerge and become dormant for a while. What is important, though, is to recognize the possible phases of conflict dynamics and the possible strategies that outside parties, such as diasporas, may help with at each phase.

Diasporas and conflict: Analysing patterns of influence

How can a diaspora in one part of the world affect, influence or modify a conflict in another part of the world? Diasporas, like other political actors, can play a constructive role in any conflict by introducing norms and practices of cooperation, helping to reframe a conflict, and generally supporting moderate positions, or they can play a destructive role, for example by exacerbating feelings of hostility or offering support for extremist positions. A diaspora's role in a conflict will clearly depend on many factors, such as its strength and level of political organization in the host country, the issues at stake in the conflict, its ability to exert political pressure in the home country, and the international attention given to the conflict. The best way to conceive of the role of diasporas in conflict is to think of the various phases or stages of a conflict and then to evaluate the possible role a diaspora might play in each phase. Thus, we may want to know what diasporas can, or cannot, do in the early phases of a conflict, when preventive measures are most appropriate; their effects on an escalating conflict, when different instruments of influence are needed; their effects in the conflict termination phase; and, finally, the modalities and activities of diasporic communities in post-conflict restructuring and

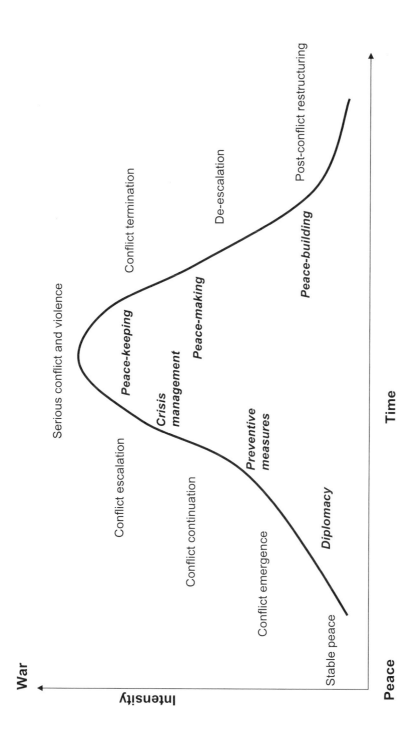

Figure 2.1 Conflict phases and approaches to conflict management.
Source: Adapted from M. Lund, *Preventing Violent Conflicts*, Washington, DC: United States Institute of Peace Press, 1996.

27

peace-building. This sharpens our thinking about diasporas and conflict resolution and forces us to identify the different effects that different diasporas may bring to bear at different phases of a conflict.

Related to the phase of a conflict are the possible arenas in which diasporas may exercise influence. I would suggest that there are four basic arenas in which diasporic communities can exercise influence in the course of a conflict – political, military, economic and socio-cultural. In each of these arenas a diaspora may exert influence directly in its host societies or indirectly over its homeland. A diasporic community's effects on a conflict can be positive (by positive I mean contributing only to the cessation, termination or resolution of a conflict), negative (by which I mean having only a bad impact on the conflict, making it worse), or neutral (in other words, it does not change too much about either the course or the termination of a conflict). Schematically, combining the phases of a conflict with the possible arenas for influence results in a comprehensive framework for analysing the role, manner and effects of diasporas in conflicts. This is represented in Table 2.1. In the following section, some of the features of this framework will be highlighted.

Conflict prevention phase

What can diasporas do to affect the conflict prevention phase of a conflict? This is the phase where a conflict is latent but some differences and incompatibilities, over such issues as territory, resources or the nature of governance, are beginning to be felt by the parties. Clearly, it is in the interests of the parties concerned and any outsider to prevent a conflict from becoming violent or from escalating into war. A diasporic community can take measures to reduce the risks of a conflict.

Political and diplomatic measures

Diasporas can be mobilized for positive action before violent conflict breaks out. They can lobby governments and international organizations to establish fact-finding missions, call upon the United Nations to give logistical and technical support to the parties, and establish informal forums and channels for dialogue and negotiation. Diaspora groups have the potential to aid conflict prevention by emphasizing non-violent alternatives to conflict. They can make it hard to forget about a conflict, and force the international community to face it.

Diaspora groups can contribute to conflict prevention through their advocacy activities. Diaspora organizations can mobilize for the purpose of influencing international public opinion and building political support for non-violence, human rights, justice and political freedoms – all of which play an important part in conflict prevention. Diaspora groups can mobi-

Table 2.1 The influences of a diaspora in different phases of a conflict

Phase of conflict	Political influences Positive/Neutral/ Negative	Military influences Positive/Neutral/ Negative	Economic influences Positive/Neutral/ Negative	Socio-cultural influences Positive/Neutral/ Negative
Conflict emergence				
Conflict continuation				
Conflict escalation				
Conflict termination				
Post-conflict reconstruction				

lize international civil society as well as their host governments and international organizations to focus attention on a possible conflict, and to do all in their power to stop it. Shain argues that some diasporas have essentially been "commissioned" to export and safeguard Western values abroad and are expected to become the moral conscience of new democracies or newly established states in their homelands.[18] Democracies function best as conflict prevention mechanisms.

Economic measures

Economic assistance can be considered an important tool of conflict prevention in so far as it contributes resources to parties who may feel deprived of them. Many of the conflicts and wars today are fought in the underdeveloped and least developed countries. Poor countries have fewer economic and political resources with which to manage conflicts. Strategies to reduce poverty and to achieve broad-based economic growth are an essential part of conflict prevention. A diaspora can raise money in its host countries and transfer it to its homeland. Such remittances are an important economic source (in some poor countries remittances account for a substantial proportion of total income), making parties more reluctant to engage in conflict and risk losing such money.[19]

Conflict emergence and continuation

This is the phase where conflict becomes manifest, positions harden, and coercive and violent behaviour may well result. Here the parties have decided that they may have more to gain from pursuing the conflict than from preventing it. Public notices are made, resources are mobilized, and actual fighting may take place on several fronts. At this stage the conflict is a very serious issue indeed for diasporas and their respective homelands. The conflict may now affect in a very real way the lives of those in its immediate environment, as well as those many miles away. Is there anything a diaspora can do at this stage to change or modify a conflict so as to bring it closer to a resolution? Or are there steps a diaspora may take that will actually exacerbate an emerging conflict and prolong it?

Political influence

There are various political ways in which a diaspora can work at the conflict emergence and continuation stage to advance the interests of its homeland government. It can actively lobby its host government and other international organizations to take action against its real or perceived enemy at home. It can advocate an economic boycott of enemy produce in the hope of weakening its capacity to wage war (for many years Arab states have encouraged all Arabs overseas to boycott Israeli goods and services). It can make information and intelligence gathered by its host government available to its homeland.

Once a conflict is ongoing, diasporic communities can galvanize their members to undertake various political measures in support of their sisters and brothers in the homeland. They can lobby their local representatives, they can engage in media campaigns, they can take to the streets in massive demonstrations, or they can simply call for shows of political unity and a determination to reward political parties or personalities who will advance their cause. Diasporas can undertake just about every measure that is legal and permissible in their host country to make the plight of their homeland a central issue to their hosts.

Economic support

Once a conflict emerges and intensifies, the costs of waging it tend to mount by the day. It is here that diasporas can play a very meaningful role. Remittances from diaspora communities do in effect give both conflict parties more resources with which to wage a conflict. Such remittances may be used in the conflict prevention phase to get better education for all and to reduce poverty, but they may also be used, in the conflict escalation phase, to encourage more bellicosity and create further instability. Palestinians, Jews, Tamils, Lebanese, Kurds, Armenians and many other diasporic communities have all contributed substantial economic resources to their homelands and have all allowed conflicts in their war-torn societies to become even worse. Economic support during conflict emergence and escalation cannot but create further problems for all concerned.

Economic support during this phase of the conflict could be vital for rebel groups, insurgents or even the military in one's homeland. Such support by a dedicated and concerned diaspora can increase the risk of further escalation and a recurrence of the conflict at higher levels of intensity.[20]

Military support

During the escalation phase of a conflict, diasporas can offer direct military support by providing weapons, training or even personnel. In order to show their loyalty to their cause, some diaspora groups (e.g. Tamils, Irish) are alleged to be collecting guns and shipping them to the conflicts. Both Protestant and Catholic rebel military organizations of Northern Ireland have actively raised funds in North America, and a number of the guns used in shootings turned out to have come from the Boston police department.

Diasporas also serve as a source of recruits by providing volunteer combatants. A feature of the Bosnian war was the weekend fighters who travelled from Germany to fight. When Israel was at war with its Arab neighbours in 1973, and the initial setbacks started to make headlines, a number of Jews from overseas went to Israel to take part in the overall war effort. Diasporic communities are often able and more than willing to offer any level of military support their homelands may require. The overall effect of such support on the conflict itself can hardly be positive.

Termination phase

The termination phase of a conflict occurs when the parties, having experienced some losses and costs in the previous phase, recognize that the only way to deal with their conflict is to bring it to an end, and to do so non-violently. Here the parties may be engaged in a variety of direct or indirect negotiations or other diplomatic activities to terminate a conflict and to cut losses. Conflict termination is driven by a myriad of forces, some internal (e.g. exhaustion by parties), others external (e.g. diasporas). At this stage, there is a conscious search for a compromise or an acceptable settlement. The challenge is to do so in a way that meets some of each party's interests and values.[21] What role can a diaspora community play in this phase?

Political measures

Although diasporas may be a force in sustaining violent conflicts, they have the potential to support the conflict's termination and to contribute to the sustainability of the peace process. Diaspora perceptions of homeland conflicts can be reframed and made more complex through a process of dialogue or awareness that the conflict has gone on long enough. In this case, the diaspora's role in the conflict may be a very positive one. In addition, a diaspora group may shift its political support from the militant leaders and organizations engaged in the homeland conflict towards a position that supports the leaders and movements seeking peace. The support that diasporas give to rebel groups is often viewed critically, but diasporas can also make a positive contribution to conflict termination.

The termination of a conflict requires an audience beyond the geographical boundaries of the conflict arena to be addressed. The Jewish Diaspora has contributed to the debate on conflict resolution for many years. During the years of the Oslo peace process, many Jewish Americans lobbied to reward Arab and Islamic states that normalized relations with Israel and encouraged others to do the same. These actions were done of their own accord, without the support of the Israeli government. The Jewish Diaspora is not, however, cohesive and, although many Jewish Americans were supportive of the peace process, others, in particular the orthodox religious conservatives, campaigned vigorously against Prime Minister Rabin, even labelling him a traitor.

Diasporas may be part of the conflict termination and peace process. For example, the Irish American diaspora played a major part in financing the conflict in Northern Ireland, but it has also been important in its termination. The Irish Northern Aid Committee was dedicated to supporting the militant factions of the Irish Republican Army (IRA) by raising funds and acting as a conduit for drug smuggling. In 1991, Americans for a New Irish Agenda was founded, an organization that spoke out publicly and financially supported the peace process in Ireland. When the peace faction within the IRA initiated the peace process, its leader went to Boston, and the British and Irish governments chose Senator Mitchell to chair the peace negotiations.

Diasporas can help conflict termination by promoting dialogue and other processes that break down inflexible perceptions of the conflict. A diaspora may encourage mediation at this stage, it may appeal to the international community or the United Nations for support with conflict resolution activities, or it may just communicate discreetly with élite members in its homeland to inform them of the desirability and feasibility of conflict termination.

Members of a diaspora can have a constructive influence on the conflict resolution process by becoming involved in problem-solving workshops. Such workshops bring together unofficial but influential parties to explore different perceptions and ideas about conflict termination. In the United States, for instance, Herb Kelman and his associates have for years brought together American Jews and Palestinians at Harvard in a series of informal problem-solving workshops, and many of the ideas discussed by the participants fed into the Oslo process.[22] Diaspora leaders, women's groups or even student groups can all be mobilized at this stage to engage in dialogue and to facilitate better termination terms and structure a better settlement. Efforts by diaspora communities in the conflict termination phase are widespread, extensive and highly visible. On many occasions they are also effective.

Post-conflict phase

The post-conflict phase is the final phase of a conflict cycle. It describes patterns of activities and interactions that occur after a conflict has ended and a settlement of sorts or a compromise has been agreed to, when efforts are made to ensure that the conflict will not erupt again. This is when a long-term perspective is being looked at. Most conflicts come to an end, but maintaining the peace is a difficult task indeed.[23] Where many of the pre-existing conditions that produced the conflict in the first instance remain intact, there is a strong chance the conflict will become violent again. Hence, there is a need at this stage to create structures and mechanisms to ensure not only compliance with the terms of an agreement but a radical rebuilding of a more peaceful structure. How can diasporas help with this important task of avoiding conflict repetition?

Political measures

How can we ensure that a once conflict-ridden society can now become, at the end of a conflict, well integrated? This is a broad agenda and may require many activities. Strengthening civil society, for instance, is an important aspect of post-conflict peace-building. Diasporas can make an important contribution to the development of a healthy and vibrant civil society in the wake of a conflict. In many post-conflict situations a UN presence may be required, and this is something a diasporic community can impress on its homeland. Ideas such as democratic institutions, free media, respect for human rights and gender equality can all be emphasized as the best guarantees for avoiding a repetition of the conflict. Diasporas in democratic countries can inform members of their group in the homeland of the norms, values and institutions which define a democratic polity and which provide equal rights to all.

Peace needs political support if the cycle of conflict is to be broken. Diasporas can provide some of this support by challenging repressive regimes in their own homelands, by challenging corruption, by speaking publicly about the need for new state structures, structures that are respectful of people, ideas and differences. The post-conflict phase is essentially one of political education and economic restructuring. A diaspora can do much in both these areas.

Economic support

Diasporas can play a major economic role in the post-conflict and reconstruction phase. Diasporas, especially those in rich countries, can offer financial support in this phase to undo the effects of a conflict and to help bring about a process of disarmament and demobilization. Allowing former soldiers to find a more productive role in their homeland is an expensive process that many poor countries can ill afford. This is where remittances from a diaspora in the post-conflict phase can come in so useful. A diaspora community can promote economic recovery and thus consolidate the foundations of peace. Post-conflict rebuilding may be a good time for a diaspora community to invest heavily in its homeland. Such investment can revive business confidence and boost the economy, aiding reconstruction and recovery and the long-term goal of a durable peace. Business links and projects can be established with an explicit role for diaspora organizations. There is some evidence that economic aid from outside, whether from a diasporic community or from other external donors, in this phase of a conflict is more effective than aid in the initial or

escalating phases of a conflict.[24] The wealth of expertise and financial resources within the diaspora community are major resources to be tapped
into in the post-conflict phase. Post-conflict remittances and aid from a
diaspora can encourage the homeland government to adopt policies and
embrace political structures that secure and sustain peace. Such policies
reduce the risk of repeat conflicts and enhance opportunities for participation and political improvement. A diaspora can thus be a major asset
to conflict resolution in the restructuring phase.

Socio-cultural influences

An important aspect of diasporas' work and effectiveness in the socio-
cultural arena concerns the promotion of justice, truth and reconciliation
in the post-conflict phase. One way for parties in conflict to come to
terms with a violent past is to honour the memory of the victims by talking about them openly and honestly. This means searching for the truth,
not with a view to punishing anyone, but with a view to gaining a better
understanding.[25] Reconciliation is the means to heal people and rebuild
the webs of relationships, which have been broken down by years of
hatred and violence. When it comes to reconciliation, people in the homeland are more accepting and willing to listen to advice from members of
the diaspora rather than other foreigners. Members of the diaspora can
offer expertise, knowledge and understanding of cultural norms and a
deeper appreciation of the situation in their homeland. Diasporic literature, publications and other cultural production can contribute to the
process of healing by countering negative images. An added feature of
expatriate involvement is that it may lead to repatriation, as diaspora
members lay the groundwork for the kinds of institution they would like
to participate in as they fulfil dreams of returning to their homeland.

   An important part of the reconciliation process involves dealing with
the psychological trauma of violent conflict and human rights abuses.
Diaspora groups have a role to play in the socio-psychological rehabilitation of victims of conflict, as illustrated by the Sierra Leone War Trust for
Children (SLWT). Members of the Sierra Leone diaspora living in the
United Kingdom established the SLWT, which is committed to improving the welfare of war-affected children through the rehabilitation of villages in Bombali province, which were completely destroyed through 10
years of civil war. Children have suffered from severe human rights violations; half of those killed during the civil war and 20 per cent of those
disabled were children. The project provides opportunities for collective
social activity as a means of trauma management. It has organized sports
tournaments and cultural events, set up community centres and provided
primary school education for all children in the area. A diasporic community can work with its brothers and sisters in the homeland towards truth

and justice in the post-conflict phase and in this way bring a much desired peace.

Conclusion

For a very long time political scientists viewed conflicts in international relations as involving essentially two states, each led by rational leaders and each of which is free to pursue its interests unencumbered by any other considerations save those within its territorial borders. That image is just not valid any more. State structures are hardly that coherent, nor are states so independent that they can ignore the realities of a complex international system. But above all, in an era of migration, globalization and ethnic conflicts and diversity, often a considerable number of citizens of states in conflict are dispersed abroad. These citizens may have political power, resources, influence and, above all, an abiding interest in, and concern for, the state or group they left behind. Staying involved in the affairs of a homeland may be one way for members of a diaspora community to remain close to their original values and perform a vital role in maintaining their identity. Such citizens may be prepared to go to great lengths to ensure the success and survival of their homeland. Few situations threaten the basic structure of the diaspora–homeland relationship more acutely than conflict – hence the very significant influence diasporas may exercise on a conflict. This is why it behoves us to understand how diasporas affect a conflict.

To appreciate whether diasporas are likely to help or jeopardize an original conflict situation, and how precisely they can do so, we need to go beyond single case-study descriptions. Diasporas today are real actors, real entities with real interests; they are not "virtual actors". Their actions, in words and in deeds, are based on deep-rooted feelings, emotions and historical affinities. What is more, the number of diaspora communities is increasing yearly. I have argued above that the best way to comprehend the relationship between homeland, diaspora and conflict is to develop a framework that takes into account the essential features of any conflict and the modalities of possible influence between states and diasporas. Such a framework allows us to examine any conflict situation in which a diaspora is involved either directly or indirectly.

The relationship between diasporas and homelands is not quite a relationship between two autonomous entities, nor is it a uniform relationship of subservience in which a diaspora is just expected to prop up a homeland in any case or conflict. It is a complex relationship that depends on contexts and specific situations. It is characterized by a struggle over political, economic, military and cultural questions. As in any relationship, tensions and confrontations are typical of this relationship. There is no uniform template that can capture the complexity of this relationship. This is why the study of diasporas in conflict raises so many important definitional, methodological and comparative issues. I hope some of them have been answered above. Many more will be answered in the chapters that follow.

Acknowledgements

The first draft of this chapter was prepared for the UNU–USIP Workshop on "The Diaspora Conundrum" held in Macau, 19–21 September 2004. I am grateful to the workshop participants and to the editors for their comments and suggestions. Special thanks are due to Hazel Smith for her careful reading of my chapter and numerous helpful suggestions for improving it. Any errors are of course mine alone.

Notes

1. See Mary Kaldor, *New and Old Wars: Organized Violence in a Global Era*, London: Polity Press, 1999.
2. See Gabriel Sheffer, *Diaspora Politics: At Home Abroad*, Cambridge: Cambridge University Press, 2003.
3. Ibid., p. 83.
4. See James Fearon and David Leitin, "Ethnicity, Insurgency and Civil War", *American Political Science Review*, 1994, 79(1): 75–90. See also Jacob Bercovitch, "Managing Ethnic Conflicts: The Role and Relevance of Mediation", *World Affairs*, 2003, 166(3): 56–69; and Terry Lyons, "Globalisation, Diasporas and Conflict", Institute for Conflict Analysis, George Mason University, draft paper, January 2004.
5. Laura Basch, Nina Glick Schiller and Cristina S. Blanc, *Nations Unbound*, New York: Gordon & Breach, 1994, p. 7.
6. Ibid.
7. Saskia Sassen, *Losing Control: Sovereignty in an Age of Globalisation*, New York: Columbia University Press, 1997, p. 29.
8. See Yossi Shain, "The Role of Diasporas in Conflict Perpetuation or Resolution", *SAIS Review*, 2002, 22(2): 115–143. See also Gunther Baechler, "Civilian Conflict Resolution in the Context of International Peace Promotion in the 1990s", in Gunther Baechler, ed., *Promoting Peace. The Role of Civilian Conflict Resolution*, Berne: Staempfli Publishers, 2002, pp. 8–19.
9. See Louis Kriesberg, *Constructive Conflicts*, Lanham, MD: Rowman & Littlefield, 1998.
10. For figures on conflict and its consequences, see Peter Wallensteen, *Understanding Conflict Resolution*, London: Sage Publications, 2002.
11. See Jacob Bercovitch, *Social Conflicts and Third Parties*, Boulder, CO: Westview Press, 1984.
12. See Morton Deutsch, *The Resolution of Conflict*, Yale: Yale University Press, 1973.
13. See Hugh Miall, Oliver Ramsbotham and Tom Woodhouse, *Contemporary Conflict Resolution*, London: Polity Press, 1999.

14. On this phase and its features, see I. William Zartman, *Ripe for Resolution: Conflict and Intervention in Africa*, New York: Oxford University Press, 1996.

15. For a good analysis of these phases and the dynamics of a conflict, see Kriesberg, *Constructive Conflicts*.

16. On this concept and its applicability to the real world, see Michael Lund, *Preventing Violent Conflicts*, Washington, DC: United States Institute of Peace Press, 1996.

17. This useful way of thinking about conflict dynamics and the measures that may be undertaken at each phase of a conflict was first suggested by UN Secretary-General Boutros-Ghali. See Boutros Boutros-Ghali, *An Agenda for Peace*, New York: United Nations, 1992. See also Kumar Rupesinghe, *Civil Wars, Civil Peace*, London: Pluto Press, 1998.

18. Democratic political institutions are stable, and stable political institutions are peaceful. See Shain, "The Role of Diasporas in Conflict Perpetuation or Resolution".

19. See Paul Collier and Anke Hoeffler, "Aid, Policy and Peace: Reducing the Risks of Civil Conflict", *Journal of Defense Economics*, 2002, 13(6): 435–450.

20. See Martin J. Esman and Robert J. Herring, eds, *Carrots, Sticks and Ethnic Conflict*, Ann Arbor: University of Michigan Press, 2001.

21. For a fuller analysis, see Chester Crocker, Fen Hampson and Pamela Aall, *Taming Intractable Conflicts*, Washington, DC: United States Institute of Peace, 2004.

22. For an account of these, see Herb Kelman, "Interactive Problem-Solving: Informal Mediation by the Scholar-Practitioner", in Jacob Bercovitch, ed., *Studies in International Mediation*, London and New York: Palgrave/Macmillan, 2002, pp. 165–192.

23. See Virginia Fortna, *Peace Time: Cease-Fire Agreements and the Durability of Peace*, Princeton, NJ: Princeton University Press, 2004.

24. See World Bank Report, *Breaking the Conflict Trap: Civil War and Development Policy*, Washington, DC: Oxford University Press, 2003.

25. See Andrew Rigby, *Justice and Reconciliation: After the Violence*, Boulder, CO: Lynne Rienner, 2001.

3

Gender, diasporas and post–Cold War conflict

Nadje S. Al-Ali

Introduction

This chapter adds a gender dimension to the question of whether diasporas are peace-wreckers or peace-makers. Yet, writing about gender and diasporas in the context of post–Cold War conflicts involves much ambiguity. It reflects the heightened sensitivity to the fact that gender matters: men and women are positioned differently in societies prior to, during and after conflict. War and conflict might affect men and women differently. Gender – the social and cultural construction of what it means to be a man and a woman – also comes into play during the flight from a war-torn country, the upheavals of migration and settling in a new environment. And, finally, the specific relations and activities of diasporic communities and individuals are gendered. What is puzzling, however, is the fact that much of the literature and political debates on diasporas, conflict and peace-making continues to be gender blind. Rather than a gendered lens being incorporated into "mainstream" analyses and policy-making, gender still tends to be ghettoized and treated as an appendix or afterthought.

Nevertheless, feminist scholars and activists have increasingly put gender on the map. Common to a wide range of feminist gender analyses is the view that the differentiation and relative positioning of women and men is an important ordering principle that pervades systems of power and is sometimes its very embodiment. Gender also has expression in prevailing ideologies and norms, in laws, in citizenship rights, in political dynamics and struggles and, of course, in economics – how money, prop-

Diasporas in conflict: Peace-makers or peace-wreckers?, Smith and Stares
(eds), United Nations University Press, 2007, ISBN 978-92-808-1140-7

erty and other resources are distributed between the sexes. However, it is important to point out here that gender does not necessarily constitute the most significant factor. Economic class, ethnic and religious differentiation, sexual orientation and political affiliation also shape power hierarchies and structure political regimes and societies. And these differentiating factors, in turn, are gendered and are part of the specific constructs of men/masculinities and women/femininities.

Looking at the roles and involvements of post–Cold War diasporas through a gendered lens, I intend to explore different phases of conflict, ranging from pre-conflict and pre-escalatory phases, to acute conflict and war, and to peace-making and post-conflict reconstruction. Recognizing that diaspora women, just like men, do not constitute homogeneous entities that act uniformly, I will not focus on the question of when and in which circumstances diaspora women and men engage in peace-making or in the prolonging of conflict. Rather I will examine the relationship between gender ideologies/relations and diaspora women's political mobilization. In other words, my main questions are: (1) what are the conditions and circumstances shaping women's political involvement, or lack thereof; and (2) what are the predisposing or influencing factors that shape women's and men's relations to violence and peace?

It is my argument throughout that existing gender relations and ideologies in the country of origin and the receiving country influence the way men and women relate to their country of origin and the conflict waging within it. Rather than looking at "hot conflict" on its own, it is important to contextualize prevailing gender ideologies and relations in terms of pre-conflict, conflict and post-conflict periods and developments.

In my theoretical stipulations, I shall draw on numerous published case studies. My own research on diasporic communities from Bosnia-Herzegovina and more recently on Iraq will constitute the basis for most of my empirical examples. However, rather than aiming to present specific case studies, this chapter is intended to illuminate some important general issues that need to be taken into consideration in analyses of the actual political mobilization of diasporas. Because I see diasporas in terms of a process and in transnational terms, I shall discuss conditions and circumstances within the country of origin as significant factors with respect to the political interventions of diasporas. I shall start by providing a working definition of diaspora.

Diasporas in conflict

Defining diaspora

In the context of post-modern and post-colonial approaches and the increasing appeal of cultural studies, the terms "diaspora" and "diasporic communities" have gained new meanings and dimensions. "Diaspora" denotes experiences of movement and displacement, and the social, cultural and political formations emerging out of this displacement. More and more, it has been used in a metaphorical sense, referring to hybrid identity formations,[1] arguing against reifications of ethnicity and culture and explaining cultural shifts in general. For the purpose of this chapter, the term "diaspora" is defined much more narrowly because I am specifically focusing on conflict-generated diasporas: diasporas that originate in conflict and have emerged through forced migration. Unlike some authors, however, I argue that "forced migration" cannot simply be contrasted with voluntary or economic migration. Rather, there exists a continuum between flight in a situation of acute danger and "hot conflict" and migration in a pre-conflict yet tension-ridden period. Economic necessities and crises force people to migrate, as do armed conflict and violence.

Conflict-generated diasporas tend to involve identities that emphasize links to symbolically valuable territory and an aspiration to return once the homeland is freed or conflict has subsided. Aside from constructions of identities bound up with the "homeland", social mobilization is also generally linked to a territorially defined country of origin. This mobilization could take many forms – political, economic, social, cultural and military. It could aim to end conflict and war and promote peace and reconstruction, or it could support armed struggle and conflict, and even hinder peace initiatives. Diasporas rarely constitute homogeneous political and social entities or communities. Different elements of a specific diaspora could pursue opposing aims and strategies. Again, gender is only one among many differentiating factors within a diaspora, others being class, ethnic and religious background, political affiliation, place of origin and the specific experience of conflict. Those who have had traumatic experiences of violence might have a very different emotional and political attitude towards conflict from those who did not experience violence directly. And it could go in both directions: experience of violence might radicalize a person and create militant supporters of armed struggle, or it might create people who abhor violence and promote peace. Although this holds true for men and women alike, there are certain indications and possible predisposing conditions in societies prior to the outbreak of conflict that might shape the way men and women react and act during conflict and in the aftermath.

By engaging in economic, social, cultural and political activities that span national boundaries, members of diasporas might contribute to accelerating or prolonging war and conflict as well as create new possibilities and opportunities for peace-making and reconstruction. Although transnational migration as a process linking migrants to their countries of origin has always existed,[2] the nature and quality of transnational ties have undergone significant changes over time, being shaped by the re-structuring of the global economy and the transformation of processes of capital accumulation, as well as by the expansion of and broader access to new technologies of travel and information. However, little attention has been paid to the various ways in which transnational fields and activities are gendered, i.e. the ways in which women and men are positioned differently in terms of prevailing gender ideologies and relations within the country of residence and the country of origin. In order to grasp the gender dimensions significant for the political mobilization of diasporas, it is important to explore predisposing conditions prior to the outbreak of armed conflict and war, during hot conflict and in its aftermath.

Moreover, Brah's notion of "diaspora space" allows us to connect locations of violent conflict with people living "in peace" elsewhere:

> Diaspora space is the intersectionality of diaspora, border and dis/location as a point of confluence of economic, political, cultural and psychic processes ... [It] is "inhabited" not only by those who have migrated and their descendants but equally those who are constructed and represented as indigenous.[3]

Finally, I conceptualize conflict-generated diasporas in terms of an ongoing process rather than a state of being. Diaspora formations happen over a period of time and many diasporas do link in with previous migration waves of either refugees or labour migrants. Because post–Cold War conflict-generated diasporas are relatively young or are built on older communities, they are partly in the making (and un-making). I take the view that it is necessary to examine the conditions and circumstances in the country of origin as well as in the receiving country in order to grasp the many dimensions shaping diaspora politics from a gender perspective.

Diaspora politics, transnationalism and competing images of the nation

What needs to be emphasized is that diasporic transnational identities are not always counter-hegemonic to nationalist discourses and formations. Although diasporic communities might not share the prevailing images of the nation amongst those left behind, they often do engage in exclusivist and chauvinistic constructions of the nation.

One of the pitfalls of the literature of diasporas and transnationalism is the tendency to perceive transnational state-building processes in homogeneous terms, neglecting the variety of discourses and "imagining" of the nation. People have different ideas of what constitutes a nation and who belongs to it. Central to this investigation are the ways in which different imagined communities come to constitute different ideas of nation, which are discursively constructed as resulting from the experience of exile and displacement that people encountered. Research findings from within Bosnia and Herzegovina suggest that refugees are often perceived as "traitors", who fled during the war and failed to defend their homes.[4] This attitude was especially widespread within Sarajevo, a city that was under siege by Serb troops for more than three years. It is also obvious in the way Iraqi exiles, who have been encouraged by the Coalition forces to get involved in the interim government in Iraq, are largely rejected by the Iraqi population.

A careful analysis of transnational practices should also interrogate the gendered ways in which national norms construct diasporas as temporary, illegal or permanent. More broadly, we need to investigate the ways in which members of diasporas are incorporated or excluded within their country of settlement as well as the ways in which these conditions limit or forge transnational practices and mobility. For instance, whereas some migrants/refugees might develop transnational practices by virtue of their double citizenship, which allows them a degree of mobility and political participation between and within two countries, others are either limited in or impeded from maintaining relations with their country of origin.

In the case of Bosnian refugees, developments in post-Dayton Bosnia as well as factors within their current country of residence have shaped refugees' shifting strategies and practices. A sense of political and economic security within the particular country of refuge can give rise to the confidence needed to create and maintain transnational links between households and families. In contrast, a sense of anxiety, which arises in relation to the question of the legal status of refugees, can play a very big role in hindering the space from which transnational practices can occur. As long as refugees are not certain about their legal status, that is, their right to reside permanently in the country of refuge, they will tend to avoid anything that might jeopardize their status.

I have argued elsewhere that forced migration sometimes leads to "forced transnationalism".[5] For example, family responsibilities and/or bureaucratic affairs, such as a property claim, might push members of a diaspora to a substantial involvement with their home country even in the absence of any desire to return. Assisting families and friends financially or with goods, such as medicine and clothes, is also often perceived to be a responsibility, occasionally even a burden. An element of social pressure not only arises with regard to individual financial assistance, but also becomes even more obvious in relation to collective donations amongst diasporic communities. Community organizations can work as a channel to contribute to development in the home country. They can also, however, be domains that restrict migrants' or refugees' individual choices and exert pressure to display loyalty and compassion for the home country.[6]

Pre-conflict conditions affecting diaspora mobilization

Nationalism and national identities: Gendered perspectives

One of the key issues in delineating gender differences in the run-up to "hot conflict" is the relationship between nationalism and gender, that is, the ways in which nationalism and the nation-state are gendered as well as the various ways in which women participate in or challenge nationalist processes. Case studies of women in a variety of geographical and political contexts substantiate the theoretical model sketched out by Yuval-Davis and Anthias to describe the various ways in which women can and do participate in ethnic and national processes: (1) as biological reproducers of members of ethnic collectivities; (2) as reproducers of the boundaries of ethnic and national groups; (3) as actors in the ideological reproduction of the collectivity and as transmitters of its culture; (4) as signifiers of ethnic and national groups; and (5) as participants in national, economic, political and military struggles.[7]

The most "natural" way in which women participate in national and ethnic processes is the "biological reproduction of the nation", which corresponds to the notion of *Volksnation* – a nation of common origin, common "blood and belonging".[8] The relationship between cultural reproduction and gender relations can be articulated in terms of a *Kulturnation*. Here, gender relations are at the centre of cultural constructions of social identities and collectivities, where women tend to constitute the symbolic "border guards". Being constructed as carriers of the collectivity's "honour" and the intergenerational reproducers of its culture, specific codes and regulations delineate the "proper women" and "proper men".[9] Often women are perceived to be both biological and cultural reproducers of a nation. In Iraq, for example, women were asked by the regime of Saddam Hussein to "produce" future soldiers, and they were also increasingly being used as symbols for the honour and stamina of the nation.

Cockburn argues convincingly that, the more primordial the rendering of people and nation, the more are the relations between men and women essentialized: "Women are reminded that by biology and by tradition they are the keepers of hearth and home, to nurture and teach children 'our ways'. Men by physique and tradition are there to protect women and children, and the nation, often represented as the 'motherland'."[10] The essentializing of gender cuts across the "homeland" and the diaspora and shapes the spaces available for women to act, to resist or to reproduce prevailing gender ideologies, nationalist rhetoric and violence.

Gender and citizenship

State citizenship as a criterion for membership in the national collectivity could potentially be "the most inclusive mode of joining a collectivity, because in principle anybody – of whatever origin or culture – might be able to join".[11] In reality, however, state citizenship is exclusive and tends to favour those with socio-economic resources. Gender is one of the many factors (others are ethnicity, class, sexuality, ability, place of residence) that affect people's citizenship and the distribution of resources. Within any given nation-state, women tend to be subjected to specific laws and regulations, despite being included in the general body of the citizens.

The private/public dichotomy, which has placed women within the sphere of the family and placed men in public life, exists to varying degrees in societies and has an impact on women's options for getting involved in war or peace activism. It has been a highly contested issue among feminist scholars. Yuval-Davis, for example, cautions us to look more carefully into this dichotomy, and contends that the division between the "public" and the "private" constitutes "a political act in and of itself".[12] States have the power to demarcate that which is "private", thereby justifying intervention and non-intervention alike.

In the context of diasporas, unequal citizenship rights for men and women might hold true in the context of both the country of origin and the country of residence. The gendered concept of citizenship that women embody and the status they are accorded in the host country forge or impede their activities and movements while in the diaspora. The conditions for being involved in transnational social fields and activities or moving transnationally are not always available to women, or are limited or framed within a set of normative and cultural gendered rules.[13] Women's activities might be conditioned by a set of regulations based on hegemonic interpretations of gender roles within both their country of settlement and that of origin. These regulations condition their activities, their identities and their likelihood of getting involved in activities that fuel conflict or foster peace. For example, women are assigned duties and responsibilities in the reproductive spheres, which they are expected to carry out whether in their country of origin or in the diaspora. The obstacles posed by social customs and normative rules might prevent them from keeping up links with what is perceived to be "back home".

On the other hand, gender ideologies and cultural norms might enable women to engage with women from different ethnic or religious backgrounds or political convictions more easily than would be the case for their menfolk. This has certainly been the case amongst the Bosnian and Iraqi women and men I interviewed. Because women were perceived to be less significant for political processes, their transgression of "talking to the other side" was less threatening than if men had done it. Moreover, some women appeared to have been more willing and eager to build bridges and mobilize as women, rather than in terms of their ethnic and religious affiliation or political parties. This is despite the fact that women who reach out to "the enemy" are frequently branded traitors and "loose women". Korac, for example, alerts us to the commonly made distinction in the former Yugoslavia between "patriotic women" and "disloyal women".[14] The former were those through whom the nation could rebuild links with the "honourable histories, religions and traditions", whereas the latter betrayed the "ethnic-national collective" by seeking to initiate or maintain solidarity across ethno-national boundaries.[15]

The continuum of violence

Instead of thinking about armed conflict and warfare as isolated instances of violence, feminist scholars and activists have alerted us to the "continuum of violence". On one level, many societies experience what has been called "structural violence" in the period prior to open conflict. According to this conceptualization, violence exists whenever the potential development of an individual or a group is held back by the conditions of a relationship, and in particular by the uneven distribution of power and resources.[16]

Many war-torn countries in the post–Cold War era have experienced severe economic crises as a result of the disintegration of the Soviet Union as well as structural adjustment programmes imposed by the International Monetary Fund. The countries of the former Yugoslavia, for example, witnessed high unemployment, depressed wages and a general economic crisis prior to the outbreak of war. During this time, women were urged to leave paid employment and pursue their "natural roles", with restrictions imposed on their reproductive freedoms.[17] The developments in former Yugoslavia parallel state rhetoric and policies towards women and gender during the period of economic sanctions (1990–2003) in Iraq. Here too, once the country was faced with a severe economic crisis, the government retreated from its previous policies of social inclusion of women and mobilization of the female workforce. Instead, Iraqi women were told to leave their workplace to let men take over and to return to their "natural place" at home as mothers of future citizens and soldiers.

Feminist scholars have also argued that, in addition to "structural violence" based on the unequal distribution of resources, women experience the gendered phenomenon of violence within the context of patriarchal social relations.[18] According to some analysts, all such violence should be situated within a "sexual violence approach",[19] even where no overtly sexual act is involved. In this interpretation, a whole set of violent acts is subsumed under a broad definition of male sexual violence[20] – "Violence which takes place in the home or the workplace and on the street corner; violence involving racism, homophobia, xenophobia and other prejudices; violence on international and global levels including trafficking in women and women's experiences of war violence."[21]

However, I concur with the view of some authors that this approach essentializes men and masculinities as well as glosses over the multiple causes of violence, which are not rooted merely in male sexuality. This is not to deny the relationships between forms of violence within the home, on the street and within society at large and the violence occurring during conflict and war. But it is important to recognize the complex causes of violence and to acknowledge that men and women can be active agents in perpetrating and resisting violence. Lentin, for example, argues that "[v]iewing women as homogeneously powerless and as implicit victims does not allow us to theorise women as benefactors of oppression, or the perpetrators".[22] Nor does it help us to theorize and explain women's agency with respect to peace initiatives and resistance to patriarchal gender ideologies and relations.

The links between patriarchy,[23] nationalism and the militarization of society have been widely demonstrated.[24] Militarism is the culture, and national militaries supply the force that tends to sustain national movements and help them to achieve their goals.[25] Militarism, like any ideology, entails a whole set of core beliefs that are tied up with militarized gender regimes[26] – that is, institutionally manifested gender relations. Among these core beliefs are:

a) that armed force is the ultimate resolver of tensions; b) that human nature is prone to conflict; c) that having enemies is a natural condition; d) that hierarchical relations produce effective action; e) that a state without a military is naïve, scarcely modern and barely legitimate; f) that in times of crisis those who are feminine need armed protection; and g) that in times of crisis any man who refuses to engage in armed violent action is jeopardizing his own status as a manly man.[27]

Militarized gender regimes often exaggerate gender differences and inequality, and dictate complementary worlds for men and women, prior to, during and after wars. Men are frequently equated with the worlds of arms and glory, while women are relegated to birthing and mourning.[28] Although militarized gender regimes generate a form of masculinity that tends to be oppressive to women and prone to violence, it is important to differentiate hegemonic masculinities from marginalized, subordinated and even subversive masculinities.[29] Masculinity is not a homogeneous entity but, like femininity, differentiated by economic class, education, religious, racial and ethnic background, sexual orientation, and political affiliation.

At times of socio-political tension and economic crisis prior to conflict, as well as during conflict itself, hegemonic militaristic masculinities are celebrated and promoted more than others. Yet male experiences of the military are fundamentally shaped by "race"/ethnicity, sexuality[30] and class. The disproportionate number of Afro-American and Hispanic soldiers in the US army is telling of the racial, ethnic and class differences within the United States, where impoverished communities tend to provide more male soldiers than do privileged communities. In the context of so-called "new conflicts", young men and boys are often subjected to forcible recruitment.

For those in the diaspora, gender differences may be even more accentuated as communities try to maintain their "authentic culture" and solidarity vis-à-vis their country of origin. However, in some instances, as was evident amongst Bosnian women refugees in the Netherlands or some Iraqi women refugees in the United Kingdom, the more liberal and less militarized societies of residence did help women (and men to some extent) to challenge previously prevailing gender ideologies and relations. In both diasporic communities, some women were active promoters of war. In the Bosnian case, many women refugees who managed to escape before the onset of the worst violence organized collections and donations of money and goods to sustain the war efforts of their male relatives. Iraqi women in the diaspora were amongst the active promoters of the recent US-led war and occupation, and mobilized in the context of both political parties and women's organizations.

Increased nationalist rhetoric and militarization also provoke increased mobilization of pro-peace activists and organizations. Owing to the lack of democratic spaces and to increasing tensions in the country of origin, this is sometimes easier for those who have left during a previous conflict or in the build-up to conflict. Women have been active in peace movements (both in mixed and in women-specific organizations), often drawing moral authority from their roles as mothers, wives, carers and nurturers, but not exclusively so. Women also draw their strength and motivations from political positions either as pacifists or as feminists. Iraqi diaspora women, for example, have been mobilizing all over the world, but most notably in the United Kingdom and the United States (the countries with the largest Iraqi diaspora populations), to raise consciousness about the humanitarian situation caused by the current occupation and militant resistance, the legacy of economic sanctions and the regime of Saddam Hussein. Yet, anti-occupation women are not necessarily all anti-war. Iraqi women in the diaspora are divided over the question of military armed struggle against occupation. Whereas some women reject the increasing violence on the basis that it only prolongs conflict and that innocent civilians lose their lives as a consequence of road-side bombs and sniper attacks, some women support the militant resistance, seeing it as the only way to oppose the occupation of Iraq by the Coalition forces.

The differences are not easily attributable to particular variables, because personality and personal disposition play a role in addition to previous political experiences and education, actual experiences of war and conflict, socialization and the current political milieu in the society of residence. Alliances and links with women's or anti-war organizations in the country of residence might shape the specific attitudes towards violence and conflict. Members of the London-based group "Act Together: Women's Action on Iraq", for example, have been very much influenced by their alliance with Women in Black (WIB) – a worldwide network of women opposing war and campaigning for peace with justice. Although WIB is not homogeneous in terms of the political orientation and background of its members, it does project and mobilize around non-violent resistance. Its analysis has had an impact on Iraqi members of Act Together, although differences do exist in terms of attitude towards "the resistance".

Gender in war and conflict

Gender and violence

When violence and conflict erupt, women tend to suffer in gender-specific ways in addition to the suffering endured by all of the population. Men continue to be the major decision-makers, politicians, generals, "leaders" and soldiers involved in "making war". Yet, war casualties are often civilians, many of whom are women and children. Increasingly, wars are fought on the home front. In both Iraq and Bosnia-Herzegovina, for example, market-places and bridges were bombed, as well as houses and shelters.

Sexual humiliation and mutilation, forced prostitution, rape and forced pregnancy are amongst the gender-specific acts of violence occurring during wars. Historically, rape has certainly been the most widespread form of gender-specific violence. It can occur as a random act within the context of general lawlessness, anarchy, chaos and aggression. However, rape has also been used systematically as a deliberate weapon of war and means of torture to inflict maximum harm. Rape is used not only to attack and humiliate the "enemy woman" but, through her, to attack her supposedly male protectors. With women being universally used as symbols of a nation's honour and pride, raping a community's womenfolk traumatizes and violates women individually and also humiliates and attacks the whole community.

Rape was used in former Yugoslavia in all communities, but particularly against Muslim women from Bosnia-Herzegovina to terrorize Bosniaks and inflict humiliation on communities. But it was women who suffered the actual act of violence, the physical and psychological trauma, possible pregnancies, and the shame and stigma attached to rape. Many women felt excluded and shunned by their communities in the aftermath of their ordeals, because they embodied the failure of the militarized men to "protect" their homeland:[31] "In Bosnia the women who are raped are feared, hated and despised ... This is all the more extraordinary given the close, integrated communities that existed before the conflict and the fact that the perpetrators are previous friends, colleagues and teachers of the women they later rape and kill."[32]

In the case of the wars in former Yugoslavia, women's bodies were used as "ethnic markers" in nationalist ideology.[33] Yet, when men are raped or sexually abused and humiliated, as also happens during wartime, these acts are also gendered. Aside from the individual abuse, it is the enemy's masculinity and ability to protect the nation that are under attack. These acts of aggression and humiliation are particularly devastating in societies where sexuality is perceived to be taboo and associated with shame. However, it would be misleading to overemphasize culture or religion: it is not only Iraqi men in Abu Ghraib prison who experienced severe humiliation and a sense of emasculation; any Western man who experiences rape experiences similar trauma.

Gendering refugees and displaced people

A high percentage (50–80 per cent) of international refugees are women and children, often exceeding the average number of women and children in a country.[34] One of the reasons is that men are more likely to be involved in the actual fighting or are killed as civilians, whereas women and children might be expelled instead. Accounts of the 1995 massacre of Bosnian men in Srebrenica are one example of this pattern.[35]

Voluntary migration, on the other hand, has traditionally been a male-dominated phenomenon, despite the recent feminization of labour migration. Moreover, some resettlement programmes, as in the case of Eritrean refugees, for example, were initially male dominated. As the boundaries become blurry where war-torn economies are concerned, diasporas are often mixed in terms of gender. The longer a diaspora exists, the more mixed it becomes in terms of both gender and generation. Yet, in many cases, flight and migration lead to the disruption of families and an increase in women-headed households.

Throughout the process of diaspora formation – including the actual flight, the possible stay in a refugee camp, the journey to the "host country" and the process of settling within a new country – gender constitutes one of the factors structuring agency and mobilization. In the process of forced migration, social structures and institutions are unravelled or undergo significant changes. This might make women even more vulnerable to poverty and violence and increase their dependence on male refugees, or it might open up new spaces as women and men are forced to give up previously accepted norms, modes of behaviour, divisions of labour and responsibilities.

It is important to understand the gendering of refugees and diasporas not merely in terms of women, but to think about it also in terms of relations of power and privilege informed by situations of maleness and femaleness,[36] otherwise we run the risk of "refugee women" being "comfortably categorised as a comparatively invariant of 'multiple minority', victimised as 'women' in their source and host cultures and as 'refugees'. Systematic neglect of the class, subcultural, and situational variability of women would be an almost automatic consequence."[37] One of the ways in which relations of power and privilege are even more tipped in favour of men during times of hot conflict is in terms of women's vulnerability where violence is concerned.

It is extremely difficult to generalize about the gendered dimension of what happens in circumstances of war and forced migration. This is because different refugee populations have different initial economic resources and access to power, encounter different conditions, and are informed by varying cultural and social notions and norms. In the context of the forced migration and diaspora formation of rural people in Africa, Koenig hypothesizes the following:

1) Women are vulnerable to greater physical violence from husbands and other close male kin, given the frustrations of the period and that anger is projected onto available targets.
2) Women's rights to property are likely to be undercut by their own ideas of appropriate behaviour as well as deliberate policy decisions.
3) Gendered assumptions about familial roles will restrict access to economic resources so that women are likely to make their gains through using exist-

ing skills to occupy less lucrative economic niches not immediately usurped by male competitors.

4) Since resettlement almost invariably brings migrants into greater contact with outsiders and greater immersion in a market economy, old ideas about gendered relationships will be profoundly changed as people live in new areas and compare their lives with those whom they see as more privileged.

5) The processes of renegotiating relationships will be anything but easy, for those with power will rarely cede it willingly, especially if the power remaining is control of women.[38]

Diaspora formations in urban contexts might affect women and men similarly to the processes described by Koenig. However, the question of increased vulnerability or empowerment very much depends on the legal and civil rights as well as the available infrastructure in the place of settlement. The potential for political mobilization of women is greater in situations where livelihood and survival are not the predominant concern. This is often the case for members in diasporas who are settling in developed countries where there is some basic provision of housing, healthcare, income support, and so on. Countries with active and diverse women's movements might also be more conducive to the political mobilization of diaspora women than countries in which women-specific activism is marginalized or suppressed.

Gender and post-conflict periods

Feminist definitions of peace

Peace for women does not mean the cessation of armed conflict. Women's security needs are not necessarily met in "post-conflict" situations because gender-based violence remains rampant in reconstruction periods.[39] Enloe's definition of peace is "women's achievement of control over their lives".[40] Peace, as defined by Enloe, would require not just the absence of armed and gender conflict at home, locally and abroad, but also the absence of poverty and the conditions that create it.[41]

In reality, women often experience a backlash in post-war situations when traditional gender roles inside the home or outside are evoked. Violence against women is often endemic in post-war situations, partly owing to the general state of anarchy and chaos but also as an element of heightened aggression and militarization and prevailing constructions of masculinity promoted during conflict. An extreme example of this situation is contemporary Iraq, which, despite the official ending of military conflict, is extremely violent and insecure. As a matter of fact, the level of everyday experienced violence is even greater now than during the period of formal military intervention. Women have suffered particularly from the chaos, lawlessness and lack of security and have been subject to increased harassment and abductions as well as sexual abuse and rape.

For women at home and within the diaspora, it often seems as if the challenges posed to traditional gender ideologies and roles during times of war become too great for patriarchal societies to accept in peace. Women often have less political space to challenge gender relations and to contribute to political processes in the aftermath of conflict. According to Donna Pankhurst:

> The ideological rhetoric is often about "restoring" or "returning" to something associated with the *status quo* before the war, even if the change actually undermines women's rights and places women in a situation that is even more disadvantageous than it was in the past. This is often accompanied by imagery of the culturally specific equivalent of the woman as "beautiful soul", strongly associating women with cultural notions of "tradition", motherhood, and peace.[42]

Historically, women rarely sustain wartime gains in peacetime. Societies neither defend the spaces women create during struggle nor acknowledge the ingenious ways in which women bear new and additional responsibilities. In the diaspora, in contrast, the potential to challenge traditional gender ideologies and relations, and thereby increase women's political mobilization, might be greater. This, however, is possible only if gender ideologies and relations in the receiving country are far more liberal and progressive. Even then there is a risk of a hardening of notions pertaining to "cultural authenticity" and "traditions", depending on the specific circumstances of the diaspora within the new country of settlement.

The absence of women in formal reconstruction processes

In many post-conflict settings, women have been sidelined or marginalized from formal peace initiatives, political transitions and reconstruction efforts. Formal peace negotiations among warring parties and their mediators serve to define basic power relations and to identify priorities for immediate post-war political activity. Traditional militarized gender regimes tend to endow men with the power in politics and locate women's importance within the family.[43] However, women within conflict-ridden societies as well as within diasporic communities do find ways to work for peace and reconciliation through grassroots activism. Women from all walks of life participate in this informal peace-building work, although their activities are often classified as "social" or "charitable", even when they actually have a political impact.

UN Resolution 1325, passed in October 2000, stated the importance of the inclusion of women and the mainstreaming of gender in all aspects of post-conflict resolution and peace operations. The reality of post-conflict situations is often quite different. If at all, UN Resolution 1325 tends to be translated into the addition of a few women in governments and ministries. Yet, the mainstreaming of gender would involve the appointment of women to interim governments, ministries and committees dealing with systems of local and national governance, the judiciary, policing, human rights, allocating funds, free media development, and all economic processes. It also aims at encouraging independent women's groups, nongovernmental organizations (NGOs) and community-based organizations.

In some post-conflict settings, especially with respect to Muslim societies, the stress on UN Resolution 1325 might be perceived to be part of a Western plot to destroy a society's traditional culture and values. This is particularly the case in contexts of US-led military intervention, such as in Afghanistan and Iraq. Paradoxically, people who might otherwise be sympathetic to issues pertaining to women's rights and women's equality may express strong opposition to women's inclusion in post-conflict reconstruction if this is one of the aims of the occupying powers. The political involvement or even return of diaspora women might evoke resentment and a backlash for local women's rights activists. This trend has been particularly evident in the Iraqi context, where the diaspora has played a disproportionate role in the new Iraqi leadership supported by the United States. Diaspora women have tried to put their mark on emerging women's organizations within Iraq, but have frequently been perceived as patronizing and being part of a Western ploy.

Diaspora mobilization during and after conflict

Women in the diaspora who have experienced killings, rape or other forms of violence might be too traumatized to mobilize politically. The physical and psychological effects of violence may evoke a state of paralysis, deep depression and anxiety, which are not conducive to political activism, whether to promote peace or war. I spoke to several Bosnian women in the United Kingdom and the Netherlands who had directly experienced violence – whether in terms of rape or seeing a relative or close friend being killed. Many were reluctant to speak about their specific experiences but made it clear that in no circumstances would they ever want to return to the place where the violence occurred. Unlike their male relatives, who had a closer territorial attachment to their "homeland" and were often involved in diaspora politics, most of the women I talked to were eager to start a new life and create a new home within their new country of residence.

Other Bosnian women, however, did mobilize, mainly to organize humanitarian aid to their families, friends and communities back in Bosnia-Herzegovina, both during the war and in the aftermath. Some even linked up with local and international anti-war women's organizations, such as Women in Black, in order to express their opposition to war and to promote peace. This has also been the case amongst Iraqi women in the diaspora. Greater in numbers than the Bosnian diaspora and with a much longer history, some members of the Iraqi diaspora opted to engage in diaspora politics through existing political parties or to form their own anti-war groups and organizations. Act Together: Women's Action on Iraq was formed originally by anti-regime Iraqi exile women who were opposed to economic sanctions and military intervention in Iraq. In the current situation of occupied Iraq, members of Act Together have been campaigning against both military occupation by the Coalition forces and also violence in the context of resistance and Islamist movements.

Experiences of violence might radicalize women and turn them into either peace activists or active promoters and supporters of violent conflict. Especially in a situation where conflict is perceived as a war of liberation and where women are actively involved in military struggle, as is the case in Palestine and Eritrea, women's experiences of violence might have the effect of making them active supporters of armed violence.

Changing gender relations in the country of origin and in the diaspora

During periods of hot conflict, family structures and compositions change and social networks are often disrupted or even destroyed. The traditional sexual division of labour tends to be challenged, with women entering previously male-dominated professions, fields of responsibilities and public spheres. Women's role as provider of the everyday needs of the family frequently becomes much more difficult, dangerous and strenuous. Shortages of food, healthcare, water, electricity and fuel mean a greater burden and heavier workload on girls and women. Male non-combatants, on the other hand, may experience stress and frustration if they are unable to fulfil their traditional role of provider for the family.

These changes might open up new spaces for women to challenge previously prevailing gender ideologies and relations. Women often take on more active public roles, initially with respect to the survival of their own families but also within their neighbourhoods and wider communities. They get more involved in the provision of healthcare and humanitarian aid, but also mobilize politically, either to support the prevailing politicians and militaries or to oppose war and violence and promote peace initiatives.

For those in the diaspora, an analysis of changing family dynamics helps to shed light on the multifarious ways in which the circumstances of flight from a war-torn country, becoming a refugee and trying to create and maintain everyday life in the receiving country shape not only gender relations but also the links to the "home country". Relationships with families, and disruptions thereof, are often linked to conceptualizations of "home" that might also relate to a particular nation, place and dwelling. Bosnian refugee households, for example, tend to diverge from more traditional extended family ties and frequently create strong nuclear family units. This pattern also holds true for Iraqi refugees in the United Kingdom. Many refugees experience tensions between their loyalties to extended family members who have remained "at home" and their wish to optimize their capabilities and improve their living conditions within their country of refuge.

The pattern of wives feeling more isolated than their husbands and trying to compensate by having contact with friends and family was widespread among many Bosnian and Iraqi refugee couples interviewed. On several occasions I spoke to women who had been professionals in their "home country" and found themselves stuck at home upon arrival in the receiving country. Several women described a vicious circle of initially being in shock (owing to war, the circumstances of their flight and separation from family and friends), insecurities related to language barriers and the perceived strangeness of their physical and cultural surroundings, and a sense of feeling isolated.

In other cases, women proved to be more resourceful and adaptable while their husbands appeared to suffer from greater levels of isolation, loneliness and a sense of "living in limbo". This was particularly true for several Bosnian women in the Netherlands, who reported that it had been much easier for them to find work than it had been for their husbands. Despite the fact that most jobs were not related to their actual professions – many Bosnian women refugees work as cleaners or nannies – they stressed that their work enabled them to leave the house, improve their language skills, get in contact with the local population and gain some financial independence and decision-making power.[44] This in turn gave many the confidence and willingness to become involved in diaspora politics, in the form of either humanitarian aid, political lobbying within the Netherlands or involvement with Bosnian political parties.

Diaspora men similarly express a broad range of attitudes and perceptions. For the majority, being in the diaspora has meant a break with their traditional roles as head of household and main breadwinner. Being dependent on income support or engaging in low-paid wage work different from their actual professions is often experienced as a loss of identity and "manhood". The alleged emotional attachment and commitment to a home country, such as Bosnia, sometimes appear to fill the gaps within the domain of identity previously occupied by a range of factors including profession, family ties and local origins. In other words, ethnic, national and political identities become especially significant in light of the loss of other identifiers traditionally associated with the "male sphere".[45] Many men reported being regular visitors to Bosnian community associations in which, next to social and cultural events, diaspora politics were high on the agenda.

This is not to fall into the trap of reproducing a strictly defined public versus private sphere supposedly categorizing male and female domains. Diaspora women also experience a great loss of identity and self-esteem when losing their work and not being able to practise their professions. However, as has been widely demonstrated in numerous case studies, women tend to be less conscious of status deprivation because of their responsibility for maintaining household routines.[46]

Nonetheless, diaspora men cannot be characterized merely by their sense of loss and their sense of national belonging. In fact, many husbands living with their families abroad are much more concerned with their immediate family than with political issues pertaining to the future of their home country. Some Bosnian and Iraqi men profess that they enjoy the time they spend with their children and are much more involved in childcare and household chores.

Acknowledging that women may gain or lose status depending on the particular migration context and cultural background,[47] the prevailing literature appears to group migrant and refugee women in one of two categories: those who have gained in status and importance within the family owing to new economic and social responsibilities, and those whose role in the family has been undermined.[48] However, as findings in the context of Bosnian and Iraqi refugee families show, gender relations and family dynamics have shifted in various directions, accounting for empowerment and increased opportunities as well as impediment and loss among migrant and refugee women. It should be stressed here that gender relations should be equated not with women per se, but rather with the power relations between men and women as well as with underlying notions of femininity and masculinity.

These changing family and gender dynamics are significant in trying to understand diaspora politics and the ways in which men and women might relate differently to their country of origin. However, it is difficult to draw generalized conclusions about involvement in diaspora politics and the more specific question of peace activism as opposed to activism in support of war.

Concluding remarks

What should be stressed is that, within any conflict-generated diaspora, men and women do react and act differently. There might be a particular trend in either direction recognizable in terms of numbers, but hardly any diaspora community will be homogeneous as regards their homeland politics. As argued in the introduction, one of the crucial factors influencing how men and women relate to their country of origin and the conflict being waged within it is existing and changing gender relations during the period of war within the country of origin as well as in the context of migration and living in the diaspora. However, as previously mentioned, social class background, place of origin, country of settlement, political affiliation and orientation, as well as specific experiences of war and conflict, also shape homeland politics.

This chapter has shown clearly that women's and men's experiences of war, flight and diaspora formation are never unidimensional. Women should not be viewed solely as victims of war. They assume the key role of ensuring family livelihoods in the midst of chaos and destruction, they are active in peace movements at the grassroots level, they provide support for male soldiers, and they are themselves perpetrators of violence and killing.

In many circumstances of open war and conflict, sections of the population oppose violence and try to promote peace. Some men try to dodge the draft or desert from the military. Some women and men may shelter, feed and look after people who are defined as "the enemy". Although men and women are involved in these peace movements and organizations, many women prefer to mobilize separately as women. There are several reasons for forming separate women's groups and organizations, both within the country of origin and within the diaspora: (1) women might feel solidarity as women, as mothers or as feminists; (2) women might oppose the hierarchical and non-democratic political structures prevalent in male-dominated groups and organizations; (3) women might feel safer and more confident in women-only environments.

To encourage the political mobilization of diaspora women, especially with respect to peace initiatives and reconstruction efforts, more should be done to ensure that women are perceived not merely as helpless victims but also as agents. Diaspora women's vulnerability may be decreased in the receiving countries by ensuring that women are equally entitled to legal rights where residence and access to welfare and resources are concerned. Enabling women to gain access to information about their homeland, other than that circulated by nationalist leaders, might also help to channel activism away from support for conflict and warfare. Moreover, local and international peace movements and NGOs involved in reconstruction might involve diaspora women not only as individuals but also as groups or organizations. Finally, the recognition of difference and heterogeneity amongst diasporic communities might encourage a shift away from the tendency to portray elder male political leaders as representative of the communities' views, politics and aspirations.

Notes

1. Stuart Hall, "Cultural Identity and Diaspora", in Jonathan Rutherford, ed., *Identity: Community, Culture, Difference*, London: Lawrence & Wishart, 1990.
2. See, for example, Nina Glick Schiller, "Transmigrants and Nation-States: Something Old and Something New in the U.S. Immigrant Experience", in C. Hirschmann, P. Kasinitz and J. DeWind, eds, *The Handbook of International Migration*, New York: Russell Sage Foundation, 1999, pp. 94–119; and Steve Vertovec, "Transnationalism and Identity", *Journal of Ethnic and Migration Studies*, 2001, 27(4): 573–582.
3. Avtar Brah, *Cartographies of Diaspora: Contesting Identities*, London: Routledge, 1996, p. 181.
4. Nadje Al-Ali, "Transnational or A-National: Bosnian Refugees in the UK and the Netherlands", in Nadje Al-Ali and Khalid Koser, eds, *New Approaches to Migration: Transnational Communities and the Transformation of Home*, London: Routledge, 2002.
5. Ibid.
6. Nadje Al-Ali, "Losses in Status or New Opportunities? Gender Relations and Transnational Ties among Bosnian Refugees", in Deborah Fahy Bryceson and Ulla Vuorel, eds, *Forging New European Frontiers: Transnational Families and Their Global Networks*, Oxford: Berg Publisher, 2003.
7. Nira Yuval-Davis and Floya Anthias, eds, *Woman, Nation, State*, London: Sage Publications, 1989, p. 7.
8. Ibid.
9. Nira Yuval-Davis, *Gender and Nation*, London: Sage Publications, 1997, p. 67.
10. Cynthia Cockburn, "Background Paper: Gender, Armed Conflict and Political Violence", World Bank Conference on Gender, Armed Conflict and Political Development, Washington, DC, 1999, p. 8.
11. See Yuval-Davis, *Gender and Nation*, p. 24.
12. Ibid., p. 80.
13. For example, referring to the Middle East, Joseph has argued that women "are recognised and addressed as citizens in the context of their positions within patriarchal structures, as subordinate mothers, wives, children or siblings" (Suad Joseph, "Patriarchy and Development in the Arab World", *Gender & Development*, 1996, 4(2): 14–19, at p. 7).
14. Maja Korac, *Linking Arms: Women and War in Post-Yugoslav States*, Uppsala: Life and Peace Institute, 1998.
15. Ibid.
16. Johan Galtung, *Essays in Peace Research*, vols 1–5, Copenhagen: Christian Ejlers, 1975–1980, cited in Cockburn, "Background Paper: Gender, Armed Conflict and Political Violence", p. 6.
17. See Korac, *Linking Arms*.
18. See Liz Kelly, "Wars against Women: Sexual Violence, Sexual Politics and the Militarized State", in Susie Jacobs, Ruth Jacobson and Jennifer Marchbank, eds, *States of Conflict: Gender, Violence and Resistance*, London: Zed Books, 2000.

19. J. L. Radford and M. Hester, "Introduction", in M. Hester et al., eds, *Women, Violence and Male Power*, Milton Keynes: Open University Press, 1996, p. 3.

20. Jacobs et al., eds, *States of Conflict*, p. 2.

21. C. Corrin, "Introduction", in C. Corrin, ed., *Women in a Violent World: Feminist Analyses and Resistance across "Europe"*, Edinburgh: Edinburgh University Press, 1996, p. 1.

22. Ronit Lentin, *Gender and Catastrophe*, London: Zed Books, 1997.

23. Recognizing that patriarchy is a contested concept, I have adopted the definition as "a set of social relations which has a material base and in which there are hierarchical relations between men, and solidarity between them, which enable them to control women. Patriarchy is thus the system of male oppression of women" (see Heidi Hartmann, "Capitalism, Patriarchy and Job Segregation by Sex", in Zillah Eisenstein, ed., *Capitalist Patriarchy and the Case for Socialist Feminism*, New York: Monthly Review Press, 1979, p. 232). It is important to stress, however, that forms of patriarchy vary historically, cross-culturally and according to class standing.

24. See, for example, Cynthia Enloe, *Maneuvers: The International Politics of Militarizing Women's Lives*, Berkeley: University of California Press, 2000.

25. Cynthia Cockburn and Dubravka Zarkov, "Introduction", in Cynthia Cockburn and Dubravka Zarkov, eds, *The Postwar Moment: Militaries, Masculinities and International Peacekeeping*, London: Lawrence & Wishart, 2002, p. 12.

26. Robert Connell, *Gender and Power*, Cambridge: Polity Press, 1987.

27. Cynthia Enloe, "Demilitarization – or More of the Same? Feminist Questions to Ask in the Postwar Moment", in Cockburn and Zarkov, eds, *The Postwar Moment*, pp. 22–24.

28. See Cockburn and Zarkov, eds, *The Postwar Moment*.

29. See Robert Connell, *Masculinities*, Cambridge: Polity Press, 1995.

30. Francine D'Amico, "Citizen-Soldier? Class, Gender, Sexuality and the US Military", in Jacobs et al., eds, *States of Conflict*.

31. Kelly, "Wars against Women".

32. G. Mezey, "Rape in War", *Journal of Forensic Psychiatry*, 1995, 5(3): 589, quoted in Kelly, "Wars against Women", p. 53.

33. Silvia Meznaric, "Gender as an Ethno-Marker: Rape, War and Identity Politics in the Former Yugoslavia", in Valentine Moghadam, ed., *Identity, Politics and Women: Cultural Reassertions and Feminisms in International Perspective*, Oxford: Westview Press, 1994.

34. See, *inter alia*, Women's Commission for Refugee Women and Children at ⟨http://www.womenscommission.org⟩ (accessed 26 September 2006).

35. Mark Danner, "The Killing Fields of Bosnia", *New York Review of Books*, 1998, 45(14): 63–77.

36. Doreen Indra, ed., *Engendering Forced Migration*, New York: Berghahn, 1999.

37. Ibid., p. xiv.

38. D. Koenig, "Women and Resettlement", in R. S. Gallin, A. Ferguson and J. Harper, eds, *The Women and International Development Annual*, No. 4, 1995, pp. 21–49, quoted by Elizabeth Colson, "Gendering Those Uprooted by 'Development'", in Indra, ed., *Engendering Forced Migration*, p. 38.

39. Myriam Gervais, "Human Security and Reconstruction Efforts in Rwanda: Impact on the Lives of Women", in Haleh Afshar and Deborah Eade, eds, *Development, Women, and War: Feminist Perspectives*, Oxford: Oxfam, 2004, pp. 301–314.

40. Cynthia Enloe, "Feminist Thinking about War, Militarism and Peace", in B. Hess, ed., *Analysing Gender: A Handbook of Social Science Research*, Newbury Park, CA: Sage, 1987, p. 538, quoted in Kelly, "Wars against Women", p. 48.

41. Kelly, "Wars against Women", p. 48.

42. Donna Pankhurst, "The 'Sex' War and Other Wars: Towards a Feminist Approach to Peace Building", in Afshar and Eade, eds, *Development, Women, and War*, p. 19.
43. Cockburn and Zarkov, "Introduction", p. 13.
44. Al-Ali, "Losses in Status or New Opportunities?", pp. 83–102.
45. Ibid.
46. Gina Buijs, "Introduction", in Gina Buijs, ed., *Migrant Women: Crossing Boundaries and Changing Identities*, Cross-Cultural Perspectives on Women Vol. 7, Oxford: Berg, 1993, p. 5.
47. Ibid.
48. Ibid., pp. 8–9.

Part II

The case studies

4

The Jewish Diaspora and the Arab–Palestinian–Israeli conflict

Gabriel Sheffer

Most diasporas are frequently, in fact almost constantly, involved in various stages of acute conflicts.[1] They are not only engrossed in conflicts in their homelands and host lands.[2] Occasionally diasporas are involved in conflicts in other countries where their brethren reside and where their culture, ideals and rights, as well as their practical interests and those of their kin, are seriously jeopardized or threatened. Furthermore, because of the current growth and enhanced socio-political and economic powers of diasporas, their members also become immersed in conflicts at the regional and global levels. This applies, of course, also to one of the oldest, most exposed and therefore endangered diasporas, though at the same time one of the most enduring and active – the Jewish Diaspora.

Here it should be noted that, until fairly recently, many identified the term "diaspora" exclusively with the dispersed Jews. Others typified the Jewish Diaspora as the ultimate "classical diaspora".[3] Recently, however, the Jewish Diaspora is more accurately viewed as sharing several characteristics with other diasporas and, like them, having both sad and happy experiences.[4] Thus, like other diasporas, each of the Jewish diasporic communities residing in different host lands has had to deal with harsh conditions in their host land, with the perilous situation of Jews in other host lands, with dangerous regional and international developments, and with constant conflicts in and related to their ancient homeland.

In this comparative context it should be noted that, like some other similar enduring diasporas, such as the Chinese, Indian and Armenian

Diasporas in conflict: Peace-makers or peace-wreckers?, Smith and Stares
(eds), United Nations University Press, 2007, ISBN 978-92-808-1140-7

diasporas, as well as some newer diasporas,[5] from the very early days of its existence until the late nineteenth century the Jewish Diaspora was caught up mostly in externally imposed conflicts in its various host lands and in its historical homeland. All these conflicts related mainly to the Diaspora's controversial (and often detested) culture, beliefs, values, historical background and human and socio-political rights. Since the end of the nineteenth century, however, some segments of the Jewish Diaspora and of their kin in their homeland – Palestine/Eretz-Israel – have also contributed quite substantially to the emergence and continuation of the multifaceted Middle East conflict system (henceforward "the Conflict").

This Conflict has attracted considerable attention among wide publics in the Middle East itself and elsewhere, as well as of politicians and academics worldwide. Consequently, the coverage of this Conflict has been impressive.[6] However, except for a few publications and references, the role of the Jewish Diaspora in the current conflict system in the Middle East has been under-studied.[7] This is certainly the case as regards analyses intended to contribute to a more theoretical view of diasporas' involvement in post–Cold War conflicts and their policy implications, which is the goal of this volume.

The main purpose of this chapter, therefore, is not only to redress the specific lacuna regarding the Jewish Diaspora's involvement in various conflicts, especially those pertaining to its homeland, but also to contribute to the analysis and theorization of the general phenomenon of diasporas' involvement in post–Cold War conflicts, particularly in their homelands.

In this vein, the chapter's main conclusions, which should contribute to that attempt at theorization, will be based on answers to four general questions: first, the extent to which the Jewish Diaspora can play the same role in the present stage of the Conflict, which involves the problematic gradual termination of the multifaceted Conflict, as it did in the previous stages of the Conflict's emergence and continuation; second, the extent to which Israel's present posture in international affairs has contributed to the diminishing role of the Jewish Diaspora in the current Conflict in general, and particularly in the Israeli–Palestinian conflict; third, the extent to which the more limited contribution of the Diaspora to the development of the recent stage of the Conflict should be attributed to deep attitudinal and perceptual splits in the Diaspora vis-à-vis its homeland, in general, and the termination of the conflicts in which it is involved, in particular; fourth, the extent to which contemporary processes of globalization and liberalization have a significant impact on the Diaspora's behaviour in relation to the Israeli–Palestinian conflict.

Following fairly strictly the general analytical framework of this volume,[8] and in accordance with the intention to contribute to the theorization of the phenomenon, the structure of this chapter is as follows: the first section focuses on the characteristics of diasporas in general and of the Jewish Diaspora in particular; the second section characterizes the Jewish Diaspora as a trans-state global entity and reviews its relevant historical background, which is crucial for an accurate understanding of the Jewish Diaspora's changed position vis-à-vis the Conflict and its current role in it; the third section ponders the Jewish Diaspora's political intervention in the Conflict; the fourth section deals with the Diaspora's role in the Conflict's "prevention" phase; the fifth section focuses on the Diaspora's role in the Conflict's emergence and continuation; the sixth section outlines the current main elements of the Conflict, the main contested issues, the global and regional environment of the Conflict, the current participants and the Conflict's dynamics; the seventh section generally considers the ability of the Jewish Diaspora to contribute to the termination of the regional Conflict; the final section discusses the possible policy implications and some general theoretical aspects stemming from the analysis of the role of the Jewish Diaspora in what is now probably the world's most enduring conflict.

On diasporas and the Jewish Diaspora

In this section I shall start with some general comments about certain relevant aspects of the diaspora phenomenon and about diasporas' involvement in politics and conflicts.[9]

There is never a single common reason for the involvement of diasporic entities in politics and conflicts. To put it another way, there are always combinations of factors driving diasporas to get involved, or to withdraw from involvement, in politics and hence in conflicts. The reasons for their involvement or withdrawal may be connected to the situation in their homelands, in their host countries, in other countries hosting their particular diaspora's brethren, or in regional and international affairs. Consequently, the patterns of their decision-making and political, social and economic behaviour are complex, not always very clear and changing.

Contrary to certain quite widespread views, it is important to note that individuals, groups and organizations within diasporic entities make autonomous decisions concerning many critical issues. Their autonomous capability to determine their strategy and tactics and to act accordingly further limits the ability of outsiders and non-members to have much influence over the activities of such groups. In many cases the incentives for actual action or passivity by diasporans and the diasporic entities are connected to their desire to overcome the inherent disadvantages involved in being "others" in their host countries. Also, because of their inherent links to their homelands, diasporas and diasporans strive to gain political and economic autonomy, or to achieve independence, or to assist in implementing political reforms in their homelands. Thus, these entities are inclined to cope actively with various repressive measures affecting their brethren in their homelands imposed by hostile organizations, societies and governments.

There are noticeable differences between the behaviour patterns, strategies and tactics of stateless and state-linked diasporas, as well as between the same diasporas at different stages of statelessness and being state-linked. Stateless diasporic entities are likely to support irredentist, secessionist and national liberation movements in their homelands, even if these are actively involved in bitter conflicts. In some cases they use or support violence and even terrorism to attain these goals.[10] In comparison with state-linked diasporas, such stateless communities more frequently use their trans-state networks to transfer or extend a variety of resources to their combative brethren, including fighters and other recruits, weapons, intelligence and laundered money. These globalized networks make it easier to launch violent attacks in both their host countries and other states. Some segments in these diasporas would opt for the continuation rather than the termination of the conflicts involving their entire nation. State-linked diasporas, in contrast, would be much more interested in the termination of conflict or at least in its management.

To a certain extent, post–Cold War "new politics" at the local, state, regional and global levels provides more opportunities for diasporic individuals and groups to use the means at their disposal (in this context, "new politics" means the relative weakening of nation-states; the formal and informal legitimization of pluralism, and in a few societies of multi-culturalism, all of which, in turn, enhances the assertiveness of individual diasporans and diasporic communities; liberalization; increasing demands for political and social rights; and attitudinal contagion). However, these developments do not mean that all diasporans are politically, diplomatically or economically active on behalf of their homelands that are immersed in conflicts, or that new politics is a fundamentally dangerous or undesirable phenomenon for their hosts.

To be really effective either in encouraging the emergence and continuation of conflicts or in managing or terminating them, these diasporas must have dedicated leaderships; no less importantly, they must be highly organized. Such leaders and organizations usually are responsible for the mobilization of human, physical and economic resources and for launching various activities on behalf of or against the people and governments in their homelands and host countries in the context of the various conflicts in which they are involved.

In view of these general comments, it is appropriate to turn now to the Jewish Diaspora. The following is a one-sentence definition of this entity: *The Jewish minorities permanently residing outside Palestine–Israel constitute an ethno-national-religious trans-state diaspora.* Short, elegant definitions such as this may capture the attention of observers and readers and gain approval, or they may be rejected. However, because of the great complexity of the diasporic phenomenon, including the Jewish Diaspora, such a definition is not adequate.[11] Thus, there is a definite need for a more comprehensive profile of diasporas in general and, in this case, of the Jewish diaspora.

Before presenting this profile, it should be noted that, as in the other diasporas, there have been two distinct periods in world Jewry's history in the twentieth century: the period before the establishment of the State of Israel, and the period since its establishment. As in the other diasporas, the establishment of the sovereign Jewish state marked a fundamental transformation in the Jewish Diaspora's status, positions and behaviour. In the pre-1948 period, world Jewry constituted a historical *stateless* diaspora, whereas since the establishment of the State of Israel, world Jewry has become a historical *state-linked* diaspora. With that change the Jewish Diaspora has demonstrated a greater similarity to other historical state-linked diasporas, such as the Irish, Armenian and Greek diasporas. The argument here will be that this changed posture influenced the way in which the Jewish Diaspora has treated politics and conflicts at home and abroad.

In addition, like other historical ethno-national diasporas, world Jewry has been an entity whose core members' identity is anchored in noticeable non-essentialist-primordial and collective-symbolic foundations. These include the idea of a common ancestry, biological connections that are maintained through endogamy, shared cultural and behavioural patterns, a historical language, collective historical memories, a discernible degree of national solidarity and shared patterns of collective behaviour. All these elements of the Diaspora's identity, especially, in the context of this chapter, the deeply rooted connection to Jewry's ancient homeland, have a critical impact on its involvement in the politics of the Conflict. However, the Jewish Diaspora's identity and behaviour are also influenced by instrumental factors, such as the practical impacts of globalization and glocalization, external and internal societal pressures, deprivation, economic considerations, and self-perceived national needs and interests.[12]

In combination, these non-essentialist-primordial, collective-psychological and instrumental factors contribute to recurrent transformations in the nature and patterns of activity of the Diaspora, including its positions and activities regarding politics in general and the politics of the Conflict in particular. Moreover, these basic formative factors have determined the identification patterns, the overall strategy that the Diaspora has adopted in its various host countries, the emergence of its numerous organizations, and its active trans-state networks, which are intended to protect and promote its cultural, political and economic interests. These are all elements of the Diaspora's profile.

As noted above, the following multivariate profile is based on my own and other studies of diasporic entities. It fits the Jewish Diaspora and most other "historical diasporas" (diasporas formed in antiquity or during the Middle Ages), "new diasporas" (diasporas formed since the industrial revolution and modernization) and "incipient ethno-national diasporas" (diasporas that have been established more recently or are being established now), whether these are stateless or state-linked. For the specific purposes of this chapter, the profile, which was originally intended to characterize all ethno-national diasporas, has been amended to characterize the dispersed Jewish people.

The Jewish Diaspora was created as a result of both voluntary and forced migration out of its homeland and other host lands. It was formed as a result of permanent settlement in many host lands, and has remained a minority in all of its host countries. Although permanently settled in host countries, core members of the Diaspora have maintained their ethno-national identity. This ethno-national identity has been buttressed by strong religious beliefs, including that regarding the holiness of the Land of Israel–Palestine. Now most core members of this Diaspora do not regard their existence in their host countries as one of exile. Based on a combination of primordial and instrumental basic factors, a sense of solidarity has emerged, especially among core members. This solidarity facilitates continuous links between the élites, leaders, organizations and active members at the grassroots level, and relates to cultural, social, economic and political matters. In turn, these factors determine the Diaspora's relations with its host lands, homeland and other international actors.

The ethno-national identity, identification, solidarity and continuous interactions serve as the bases for organization and collective action, whose essential purpose is to ensure the Diaspora's ability to promote its interests in both its host lands and its homeland as well as to maintain cultural, social, economic and political connections with its homeland and with other segments of world Jewry. Wherever and whenever core members are free to act autonomously, they tend to adopt distinct strategies and tactics concerning their existence in their host country and relations with their homeland. In most cases, members of the Jewish Diaspora have adopted a communalist strategy, which is intended to ensure their integration rather than assimilation in their host country. This strategy, coupled with the general wish to maintain contacts with the homeland, determines the nature and behaviour of the organizations that the Diaspora has established. This has led the dispersed Jews to set up elaborate and sometimes labyrinthine trans-state networks.

The establishment of overarching institutions, front organizations, specialized organizations and local communal organizations enables the Diaspora to play non-marginal political, diplomatic and economic roles in its homeland, in some host lands and in other countries. These organizations perform three types of essential function relevant to the analysis here – legal and physical defence; social, religious and financial maintenance; and promotion of communal cultural, social and political interests.

The existence of these organizations and trans-state networks, and their subsequent activities, raise complex and delicate issues of loyalty. The Diaspora's loyalties can be ambiguous, divided or dual, and may alter in the light of changing circumstances. To avoid and prevent undesirable clashes between the Diaspora and its host lands' governments concerning the laws of the land and the norms of the dominant segments in host societies, the Diaspora's core members usually accept these norms and comply with those laws. Nevertheless, during certain periods, especially when their homeland or host lands are embroiled in crises and conflicts, or when the Diaspora encounters severe difficulties, certain segments in the host society may develop negative perceptions about the Diaspora's "disloyalty". On occasion, such tensions and clashes lead to the homeland's intervention on behalf of its Diaspora or to meddling in the Diaspora's affairs.

The relevance of the various elements of this profile to the analysis and theorization of the Diaspora's involvement in the Middle East conflict system will be analysed and demonstrated below.

World Jewry as a global trans-state diaspora

At the beginning of the twenty-first century, the majority of the Jewish people live outside Israel. Compared with about 5.2 million living in Israel, there are about 5.3 million in the United States and about 3 million in all other host lands (about 500,00 in France, 370,00 in Canada, 300,000 in the United Kingdom, 250,000 in Russia, 180,000 in Argentina, 120,000 in Germany, and the rest in other countries worldwide).[13] The majority of the members of the Jewish Diaspora, especially in Western democracies, reside in relative security. They enjoy political rights, economic prosperity and cultural progress.

These demographic and socio-political factors have raised the issue of the location of the Jewish national centre, which is directly connected to the relative roles of the Diaspora and Israel in politics and the Conflict. During the first two decades after the establishment of Israel, the Diaspora generally recognized the new nation-state as the main Jewish centre. Implicitly, the Diaspora accepted the notion that Israel's policies and actions might well determine developments in the Diaspora. Now, over fifty years later and under the influence of recent processes of globalization and glocalization, Israel has lost its central position. There are currently five major Jewish centres – American, Israeli, French, British and Russian. There is implicit and explicit competition among these centres, and some other emerging centres such as in Germany, over predominance in the entire nation, which means that it is more difficult for Israel to impose its positions and policies on all the Diaspora's communities, and to control their loyalties and their autonomy in determining and pursuing their own strategic and tactical policies and decisions.[14]

Moreover, the Jewish Diaspora faces serious questions concerning its continuity. Grappling with this existential issue has already led to some far-reaching changes in the perception of communal needs, and consequently also in the activities and the proportional allocation of resources for the homeland and the Diaspora's needs. This development, coupled with criticism of the general policy vis-à-vis the Arabs and Palestinians pursued by rightist Israeli governments in the 1980s, the 1990s and the early years of the twenty-first century, does much to explain the main pattern of the Diaspora's involvement in the post–Cold War Middle East conflict system.

The Jewish Diaspora in conflict politics

Immediately after the Holocaust during World War II, while the Jews still constituted a historical stateless diaspora, large sections in various Jewish communities adopted a strategy focused on the homeland. Accordingly they intended to assist in establishing and strengthening a Jewish state there. Not surprisingly, this strategy has changed since the establishment of Israel in 1948 and especially after Israeli successes in the 1967 war. Now, in most democracies and democratizing states, Jewish communities adopt a communalist strategy focused on their own needs in their host lands. Essentially, this strategy entails not only intra- and extra-communal liberal social, political and economic behavioural patterns, but also a different approach to Israel and to the Conflict in which it is involved. This change has meant a greater willingness, readiness and ability to adjust to the prevailing socio-political conditions in their host countries and less attention to the changing conditions and positions in Israel.

Thus, on a spectrum of strategies that runs from an assimilationist pole to a return to the homeland pole, the middle way of the communalist strategy is regarded as one that poses no major threats to its host lands, does not totally alienate the homeland, and does not impose too great a demand on the members of the Diaspora. By adopting this strategy, the Diaspora implicitly, and at times also explicitly, is pronouncing that it accepts the main social, political and economic rules of the game in its host lands and that only in extreme circumstances would it adopt moderate forms of dual loyalty. When fully implemented, this pattern also reduces potential and actual controversies and clashes between the Diaspora and the homeland, but at the same time also diminishes the Diaspora's readiness to get involved in the management or termination of the Conflict.

Despite the basic similarities between the Jewish Diaspora and other ethno-national diasporas, the Jewish Diaspora is also characterized by some unique collective traits: the Holocaust as a decisive basic traumatic memory; the prevailing memories of the Diaspora's major role in the establishment of Israel; the relatively large number of Jewish returnees to Israel; and continued personal and inter-organizational contacts between the Diaspora and the Jewish state. Some connections are related to the Jewish Diaspora's role in the Arab–Palestinian–Israeli conflicts and its influence, or lack of influence, on them.[15]

The Diaspora's role during the Conflict's "prevention" phase

Accurately to understand the changes in the Diaspora's positions and activities in relation to the current ongoing Conflict, it is necessary to contextualize them by briefly reviewing the history of its involvement.

Diaspora Jews were involved in historical conflicts that occurred in and about Eretz-Israel/Palestine during the rule of the Babylonian, Persian, Greek and Roman empires over that highly contested territory. During the Middle Ages, however, the Diaspora was more widely scattered, stateless, non-organized and thus much weaker, and was almost incapable of becoming involved in conflicts occurring in its historical homeland or in relation to it. On the other hand, as noted, Jews were deeply engaged in externally imposed conflicts relating to their own survival in host countries.[16]

Major change occurred only in the mid-nineteenth century, and became more evident toward the end of that century. At that time, two more integrated, stronger and better-organized Jewish diasporic communities in particular – those in Britain and later in the United States – became interested, and were able to react politically, economically and diplomatically to the dangerous processes and events affecting the Jews living in Palestine.[17]

The Diaspora was successful in some of these interventions. However, it could not prevent or terminate the conflicts there, being able merely to ameliorate them during certain phases. This should be attributed to a number of factors: individual, mostly rich, Jewish activists' greater awareness of what was happening to their brethren in other parts of the world, including in Palestine, which at that time was ruled by the Ottomans; Jews' growing readiness to become involved in such conflicts; their enhanced economic and political integration and control of resources, particularly in Western societies; their easier access to politicians and governments in their host lands; their more comprehensive and efficient organization; and the improving worldwide communication systems which enabled them to obtain information concerning the situation of their dispersed brethren and to mobilize in order to tackle conflicts and intervene when needed. Most of these factors still influence the Diaspora's behaviour today.

The Jewish Diaspora's intensified and organized involvement in Palestine, and thus in the very early stages of the Conflict, began only after the formal setting-up of the World Zionist Organization in 1897. A major result of the establishment of this nationalist organization was waves of Jewish immigrants to Palestine, which at that time was settled mostly by Palestinian Arabs. Before World War I there were three such waves of immigrants, which increased the size of the small Jewish community in Palestine. Most, but not all, of these immigrants were Zionists who purchased land, established settlements, and built new towns. The development of the Yishuv (the Jewish community in Palestine) was dynamically supported – organizationally, financially and diplomatically – almost exclusively by Zionists, then a tiny minority in the entire dispersed Jewish nation, and by the families of the immigrants in the Diaspora. Zionists were also active in the political and diplomatic endeavours to protect the growing Yishuv, and in attempts to manage, rather than prevent, the looming local conflicts that occurred in Palestine as a result of Jewish immigration and settlement.[18]

Though an animated debate continues concerning the exact historical timing, it is clear that an embryonic Palestinian Arab national movement emerged in Palestine at the same time as the appearance of organized Zionism, the early waves of immigration to Palestine, the first Jewish settlements there, and the gradually growing involvement of Diaspora Jews in Palestinian affairs.[19] Until World War I there were no major or recurring violent clashes between the two separate emerging national communities that would have dictated a more intensive involvement on the part of the Jewish Diaspora. Nevertheless, tension was gradually growing, especially in view of further purchase of land by Jews, the continuously growing numbers of Jewish immigrants arriving in Palestine, and the economic development of the Yishuv. In fact, these are the historical roots of the Middle East conflicts, which are referred to as "the century-old confrontation" between Arabs and Palestinians, on the one hand, and Jews, on the other. Some of these factors are still relevant at the beginning of the twenty-first century.

While the conflict over Palestine was slowly brewing, direct involvement of a-Zionists and anti-Zionists in the Diaspora and of Arab politicians in the neighbouring countries was generally insignificant. Thus, neither the Arab leaders nor the non-Zionist segments in the Jewish Diaspora could have prevented the conflict or stopped its emergence, acceleration and continuation. Hence, the acute Conflict's relatively slow emergence and development and the ensuing initially non-violent and fairly limited clashes between Arabs and Jews in Palestine did not persuade the basically uninterested non-Zionist majority in the Diaspora to intervene effectively.

The Jewish Diaspora's role in the Conflict's emergence and continuation

The major changes in Palestine during and immediately after World War I did not lead the non-Zionist majority in the Diaspora to change its position regarding involvement in the emerging Conflict. This was the case even when, in response to the vast post-war growth of the Jewish community, the Palestinians initiated a series of violent clashes directed at both the British rulers of Palestine and the Jewish community in 1920, 1921, 1929 and 1932, culminating in the 1936–1939 Arab Rebellion. These clashes were intended to stop the development of the Yishuv and to block the Diaspora's involvement in Palestinian affairs. The self-imposed and almost total social and political separation between the two communities in Palestine intensified the Conflict and widened its scope to the neighbouring Arab countries.[20] All attempts to bring the intensifying Conflict to an end through negotiations and agreements with the Palestinians, including suggestions for the establishment of a bi-national state and the 1937 British-sponsored Partition Plan, failed miserably.[21] Yet, the majority of the Jewish Diaspora was still either not interested or passive. It was largely the World Zionist Organization that extended assis-

tance to the struggling Yishuv in the form of manpower, political and diplomatic action and money.

A fundamental change in the Diaspora's position occurred in the aftermath of World War II when the conflict flared up again against the background of the Holocaust, further increased Jewish immigration (legal and
illegal) into Palestine, and renewed proposals for the partition of the
country and the establishment of two independent states.[22] As long as
the British were in control of Palestine it was only natural that the British
branch of the Zionist movement, led by one of the founding fathers of
the movement and later of Israel, Chaim Weizmann, should be deeply involved in the social, political and economic developments in Palestine
and the ongoing Conflict.

The Conflict itself then became existential, involving a clash of two
thriving national movements, two cultures, two distinct social, political
and economic structures, and growing aspirations.

During World War II, and especially in its aftermath, the British branch
of the Zionist movement and the British Jewish community lost their predominance in the political processes concerning Palestine. Instead, the
American-Jewish community, then the largest entity in world Jewry,
began to play a greater and more decisive role in Palestinian affairs and
in the Conflict, which had already fully emerged and was now in the continuation phase.[23] This major change in Jewish involvement was related
to the United Kingdom's loss of its hegemonic position in the Middle
East, including Palestine, and to the United States' new deeper involvement in Middle Eastern politics at large, and in developments in Palestine in particular.

Simultaneously, most of the American-Jewish anti- or non-Zionist organizations altered their previously uninterested or negative positions.
These organizations became deeply involved in Palestinian politics and
in the Conflict. Subsequently, and partly interrelatedly, the US role in
the region continued to grow as well. However, the leaders of this Diasporic community remained extensively heterogeneous as regards their
positions vis-à-vis the Conflict. Their involvement grew further during
the period when the Conflict reached a new peak during the 1948 war,
the establishment of the State of Israel, and the annexation of the West
Bank to Jordan and the Gaza Strip to Egypt. These were the developments that the Palestinians refer to as the *Nakba* ("the cataclysm"),
which caused their intransigent enmity toward Israel.[24]

The unavoidable interim conclusion is that the limited interest prior to
World War II of large Jewish diasporic groups, leaders and organizations
in the Yishuv and in what was occurring in Palestine, in the Yishuv's continued intertwined conflicts with the Palestinians and Arab states, and in
their gradual escalation explains the lack of any serious attempts on the

part of the Jewish Diaspora to prevent the conflicts and then to terminate them. As noted, at most the Diaspora contributed to some low-key attempts to manage the conflicts.

As far as the Diaspora's relations with Israel, and thus its involvement in the Conflict, are concerned, the period from 1948 to the early 1990s should be divided into a number of sub-periods. During the first sub-period – 1948 to the 1956 war – the entire Jewish Diaspora extended much greater political, diplomatic and economic support to the beleaguered new state (here it should be noted that, in the meantime, the opposition of large segments in the Diaspora to the establishment of the Jewish state and to its development had almost totally disappeared).[25] However, the Diaspora's impact on the Conflict was still rather limited. The Diaspora provided inconsequential diplomatic assistance to the Yishuv and to Israel in the United Nations during the exhausting discussions about the results of the 1948 war and the determination of the 1949 ceasefire boundaries of Israel. In fact, only a few attempts were made by Jewish diasporic organizations and leaders to mediate between Israeli and Arab leaders. These were initiated by the Israeli governments. And, not surprisingly, the mediatory efforts did not have any major impact on the Conflict.

The main Jewish organizations, such as the newly established Conference of Presidents of Major American Jewish Organizations, became more active in lobbying on behalf of Israeli positions and policies in light of the Eisenhower administration's more favourable policies towards the Arab states, which then became more deeply involved in developments in Palestine. Nevertheless, the impact of these attempts was also relatively negligible.[26]

The 1956 war was initiated and carried out by Israel, the United Kingdom and France. During and immediately after that war, a majority of core members of the Diaspora were happy with its results – the Israeli occupation of the entire Sinai Peninsula. The pro-Israeli American activists and organizations lobbied in favour of the continuation of US financial support for Israel, which the Eisenhower administration threatened to block and cut. By the same token, they supported the Israeli policy of non-withdrawal from the Sinai. Later, however, when the United States and the Soviet Union imposed intensive pressure to ensure a rapid Israeli withdrawal from the Sinai, the leading American-Jewish organizations changed their position and generally accepted the administration's policy.[27] The adoption of this position contributed to the eventual imposed Israeli withdrawal from the Sinai.

A lull in the active involvement of the Diaspora in the Conflict followed until the eve of the 1967 war. This was directly connected to the fact that this was perceived to be and actually was one of the more relaxed periods in relations between Israel and its Arab neighbours.[28] On the eve of the 1967 war, however, it looked as if Israel was in great danger of being defeated by Egypt and its Syrian ally. This perceived existential danger galvanized the Jewish Diaspora, especially the highly organized American-Jewish community.[29] It led to a distinct change in the previous relative indifference of large segments of the Diaspora. There was an outpouring of almost unqualified ideational and practical support for the threatened Jewish state – the money transferred to Israel reached a peak and political and diplomatic assistance was substantial.

Following the 1967 war, the majority of Diaspora Jews were in favour of the continuation of the occupation of the West Bank, the Golan Heights and the Gaza Strip. Even more emphatically, Diaspora Jews accepted and defended all the means that Israel used against the Palestinians in general and the Palestine Liberation Organization (PLO), led by Yasser Arafat, in particular, such as retaliations for their attacks on Israelis. Moreover, the main Jewish organizations vehemently opposed small "leftist" Diasporic groups, such as Briera, that had tried to conduct a dialogue with the Palestinians and supported Israeli "leftist" parties and organizations that were against the occupation and the new Jewish settlements in the West Bank and the Gaza Strip.[30] This trend of almost complete support for Israeli positions regarding the Conflict continued until the highly problematic 1973 war.

Yet, at the same time, led by small groups such as Briera, a slow movement started inside the Diaspora towards less admiration and greater criticism of Israeli policies. This growing dissatisfaction with the Israeli government was caused and then exacerbated by Israel's questionable military and political conduct during the early stages of the 1973 war; the lack of serious attempts to find a solution to its relations with the Arab states, especially Egypt; the continued occupation of the West Bank and the Gaza Strip; and the numerous clashes with the Palestinians. After the 1973 war, some Diaspora organizations supported the initial talks about a peace treaty between Israel and Egypt. Moreover, there emerged growing agreement with the US government's position regarding the ongoing conflict.[31]

The Jewish world was turned upside down after the 1973 Israeli–Arab war and the outcome of the 1977 elections in Israel, which marked the beginning of the political hegemony of the Israeli nationalist right.[32] As a result of this political transformation, profound disagreements emerged among various groups in the Diaspora, again especially in the United States. These disagreements, and even deeper splits, were over how Israel should deal with its still unresolved conflicts with the neighbouring Arab states (Jordan, Syria and Lebanon) and especially with the Palestinians.

The debates in the Diaspora further intensified in the light of Israel's continued occupation of the Sinai, the Golan Heights, the West Bank and the Gaza Strip and the increased Jewish settlement in these areas. Initially, the majority in the organized Diaspora supported the rightist government's inherent opposition to ending the occupation. Thus, for example, the American-Jewish Diaspora opposed President Carter's criticisms of the Israeli positions and his plans for the termination/ resolution of the Conflict. But President Anwar Sadat's unexpected and awe-inspiring peace initiative led many Jewish diasporans to change their attitude to peace treaties with Arab states and even regarding negotiations with the Palestinians.[33]

During the three-sided negotiations (Israeli–Egyptian–American) on a peace treaty with Egypt, a majority in the Diaspora supported the ending of this Conflict through a withdrawal from the Sinai and its neutralization. Indeed, eventually this was the essence of the Israeli–Egyptian peace treaty. However, the Diaspora faced a growing dilemma concerning its position on US pressure on Israel to change its policy towards the Palestinians and to consider withdrawal from all occupied territories. The splits within the Diaspora became clearer, and political, diplomatic and economic support for Israel gradually began to diminish. The Israeli invasion of Lebanon in 1982 widened the splits in the Diaspora and increased the inclination of certain "liberal" groups openly to criticize the Israeli government for its uncooperative policies and actions. Reactions to the Sabra and Shatila massacres were even stronger and intensified criticism of the Israeli government's policies.[34] Simultaneously, Diasporic criticism of Israeli treatment of the Palestinians also grew. According to public opinion surveys, the American-Jewish community was by then evenly split over Israel's rejection of President Reagan's plans for the establishment of a Palestinian state side by side with Israel.[35]

It is hardly necessary to mention that more or less the entire Jewish Diaspora warmly welcomed the peace treaty that Menachem Begin's government signed with the Egyptian government led by Anwar Sadat. This may partly be attributed to feelings in the Diaspora that Israel would be in a much better security, political and economic situation and that, in addition, the Diaspora would be relieved of some of its political, diplomatic and economic responsibilities towards the Jewish state. Yet this peace treaty was reached and signed without any major intervention by or influence of the Diaspora. It was signed as a result of direct contacts between Israel, Egypt and the United States.

On the other hand, large segments in the Diaspora increased their explicit criticism of the treatment by the Israeli national unity government (led by Yitzhak Shamir of the rightist Likud and then by Yitzhak Rabin of the centre–left Labour Party) of the Palestinians, who launched their first Intifada (uprising) in December 1987. However, the impact of these critical expressions on actual developments in the Conflict was fairly limited. One of the main reasons was that Israeli politicians had established direct links with the US administration, including the presidents, thus diminishing the need for lobbying and the extension of political and diplomatic support by the Diaspora. Yet, the rightist Likud governments in particular, which were reluctant to discuss withdrawal from the occupied territories, granting interim concessions to the Palestinians and offering them greater freedom of movement, were hoping for the support of the Diaspora in view of their recurrent clashes with the US government.

In conclusion, what emerges from this brief historical review to contextualize the current state of the Conflict and the Diaspora's positions and intervention in it is that from the late 1940s until the late 1970s there occurred a gradual intensification of the Jewish Diaspora's concern and sympathy for Israel, and consequently of the Diaspora's political and economic support for Israel. Hence, dedicated Jewish diasporans did not make any significant attempts to intervene in order to push Israeli governments seriously to try to resolve or terminate the Conflict.

Towards the end of the Cold War era, however, the Diaspora's positions on the Conflict and the Israeli government's policies towards it became split. Generally, the Diaspora still felt obliged to offer moral, political, diplomatic and economic support to Israeli governments, which found themselves under pressure to terminate the Conflict both by their Arab or Palestinian neighbours and by foreign governments, especially the US administration. Nevertheless, implicitly, and sometimes explicitly, the Diaspora's fundamental view and position were in favour of managing the Conflict in a manner that was not totally hostile to Israel but that at the same time would lead to the resolution or termination of the Conflict.

The post–Cold War Israeli–Arab–Palestinian conflicts

The global and regional changes that occurred in the wake of the collapse of the Soviet Union and its empire, which marked the beginning of the post–Cold War period, also had an effect on the general situation in the Middle East and on Israel and its conflicts with the surrounding Arab states (except for Egypt, which, as a result of its peace treaty, continued to maintain a cold peace with Israel) and with the Palestinians.[36]

The 1990s opened with the crisis in the Persian Gulf caused by the Iraqi invasion of Kuwait. By dint of the dramatic events in the Gulf area, attention shifted from the interlinked Israeli–Arab–Palestinian conflicts and the first Intifada to the events in the Persian Gulf. Nonetheless, the

Palestinians, who generally supported Saddam Hussein and had received some financial aid from Iraq and the Palestinian diaspora in the West, and who were frustrated at the lack of any easing in their situation (in particular at the suspension of talks between the United States and the PLO), increased their terrorist attacks on Israel. This led to the intensification mainly of the Israeli–Palestinian conflict. The resulting change in US policy, and in particular the suspension of the American–PLO dialogue, should be partly attributed to the close connections of the Israeli government with the US administration and to lobbying by some American-Jewish organizations in Washington. During that period, the American Israel Public Affairs Committee (AIPAC) was particularly effective. Other Jewish organizations were far less influential.

The Gulf crisis had adverse effects on Israelis and their government too. Thus, the Palestinians' vocal support of Saddam Hussein and their hostile acts against Israel only strengthened the position of the ultra-rightist government in Israel.[37] Yet, under the constant pressure originating in the George Bush administration and applied by some American-Jewish leaders, even the ultra-rightist government of Yitzhak Shamir had to participate in the October 1991 Madrid peace talks, which continued until 1993. Various aspects of the Israeli–Palestinian conflict were discussed in these talks, but no clear and practical results were achieved.

Despite the Gulf crisis and the exacerbation of Israeli–Palestinian relations, a major new change in the conflict system occurred when, after 15 years of rightist Likud and national unity governments (mainly based on a Likud–Labour coalition), the Labour Party, led by Yitzhak Rabin, won the 1992 elections by an impressive margin and formed a Labour government. This centre–left government simultaneously employed a tough military policy, including the killing and arrest of Palestinian activists, and attempted to negotiate with the Arabs and the Palestinians.[38] Subsequently, the Rabin government became involved in the Oslo talks concerning the resolution of the Israeli–Palestinian conflict and in the resulting Declaration of Principles on Interim Self-Government Arrangements (the Oslo Accords). This Declaration was signed by Israel and the PLO on the lawn of the White House in September 1993. No less important was the signing in 1994 by the Rabin government, after prolonged negotiations, of a peace treaty with Jordan. This led to a warmer peace between these two countries in comparison with the Israeli–Egyptian peace treaty.

Notwithstanding some disappointment at the failure of diplomatic contacts with Syria, the Oslo Accords and the peace treaty with Jordan were indicative of a huge change in the Middle East and in the conflict system. At the time, it seemed that the dream of a "New Middle East" was materializing. Not surprisingly, although they still expressed concern about Israel's security and other interests, 85 per cent of American Jews supported both the Oslo Accords and the peace treaty with Jordan. This demonstrated the fundamental, if not public, position of Jews concerning the need for the interlinked conflicts to be terminated. During this period, the majority of the Diaspora's leaders agreed with the policies of Israeli governments.

Rabin's assassination in November 1995, the consequent Labour failure in the 1996 elections, and the rightist Likud's renewed control of government dampened the hopes for new and far-reaching developments in the Conflict. Yet the next Likud prime minister, Benjamin Netanyahu, made some hesitant moves in this direction. It should also be noted here that the supporters of the Israeli right in the Diaspora lobbied in favour of the Netanyahu government's tough policy vis-à-vis the Palestinians in the occupied territories.

Labour's next prime minister, Ehud Barak, launched an attempt to negotiate with Syria. But he abandoned it because of Syria's adamant demands for an Israeli withdrawal from the entire Golan Heights. Barak's short term in office was nonetheless marked by partial progress in the Israeli–Arab conflict – a unilateral withdrawal from the Israeli security zone in southern Lebanon and negotiations with Yasser Arafat, which broke down completely during the Camp David talks under the auspices of President Bill Clinton.[39]

These failed negotiations, led in late 2000 to the Palestinians' second Intifada, which was triggered by the unfortunate visit of Ariel Sharon, the leader of Likud, to Temple Mount. The second Intifada was a disastrous development from any point of view for both Israelis and Palestinians. It caused tremendous losses on both sides, unprecedented mutual hatred, identical positions regarding the need for peace negotiations and at the same time for the use of force to move the other side in the "right" direction, the strengthening of extremism and ultra-extremism on both sides,[40] and an increasing number of Israeli outposts and settlements in the occupied territories, further complicating the possibility of a resolution or termination of the conflict. In Israel, the outbreak of the second Intifada paradoxically contributed to the stunning victory of Sharon and his party in the 2001 elections.

The second Intifada continued until the killing of Sheik Yassin, the leader of the extremist Hamas movement, by the Israeli army, followed by the death of Yasser Arafat, the events of 11 September 2001, the war in Iraq, and the pressure by the George W. Bush administration on both sides to accept the Road Map to Peace that he had concocted. The lull in the Intifada led to the installation of Abu Mazen, a moderate Palestinian leader, as president of the Palestinian Authority and to the decision by Ariel Sharon and his coalition government, which included a small group

of Labour Party members of the Knesset, to implement a unilateral Israeli withdrawal from the Gaza Strip. Now, after the successful withdrawal from the Gaza Strip, the most profound disagreements are over
the extent of the Israeli withdrawal from the West Bank, the urgent need
for an end to all insurgencies by the Palestinians, and the stunning electoral victory of Hamas in February 2006, which led to the establishment
of a Hamas government.

In sum, despite some major failures, a fluctuating process in the search
for a resolution/termination of the conflict, and considerable mutual enmity and suspicion, the main developments during the post–Cold War
period have contributed to some relaxation in the conflict, even if temporary and uncertain. But most Jewish Israelis and Jewish diasporans feel
and argue that there is no guarantee of further developments since the
Israeli withdrawal from the Gaza Strip. Many would agree that there is
only a small likelihood of a continuation of favourable progress toward
the resolution or termination of the three remaining interlinked Middle
East conflicts – between Israel and Syria, Lebanon and the Palestinians.

The Jewish Diaspora and the failure to terminate the Middle East conflicts

Activists in the Jewish Diaspora are concerned about two unresolved aspects of the Middle East conflicts: the lack of progress regarding peace
with Syria and Lebanon, and the ongoing Israeli–Palestinian conflict,
which despite its better management during the post-Arafat period (until
Hamas's electoral victory) is still far from ending. The most important
reason for the continuing unease of the Diaspora, on the one hand, and
its fluctuating involvement, on the other hand, is the basic fact that, until
the achievement of a full formal peace with Israel's two northern neighbours and further agreements with the Palestinians, the Diaspora's individuals and organizations are occasionally called upon to act on behalf of
Israel. To some extent, such individuals and organizations feel obliged to
comply with such Israeli calls. Thus, for example, on the eve of attempts
by Rabin and Barak to negotiate with the Syrian presidents, Hafez Assad
and Basher Assad, over a peace treaty, some Diaspora leaders tried to
mediate between Israel and Syria. However, in view of the then determined positions of the Israeli and Syrian governments, there were no evident positive effects. Similarly, some attempts have been made by Jewish
Diasporic supporters of the Oslo Accords to mediate between Israel and
the Palestinians, again to no avail. However, the possibility of clashes with
their host countries' governments, the much reduced concern for Israel
shown by wider circles in the Diaspora, the concentration on the Dias-

pora's own affairs, and the deep splits in the positions of the communities as regards the solution of the Conflict all make it more difficult for the Diaspora to intervene effectively.

Thus, it remains the case that the Diaspora's involvement in the Conflict is focused on lobbying and on attempts to influence the positions of all the actors involved. The Diaspora has taken on the "job", on the one hand, of lobbying host countries' parliaments and governments as well as international organizations, such as the United Nations, to ensure support for Israeli governments' positions and strategies, and, on the other hand, of influencing Israeli governments to adopt reasonable policies vis-à-vis Israel's Arab opponents. Put another way, the Diaspora is unable, and therefore is not asked by Israel, to supply any substantial moral, political or military support to the well-established and militarily strong Jewish state. Occasionally the Diaspora, especially particular American-Jewish organizations, such as AIPAC, is required by Israel to supply some diplomatic assistance, mainly to buttress Israeli positions against requests from host countries and demands from international organizations such as the European Union and the United Nations.

As to the question of whether the Jewish Diaspora can contribute effectively to the resolution or termination of the remaining interlinked Arab–Palestinian–Israeli conflicts, the pretty clear answer is that it is doubtful. This is because in the present circumstances, which have been created by the post–Cold War atmosphere of greater room for manoeuvre by most state actors, only Israel, Syria, Lebanon and, to an extent, the Palestinian Authority can determine the most meaningful processes and specific steps towards a satisfactory resolution of their interlinked conflicts. Since, as indicated above, there is no question that the Diaspora will continue to show its interest and demonstrate its concern about the future of Israel and the conflicts in which it has been involved, the best that it can do is to try to persuade the Israeli, Syrian, Lebanese and Palestinian publics to encourage their governments to strive more consistently for conflict resolution. In the meantime, they can attempt to improve the management of the conflicts and, as far as possible, to reduce the violent outbursts that are impairing any significant progress.

The main arguments and policy implications

Based on the description and analysis in the previous sections, the following are the main arguments that should contribute to the attempt to theorize diasporas' roles in current conflicts.

First, the historical description and analysis have shown that in the post–Cold War era the Jewish Diaspora is not playing the same role that it played in the Middle East conflicts up to the 1990s. But, as has been shown, this is only partly owing to the transformed global situation.

Second, the more limited role of the Diaspora in the Conflict is caused by the far stronger Israeli posture in the global and regional systems. Thus, as a result of the peace treaties with Egypt and Jordan and the military weakness of Syria and Lebanon, and despite the new leadership in the Palestinian community and the Iranian efforts to acquire a nuclear capability, there is no immediate existential threat to Israel that automatically compels the Diaspora wholeheartedly to support the Jewish state and act on its behalf. The homeland's stronger posture, together with the evident direct contacts between successive Israeli prime ministers and their governments and the presidents of the United States and their staff, further reduces the need for the Diaspora's lobbying and pressuring in Washington, as well as in other capitals.

Third, Israel's stronger position and the Diaspora's greater need to focus on its own affairs, such as ensuring communal continuity and revival, intensify the arguments within the Diaspora for and against Israel's policies and its need for substantial political, diplomatic and economic support by the Diaspora. These combined factors bring to the fore the deeper splits in the Diaspora's attitudes towards and perceptions of Israel, and consequently its more restrained wish and need to support Israel and to continue to be involved in the Conflict.

Fourth, contemporary processes of globalization and liberalization, which preceded the end of the Cold War era and are now in full swing, have had some impact on the Diaspora's involvement in the Israeli–Palestinian conflict. Again, this impact is not unidirectional. On the one hand, the struggle against global Muslim terrorism is pushing the Diaspora to support the Israeli insistence on the disarmament of the Palestinian armed movements and organizations as a precondition for any further progress toward the resolution and termination of the Conflict, and, on the other hand, current trends of liberalization and democratization are influencing larger segments of the Diaspora explicitly and implicitly to criticize Israel and call for it to move further on the Road Map toward the eventual resolution of the Conflict.

Finally, the following policy suggestions are not just based on the Jewish Diaspora's case analysed here; they stem as well from the study of the involvement of other diasporas in bitter conflicts.

Thus, first, since it is difficult to regard most of the existing diasporas as tightly knit homogeneous entities collectively pursuing a single strategy, any serious attempt to enlist their support in the resolution of conflicts in their homelands should take into consideration the various shades of opinion and position among the diasporans.

Second, and following on from the previous point, anyone trying to enlist the support of diasporic groups or entities should try carefully to identify and recruit the most significant activists who care about conflict management, resolution and termination.

Third, it should be remembered that truly established and integrated state-linked diasporas are engaged in activities that are intended primarily to enhance their own cultural, civic and economic well-being in their host countries, and only secondarily to improve the welfare of their host countries and homelands. Yet governments and social organizations should not stigmatize entire diasporas, thereby creating a permanently hostile environment that can make the lives of individual diasporans and of entire diasporas even harder than they usually are, and eventually push diasporans to use their power and resources to exacerbate rather than quell the particular conflict.

Fourth, host-land and homeland governments should monitor and unobtrusively follow the moods, positions, attitudes and political trends among both diasporans and their brethren in their homelands. Special attention should be paid to the formal and informal élites and leaders of diasporic entities who play a major role in these affairs. By the same token, the host-land and homeland governments should try to monitor the trans-state networks that diasporas establish in order to acquire information about any suspicious moves and actions by diasporans. In this context, particular attention should be paid to money transfers and to illegal transactions and deals.

The most obvious (almost banal) but still the most essential observation in this context is that, as long as the fundamental problems and grievances of ethno-national diasporas are not addressed and resolved, these groups will be persistently tempted to use strategies and tactics aimed at the continuation of the conflicts in which they and their homeland are involved. Therefore, there must be a constant dialogue with such diasporans and diasporas. For this purpose, constant formal and informal channels of communication should be maintained with them.

Notes

1. See, for example, Aline Angoustures and Valerie Pascal, "Diasporas et Financement des Conflits", in Francois Jean Rufin and Jean-Christophe Rufin, eds, *Economie des Guerres Civiles*, Paris: Hachette, 1996; Daniel Byman, Peter Chalk, Bruce Hoffman, William Grey Rosenau and David Brennan, *Trends in Outside Support for Insurgence Movements*, Santa Monica: RAND, 2001, Chapter 3; James Fearon, "Commitment Problems and the Spread of Ethnic Conflict", in David A. Lake and Donald Rothchild, eds, *The International Spread of Ethnic Conflict: Fear, Diffusion and Escalation*, Princeton, NJ: Princeton University Press, 1998; Michael E. Brown, ed., *Ethnic Conflict and*

International Security, Princeton, NJ: Princeton University Press, 1993; David R. Davis, Keith Jaggers and Will H. Moore, "Ethnicity, Minorities, and International Conflict Patterns", in David W. Carment and Patrick James, eds, *Wars in the Midst of Peace: The International Politics of Ethnic Conflict*, Pittsburgh, PA: University of Pittsburgh Press, 1997; Ted R. Gurr, *Peoples Versus States: Minorities at Risk in the New Century*, Washington, DC: USIP Press, 2003; Ted R. Gurr and Martin Marshall, *Peace and Conflict*, Maryland: CIDCM, 2005; Manus I. Midlarsky, ed., *The Internationalization of Communal Strife*, London: Routledge, 1992; Charles King and Neil J. Melvin, "Diaspora Politics: Ethnic Linkages, Foreign Policy, and Security in Eurasia", *International Security*, 1999/2000, 24(3); Stephen Saideman, "Explaining the International Relations of Secessionist Conflicts", *International Organization*, 1997, 51(4); Yossi Shain and Martin Sherman, "Dynamics of Disintegration: Diasporas, Succession, and the Politics of Nation States", *Nations and Nationalism*, 1998, 4(3); Yossi Shain, "The Role of Diasporas in Conflict Perpetuation and Resolution", *SAIS Review*, 2002, 22(2); Gabriel Sheffer, "Ethno-National Diasporas and Security", *Survival*, 1994, 36(1); Gabriel Sheffer, "Ethnic Diasporas: A Threat to Their Hosts?", in Myron Weiner, ed., *International Migration and Security*, Boulder, CO: Westview Press, 1993; Gabriel Sheffer, "The Study of Ethnic Conflict Resolution", *Migration*, 2003, no. 42; and see the other contributions in this volume.

2. For the distinction between trans-statism and transnationalism, see William Miles and Gabriel Sheffer, "Francophonie and Zionism: A Comparative Study in Transnationalism and Trans-Statism", *Diaspora*, 1998, 7(2); Gabriel Sheffer, *Diaspora Politics: At Home Abroad*, Cambridge and New York: Cambridge University Press, 2003.

3. John Armstrong, "Mobilized and Proletarian Diasporas", *American Political Science Review*, 1976, 70(2).

4. See, for example, Robin Cohen, *Global Diasporas*, London: UCL Press, 1997; William Safran, "Comparing Diasporas: A Review Essay", *Diaspora*, 1999, 8(3); William Safran, "The Jewish Diaspora in a Comparative and Theoretical Perspective", *Israel Studies*, 2005, 10(1); Sheffer, *Diaspora Politics*; Gabriel Sheffer, "A Nation and Its Diaspora: A Re-Examination of Israeli–Jewish Diaspora Relations", *Diaspora*, 2002, 11(3); Gabriel Sheffer, "Is the Jewish Diaspora Unique? Reflections on the Diaspora's Current Situation", *Israel Studies*, Special Issue, 2005, 10(1); Steven Vertovec, "Three Meanings of Diaspora", *Diaspora*, 1997, 6(3).

5. On conflicts involving some new diasporas, see, for example, Michael Mandelbaum, ed., *The New European Diasporas: National Minorities and Conflicts in Eastern Europe*, New York: Council on Foreign Relations, 2000; on the Kurdish role, see, for example, David McDowal, *Modern History of the Kurds*, London: I. B. Tauris, 2004; for a comparative analysis of the Jewish and Armenian diasporas' involvement in conflicts concerning their homelands, see Shain, "The Role of Diasporas"; Gloria Totoricaguena, "Basques around the World: Generic Immigrants or Diaspora?", *Euskonews & Media*, 2000, Issue 72.

6. See, for example, Nicholas Guyatt, *The Absence of Peace: Understanding the Israeli–Palestinian Conflict*, New York: Zed Books, 1998; Benny Morris, *Righteous Victims: A History of the Zionist–Arab Conflict 1881–2001*, New York: Vintage, 2001; Avi Shlaim, *The Iron Wall: Israel and the Arab World*, London: Penguin Books, 2000; Mark Tessler, *A History of the Israeli–Palestinian Conflict*, Bloomington: Indiana University Press, 1994.

7. Steven Rosenthal, *Irreconcilable Differences? The Waning of the American Jewish Love Affair with Israel*, Hanover and London: Brandeis University Press, 2003; Howard Morley Sachar, *A History of the Jews in America*, New York: Vintage, 1992; Shain, "The Role of Diasporas".

8. See Jacob Bercovich's chapter in this volume.

9. The following discussion is based on my own writings, such as Gabriel Sheffer, ed., *Modern Diasporas in International Politics*, New York: St Martin's, 1986; and Sheffer, *Diaspora Politics*; and on other books and articles, such as Robin Cohen, *Global Diasporas*; William Safran, "Comparing Diasporas"; Vertovec, "Three Meanings of Diaspora".

10. Gabriel Sheffer, "Diasporas, Terrorism and WMD", *International Studies Review*, 2005, 7.

11. On the need for complex characterizations of diasporas rather than simplistic definitions, see, for example, William Safran, "Diasporas in Modern Societies", *Diaspora*, 1991, 1(1); James Clifford, "Diasporas", *Cultural Anthropology*, 1994, 9(3); Khachig Tölölyan, "Rethinking Diaspora(s): Stateless Power in the Transnational Moment", *Diaspora*, 1996, 5(1): 5–18; Robin Cohen, *Global Diasporas*.

12. This "synthetic" approach to the question of ethnic identities is well presented in John Kellas, *The Politics of Nationalism and Ethnicity*, New York: St Martin's, 1991; for its application to the Jewish Diaspora, see Sheffer, "Is the Jewish Diaspora Unique?"; and Robin Cohen, *Global Diasporas*.

13. The Jewish People Policy Planning Institute, *The Jewish People 2004, Between Thriving and Decline*, Jerusalem, 2005.

14. William Safran, "The Jewish Diaspora in a Comparative and Theoretical Perspective".

15. See, especially, Robin Cohen, *Global Diasporas*.

16. See, for example, Avraham Malmat et al., *History of the Jewish People*, 3 vols, Tel Aviv: Dvir, 1969 (in Hebrew); Paul Johnson, *A History of the Jews*, New York: Harper & Row, 1987.

17. Howard Morley Sachar, *A History of the Jews in the Modern World*, New York: Knopf, 2005.

18. Howard Morley Sachar, *A History of Israel. From the Rise of Zionism to Our Time*, Tel Aviv: Steimatzky, 1976.

19. Yehoshua Porath, *The Emergence of the Palestinian Arab National Movement*, London: Frank Cass, 1974; Neville Mandel, *The Arabs and Zionism before World War I*, Berkeley: University of California Press, 1976; Tessler, *A History of the Israeli–Palestinian Conflict*.

20. Tessler, *A History of the Israeli–Palestinian Conflict*.

21. Shmuel Dotan, *The Debate about Partition during the Mandatory Period*, Jerusalem: Yad Ben Zvi, 1980 (in Hebrew); Norman Rose, "The Debate on Partition", *Middle Eastern Studies*, 1970/1971 (6 and 7).

22. Sachar, *A History of Israel*; Tessler, *A History of the Israeli–Palestinian Conflict*; Shlaim, *The Iron Wall*.

23. Eliyahu Elath, *The Struggle for Statehood*, 3 vols, Tel Aviv: Am Oved, 1979–1982 (in Hebrew); Rosenthal, *Irreconcilable Differences?*

24. Tessler, *A History of the Israeli–Palestinian Conflict*.

25. Zvi Ganin, *Truman, American Jewry and Israel 1945–1948*, New York: Holmes & Meier, 1979; Michael Cohen, *Truman and Israel*, Berkeley: University of California Press, 1990.

26. Zvi Ganin, *An Uneasy Relationship: American Jewish Leadership and Israel, 1948–1957*, Syracuse: Syracuse University Press, 2005.

27. Melvin Urofsky, *We Are One*, New York: Anchor, 1978; Menachem Kaufman, *An Ambiguous Partnership*, Detroit: Wayne State University Press, 1991.

28. Nadav Safran, *Israel the Embattled Ally*, Cambridge, MA: Harvard University Press, 1981.

29. Michael Oren, *Six Days of War: June 1967 and the Making of the Modern Middle East*, Oxford: Oxford University Press, 2002.

30. Rael Jean Isaac, *Briera*, New York: Counsel for Judaism, 1977.
31. Nadav Safran, *Israel the Embattled Ally*.
32. Rosenthal, *Irreconcilable Differences?*, p. 42.
33. William Quandt, *Peace Process: American Diplomacy and the Arab–Israeli Conflict since 1967*, Washington, DC: Brookings Institution Press, 2002.
34. Itamar Rabinovich, *The War for Lebanon 1970–1983*, Ithaca, NY: Cornell University Press, 1984; Zeev Shiff and Ehud Yaari, *Israel's Lebanon War*, New York: Simon & Schuster, 1984; Yair Evron, *War and Intervention in Lebanon*, Baltimore, MD: Johns Hopkins University Press, 1987.
35. Rosenthal, *Irreconcilable Differences?*
36. On the post–Cold War situation of the conflicts in which Israel and the Diaspora are involved, see, for example, David Makovsky, *Engagement through Disengagement: Gaza and the Potential for Renewed Israeli–Palestinian Peacemaking*, Washington, DC: Washington Institute for Near East Policy, 2005; Morris, *Righteous Victims*; David Shipler, *Arab and Jew: Wounded Spirits in a Promised Land*, New York: Penguin Books, 2002; Charles Enderlin, *Shattered Dreams: The Failure of the Peace Process in the Middle East 1995–2002*, New York: Other Press, 2003.
37. Tessler, *A History of the Israeli–Palestinian Conflict*; Shlaim, *The Iron Wall*.
38. Tessler, *A History of the Israeli–Palestinian Conflict*.
39. Dennis Ross, *The Missing Peace: The Inside Story of the Fight for Middle Eastern Peace*, New York: Farrar Straus Giroux, 2004.
40. See the periodic surveys conducted by Yaacov Shamir and Hallil Shikaki on the positions of Israelis and Palestinians and published by the Truman Institute of the Hebrew University of Jerusalem.

5

The Palestinian diaspora

Mohammed A. Bamyeh

The Palestinian diaspora (*ash-Shatat*) is a product of the Israeli–
Palestinian conflict. Since its beginning in the cataclysmic events of 1948,
diaspora life itself has signified for Palestinians the essence of their dispossession and one of the most compelling elements of their cause. Unlike other parts of the Levant, which had produced recognizable overseas
communities by the early twentieth century, Palestinians did not leave
their homeland in significant numbers before what they uniformly refer
to as the *Nakba*, or great calamity, of 1948. In 1948, and to a lesser extent
in 1967, large Palestinian refugee populations formed in surrounding
Arab countries. Ever since, these populations have been a veritable
breeding ground of resentment and a ready recruiting pool for various
political movements and parties. Arab governments, while expressing
sympathy for the plight of the refugees, have usually regarded these
populations as a source of potential or actual trouble. Over time, large
Palestinian communities formed throughout Western Europe, the United
States and elsewhere, though the greatest concentrations remain in Arab
countries. Today, the majority of Palestinians still live in the diaspora,
and a majority of the diaspora population are registered as refugees.

To examine the relationship of the Palestinian diaspora to the prospects of peace both historically and in the present, I shall address three
interrelated themes: the emergence within the diaspora of a particular
social psychology that has direct political implications; the role of the
diaspora in the Palestinian national movement; and the principle of the
"right of return", which is the main political demand of the diaspora.

Diasporas in conflict: Peace-makers or peace-wreckers?, Smith and Stares
(eds), United Nations University Press, 2007, ISBN 978-92-808-1140-7

My conclusion in this chapter is that an ethical rather than a practical interest underlies the Palestinian diaspora's demand for a right of return. Incorporating ethical questions into the envisioned solution of the conflict would not only address the demands of the diaspora more easily and directly than would otherwise be the case but also provide the basis for a more stable, comprehensive and lasting peace overall. I hope that in the process it will become evident that, as far as the Palestinian diaspora is concerned, meaningfully addressing what Jacob Bercovitch refers to as the "socio-cultural" arena will prove to be key to the termination of the conflict as well as to post-conflict reconstruction. However, it is a mistake to think that the diaspora's role and grievances in the history of the conflict consist simply of socio-cultural issues, because these are obviously integral to the political, military and economic mobilization of Palestinian diaspora – and those dimensions cannot be easily separated. In the final analysis, this diaspora is not the cause of the conflict. It has come into being *because* of the conflict.

The social psychology of the diaspora: Memory and reality

The emergence of a Palestinian diaspora out of war and forced migration left lasting imprints on its social psychology.

First, diasporic life tended to be seen as *temporary*, even after years of exile. The sense that life outside of Palestine is not to be regarded as a permanent fate is widely expressed among virtually all classes of diasporic Palestinian society. Even now, it is quite common to hear not only elders of the first diasporic generation but also their descendants recount how their families left all their property, furniture, businesses and other belongings intact in the expectation that they would be able to go back once hostilities were over. Relics such as ancient house keys and yellowing property deeds are maintained and displayed as symbols of this temporariness of exile.

It was in the late summer of 1948 that many Palestinian peasants living in the camps first learned that life as a refugee was going to last for a long time as they sought, and failed, to cross the new armistice borders so that they could be in their fields in time for the harvest season. As described by Lieutenant General J. B. Glubb, "[t]he Arabs returning to look for their homes were at first almost entirely unarmed. A great number of them were shot dead, without question or answer, by the first Israeli patrol they met. Others were maltreated or tortured."[1] Years after this realization, the refugees still resisted their new fate. When the United Nations Relief and Works Agency (UNRWA) attempted to transform camp dwellings from tents into built structures in the early 1950s, many refugees protested, perceiving the housing upgrade as a ploy to make the camps into permanent homes. The temporary status of diasporic life is summed up in the centrality of the slogan *'awdah*, or "return" (about which more will be said later), throughout Palestinian national discourse and Palestinian literature.

Second, diasporic life signified for Palestinians a profound sense of *injustice*. They live in their diaspora because their ancient homeland has been usurped by an aggressor, along with their homes, orchards, businesses, properties and the richly connected social life of their towns, villages and extended families. Accepting life in diaspora, therefore, is tantamount to becoming resigned to an unparalleled act of injustice. The burgeoning Palestinian Al-Awda movement, the Palestine Right to Return Coalition, in fact asserted this understanding at its second conference held in New York in 2004, at which it affirmed that the right of Palestinians to return to their homes, property and land of origin was both a national and an individual right.[2] Al-Awda stated the nature of that right in a way that most Palestinians would easily accept: being based on the natural belonging of a people to their property and place of origin, this right of return is inalienable, and as such it transcends generations, treaties and agreements, and cannot be subject to negotiation or compromise. It is defined as part and parcel of a basic national right to self-determination of the Palestinians as a whole, regardless of their place of birth or residence.

Third, diasporic life was obviously *unchosen*. It was not a product of a natural population movement or immigration. This conception of diasporic life meant that, even as many of them became prosperous in the diaspora, Palestinians continued to invest in producing a memory of Palestine for subsequent generations. Entrepreneurial success alone could not efface the unchosen nature of diaspora life. As Fawaz Turki put it in his bitter memoirs,

> [the environment] of the Palestinian family ... engendered a deep and constant hope for the return to Palestine ... In his home a Palestinian child, whether born in Beirut, Amman, or Damascus, would be instructed to identify himself as a Palestinian from Haifa or Lydda or any other town that had been his parents' birthplace, and his own experience [i.e. as a discriminated against outsider in a host society] would constantly remind him of this.[3]

Fourth, Palestinians regard diasporic life as an outcome of a *conspiracy* against them, rather than of any necessary or compelling historical logic. Their dispersion and dispossession are viewed as the purposeful result of an underhand, sinister plan by Zionists, in alliance with a powerful West and in collusion with treacherous Arab governments, to rob them of their historical homeland. The Balfour Declaration of 1917, the encouragement of the British Mandate authorities of Jewish immigration until 1939 and then again after World War II, the United Nations' partition plan of 1947, and the immediate recognition of the new state of Israel by all the great powers are readily cited as confirmation of the conviction that a powerful Western alliance had wanted for a long time to carve out an alien state in the heart of Arab lands. In addition, the otherwise inexplicably poor performance of Arab armies in 1948 seemed to confirm the other part of this conviction, namely that Arab governments, themselves appointees of colonial powers, were in effect part of the conspiracy. The assassination of King Abdullah I of Jordan by a Palestinian was an outcome of that belief, which also gained further public credence when Nasser publicly used the example of his own poorly supplied brigade as one of the reasons the Free Officers began their plot to overthrow a corrupt Egyptian monarchy. The Palestinian conviction of Arab governmental collusion was reinforced by various reports and eventually historical research that highlighted the role of a secret agreement between King Abdullah I of then trans-Jordan and Zionist leaders to divide up historical Palestine between a largely desert kingdom and a new Jewish state, which was indeed the outcome of the 1948 war.[4]

These defining features of the social psychology of the Palestinian diaspora – temporary, unjust, unchosen, accidental – powerfully informed widespread practices aimed primarily at producing and maintaining a memory oriented to keeping alive the image of Palestine and the dedication of subsequent diasporic generations to its cause. This tradition shows no abatement over time. On the contrary, it emerged at a later stage in the life of the Palestinian diaspora as a fervent effort to document Palestinian rights and the fabric of pre-diaspora society. Not only do the practices involved in producing national memory in the diaspora include the reconstruction of the networks of Palestinian society in exile, centred around the extended family. They also encompass new public intellectual practices, such as encyclopedic compendiums of Palestinian life as well as more specific city histories and city associations.

The encyclopedic compendiums constitute a distinguished and universally useful part of these practices of memory. They aim primarily at illustrating the pre-diasporic vibrancy of Palestinian society, identifying destroyed towns and villages, charting the class relations of old Palestine, mapping the dispersion of Palestinians throughout the world and, most openly, documenting concrete, legal Palestinian rights to property, infrastructure, natural resources and redress of historical injustices, massacres, forced migration and denial of all rights. The most important highlights of this literature include Walid Khalidi's richly illustrated *Before Their Diaspora* and the recently released colossus of Salman Abu Sitta, *Atlas of Palestine*.[5]

Another genre aimed at the preservation or production of memory comprises city histories and urban geography. Unlike the larger encyclopedic works and historical atlases, which are aimed primarily at documenting Palestinian rights in international arenas and thus tend to be bilingual or available in various languages, city studies appear largely in Arabic, using memories of an older generation and aiming to produce a faithful image of a lost collective life, whose reclamation could then become the task of newer generations who had grown up in the diaspora and thus knew little about Palestine first hand.[6] Another branch of city history studies aims primarily to assert the historical vibrancy of Palestinian life, in an explicit refutation of the old Zionist claim that Palestine was essentially a land without people.[7]

The practice of memory is not of course without supporting institutions that bring its relevance to the fore of community life. A remarkable feature of the Palestinian diaspora is the reconstitution within it of the honorifics associated with the class society that had prevailed in old Palestine, with the old notable families (or *a'yan*) maintaining their status even as they lost wealth and property.[8] Yet, as a shared fate, diasporic Palestinian life cast the Palestinian struggle as a collective national cause of equal relevance to *all* classes of society, because all classes had lost something. Indeed, it was precisely this sense of cross-class exposure to an outside enemy that had favoured organizations defining Palestinian nationalism in terms of a general class alliance, such as Fateh, over Marxist-style ones highlighting class analysis, which elsewhere in the third world were more popular carriers of national liberation struggles.

The PLO as a diaspora organization: Trials and tribulations

The emergence of a genuine, mass-based Palestinian resistance movement under the umbrella of the Palestine Liberation Organization (PLO) after 1967 embodied the aspirations of diaspora Palestinians, even though the goal of liberating Palestine was shared by all Palestinians. In terms of active cadres, leadership and organization, however, the PLO largely operated from the many centres of the diaspora. The refugee camps everywhere provided the most reliable and dedicated foot-soldiers of the various organizations of the national movement. For 20 years – that is, between the real birth of a national Palestinian mass movement after 1967 and the outbreak of the first Intifada in 1987 – the Palestinian diaspora was essentially the dominant feature of Palestinian nationalism.

Those 20 years (but especially up to the Israeli invasion of Lebanon in 1982 in order to drive out the PLO) witnessed a remarkable institutional revolution, in which the PLO emerged as a broadly representative worldwide structure. It incorporated professional associations, political groups, independent intellectuals and personalities, and think tanks into its various channels, and together they connected the diasporic Palestinian populations into structures of activism and consciousness unparalleled in their scope in Palestinian history. This growing institutional thickness of Palestinian diasporic life complemented the strong extended family ties that had survived into the diaspora,[9] where Palestinians from various villages and classes commingled in new networks, thereby giving a deep and often concrete meaning to national identity and promoting new ideologies and styles of struggle.

This institutional thickness was attained on two fronts: first, through the worldwide expansion of the membership and representation of professional associations that linked the work, class and gender identities of the diaspora to the umbrella framework of a single national structure, the PLO; second, by constantly broadening the representative scope of the PLO's "parliament in exile", namely the Palestinian National Council (PNC), which served as the legislative body of the PLO.

The professional associations began to emerge independently, several years before the PLO came into existence, becoming organized as global "general unions" with affiliated national branches. Some of the most prominent ones are the General Union of Palestine Students, the General Union of Palestine Teachers, the General Union of Palestine Workers, the General Union of Palestinian Women and the Society of Palestinian Engineers. Eventually all of these associations sent delegates to the PNC, which began to undergo dramatic structural change, especially as of the late 1960s, in order to reflect the new realities. These new realities included mainly the emergence of large grassroots political organizations among Palestinian refugees and other diaspora populations, as well as the declining influence of the original leaders of the PLO, who owed their offices largely to the support of Arab governments keen on keeping control over the PLO from its creation in 1964 until shortly after their defeat by Israel in 1967. Over the next three decades the PNC would increase from about 100 to well over 500 members, and it also met quite frequently. Its meetings were major events for Palestinians, because they often corresponded with moments of crisis and thus a concomitant need to forge a national consensus on new directions.

In its composition the PNC reflected the manner in which the Palestinian national movement as a whole strove to maximize its inclusiveness. In the late 1960s, a substantial number of its members were selected on the basis of party affiliation, with a set number of seats going to Fateh, the Popular Front for the Liberation of Palestine, and so on. Gradually, however, the PNC came to include an ever-growing number of independents, who within a decade constituted its majority, as well as increased representation of professional societies. In theory, principles of representation within the PNC were meant to maintain a balance between diaspora and non-diaspora Palestinians. However, given that until the Oslo Accords in 1993 the PNC met in exile and that its active members from the occupied territories had had to relocate or had been expelled by Israel, for most of its history the PNC in effect conformed to the more general pattern of domination of the Palestinian movement by the diaspora, which in any case continues to be home to the majority of Palestinians.

The outbreak of the first Intifada in 1987 marked an important redirection of the Palestinian struggle away from its diaspora-centricity. For the first time since 1970 – when the Jordanian civil war effectively blocked the PLO's major channels of communication to the occupied territories – a genuine social movement erupted within the occupied territories with little outside input. By the time of the first Intifada, the PLO had been headquartered in Tunisia for about five years, where it increasingly appeared as a distant, bureaucratic organization lacking in connection or relevance to the lives of Palestinians under occupation. Moreover, the Arab world had turned its attention to the Iran–Iraq war and also to Lebanon, which was by then embroiled in a hopeless and increasingly pointless civil war. As Samih Farsoun and Jean Landis have shown,[10] the first Intifada defied basic social science expectations, since when it broke out in 1987 none of the factors that sociologists usually identify with successful mass movements were in existence.

The first Intifada therefore, surprising as it was, re-energized the Palestinian struggle. It also developed new techniques that had not been part of the diaspora's repertoire. In essence, armed struggle was replaced by civil disobedience, daily demonstrations, boycotts, strikes, stone-throwing and use of the media. The party structure of the PLO groups, although retained, gave way to the more influential local coordinating committees that had sprung up on the scene. Old loyalties to distant leaders and structures were replaced by a new grassroots-based leadership. In every sense, therefore, the first Intifada expressed a localization of the Palestinian struggle. This development was also welcomed by diaspora Palestinians, who were becoming increasingly disenchanted with the ineffectiveness of the Tunisian-based PLO.

Israel, however, continued to regard the PLO, rather than the emerging Intifada leadership, as its main nemesis. That was obviously because of the political threat implied by the international recognition the PLO was still enjoying, which gave it a unique status as the one institution that could legitimately speak on behalf of Palestinians everywhere. Thus, by the time of the Arab–Israeli Madrid peace conference following the Gulf war of 1991, Israel was maintaining its refusal to negotiate with a much-weakened PLO, insisting that it would speak only to selected representatives of the Palestinians of the West Bank and Gaza, and then only if those representatives operated as part of the Jordanian delegation.

Although that strategy was consistent with the expressed goal of successive Israeli governments of breaking any political connections between the diaspora and local Palestinians, Palestinians regarded the composition and status of the Madrid delegation as just a necessary adjustment to demands by powerful outside powers, and not as a reflection of how they saw themselves as a single global nation. Thus, on their way to Madrid, the leaders of the Palestinian delegation, Hanan Ashrawi and Haider Abdul-Shafi, passed through Algeria in order to make a point of appearing before the PNC, which had been meeting there, and asking (even though officially they did not need to) for its backing of their mission. By giving the Madrid delegation the right to negotiate on behalf of *all* Palestinians, the PNC in effect defused the Israeli attempt to separate the diaspora and local Palestinians. The fact that Palestinians and Israelis did not see the status of the Madrid delegation in the same way was expressed with apt theatrics by Yasser Arafat, who jokingly asked PNC members to pretend that they had not seen the leaders of the Madrid delegation as he was publicly introducing them to the assembly.

Two years later, the Oslo Accords effectively, and even formally, reintroduced the diaspora into the equation, marking thereby a major rethinking of the Israeli strategy of excluding the diaspora. The Israeli aim behind that earlier strategy was to have better control over the outcome of the negotiations by identifying as negotiating partners a group of local notables with less international stature, historical legacy and popular support than the PLO. However, the Palestinian delegation in Madrid proved more difficult to extract concessions from, remaining steadfast in its commitment to *clear* solutions of Palestinian national demands. This was in contrast to the Tunis-based PLO leadership, which in the secret negotiations that led to the Oslo Accords and the setting up of the Palestinian Authority colluded, albeit perhaps unwittingly, in planting the seeds of subsequent breakdowns in the peace process by agreeing to postpone or poorly define major elements of a final settlement. Thus the Oslo Accords caught the Madrid delegation by surprise, so much so that Haider Abdul-Shafi complained publicly about being sidestepped in a secret process that resulted in Palestinian concessions of a magnitude that the Madrid delegation would never have accepted.

The open process of Madrid became redundant once the secret process of Oslo reached its conclusion. In terms of the Palestinian diaspora, Oslo also marked a significant departure from all previous Israeli policies, which mandated a refusal to talk to the PLO in particular and exclusion of the Palestinian diaspora in general from all processes. Although no right of return and no other refugee rights were recognized, the manner and whole range of symbolism involved in reintroducing the diaspora into the political equation were unmistakable. The leadership that came to preside over the Palestinian Authority (PA) returned to the occupied territories from life-long exile, and from that exile it brought with it many of its armed officers and civil servants. Literally overnight, thousands of PLO operatives accomplished the undreamed of feat of moving into the occupied territories from Tunisia, where they had been festering in isolation for years. Palestinian society itself continues to recognize the novelty, because the differences in behaviour and political culture between the "Tunisians" and the more local leaders and workers of the PA remain apparent.[11]

By reintroducing the diaspora element, the Oslo process therefore reversed not only long-standing Israeli policy but also the main accomplishment of the first Palestinian Intifada itself, which had re-centred the Palestinian struggle. Of course, what was reintroduced in Oslo was neither the entirety of the diaspora nor any of its main demands. Rather, until the Hamas government, the pattern of Palestinian governance that is associated with Oslo highlighted consistent attempts by the "Tunisians" to substitute their new PA for the grassroots organizations and the local civil society that had organized itself around the first Intifada. To that end they were helped by superior resources, including well-intentioned foreign aid, which helped the PA embark on a hitherto unfamiliar top-down process of institution-building, whereas local Palestinians had previously been used mostly to a slow, painstaking process of building their civil society institutions from the ground up.[12]

At any rate, what has become obvious since Oslo is that any final status settlement will have to address some of the main concerns of diaspora Palestinians, clustering around the right of return. During various processes in the past, the Palestinian diaspora had stood on the sidelines, supporting a unified Palestinian position whose main demand had been an independent state. However, all Palestinians always expected that any final status negotiations over such a state would include the question of refugees and in particular address the principle of the "right of return".

The right of return and the final settlement

Throughout modern Palestinian history, national struggle was encapsulated in two central slogans, *sumud*, or "steadfastness", and *'awdah*, or "return". The first applied to Palestinians who had stayed in historical Palestine, the other to diaspora Palestinians. The two slogans represented the twin understanding of the goals of Palestinian nationalism. Whereas *sumud* described a programme to resist Zionist attempts to accentuate the Jewish character of historical Palestine through encouraging Palestinians to leave by making their life difficult, *'awdah* encapsulated the desire of the diaspora to return to its former home. Whereas *sumud* evoked forbearance in the face of daily hardships and an ongoing encounter with an enemy, *'awdah* expressed the reversal of an accomplished fact of dispossession as the central goal of political life.

The PLO has always articulated the concerns of both constituencies, despite operating largely in the diaspora. Even with the Intifada, which shifted attention dramatically to the plight of Palestinians living under occupation, Palestinian nationalism did not need to make a choice between *sumud* and *'awdah*. Both programmes continued to represent complementary aspects of the Palestinian claim to a historical homeland. It was not until the Declaration of Principles of Oslo in 1993 that the first inklings could be detected that a choice would have to be made. This has become even more apparent in recent years, every time elements of a final settlement are circulated publicly.

Until recently, therefore, diaspora and non-diaspora Palestinians perceived themselves to be pursuing the same national goal, albeit with different rhetorical emphases that highlighted the specific conditions of each community. The fact that the two programmes of *sumud* and *'awdah* had been merged since the PNC meeting of 1974 under a common commitment to an independent Palestinian state served further to elide the distinction between the two programmes and, in effect, postpone any choice the national movement might have to make between them. The persistent *official* Israeli rejection of any discussion of an independent Palestinian state – which was in effect up to the Barak–Arafat summit of 2000 – also helped the Palestinians retain a unified perspective, since there was nothing on the table that would compel diaspora and non-diaspora Palestinians to see that their different goals required them to make a choice.

The years 1967–1982 witnessed the heyday of a politicized diaspora, with the PLO organizing worldwide, Palestinian civil society consolidating itself in the diaspora, and the Palestinian struggle achieving worldwide acceptance as a legitimate national struggle. Israel, however, remained determined to restrict the scope of Palestinian rights to limited self-rule for the occupied territories, and further insisted on negotiating this self-rule with local Palestinians whom it selected rather than with the PLO. There was no role in that position for the Palestinian diaspora, nor an acknowledgement of any of its demands. In this light, the 1982 Israeli invasion of Lebanon was an attempt to eliminate the diaspora equation entirely from any formula for a possible settlement of the conflict.

Yet, the Israeli success in driving the PLO out of Lebanon only gave it a determined Intifada that proved to be not only difficult to control but even more effective than the PLO in highlighting internationally the legitimacy of the Palestinian struggle as a whole.

Whereas the first Intifada highlighted the *sumud* facet of Palestinian identity, the Oslo peace process turned the Palestinian struggle back to its multiple goals. Yet a stated Palestinian consensus on the priorities was maintained throughout, and these involved first and foremost an independent state, including East Jerusalem, and an "adequate" settlement of the refugee question. Historically, Palestinians of all political stripes had resisted prioritizing the refugee issue, which was why they initially rejected UN Security Council Resolution 242, because it addressed Palestinians only as refugees rather than as a nation with a right to self-determination. Palestinians always preferred to include the refugee question under the "right of return" clause, so that the plight of the refugees would be defined not simply as a "humanitarian" issue but rather as an integral part of a national right to self-determination.

The right of return, therefore, has never been given up by any Palestinian negotiator, even though Palestinians knew that any realistic final settlement was unlikely to endorse this right. It was possible to postpone the issue because of the very structure of various peace processes. The Oslo process and the later Road Map themselves left the refugee question to the very end, thus acknowledging the complexity of the issue but also the fact that it would have to serve as a capstone of a historic process. In other words, it was implicitly understood by all parties that no peace can be finalized until the fundamental demand of the diaspora, namely the right of return, is addressed meaningfully. The lack of progress on the peace process simply postponed the issue; in other words, Palestinians experienced no urgency to reconsider even the manner in which they expressed the demand.

Yet, in the meantime, a body of scholarship has emerged on the question of the right of return, most of which is of fairly recent origin.[13] Much of this literature focuses on international law, and also on the various schemes available for resolving the issue. The typical range of possibilities includes repatriation, compensation and resettlement. Don Peretz points out that each of these presents demographic, political and economic complications of its own.[14] Repatriation is limited by Israeli resistance to changing the demographic balance not only of Israel itself but also of the whole area between the Jordan River and the Mediterranean. Compensation is hampered by difficulties of assessing the value of lost Palestinian property over time, and also by an Israeli demand that the properties of Jews who had been living in Arab countries should be included in the compensation formula. Resettlement is impeded by the political difficulties of incorporating the large refugee populations where they currently reside, a problem that is most immediately felt in Lebanon. In addition, all these schemes suffer from a common problem – the Israeli refusal to acknowledge any responsibility for turning the majority of Palestinians into refugees. Thus any repatriation, however limited, is seen by Israel as a "humanitarian" gesture rather than as an admission of guilt. Similarly, the Israeli position on compensation envisions payments to refugees being made out of an international fund rather than by Israel.

This resistance to considering the question of responsibility constitutes in effect the heart of the problem. It will prove far more detrimental to the possible success of any eventual final settlement than the details of any specific scheme to resolve the issue of the refugees in particular, and that of the diaspora's political role and socio-cultural demands generally. There is in this conflict a basic ethical issue that most negotiations have simply ignored. Diplomats generally prefer to deal with issues for which a clear solution can be identified, hence the centrality to negotiations of such material issues as land, water, borders, settlements, Jerusalem, and so on. These, of course, are not easy issues, but the parameters of a resolution are implied in international consensus and are the object of various existing proposals. Questions that are more ethical in nature, such as who is responsible for what, represent a different game altogether. Yet the conflict gains daily sustenance precisely from this unresolved issue of responsibility, and questions of innocence or guilt provide the core defining features of both Palestinian and Israeli national consciousness. It is therefore difficult to imagine how a lasting peace could take root if it failed at least to take such ethical questions into account, let alone make them central to the solution.

By far the easiest solution to the issue of refugees would be to combine a historic admission of guilt by Israel with a resettlement of the refugees, either in the Palestinian state or wherever they happen to reside now – with full citizenship rights in either case.[15] For the diaspora, the end of the conflict would not necessarily signify an opportunity to "return", which in any case might not be a practical proposition for families that had been established overseas for decades. Rather, the end of the conflict would more likely signify an opportunity for the established diaspora to contribute from afar to developing the new Palestinian state. In recent years, the contribution of the Palestinian diaspora to the economy of the occupied territories, in terms of both investment and philanthropy, has been roughly equal to all other sources of foreign aid.[16] Furthermore, the diaspora's economic links with Palestine are not simply brought about by a sense of patriotic obligation or sentimental nationalism, but are also enhanced by the well-developed, and by now traditional, global networks of extended families.[17] The fact that the diaspora is in a good position to help stabilize and develop an independent Palestinian homeland by capitalizing on its rich connections with the Palestinian homeland, structured along lines of extended kin, in itself constitutes an important element in resolving the grievances of the diaspora, which centre on its connections to Palestine being denied.

The likelihood of success of such a scenario, however, is entirely dependent on two major developments: the emergence of a viable independent Palestinian state, and satisfaction of the ethical core that in effect underlies the principle of the right of return. The "right of return", however central it may seem to be to the Palestinian diaspora's expressed demands, is ultimately based on underlying ethical commitments that can be traced to the social psychology of the diaspora, which I addressed earlier.[18] In the final analysis, these ethical commitments are the issue. That is to say, if for Palestinians a core defining element of their diaspora is its injustice, then an elementary point of departure would be that the perpetrator must admit to having caused the injustice. There is nothing unusually demanding in this, since revisionist Israeli historians, led by Benny Morris, have themselves shown that Israel consciously caused the Palestinian refugee problem (even though Morris expresses the issue not in terms of "guilt" but rather in terms of historical "necessity"). The *foundations* for a potential joint Israeli–Palestinian historical narrative on the refugee question thus already exist.

The other constituting elements of the social psychology of the diaspora could equally be satisfied with a joint historical narrative. The notions that the diaspora is "unchosen" and "temporary", for example, which are still maintained by a generation that never lived in Palestine, are obviously not maintained because people want to "return" to a land that they actually do not know and in the process abandon the certainly more familiar life of the diaspora. In this context, the notion of an unchosen, temporary diasporic life must express something more basic, namely a dedication to a cause that has never been resolved, and defiance of an enemy whose foundations are seen to consist in precisely denying the very existence of Palestinians. A joint historical narrative, therefore, answers precisely this element of the social psychology of the diaspora.

Finally, the definition of diasporic life as resulting from an "accident" would also be resolved by a joint Israeli–Palestinian historical narrative based on identifying guilt and making ethical questions central to a common educational process. An "accident" is by definition something altogether different from some "logic of history". If anything, an "accident" expresses a malfunction, if not a basic violation, of the logic of history. What a joint narrative does is to account for the "accident", making it possible finally to transcend the hold it has on national consciousness. In this way, "accidents" are not left standing as aberrations of the order of civilization. Rather, they are addressed forthrightly, like all transgressions should be, and accountability for them is pronounced by a joint tribunal.

None of this expresses a utopian pipedream. Questions of ethics present serious issues that unfortunately are not yet part of official peace processes, which is perhaps why so many attempts at peace have fared so poorly. Ethical considerations are in the final analysis symptoms of a solid, confident process. The conflict, of course, is not simply about ethics, but the absence of an ethical dimension from the negotiations will certainly not help in resolving it.

Is there a model for this kind of process anywhere else? There are several examples of accountability being incorporated as an element in the resolution of various conflicts, representing the emergence of a global realization that festering ethnic and national conflicts cannot be resolved if one ignores issues of ethics and accountability. One of the best examples so far is South Africa's Truth and Reconciliation Commission, whose work sought to endow the post-Apartheid era with an ethical core without which the national culture would have lacked a common narrative that would eventually become the foundation of social peace. The question of the Palestinian diaspora is one that can only be resolved through such a model of truth and reconciliation. This is central to both the Israeli state and the Palestinian resistance against it. If a lasting peace means ultimately learning how to live together, side by side, it is impossible to see how this can be done without an agreement anchored on an ethical foundation. The lack of such a foundation is an important reason for this conflict to have defied resolution when the other elements of a practical solution have been so obvious for more than three decades.

Notes

1. J. B. Glubb, "Violence on the Jordan–Israel Border: A Jordanian View", *Foreign Affairs*, July 1954, p. 556.
2. See the conference statement at ⟨http://alawdaconvention.org⟩ (accessed 4 March 2005).
3. Fawaz Turki, *The Disinherited: Journal of Palestinian Exile*, New York: Monthly Review Press, 1972, p. 39.
4. This has been well documented in various studies. For an excellent recent overview, see Eugene L. Rogan and Avi Shlaim, *The War for Palestine: Rewriting the History of 1948*, Cambridge: Cambridge University Press, 2001.
5. Walid Khalidi, *Before Their Diaspora: A Photographic History of the Palestinians 1876–1948*, Washington, DC: Institute of Palestine Studies, 2004 [1984]; Salman Abu Sitta, *The Atlas of Palestine 1948*, London: Palestine Land Society, 2005.

6. Apart from the countless works on Jerusalem, for some of the more developed studies within this genre see, for example, May Seikaly, *Haifa: Transformations of an Arab Society 1918–1939*, London: I. B. Tauris, 2002; Isbir Munir, *Al-Lid fi 'Ahdai al-Intitab wa al-Ihtilal* [Lydda between Mandate and Occupation], Beirut: Institute of Palestine Studies, 2003; Mustapha al-Abbasi, *Safad fi 'Ahd al-Intitab al-Baritani* [Safad under the British Mandate], Beirut: Institute of Palestine Studies, 2005.

7. This line of works is currently best represented by Beshara Doumani, *Rediscovering Palestine: Merchants and Peasants in Jabal Nablus, 1700–1900*, Berkeley: University of California Press, 1995; and Zuhair Ghahayem, *Liwa' 'Akka fi 'Ahd al-Tanzimat al-'Uthmaniyyah 1864–1918* [Akka Province during the Ottoman Tanzimat 1864–1918], Beirut: Institute of Palestine Studies, 1999.

8. This too is part of the practice of memory, as various publications seek to identify genealogies of prominence. For a fairly representative book in this genre, see "Adel Mana", *A'lam Filastin fin Awakher al-'Ahd al-'Uthmani (1800–1918)* [Notable Palestinians during the Late Ottoman Period 1800–1918], Beirut: Institute of Palestine Studies, 1997.

9. For one of the best documentations of the institutional restructuring of Palestinian society in the diaspora, see Sari Hanafi, *Huna wa Hunak: Nahwa Tahlil lil-'Alaqah bayn al-Shatat al-Filastini wa al-Markaz* [Here and There: Towards an Analysis of the Relationship between the Palestinian Diaspora and the Centre], Ramallah: Muwatin (Palestinian Institute for the Study of Democracy), 2001.

10. Samih Farsoun and Jean Landis, "The Sociology of an Uprising: The Roots of the Intifada", in Jamal Nassar and Roger Heacock, eds, *Intifada: Palestine at the Crossroads*, New York: Praeger, 1990.

11. In fact, it was the issue of corruption, with which the "Tunisians" are perceived to be highly associated, that was instrumental in the triumph of Hamas in the January 2006 elections.

12. For an unusually well-informed study of the relationship between the Palestinian Authority and the local civil society, see Jamil Hilal, *Al-Nizam al-Siyasi al-Filastini ba'd Oslo* [The Palestinian Political System after Oslo], Beirut: Institute for Palestine Studies, 1998.

13. See, for example, Elia Zureik, *Palestinian Refugees: A Negotiations Primer*, Beirut: Institute of Palestine Studies, 1996; Farouk Mardam-Bey and Elias Sanbar, eds, *Le Droit au Retour: Le Problème des Réfugiés Palestiniens*, Paris: Actes Sud, 2002; Ramadane Babadji, Monique Chemillier and Géraud de La Pradelle, *Haq al-'Awdah lil-Sha'b al-Filastini wa Mabadi' Tatbiqihi*, Beirut: Institute of Palestine Studies, 1996.

14. Don Peretz, *Palestinians, Refugees, and the Middle East Peace Process*, Washington, DC: United States Institute of Peace, 1993.

15. A survey in 2003 of refugee preferences seems to confirm the viability of this scenario. The question of Israeli responsibility for the refugee crisis is implied in Palestinians' attitude towards compensation and resettlement, and is openly shared by all Palestinians. See Palestinian Center for Policy Survey and Research (PSR), "Results of PSR Refugees' Polls in the West Bank/Gaza Strip, Jordan and Lebanon on Refugees' Preferences and Behavior in a Palestinian-Israeli Permanent Refugee Agreement", Ramallah, 2003.

16. For a study of the likely contribution of the diaspora to the economic health of a Palestinian state, see Nadia Hijab, "The Role of Palestinian Diaspora Institutions in Mobilizing the International Community", paper presented at the Economic and Social Commission for Western Asia (ESCWA), "Arab-International Forum on Rehabilitation and Development in the Occupied Palestinian Territory: Towards an Independent Palestinian State", Beirut, 11–14 October 2004. For some trends, see Sari Hanafi, "Palesti-

nian Diaspora Contribution to Investment and Philanthropy in Palestine", October 2000, at ⟨http://www.palesta.gov.ps/academic/publication/diaspora.htm⟩ (accessed 22 February 2006).

17. For a statistical summary of the "density" of diasporic and local family relations, see Hanafi, *Huna wa Hunak*, p. 59.

18. For a lengthier exploration of the underlying ethics of the right of return principle, see Mohammed A. Bamyeh, "Palestine: Listening to the Inaudible", *South Atlantic Quarterly*, Fall 2003.

6

The Armenian diaspora and the Karabagh conflict since 1988

Khachig Tölölyan

This chapter attempts to answer a set of linked questions: when, how and to what extent did the Armenian diaspora influence the Karabagh[1] conflict? It also asks – of necessity more speculatively – how it might help to shape the peace process. I address these questions in several steps.

First, I offer an overview of the contemporary Armenian diaspora, focusing on those portions of it that are "mobilized"[2] and institutionally saturated, and explore why it is difficult to speak of the Armenian diaspora (and, indeed, of any diaspora) as a unified actor engaged in coherent actions that result in discernible, one-cause one-effect consequences at the scene of conflict involving the distant homeland. Despite that difficulty, I argue that the prolonged, complex orientation of the diaspora towards the homeland and their mutual engagement with each other are in general consequential, and particularly so in the case of this conflict.

Second, this chapter provides an analytical narrative of the diaspora's attempts to influence the outcome of the conflict between Armenia, Azerbaijan and the initially autonomous secessionist region of Karabagh.

Third, I combine my own observations with others drawn from interviews conducted with experts on various aspects of relations between the Armenian diaspora and the homeland and offer the consensus view that is currently attainable among Armenian specialists about the role of the diaspora in the conflict. These experts live and work in Armenia, Lebanon, France, Britain, Canada, the United States and Argentina. All are scholars or analysts. Nine have been or are now affiliated with a dia-

Diasporas in conflict: Peace-makers or peace-wreckers?, Smith and Stares (eds), United Nations University Press, 2007, ISBN 978-92-808-1140-7

sporic institution that is active in transnational politics. Six have been politically active as individuals. They spoke on condition of non-attribution,
because they have been or may again be actors in the political processes that link the diaspora to the homeland in contention as well as in
cooperation.[3]

Because there have been many active groups in the Armenian diaspora, this chapter concentrates selectively on a few diasporic groups
and actions that, in my opinion and that of a majority of interviewees,
materially or psychologically affected the outcome of the conflict. However, although often there is agreement on the importance of a particular
action, assessments of the actual political consequences of the action differ; these differences will be noted. Although this chapter does not undertake to assess the "reverse" phenomenon, it is necessary to emphasize
that the post-1988 engagement of the Armenian diaspora with the homeland and the Karabagh struggle has transformed that diaspora far more
than it has changed the homeland.

Finally, this exploration of the Armenian diaspora's effect on the Karabagh conflict does not attempt to engage a contested issue that concerns other analyses of similar conflicts: does a diaspora autonomously
initiate political moves that affect homeland conflicts, or does it merely
contribute to initiatives emerging from the homeland? Gurharpal Singh,
a scholar who is reluctant to attribute a genuinely autonomous role to the
Sikh diaspora in the "Khalistan" conflict, asks: "is the diaspora the leading actor, or is it a weathervane responding to developments in Punjab
and India?"[4] There is no general, theoretical answer to this question.

Diasporic agency in international affairs

In the period of post-Soviet globalization, scholars of international relations and of the emerging discipline of diaspora studies have focused,
from quite different perspectives, on the ways in which contemporary
diasporas become active agents in international politics.[5] Whether the
investigation is framed in the discourse of international relations or with
the concepts of diaspora studies, scholars usually focus on a small number of political activities that result from the solidarity that mobilized,
transnational ethnic groups – "diasporas" – feel towards homelands
caught up in conflict.

The most visible of these activities is the way in which diasporas lobby
the governments of the countries of which they are citizens with the
intention of inducing them to conduct policies favourable to their kin-
states or original homelands. Such activity leaves diasporas vulnerable

to charges of multiple and divided loyalties. The second activity consists of diasporic attempts to influence the media and public debate of the countries they inhabit with the intention of having their homelands (and the causes or conflicts they are engaged in) represented in a favourable light. The third, most heterogeneous, activity includes, for example, appeals to supranational organizations such as the United Nations or engagement with and investment in transnational non-governmental organizations (NGOs) in order to further the security, health, environmental or developmental aims of homelands. Fourth, at least some diasporas seek to influence the behaviour of the governments of their original homelands or kin-states, especially during the transitional phase that marks the passage to sovereignty, for example in Armenia after the collapse of the Soviet Union. Some diasporas working from within Western democracies do so with the intention of furthering democracy. Often, the definition and consequences of the form of democracy promoted by the diaspora are shaped by the interests and pressures of the host state. Finally, some diasporas have agendas – usually grouped under the label of nationalism – that seem problematic to many Western scholars and governments. These diasporic attempts to influence homeland governments, or to contribute to and intervene in the economic, social and cultural life of the homeland, may have as their goal the strengthening of a particular form of national identity in both the homeland and the diaspora.[6]

This chapter contributes to the discussion of the agency of diasporas by concentrating on one case and by asking how and to what extent the Armenian diaspora influenced and may yet influence the government, élites, discourses and ordinary people of Armenia and Karabagh during the conflict between them and Azerbaijan that began in 1988 as a local political struggle, was subsequently brutalized and militarized, escalated through clashes and massacres into a war, was slowed down by a ceasefire in 1994, and remains unresolved even as the attempts to broker a peace have become fully internationalized.[7]

Multiple diasporic communities or a single diaspora?

Analysing the Armenian diaspora's influence on the conflict is immediately complicated, first by the fact that "influence" is notoriously elusive and difficult to trace when non-state entities interact with states, and second by the fact that this diaspora is neither a unified social formation nor a monolithic polity. It can safely be said that several organizations that operate transnationally in many Armenian diasporic communities had relevant programmes and policies, and also that a few diasporic individuals with skills, resources and determination played a role in the conflict. It is difficult to generalize further: the Armenian diaspora is often used loosely as a term referring to all Armenians who live, dispersed, outside their homeland. No one knows exactly, but a conservative estimate is that at the moment there are fewer than 3 million Armenians in the homeland and at least 4 million Armenians in diaspora. We need to be precise about the latter before generalizing about "diaspora" activity. Some members of the global Armenian diaspora are descended from people who left their homeland centuries ago – in Iran, people descended from a coerced exodus out of Armenia in 1604 may constitute the majority of the community. Over half of the diaspora's population is descended from survivors and refugees of the Ottoman Turkish genocide of the Armenians during World War I; this is the case for the Armenian communities of Syria, Lebanon, Cyprus, Argentina and, partly, the United States. Roughly a quarter of the contemporary diaspora consists of economic refugees who left Armenia after 1991, and of these more than half live in Russia, where they joined a much older community that began to form in the Crimea in the twelfth century and took its current shape in the eighteenth century. Thus, the Armenian diaspora is made up of a mixture of individuals and communities possessed of different histories and hybrid cultural identities, plus ethnic Armenians, exiles and migrant labourers. Each group has somewhat different commitments to Armenian issues and vastly different abilities to support them.

Furthermore, Armenians living outside Armenia are sometimes Armenian in name only; they are in fact assimilated people with vague memories of having an Armenian heritage. In France and the United States, there are thousands of such Armenians. The majority of "diaspora" Armenians in some communities, especially in the United States, are in reality ethnic Armenians. That is, they acknowledge their Armenian origin and manifest certain characteristic behaviours in daily life – in food, drink, music and social contacts. Many retain links with the symbols and institutions of their Armenian heritage, in particular the Armenian Apostolic Church. They demonstrate loyalty to that heritage on certain occasions in ritual ways, for example by attending church or annually commemorating the genocide of the Armenians by Ottoman Turkey during World War I, an event that remains shamefully unacknowledged by contemporary Turkey. They also contribute money, time and effort to communal institutions, such as schools that teach a smattering of Armenian language and history and political organizations that cultivate particular constituencies and ideologies; they make partially successful attempts to learn Armenian and to marry endogamously. But they live most of their lives as white ethnics – they are Americans for whom *home* is unequivocally the United States; Armenian identity is one of several identities that compete for their time and attention; and Armenia is a place for which they have sympathy and in which they take an interest.

Finally, there are those who are fully "diasporic" in their concerns. As a percentage of the total population in a particular community, they are usually a minority. But they are characterized by the fact that their identities and their activities are truly bi-local or multi-local. They share the concerns of ethnic Armenians, but in addition, while living in, say, Canada, Greece, Egypt or the United States, they are knowledgeable about and care for the condition of Armenians elsewhere, be it in another, troubled diaspora such as the one in Turkey, or in the homeland. These diasporic Armenians are committed; some are activists, and, on occasion, a few are militants. A few of the latter, in a very specific and delimited time and place, engaged in terrorism against Turkey (1975–1983).

What distinguishes diasporic ethnic Armenians from other ethnic Armenians is a combination of three characteristics: they care about kin in the homeland and elsewhere, so their concerns are multi-local and transnational; they create, staff and finance institutions that actively enact their caring, including through lobbying; and they make sustained efforts to "diasporize" the consciousness and identity of their ethnic kin through cultural, social and political actions. For example, during 1988, when the Karabagh conflict began to emerge and a dreadful earthquake ravaged northern Armenia, these efforts to raise ethnic consciousness, to mobilize the ethnic Armenians and to rally them to diasporic identities and institutions in the name of the homeland were especially productive. It is essential, in studying Armenian or other diasporas, to recognize that the internal boundaries and fractions of the community are not set; they are always in motion, with new immigrants usually moving towards further ethnicization and assimilation, but with reversions possible, especially during times of crisis or charismatic leadership.

Because the Armenian diaspora communities are "national" diasporas, it is necessary to think of them as remarkably heterogeneous in relation to each other. That is, the Lebanese Armenian diaspora bears the marks of its residence in Lebanon, and differs in identity, behaviour and even dialect from the Iranian Armenian diaspora, not to mention, say, the Australian Armenian diaspora. This heterogeneity extends not just to the geographical-spatial, but also to the temporal dimension. Some are *residual* diaspora communities, declining in number, ethno-diasporic sentiment and influence, such as the one in Ethiopia; and it seems unlikely that they have a future. Others are *emergent*, growing in membership, level of organization and commitment, such as those that have developed in the past two decades in Sweden and Hungary or in the past four decades in Canada. And some, such as the ones in the United States, France, Iran, Lebanon and Syria, and now perhaps in Russia and Argentina, are "dominant", thanks to their numbers, prosperity, levels of organization, institutional saturation, ideological commitment and inventiveness in cultural innovation.

On rare occasions, even in the matter of the Karabagh conflict, and certainly when less pressing commitments are at stake, these "national diasporas" diverge. For example, some leaders of important segments of the French and Argentinian communities lean to socialism, whereas most in the United States, the citadel of capitalism, are often fiercely committed to fostering free enterprise in Armenia and Karabagh, sometimes even over the objections of many locals. Similarly, diasporic nationalism is a more potent force in the Lebanese Armenian community than, say, in the UK one. In other words, diasporic communities are different from each other, and each is also internally divided on political and cultural issues.

Counteracting diasporic multiplicity: Institutional and ideological cohesion among élites

What, then, allows us to speak even tentatively of "the Armenian diaspora" as a single entity? First, those elements of popular culture that are shared across the diaspora (religion, music, some grasp of the genocide). Second, those transnational forms of discourse that circulate widely between élites and institutions across the (now partially democratized) Web.[8] Together, these discourses, cultural practices and organizations link and mobilize different proportions of ethnic and diasporic members in different communities. The majority of these practices are not explicitly political, yet the links they foster are an enabling, perhaps indispensable, precondition of politicization. This is not the place to argue in detail for the importance of élite leadership groups in the Armenian diaspora.[9] Compressing what must be both a historical and a theoretical argument, we can say that the vigour of the now-global, mobilized Armenian diaspora depends on some participation by ethnic Armenians in local community affairs and above all on intense participation by the numerically smaller diasporan contingent in the affairs of the transnational institutions that link diaspora communities to the homeland and to each other.

First among the institutions, discourses and practices that foster some diasporic "unity" across diversity is the Armenian Church, which, despite its recent decline, remains an important pan-Armenian organization that has functioned in that capacity throughout the millennial history of the diaspora's existence. Over 90 per cent of all diasporic Armenians belong to it. Funds are raised for it everywhere. Its priests are recruited and trained in seminaries in several countries (Lebanon, Jerusalem, the United States, Armenia) and are assigned to the roughly 34 countries that have a significant diasporic community. Though of necessity always adaptable to local conditions in its practices, the Church remains unified in its doctrine, rituals and discourse, and addresses the "Armenian nation" in homeland and diaspora as a people united by its particular form of Christianity and has done so since at least 1165, when an encyclical by Nersess Shenorhali, the head of the Armenian Church, first acknowledged that the diasporization begun a century earlier had become an irreversible fact of collective life, challenging an until-then territorialized Church's sense of its mission.

The Church retains its role despite the presence of Armenian Catholics, Protestants and an increasing number of sects, as well as divisions among its hierarchy and a bitter struggle over jurisdiction that began in the 1930s. The clergy constitute one of the interlocking leadership élites that staff, supervise or direct major diaspora institutions and labour to recruit both diasporic and ethnic Armenians as their constituents in local arenas, while sustaining both the myth and the reality of a single nation. Furthermore, the Church's complex discourse of martyrdom contributes importantly to uniting the older discourse of Christianity with a more recent discourse of political sacrifice.[10]

In addition to the Church and associated clerical and lay élites, the second most important organization of the Armenian diaspora is the Dashnaktsootyun or "Dashnak" Party. Founded as a revolutionary political party in 1890 in the diaspora community of Tbilisi, Georgia, with a platform that was both socialist and nationalist, this organization functioned between 1890 and 1920 as an Armenian "national liberation front", participating in armed struggle in Ottoman Turkey, in Tsarist Russia and even briefly in Persia. Between 1921 and 1988, it was the leading political organization of the diaspora, but its position was everywhere vigorously and sometimes successfully contested by other élites. Since 1988, it has been a political party in Armenia, winning between 4.5 per cent and 8 per cent of the votes cast there in presidential and parliamentary elections, but mattering more than those figures indicate. It owes its importance to a mixture of factors: the lobbying role of its diasporic component, its organizational discipline and coherence, and finally the passionate commitment of its membership to a national ideology. Currently, the Dashnak Party has deputies and ministers in Armenia's government. It also has two deputies in Iran's *Majlis* and, until recent electoral setbacks, had three deputies in Lebanon's parliament. Notably, it was able to muster an armed militia during Lebanon's civil war of 1975–1990. It still sustains a successful lobbying arm, the Armenian National Committee, in Washington, DC, and has launched a new one in Brussels to lobby the European Union. The number of card-carrying cadres of this truly pan-diasporic political party is a jealously guarded secret, but is roughly 13,000 in homeland and diaspora together. Its far more numerous sympathizers constitute a plurality in some diaspora communities (e.g. Lebanon) and an important minority in almost all others. The Dashnaks exemplify a form of "stateless power".[11]

The third major transnational organization is the Armenian General Benevolent Union (AGBU), once a conservative philanthropic organization that is now restructured like a closely held corporation led by a handful of major philanthropists but supported by others donating at least a small sum of money annually. Currently, it has an endowment of around US$500 million; in recent years, it has annually spent US$27–35 million on educational, cultural and charitable projects. It cooperates closely with the Church hierarchy in Armenia on some matters but conducts independent activities in other spheres: for example, it founded and has funded the American University of Armenia for more than a decade. That university has played a role in the training and ideological re-education of a post-Soviet bourgeoisie.

The fourth organization significant in diaspora politics has been the Armenian Assembly of America, founded in the 1970s by an unusual coalition of long-settled Armenian Americans and recently arrived Armenian immigrants from the Middle East. Its influential lobbying office in Washington represents some important segments of communal opinion in the United States. Its numerically small membership is growing through recruitment among the more prosperous members of the community. Though not transnational in structure, its impact (through its influence on US policy) is widespread.

Fifth, since the early 1990s, the Haiastan or Armenia Fund[12] has been a paradigmatically transnational creation of leaders from Armenia and the diaspora. It has been raising several million dollars a year in the diaspora and spending it in Armenia and Karabagh, where it has financed the construction of strategically important roads linking Armenia to Karabagh and portions of Karabagh (long neglected under Azeri rule) to each other.

As an account of the complex institutional saturation of the Armenian diaspora, this enumeration of organizations is inadequate, but the rest can only be sketched. One, the Armenian Relief Society, is a major women's philanthropic organization. Though linked to the Dashnaks, it operates autonomously, with NGO status recognized by the United Nations. Another is the Zoryan Institute, established in 1982, which in 1988 published the first informative texts on the history and then-current status of Karabagh and distributed them to US media and politicians.[13] There have also been numerous, inventive post-independence initiatives started by small groups of activists. Then there are the older associations that link diasporic descendants of Armenian refugees from a particular region of pre-genocide Armenia – from Marash in present-day Turkey, for example – to each other and now to kin in the homeland. They also coordinate the efforts of Armenians who have emigrated from primary diasporas in the Middle East to secondary ones in Europe and the United States: the associations of Istanbul, Iran and Kesab (in Syria) Armenians are noteworthy. Though their individual reach may be relatively small, cumulatively such groups organize and finance many cultural, educational and philanthropic activities that have indirect political effects, cementing relationships within as well as between various communities as benefactors and the homeland as recipient.

To sum up: the élites that dominate diasporic organizations, sustain their links with the homeland and mobilize ordinary Armenians are constituted by the interlocking personnel of the clergy; the wealthy philanthropists and the numerous smaller donors who fund major institutions; the politically mobilized employees and volunteers who staff those organizations; and, last but not least, the scholars, intellectuals and artists who engage in diasporic cultural production and both draw from and intervene in the culture and debates of the homeland.

This structure is supplemented by two final groups that must be mentioned. The first consists of a few charismatic individuals who act alone on the basis of their wealth, such as Kirk Kerkorian, the Armenian American billionaire who has given US$170 million to Armenia since 1988, and Charles Aznavour, the French Armenian entertainer who can rally thousands through his benefit concerts. The second group is composed of the ordinary Armenians who do not work through organizations but send money (gifts or remittances) to their relatives. The immediate economic impact of these is hard to quantify; in particular, their indirect political influence on the government of Armenia and of the de facto state[14] of the Nagorno-Karabagh Republic (NKR) is impossible to estimate. However, there can be little doubt that, incrementally, these sums have a direct material consequence in that they enable the population of a small state subject to economic blockade by Azerbaijan and Turkey to endure. They also stiffen the morale and will of at least some portions of the population of Karabagh and Armenia. Moreover, the flow of money enables both diasporan and homeland Armenians constantly to renew links within what sociologists call the "transnational social field"[15] sustained by diasporas in the era of globalization.

The preceding discussion suggests some of the reasons it is so difficult to pinpoint *the* "influence" of *the* Armenian diaspora on the Karabagh conflict. Neither the diaspora nor its major institutions have acted monolithically. Different communities and organizations within them have their own agendas. As Razmik Panossian has suggested, it can even be said that "the Dashnak Party has its own 'foreign policy'".[16] Diasporic activities on behalf of a homeland caught up in conflict and a difficult transition into a post-Soviet economy under blockade include the realm of political and diplomatic action, but also gifts, remittances, investment, humanitarian aid, educational assistance and technical innovation, as well as ideological and cultural interventions. It is difficult to gauge the specifically political consequences of this complex configuration of activities and to disentangle them from other forms of impact on social life. Empirical data are scarce and sometimes contradictory. The discussion that follows, drawing on the earlier-mentioned interviews with experts, focuses on the areas where the evidence is strong and the provisional consensus of analysts reasonably so.

Diasporic political action in the West

There is a degree of consensus in the literature and among interviewees that the early years of the transition from Soviet rule were the ones during which the actions of various diaspora communities had their greatest impact. The spheres of action include the military, the political, the economic, the humanitarian-philanthropic, and the discursive and cultural debates over national identity. All of these, in turn, influence the less easily defined psycho-social realm of collective morale and will.

As the conflict began, the intra-state Karabagh diaspora[17] was the first to act. Estimates of the number of its members range from 150,000 to 300,000; in 1988 there were sizeable groups in Baku, Azerbaijan, as well as in Armenia, Georgia, and Russia proper. Karabagh Armenians speak a dialect that is nearly unintelligible to speakers of the two major standard Armenian dialects. They tend to be fluent in Russian and to identify themselves in the intra-state diaspora as being specifically from Karabagh. This diaspora became active immediately after 20 February 1988, when the representatives of the Armenian majority of what was then, officially, the Nagorny-Karabagh Autonomous Region (with a 78.5 per cent Armenian population of 145,000 and a 21.0 per cent population of 40,000 Azeris) resolved to petition that the USSR's Supreme Soviet approve the administrative transfer of the region from the Azerbaijani SSR to the Armenian SSR. The speed with which the Karabagh diaspora began to agitate for support of the resolution suggests the strength of the links maintained with the homeland leadership; off the record conversations confirm the likelihood of prior coordination. Between 1988 and the collapse of the USSR at the end of 1991, several members of the Karabagh diaspora, above all Igor Mouratian, played a significant role in generating political support in Armenia and among Russophone Armenians in Russia.[18]

What is less frequently mentioned, even in Armenian sources, and very rarely in English ones, is the crucial military role played by the intra-state

Armenian diaspora of the Soviet Union, especially by the descendants of emigrants from Karabagh. The Armenian leadership of Karabagh proper was unprepared for the armed response by the Azerbaijani police and the militia of the ministry of the interior, let alone the full-scale war that developed as the USSR began to collapse. This lack of preparation was owing to the fact that at the outset it viewed itself as initiating a political and administrative transfer, not futile armed rebellion against the Soviet state. Given the lack of preparedness, intra-state diasporic assistance was indispensable. There is anecdotal evidence that early in the conflict the diasporic communities in the Crimea, Moscow, and later the 80,000–100,000 strong Armenian community of Abkhazia sent crucial assistance in the form of weapons and money to purchase weapons on the black market.[19] But what enabled first the ragtag Karabagh forces and then Armenia's own militia to become a disciplined army, which was more rapidly professionalized than Azerbaijan's better-financed and armed forces, were the diasporic Karabagh and Russian-Armenian officers, along with local NCOs and ordinary soldiers who had gained experience while fighting in Afghanistan.[20] The appendix to this chapter offers data on four such high-ranking officers, but four who played a pivotal role early on must be discussed here. Then-Colonel and now Major-General Arkady Ter-Tatevosian, born in the Karabagh diaspora of Georgia, was probably the first high-ranking officer to take retirement from the Soviet Army (in 1990) and move to Karabagh, where he eventually became Chief of Staff of the defence forces. Colonel-General Gurgen Dalibaltayan, also born in Georgia, retired in 1991 from his post as deputy commander for combat training of the North Caucasus Military District, then moved to Armenia, where he became Chief of Staff of the Armenian Army and is currently its inspector-general. Colonel-General Norad Ter-Grigoriants, born in the Russian-Armenian diaspora, formerly Deputy Chief of Staff of Soviet ground forces, moved to Armenia in 1992 and served as a staff officer. Finally, Colonel-General Mikayel Haroutunian, born in Azerbaijan, formerly chief lecturer on reconnaissance in the Academy of the Soviet General Staff, moved to Armenia in 1992 and is currently the Chief of Staff of Armenia's armed forces. The expertise of these officers contributed to the ability of the Karabagh forces to recover from initial setbacks in 1988–1992 and to win in 1993 and 1994.

In addition, a handful of ordinary combatants and several officers came to fight in Karabagh from Lebanon, France and the United States (see the appendix). Of these, Monte Melkonian – a Californian who had earlier joined an Armenian terrorist movement – was a charismatic leader who fascinated diaspora Armenians by the depth of his commitment and his eloquence about it. From Lebanon, a handful of fighters (the number is debated, but included no more than two dozen by most accounts) went to Karabagh. What made them significant is that many, including Lt. Col-onel Sefilian, were cadres of the Dashnak Party, which has always prided itself on its heroes and martyrs; two who were killed in Karabagh, M'her Tchoulhadjian and Vicken Zakarian, continue to be remembered by the Lebanese Armenian diaspora community as embodiments of the spirit of sacrifice that is a key element of diasporic discourse in general and Dash-nak Party culture in particular.

In politics, there have been two kinds of diasporic activity, one having to do with lobbying the United States and other governments, the second with attempts by three diasporic political organizations to become regis-tered, election-contesting parties in Armenia. In the former sphere, the strongest contribution has been that of the US Armenian community, which, in the decade of 1972–1982, had organized to lobby for its inter-ests in Washington, DC, and in particular to press the US government to acknowledge the Turkish genocide of the Armenians during World War I. After 1988, although genocide-related lobbying continued, lobbying on behalf of the diplomatic and economic advantage of both Armenia and the NKR became primary. Two lobbies have operated effectively.[21] One, the Armenian National Committee, represents the Dashnak Party's viewpoint. It has considerable grassroots support in California and Mas-sachusetts and some in New York, New Jersey and Michigan, as well as reasonable funding, and in recent years has become increasingly skilled. The other, the Armenian Assembly of America, was always well funded by a small group of wealthy contributors; it is now broadening its initially narrower popular base; its organizational and lobbying skills are first-rate, and it can rightly claim to be the primary architect of Section 907 of the Freedom Support Act, signed into law on 24 October 1992, as Pub-lic Law 102-551.

The strictly material impact of Section 907 was not all that great, espe-cially for an increasingly oil-rich Azerbaijan. It placed restrictions on some kinds and amounts of aid the United States could extend to Azer-baijan, while significant non-military assistance (US$80–105 million per year) went unimpeded to Armenia, where it made a real contribution to the Armenian economy. At the same time, fiscally trivial but symbolically and politically significant US funds also went to the NKR. After years of Azerbaijani and Turkish lobbying and White House pressure, in October 2001, in the aftermath of 9/11, Congress loosened and modified but did not entirely rescind the restrictions, even as their principal architect, the Armenian Assembly, stopped opposing the waivers.[22] The President can now waive, at his discretion, the restrictions for a one-year period on the grounds that aid to Azerbaijan would serve overriding national security interests; each year since 25 January 2002, the White House has waived the section.

Section 907 has come to stand for the efforts of the US Armenian diaspora to secure political and diplomatic support for Karabagh's right to
self-determination. A remarkably large proportion of the experts con-
sulted for this chapter in both Armenia and the diaspora identify it as a
major factor in the conflict, shaping the homeland's diplomacy and morale to some degree. It has come to stand for (and sometimes even to
lead to a lack of recognition of) other important actions by the US
diaspora, such as its success in speeding recognition of the Republic of
Armenia and especially in establishing a fully functioning embassy in
Washington, DC, at a time when the Republic lacked the funds to purchase an appropriate building. Even the stubbornly continuing, if ultimately unsuccessful, attempts of the US (as well as French and Canadian
Armenian) lobbies to obtain recognition for the genocide committed by
Ottoman Turkey trouble Azerbaijan, not only because of its close identification with Turkey but also because the persistence and near-success of
the enterprise are taken as evidence of Armenian diasporic power.[23]

In related efforts, the US diaspora combined political work and financial assistance to enable the de facto state of the NKR to maintain offices
and have representation in Washington, Moscow and Paris. No other
Eurasian separatist state – Abkhazia, South Ossetia, Transdnistria, let
alone Chechnya – enjoys the level of quasi-official representation in several capitals that the NKR has enjoyed since 1991 (the collapse of the
USSR), thanks primarily to the efforts of the Armenian diaspora. During
this time, Congressmen belonging to the congressional Armenian Caucus
have repeatedly spoken out in favour of Karabagh's self-determination
on the floor of the House. UK notables such as Lady Caroline Cox have
frequently visited the area on humanitarian missions while calling attention to the unresolved conflict and what a just resolution of it might be.
Even recently, after the waiver of Section 907, the Armenian diaspora
continues to send delegations to the NKR that are sometimes accompanied by US Congressmen and French officials, without asking for Baku's
permission; this has its impact in Azerbaijan, which protests each visit to
the NKR, over which it retains de jure sovereignty. Together, these
events serve as a reminder that if the "front" in the conflict is the ceasefire line, the "home front" of Karabagh encompasses both Armenia and
significant portions of the Armenian diaspora.

Overall, these efforts have kept Baku, Ankara and their allies in Washington aware that the US Armenian diaspora, in particular, has been, is
and will remain a factor in the debate contesting what US actions in
the Transcaucasus would best serve America's national interest. One of
the scholars interviewed for this chapter recalled a closed seminar in the
United Kingdom in 1997 during which UK officials criticized the senior
participating US diplomat for failing to overturn Section 907. Exasper-

ated, the official replied: "If you had to deal with a million Armenian citizens every day, you'd behave differently, too." Although the true figure is closer to 800,000, the remark encapsulates a reality. The US Armenian diaspora is an actor in the political arena where the interests of the United States in the NKR conflict are formulated and acted upon. This participation may be more important than the exact tally of votes won and lost in individual cases. It matters to the mobilization of the diaspora in the United States and elsewhere (especially in France and now, increasingly, at the European Union in Brussels). It almost certainly matters to the calculations of Baku and Ankara. And it has certainly strengthened, albeit to an incalculable degree, the political will of Armenia and the NKR.

Diasporic influence on Armenian participants in the conflict

The diaspora's political actions have not been limited to lobbying outside the homeland. They have extended to Armenia proper. In February 1988, the Karabagh movement began; in December 1988, a catastrophic earthquake rocked northern Armenia. Both were badly handled by Gorbachev's government. From then until December 1991, the diaspora sent medical and humanitarian assistance at the same time that its organizations interceded politically both abroad and in the homeland. (The latter was regarded by many locals as interference.) Diaspora groups (especially from France) exerted effective pressure on Gorbachev, through the European media and the EU parliament, to free the arrested members of the Karabagh committee, whose leadership, headed by Levon Ter Petrosyan, later became the first government of Armenia. Several diaspora organizations that rarely cooperate nevertheless signed a joint statement calling on homeland Armenians advocating independence to move cautiously, arguing that the Soviet Army was the guarantor that Turkey and Azerbaijan together would not launch an attack, even a second genocide. The appeal was not heeded and it became a paradigm for many in Armenia for what they came to view as the negative nature of some of the diaspora's political actions: ignorance of local dynamics combined with insistent advice that was then followed by indignation when diasporic views were not welcomed.

Soon after 1988, the major diasporic organizations felt a strong need to be active in Armenia through their own official representatives. Faced with the likelihood that the diaspora's political dynamic would itself undergo massive upheaval in response to the homeland's move towards independence, they wished to have a role in the process, invested funds and sent personnel to Armenia in order to secure a foothold on the ground where questions of Armenian identity as well as transnational politics would henceforth be contested.[24] The Ramgavar Party (the Armenian Democratic Liberals) failed to establish a strong position, but a newspaper it launched, *Azg* (Nation), is now one of the most trusted and influential in Armenia. The Dashnak Party contested the first presidential election, in which it won an embarrassing 4.5 per cent of the vote, but it persisted, was prosecuted by the government for reasons and circumstances that remain obscure, and recovered. It participates in parliamentary elections, has deputies and ministers in the government, is currently a junior partner of President Kocharian's government, and functions as an extraordinary transnational organization, both global and local, with offices in communities ranging from Los Angeles, Washington, DC, and New York to Paris, Moscow, Yerevan, Beirut, Teheran and beyond.

Meanwhile, as in other formerly communist countries, ranging from Estonia to Croatia, talented and ambitious individuals went to work in Armenia. Both the first foreign minister of Armenia, Raffi Hovannisian, and the long-serving current foreign minister, Vartan Oskanian, are diaspora Armenians, as is Jivan Tabibian, Armenia's ambassador to Austria, and as was Sebouh Tashjian, another minister. Hovannisian, who remains active in Armenia, resigned from President Ter Petrosyan's government over a dispute concerning the extent to which the question of genocide could be tacitly put aside in order to make negotiations with Turkey more productive. His brief tenure established one of the paradigmatic problems that haunt Armenia's relations with the diaspora, where so many are descendants of genocide survivors. In Armenia, the genocide matters a great deal, but the dangers to Karabagh are not primarily envisaged in those terms, whereas a form of "never again" (whether realistic or not) continues to underpin many diasporic Armenians' commitment to Karabagh. In effect, the realistically fearful analogy that leads to Armenia's prevailing view – "Armenians must not be ethnically cleansed from their land of Karabagh as they were eliminated by genocide from western Armenia" – becomes something more emphatically dominated by the grievous memory of genocide in some diaspora rhetoric.

Hovannisian's career can be usefully contrasted with that of Jirair Gerard Libaridian, a Lebanese-born US citizen who became, with Levon Ter Petrosyan, the architect of Armenia's foreign policy and its most important negotiator on Karabagh in the first five years of Armenia's independence. The aim and achievement of this foreign policy was to maintain balance, to secure US aid (an average of close to US$100 million a year) with the help of the US-Armenian lobby, while also securing Russian assistance to arm both NKR's and Armenia's military, to establish full diplomatic relations with Turkey (rebuffed by Ankara) and to find a formula that would let Azerbaijan retain de jure sovereignty over NKR while also accommodating the near-independence of the de facto state that has emerged. This effort came close to success, but ultimately failed because of multiple forms of intransigence in Armenia, Turkey and Azerbaijan. An important faction in Armenia, backed by the Dashnak Party and much of the diaspora's public opinion, believed and continues to believe that time is on the NKR's side, that Russia's restored power and its willingness to help Armenia, along with resettlement and prosperity in Armenia and the NKR,[25] will eventually create irreversible geographical, economic, demographic and political facts on the ground. Azerbaijan's leadership has been at least equally misled by a notion that time is on its side. Several factors have contributed to this conclusion. Baku has come to believe that oil wealth, plus the Western arms (especially air power) that wealth will buy, will eventually result in military superiority. Its optimism about the future also results from a belief that assistance from Turkey and the United States will continue even as Russian influence in the region weakens. Finally, this optimism about the future counts on the abiding primacy of the principle of territorial integrity. President Levon Ter Petrosyan predicted in 1994, in an interview with me, that each side's belief that "time is on our side" would lead to what he called "*Kipratsoom*" – "Cyprusization", in Armenian. It appears he was right. A faction of the diaspora, most vigorously but not exclusively represented by the Dashnak Party, has had a significant though not determining role in the process of promoting that view and freezing the situation.

The differences between the positions taken by Ter Petrosyan and Libaridian and those held by both the Dashnak Party and many others in the diaspora have been constitutive, determining the approaches of many diasporic groups to conflict resolution. For the first camp, of which Libaridian has been the most eloquent theorist, distinctions between the proper roles of the government of Armenia and of the diaspora are and must remain clearly demarcated. This camp views Armenia's government as primarily the government of the citizens of Armenia, responsible for them and obligated to prioritize their interests and issues. By contrast, many in the diaspora look for leaders in Armenia who will commit themselves not just to local citizens but also to the interests of "the Armenian people/nation" (terms that encompass ethnic Armenians living in Armenia, Karabagh and the diaspora). They imply that they have the best insight into the pan-national (*hamazgayin*) interests at stake in the Karabagh conflict. This position is partly shared by those in Armenia's government and élites who either agree with it or, more commonly, profess agreement because they believe that to declare solidarity with the view strengthens their position as they pursue more local interests. Still others, both in the homeland and in the diaspora, oppose the position taken by Ter Petrosyan and Libaridian because they think, rightly, that the way it was articulated unnecessarily alienated the diaspora. Individuals holding one or more of these positions currently influence President Kocharian's policy, paying lip-service to the notion that, though the combatants in the conflict are locals, the cause is pan-national.

In the early 1990s in the NKR, the diasporic Dashnak Party assisted and influenced several of the early dissidents, fighters and administrative leaders of the emerging regime (most prominently Arthur Mkrtichyan, but also Ashot Ghulyan, Manvel Sargsyan and Maxim Mirzoyan). Once again, this was a case not of a diaspora organization shaping local realities, but rather of "meshing with"[26] and so to some extent directing an already existing movement. Here, as in Armenia, it is essential to underscore that the positions of the diaspora and/or of the Dashnak Party have not been decisive on their own. Rather, dominant diasporic factions have formed *alliances* with some major factions in the NKR and Armenia who fought and won the battles. Rhetoric and convenience shape that alliance as much as or more than fully shared views. Part of the ongoing political, ideological and cultural contestation has to do with whether those views will converge and become a new, hegemonic, transnational Armenian view of the political interests at stake in the Karabagh conflict.

No overview of the diaspora's influence on the NKR conflict, whether directed or mediated through Armenia, can neglect the economic dimension. First, the two Armenian lobbies in Washington have been crucial in securing over US$1 billion in US aid for Armenia since 1991. A small part of that would have gone to Armenia without such lobbying, but not most of it. That averages about US$86.5 million a year for a government whose budget sank to less than US$200 million at its nadir in 1994 and whose gross domestic product was US$1.2 billion; by 2005, the budget had grown to US$900 million and GDP to US$4.86 billion, but dependence on diasporic sources remains strong. Currently, remittances to Armenia from Armenians working abroad, primarily in Russia, are the largest source of foreign currency and are estimated at US$940 million for 2005, one-fifth of GDP. Analogous figures are not available for the NKR, but likely to be comparable. Tourism (318,000 in 2005, mostly by Armenians, either post-1988 emigrants returning for a visit or members of the older diaspora) contributed an estimated US$250 million to GDP. Philanthropic organizations such as the Hayastan Fund, the AGBU, the United Armenian Fund and the Armenian Relief Society have also contributed millions, though here the figures are less reliable because much of the assistance came in the form of donated goods, from ageing kidney dialysis machines to computers to clothes and medications.

In these various ways, the old and new diasporas together contribute significantly to Armenia's and the NKR's GDP. These sums are of material significance. They raise morale and the will to resist an unfavourable settlement of the Karabagh issue. And that difference in morale has been a major factor throughout the conflict. Not surprisingly, Azerbaijan's leadership has taken steps to promote the organization of its own dispersed emigrant populations into a diaspora.[27]

What does this record of diasporic influence on Armenia and Karabagh enable us to say about the future of conflict resolution? First, that, though the diaspora does not speak with one voice, some solidarities emerge around certain positions: I know of no group that envisages a simple return of the NKR to Azerbaijani control – a control that is universally regarded as guaranteeing bureaucratic persecution that would coerce Armenians to emigrate from the territory, as happened between 1921 and 1989, when an overwhelming Armenian majority declined to 78.5 per cent. This consensus forms the core ground for cooperation. In addition, homeland and diaspora Armenians agree that the *security* of Armenia and Karabagh must be guaranteed by creating a situation in which violence and economic blockade will no longer continue to coerce Armenians into leaving their ancestral lands.[28] Beyond such consensus, diasporic views diverge. Most groups agree on the importance of "well-crafted third party mediation".[29] The Armenian Assembly and the shapers of Armenian foreign policy have both felt that involving the Organization for Security and Co-operation in Europe, especially Russia, the United States and France, is likely to guarantee a more just mediation, even if it might take longer to achieve unanimity. Interestingly, much of the leadership of the diaspora as well as of the homeland is wary of advocating mediation by one country, even if that were Russia, currently Armenia's ally (which it was not between 1988 and 1993). In this, the Armenian parties to the Karabagh conflict differ significantly from Western theorists of conflict resolution.[30] Although agreeing that conflicts may be resolved more rapidly when the number of influential secondary parties to the conflict is kept small, they believe that a just and lasting peace requires a larger participation and endorsement.

On other issues, such as the form and direction of state-building in Armenia and the NKR during and after the conflict, there is more disagreement: presidencies on the Yeltsin–Putin model, which weaken the parliament in which the Dashnaks have power, are unsurprisingly opposed by the Dashnaks. An ever-larger number of diasporic intellectuals are voicing their unease about corruption (which is easy to condemn in general terms) and governmental abuse of concentrated power, both because they are immoral in themselves and because they lead to the disillusionment of the general population, who may come to neglect the distinction between fighting for Karabagh and fighting for the corrupt élites that rule it and Armenia. A similar disenchantment of ordinary Azeris with their own oil-rich élites also exists; curiously, this may contribute to the freezing of the conflict, as neither side is eager to test the true resolve of immiserated and disenchanted populations during active and prolonged combat. In earlier years, the crisis of war and economic blockade silenced criticism because there was a country to be saved. Now that there is a state to be built and a society to be reconstituted, diversity of opinion is becoming more vocal. It is helpful to recall that diasporas often sustain their homelands while opposing particular governmental measures. Such opposition is now forming.

Three final generalizations can be ventured. First, the diaspora feels itself to be important to Armenia and Karabagh and to the ability of both to resist a resolution of the conflict that is unjust to Armenians. Armenia's leadership tries to downplay that (sense of) importance while maximizing the forms of support it can extract by accommodating it to some degree. Kocharian's current regime, more than Ter Petrosyan's, understands that to maximize the diaspora's contributions requires not puncturing its sense of importance, even when it would be possible and justifiable on some specific occasions to do so. Vartan Oskanian, the foreign minister, himself of diaspora origin, has proved adept in this matter. Second, any diasporic group's attempt to influence either Armenia or the NKR is maximized when it can ally itself with a local group strong enough to establish a movement, but not strong enough to win by itself. Smaller diaspora groups that lack resources to bring to the homeland table, to make a consequential difference, cannot find partners and are sidelined – that is what happened to the Hnchags, an old and once-prestigious diasporic political organization (founded 1887) that has been unable to insert itself into the power structure in Armenia. Third, the major diasporic lobbies and organizations (including new ones emerging in Moscow) will have a role to play in reminding the likely international mediators that "settlement is possible only if it is premised on some form of acceptance of the current existence of the de facto states".[31]

There is no agreement about how this settlement of the conflict is to be accomplished, because each action that reinforces these de facto states can have a backlash. For example, some in Armenia and many in the diaspora opt for increasing settlement of immigrant Armenians, not only in the NKR but also in the areas of historical Karabagh that are now occupied by the joint forces of the NKR and Armenia but were not part of the pre-1988 NKR. As the Israeli example shows, the settlement of occupied territories is a double-edged sword. On the one hand, it alters the facts on the ground and forces those in Azerbaijan and the West who continue to wish to deny "the bad secessionist", Karabagh, its proper place at the negotiating table, and to minimize Armenia's power, to take both into account. But to construct such facts on the ground is also to give a hostage to the future; it becomes ever more traumatic to dislodge settlers, who themselves resist, as does a diaspora that fears that the settlements, roads, canals and power lines it has funded will be torn up by bulldozers or turned over to the other side. The key problem, for the diaspora, for Armenia and for Azerbaijan is to see that time is not *predictably* on anyone's side. The key problem for even the best Western analysts and government negotiators is to see that the recognition of the de facto independence of Karabagh will require not only words on paper as a guarantor of security but, for at least a generation, some small number of reliable troops acceptable to both sides in and on the borders of Karabagh. There is still work for NATO to do.

Appendix: High-ranking diasporic Karabagh and Russian-Armenian officers who joined the armed forces of Armenia or Karabagh

Armenian officers of high rank include

Major General Enriko Apriyamov. Born in Georgia. He commanded a Soviet "missile artillery" division. Moved to Armenia in 1992, where he serves as Deputy Chief of Staff of the Armed Forces.

Lieutenant General Hrachya Andreasian. Born in Russia, former chief representative of Warsaw Pact HQ to the Czechoslovak Armed Forces. Retired in 1990, moved to Armenia in 1992, served as Chief of Staff of the Armed Forces. Died in 1999.

Major General Vagharshak Haroutyunian. Born in Georgia, served as a Naval Captain, 2nd rank, in the Soviet Pacific Fleet. Moved to Armenia in 1991. Served as Armenia's representative to Russia, and as defence minister. Discharged, lives in Yerevan.

Lieutenant General Khristofor Ivanian. Born in Georgia. A veteran of World War II, he served as director of a Soviet artillery and missile school and retired in 1979 to live in Leningrad. Moved to Karabagh in 1992, where he served as Chief of Staff of the defence forces. Died in 1999.

Officers from the non-USSR diaspora

Colonel Hovsep Hovsepian. Born in France. Moved to Armenia in 1991, commanded a regiment. Retired, lives in Yerevan.

Monte Melkonian. Born in the United States. Moved to Karabagh in 1991, commanded the 3rd Defence Region (*Pashtpanakan Shrjan*) of Martuni. Killed in action June 1993.

Lt. Colonel Jirair Sefilian. Born in Lebanon. Commanded the Dashnak Party's irregular units in Karabagh, then the 7th Defence Region, which includes the occupied Azerbaijani territory of Kelbajar. Retired, withdrew from the Dashnak Party, lives in Yerevan and is a member of a group for "the defence of the liberated territories".

Acknowledgements

I wish to thank Hazel Smith for the guidance she offered during revision of this chapter and the scholars and analysts who supplied information and offered views that greatly enhanced my analysis, alphabetically: Khatchik Der Ghougassian, Richard Giragosian, Arman Grigorian, Richard Hovannisian, Hovsep Khourshoutian, Jirair Gerard Libaridian, Robert Owen Krikorian, Van Krikorian, Gaidz Minassian, Razmik Panossian, Simon Payaslian, Hovan Simonian, Emil Sanamian, Ara Sanjian, Hratch Tchilingirian and Ross Vartian.

Notes

1. This region is described by several names. The use of any particular name signals to at least some of those involved in the conflict a political commitment that may or may not be intended by those who use the term. Artsakh is the old Armenian name used for this and some adjacent regions and is preferred by more nationalistic Armenians. Karabagh or Karabakh are variant transliterations of Gharabagh, a word of Azerbaijani Turkish origin used by most Armenians as well. It is compounded of kara/ghara ("black") and "bagh" ("garden"). Gharabagh has been applied since around 1386 by the Turkic Muslim conquerors of the region to both Lower or Plains Gharabagh (in Armenian, Dashtayin), a large and fertile territory, and to what became under Russian administration Nagorno-Karabagh (Upper or Higher Karabagh; in Armenian, Lernayin), a smaller region. The latter is the area in which Armenians have constituted an absolute majority throughout history.
2. The term is first used in John Armstrong, "Mobilized and Proletarian Diasporas", *American Political Science Review*, 1976, 70: 393–408.
3. They are named in my acknowledgements.
4. Gurharpal Singh, "A Victim Diaspora? The Case of the Sikhs", *Diaspora*, 1999, 8(3): 204. He was criticizing Darshan Singh Tatla's claims in *The Sikh Diaspora*, Seattle: University of Washington Press, 1999.
5. Gabi Sheffer and the contributors to the volume he edited, *Modern Diasporas in International Politics*, New York: St. Martin's Press, 2002 (first published 1986), did pioneering work. So did the prolific Myron Weiner, whose work, for example the edited volume *International Migration and Security*, Boulder, CO: Westview, 1993, on migrants, refugees and demography, has implications for the study of diaspora politics and international relations. Yossi Shain's work has been the most sustained and sophisticated study of the connections between diasporas and international affairs.
6. Yossi Shain, "American Jews and the Construction of Israel's Jewish Identity", *Diaspora: A Journal of Transnational Studies*, 2000, 9(2): 163–202; Patricia F. Goff and Kevin C. Dunn, *Identity and Global Politics: Theoretical and Empirical Elaborations*, New York: Palgrave Macmillan, 2004, provide an overview of the ways in which diasporic political activity is often inseparable from "identitarian" concerns. Identity concerns and political actions reciprocally shape each other.

7. By now, there is a considerable literature in Armenian on this war, scattered in the diaspora's numerous and lively newspapers. In English, there are useful articles by Edward Walker ("No Peace, No War in the Caucasus: Secessionist Conflicts in Chechnya, Abkhazia and Nagorno-Karabakh", Occasional Papers of the Strengthening Democratic Institutions Project, Harvard Center for Science and International Affairs, Cambridge, MA, 1998) and Charles King ("The Benefits of Ethnic War: Understanding Eurasia's Unrecognized States", *World Politics*, 2001, 53: 524–552) and helpful books by Thomas De Waal (*Black Garden: Armenia and Azerbaijan through Peace and War*, New York: New York University Press, 2003) and Dov Lynch (*Engaging Eurasia's Separatist States: Unresolved Conflicts and De Facto States*, Washington, DC: United States Institute of Peace Press, 2004). However, even Lynch's excellent analysis lacks a thorough understanding of the Armenian diaspora's role.

8. Khachig Tölölyan, "Elites and Institutions in the Armenian Transnation", *Diaspora: A Journal of Transnational Studies*, 2000, 9(1): 107–136.

9. For an overview of the role of élites in the Armenian diaspora's history, see Tölölyan, "Elites and Institutions in the Armenian Transnation". For a theoretical analysis of the enduring importance of élites in democratic societies, see G. Lowell Field and John Higley, *Elitism*, London: Routledge & Kegan Paul, 1980. Though they focus on Western states and societies, their ideas can be adapted for an exploration of the role of business, religious and intellectual élites in guiding more mobile and stateless diasporic social formations.

10. Khachig Tölölyan, "Cultural Narrative and the Motivation of the Terrorist", *Journal of Strategic Studies*, 1987, 10(4): 217–233; Khachig Tölölyan, "Martyrdom as Legitimacy: Terrorism as Symbolic Appropriation in the Armenian Diaspora", in Paul Wilkinson and Alasdair Stewart, eds, *Contemporary Research on Terrorism*, Aberdeen: Aberdeen University Press, 1987, pp. 89–103.

11. Khachig Tölölyan, "Rethinking Diasporas: Stateless Power in the Transnational Moment", *Diaspora: A Journal of Transnational Studies*, 1996, 5(1): 3–36.

12. Armenia is *Haiastan* in the Armenian language, and an Armenian is a *Hay* or *Hye*, pronounced "High".

13. This volume, edited by Gerard J. G. Libaridian (*The Karabagh File: Documents and Facts on the Question of Mountainous Karabagh, 1918–1988*, Cambridge, MA, and Toronto: Zoryan Institute for Contemporary Armenian Research and Documentation, 1988), was of primary importance. It was accompanied by a flurry of lesser publications and community lectures and seminars that helped to educate and mobilize a newly committed ethno-diasporic, usually quite young, sector of the community.

14. Lynch, *Engaging Eurasia's Separatist States*.

15. The term was popularized by Linda Basch, Nina Glick Schiller and Cristina Szanton Blanc, *Nations Unbound: Transnational Projects, Postcolonial Predicaments, and Deterritorialized Nation-States*, Langhorne, PA: Gordon & Breach, 1994.

16. Personal communication with the author.

17. The term is used for people living away from their homeland but in the territory of the empire that rules the homeland – therefore not in transnational, trans-state diaspora. The Karabagh Armenians were an exclusively Soviet diaspora. Earlier, the Armenian intra-state diasporas of Tbilisi, Georgia (in Tsarist times), and of Istanbul in the Ottoman Empire played decisive roles in modern Armenian history. See Khachig Tölölyan, "Exile Government in the Armenian Polity", in Yossi Shain, ed., *Governments-in-Exile in Contemporary World Politics*, New York: Routledge, 1991, pp. 166–187.

18. Abel Aghanbekian, head of an important economics institute and adviser to Gorbachev, is of Karabagh origin. Russian in outlook and speech, he is said to have cautiously sup-

ported the transfer of Karabagh to Armenian sovereignty. If so, he illustrates the way in which almost fully assimilated ethnics can, in moments of crisis, rally to the homeland.

19. A small but symbolically important shipment of weapons – 250 Kalashnikovs – was sent from Lebanon by the Dashnak Party in 1991, according to two scholars familiar with local fighters in Karabagh. A resourceful and prosperous Armenian from Greece is also generally acknowledged to have been responsible for crucial early shipments of weapons, for which he was decorated by the de facto state of Karabagh.

20. In general, Armenian soldiers of all ranks saw more combat service in Afghanistan than the often only nominally Muslim Azeris, whom the Soviet Army was nevertheless apparently reluctant to assign to combat against fellow Muslims. It should be noted that a majority of the Armenian officers serving in the Soviet Army were in logistical and technical branches, given the extent and skill of Armenia's industrial and computer cadres. Nevertheless, more had combat experience than Azeris of equivalent rank.

21. One index of this effectiveness is the size of the Armenian Caucus in the House of Representatives. As of 8 September 2005, 147 Congressmen belonged to it, or 33.5 per cent of its membership. See ⟨http://www.aaainc.org/press/⟩. Armenians comprise 0.3 per cent of the total US population.

22. In private, members of the group state that they believed Section 907 had run its course and would no longer repay efforts to keep it in force after the cataclysm of 9/11. There was some criticism of the Assembly's action, but on the whole the lobbyists have refocused their efforts elsewhere, successfully continuing efforts to retain US economic assistance for Armenia.

23. Armenian diasporic groups have achieved partial successes in "genocide recognition" in Uruguay, the European Union, France, Canada, Germany and Argentina.

24. Diasporic intellectuals, artists and some political leaders have come to realize that henceforth new diasporic Armenian identities and commitments will be shaped to some extent in Armenia and Karabagh, as well as through the transnational migration and cultural circuits that are rapidly altering Armenia's own identity. The uneven but reciprocal penetration of the homeland by the diaspora and of the diaspora by the homeland is accelerating, as is globalization. While the homeland has new emigrants who are citizens of Armenia as well as having embassies in countries with large Armenian diasporas, the diasporic organizations have a presence in the homeland as well: cadres, media, money, ideologies. Shain, "American Jews and the Construction of Israel's Jewish Identity", closely examines analogous Jewish diasporic penetration of Israeli society, motivated by concerns over identity.

25. Much of Armenia and the NKR remain immiserated, but money, especially from Iran's diaspora, is being invested heavily in the respective capitals of Yerevan and Stepanakert. In the former, apartments in the central city quadrupled in value between 2000 and 2005; in the latter, values quintupled.

26. The term is John Antranig Kasbarian's (in personal correspondence). His unpublished dissertation on Karabagh ("We Are Our Mountains: Geographies of Nationalism in the Armenian Self-Determination Movement in Nagorno-Karabakh", Rutgers University, Geography Department, 2004) is a source of helpful detail.

27. See ⟨http://www.regnum.ru/english/607105.html⟩.

28. War, a desire to avoid the draft, blockade, economic collapse, corruption and unemployment have already led to the emigration of close to 1 million Armenians since 1989.

29. Lynch, *Engaging Eurasia's Separatist States*, p. ix.

30. Such as Hugh Miall, Oliver Ramsbotham and Tom Woodhouse, *Contemporary Conflict Resolution*, London: Polity Press, 1999.

31. Lynch, *Engaging Eurasia's Separatist States*, p. 9.

7

A reluctant diaspora? The case of Colombia

Virginia M. Bouvier

The relationship of Colombians living in the United States to the conflict in their country of origin is multifaceted, changing and mainly characterized by a reluctance to engage. This chapter analyses this relationship. I begin with a general discussion of the nature and evolution of the decades-old internal armed conflict in Colombia, focusing particularly on changes in the past decade. I then analyse characteristics and patterns of Colombian migration to the United States and its relationship to the conflict. Finally, I analyse incipient signs of increasing engagement of the diaspora communities in the economic, social, intellectual and political life of the home country, and I consider the potential for this increased engagement to provide new, creative and largely unexplored opportunities for conflict mitigation, peace-making and reconciliation options at home.

The Colombian conflict

Colombia's conflict is a highly complex internal armed conflict that has its roots in inequitable political and economic structures and that has evolved over more than half a century. At first, 40 years ago, political partisanship and ideologies provided the backdrop for a largely rural guerrilla war. The guerrilla movements that emerged at that time – including the still-active Fuerzas Armadas Revolucionarias de Colombia (FARC) and the Ejercito de Liberacion Nacional (ELN), as well as a

Diasporas in conflict: Peace-makers or peace-wreckers?, Smith and Stares (eds), United Nations University Press, 2007, ISBN 978-92-808-1140-7

plethora of other smaller groups – challenged the traditional practices of political exclusion and marginalization.

Since the mid-1990s, socio-economic and political platforms have become interwoven with agendas of violence, power, corruption, vengeance, drugs, oil and greed. Violence in Colombia has escalated to unprecedented levels and the conflict has penetrated regions of the country that had previously been unaffected.[1] The conflict continues to be particularly acute in much of the Colombian countryside, where multiple insurgent groups engage in a war against the government and right-wing paramilitary groups. In many rural communities, conflicts over resource-rich lands and intensive US-backed fumigation programmes have caused massive displacement and put poor rural populations previously neglected by the state in the line of fire.

Displacement has been a consequence and, increasingly, threatens to be a further source of Colombia's deepening conflict. With some 3 million internally displaced people (IDPs), Colombia is home to one of the largest humanitarian crises in the Western hemisphere, and its IDP population is surpassed only by that of Sudan and the Democratic Republic of Congo.

Regionalism, ethnicity, gender and rural–urban tensions also permeate the fractures of Colombian society. Regional identities and family loyalties tend to be stronger than national allegiances and a handful of élite families from three regions – Antioquia, Cundinamarca (which includes the capital city, Bogotá) and Magdalena Medio – dominate national politics, often to the detriment of other regions. Although Colombia's conflict is not primarily an inter-ethnic conflict, it does have ethnic dimensions, since Afro-Colombians (the largest minority group in Colombia, constituting about 25–30 per cent of the population) and indigenous communities (about 2 per cent of the population) suffer disproportionate poverty, displacement, environmental degradation, ill health, food insecurity and historical neglect by the state. Gender dimensions of the conflict can be seen in the efforts of rural paramilitary forces to impose a social ideology at the community level that proscribes deviation from traditional gender roles for both men and women. The weapons of war have included violence against women, who have been the victims of rape and intimidation; the majority of the internally displaced are women and children. Furthermore, the Colombian conflict (some would argue that it is a civil war) increasingly has acquired international dimensions. The conflict has pushed hundreds of thousands of refugees across Colombia's north-eastern border with Venezuela and its shorter south-western border with Ecuador and, as we shall see later in this chapter, has propelled millions of Colombians abroad.[2]

The United States has become more engaged in the conflict since the late 1990s, when US aid to Colombia escalated dramatically from US$50 million in FY2000 to a total of nearly US$4 billion in 2000–2005, with some 80 per cent of that aid going to Colombia's military and police for training, weapons, equipment and intelligence operations.[3] Three dimensions of Colombia's conflict – namely oil, insurgency (recently recast as "terrorism") and drugs – have particularly attracted US interest. Colombia is one of the top 10 oil sources for the United States and an increasingly important alternative to other areas of the world, such as the conflict-torn Middle East. Three of Colombia's illegal armed groups – the FARC and ELN guerrillas, as well as a right-wing paramilitary coalition known as the Autodefensas Unidas de Colombia (AUC) – have been designated as "terrorist" groups by the US State Department. In the aftermath of 9/11, US policy-makers have given heightened priority to counter-insurgency and counter-terrorism worldwide. Finally, Colombia is the single largest supplier of cocaine to the United States in the world. Today, over 90 per cent of the cocaine (and about half of the heroin) consumed in the United States is reportedly produced in or transits through Colombia.[4]

Although the conflict in Colombia pre-dates the cocaine and heroin boom and drugs were not an initial source of the conflict in Colombia, an expanding and ever more prosperous narcotics and contraband trade appears to have added to the conflict's intractability. All of Colombia's armed actors now benefit, albeit to different degrees, from the lucrative drug trade. Paramilitary leader Carlos Castaño has claimed that 70 per cent of the income of the AUC (estimated at US$20–200 million annually) is from drug-related activities.[5] Coca "taxes" and other drug-related revenue financed FARC's dramatic expansion in the 1990s, and were said to yield some US$1.5 million a day by the late 1990s and to account for half of FARC's income.[6] Some 8 per cent of the income of the ELN, Colombia's second-largest guerrilla group, is said to come from drugs – with kidnapping and extortion of tributes from oil companies, wealthy individuals and multinational companies accounting for most of the remainder.[7] Furthermore, drugs and the related scourges of corruption and violence are also undermining legal and political institutions.

The thriving narcotics trade, the multiplicity of armed illegal actors, high levels of violence and displacement, and the increased militarization of the conflict have all shaped the Colombian landscape in recent years. Clashes continue between guerrillas and paramilitary groups over control of natural resources and land in many rural areas, and the violence has spread to new areas of the countryside, as has the growth of illicit crops.[8] Paramilitary "self-defence" groups, initially encouraged by the state, have consolidated their economic and political power; by 2005, they were said to claim over one-third of the seats in the Colombian national legislature, a proportion that observers believe is likely to grow in the aftermath of the controversial demobilization of the AUC in 2005–2006 and following the 2006 presidential and congressional elections.

Colombian migration to the United States

Displacement and migration have been directly linked to the ebbs and flows of Colombian violence, internal conflict and economic indicators. Colombian migration to the United States since the 1940s can be broadly divided into three or four waves.[9] The first major wave of Colombian migration to the United States appears to date back to the particularly brutal decade of Colombian history known as "La Violencia" – the period from 1948 to 1958 when partisan violence between the Liberal and Conservative parties took the lives of some 200,000 Colombians. La Violencia and its aftermath sent large numbers of Colombians abroad. Between 1945 and 1965, the United States admitted some 55,000 Colombian immigrants, with more than four-fifths of that total arriving after 1955.[10] This first wave from Colombia – motivated partly by conflict at home and by new US immigration laws and work opportunities – continued until the late 1970s. Legal migration was at its peak in the period from 1966 to 1975, when the United States accepted just over 64,000 Colombian immigrants.[11] Throughout the 1960s, middle-class and skilled blue-collar workers (sometimes recruited to work in the manufacturing sector of the north-east United States) predominated, although the wave also included a significant number of professionals, especially doctors and engineers, many of whom settled in the metropolitan tri-state area of New York/New Jersey/Connecticut or in southern Florida.[12] Gender-disaggregated data, available beginning in 1960, show that consistently more than half of Colombia's legal immigrants to the United States have been female, and that women's numbers surged in response to provisions for family reunification.[13] Illegal migration may tell a different story.

Official statistics based on numbers of immigrants admitted into the United States capture only a part of Colombian migration flows. Ever since passage of the 1965 Immigration Act, which assigned national quotas and for the first time restricted in number and kind which migrants from the Western hemisphere could establish legal residency in the United States, illegal immigration from Colombia and other Latin American countries has far surpassed legal migration.[14]

As the conflict in Colombia grew deeper and more violent in the late 1970s, a second wave of Colombians migrated (now primarily illegally) to the United States. Colombian migration in this period reached its height in 1990, when the United States granted immigrant status to nearly 25,000 Colombians, bringing the total number of Colombians who were residing in the United States legally to 378,726.[15] Although this wave of migrants again included all economic groups, it was characterized by a growing number of middle-, upper-middle- and upper-class Colombians – many of whom migrated to Florida and then moved on to New York or to an expanding number of other US cities.[16]

Some of Colombia's migration in this period was tied directly to the job opportunities created by the growing drug trade. The heightened demand for drugs and the expansion of the international drug market and related money-laundering activities generated a need for workers both within and outside Colombia who could carry out the commercial operations and transnational logistics that the growth of the industry required. Urban gangs contracted by the major drug cartels sometimes established criminal operations abroad. Colombian drug-traffickers created tight networks of collaborators within major urban centres, especially Miami and New York, which enabled them to penetrate the US drug market in the 1980s.[17] The hub of the Cali cartel in the United States was based in the greater metropolitan area of New York City, where it relied on resident Colombian and Dominican communities for links with local traffickers and for assistance in laundering income from drug sales. Colombian residents in New York sometimes headed up the US-based cartel cells involved in such illegal activities.[18] Their families back home served as collateral that ensured their continued loyalty and cooperation.

US drug policies designed to address the sudden surge in drugs on US streets inadvertently helped to internationalize the drug trade. A major offensive carried out by the United States and Colombian governments against the 10–15 major drug cartels operating in Cali and Medellín in the 1980s had the unanticipated consequence of democratizing the narcotics industry, leading to the emergence of more than 200 smaller drug cartels, and shifting power at least temporarily to the Mexican cartels.[19] This new environment opened up even more jobs and opportunities. In places such as Cali and Pereira, two of the key sending centres in Colombia, migration in the late 1980s skyrocketed and became more socially heterogeneous as a result of the growing need for a mobile labour force to facilitate transnational drug transactions.[20] In their study of transnational migration, Guarnizo and Díaz concluded, "In the same way that organized crime became a means for upward mobility for many immigrant groups in the United States, drug trafficking has become one of the widest, most 'democratic' machines for upward mobility for many Colombians, from unemployed or underpaid professionals, to marginalized and disenfranchised urban dwellers."[21]

By the end of the decade, furthermore, Colombia's national economy was beginning to show signs of deterioration that would exacerbate the conflict. Neo-liberal economic reforms and an agricultural crisis linked to plummeting coffee prices led to the bankruptcy of thousands of businesses, skyrocketing unemployment and a dearth of job opportunities – especially for university graduates, youth and women.[22] National economic restructuring was devastating local economies and pushing larger numbers of Colombians abroad, lured by prospects of work, peace and prosperity.

Although a new Constitution approved in 1991 opened the political process at least initially to many of Colombia's disenfranchised sectors, and migration slowed for a time, mounting economic and political crises made this interlude short-lived. The successful dismantling of the Medellín cartel in 1993 and the arrest of six of the Cali cartel's seven top leaders in 1995 caused local markets to contract rapidly. In Cali, unemployment nearly doubled from 95,000 to 165,000 in an 18-month period from 1995 to 1997.[23] In 1999, national unemployment rates jumped 5 per cent to 20.1 per cent and GDP fell 4.8 per cent – its steepest decline in a decade. Between 1999 and early 2000, the Colombian economy suffered its worst recession in 70 years.[24]

The economic crisis – combined with growing violence related to drugs, delinquency, politics, organized crime and a counter-insurgency and counter-narcotics war being played out within Colombia – created a heightened sense of insecurity and prompted a third wave of Colombian migration to the United States that began in the mid-1990s and escalated in subsequent years. Between 1996 and July 2003, 1.6 million Colombians "permanently" left Colombia, with 49 per cent of the total emigrating between 1999 and 2001.[25] By 2002, a total of more than 5.2 million Colombians (over 10 per cent of Colombia's population of 43.8 million) were living in more than 25 countries on four continents.[26] Of these 5.2 million Colombians, 44 per cent resided in Venezuela, 38 per cent in the United States, and 4.6 per cent in Spain.[27]

Between 2000 and 2003, the United States became a refuge for an estimated 200,000–300,000 Colombians.[28] The Colombian Bureau of Statistics (DANE) indicates that some 1,125,000 Colombians, of whom up to 500,000 are without documents, are currently living in the United States.[29] The latest available US census data (2000) show that 470,682 Colombians are living legally in the United States, an increase of 91,956 people (24.3 per cent) since 1990.[30] They reside primarily in New York, Florida, New Jersey, California and Texas.[31] A large and growing number of these migrants are settling in the southern part of Florida (Miami-Dade, Broward, Palm Beach and Monroe) as well as in some relatively new destinations, including Atlanta, Chicago, Houston and the San Francisco Bay area.[32]

From its inception, Colombian migration to the United States has been marked by its heterogeneity. This latest wave of migrants – the largest in the history of Colombia – is once again made up of a broad cross-section of Colombian society, including university-educated professionals, businessmen and young middle-class students, as well as representatives of marginalized sectors of society, petty thieves, drug-traffickers and contracted killers.[33] A disproportionate number of these immigrants are from the middle and upper-middle class.[34] In comparison with other Latin American immigrant groups in the United States, Colombians in the United States appear to have the highest, albeit still modest, income levels.[35]

Members of a largely conflict-generated diaspora, Colombians in the United States today are a highly diverse group. As a group, they are marked by many of the same class, race, ideological, ethnic and regional divisions that also permeate their country of origin and that have contributed to the intractability of the conflict within Colombia.

The conflict and the diaspora

The case of Colombia posits a variety of distinct, discrete coordinates that challenge the representation of the evolution of conflict and conflict interventions along the familiar bell-curve.[36] Low-intensity conflict, hot conflict and post-conflict thrive simultaneously in Colombia, as do their remedial interventions. The stages of conflict prevailing at a given time vary tremendously according to regional and local circumstances. Local negotiations have created precarious pockets of peace in some areas; in other regions of active conflict, communities have teamed up with the government and the international community to design and implement early warning systems for the prevention of conflict.[37] Furthermore, for nearly 25 years, Colombia's national governments have engaged in negotiations that have led to the disarmament, demobilization and reintegration of some of the armed groups. What is unusual in the Colombian case is that these processes have occurred and are occurring in the midst of an ongoing conflict that continues to produce new waves of refugees, displacement and the de facto "recycling" of demobilized individuals. In Colombia then, conflict, conflict prevention, conflict mitigation, conflict resolution and post-conflict reconstruction exist simultaneously and, theoretically, each provides an access point for the diaspora community to engage or intervene.

As we saw earlier in this chapter, Colombia's diaspora population is in large part conflict generated, and its size swelled in the late 1990s and early 2000s with the increasing militarization at home. The participation of Colombian migrants in the drug trade may have contributed to the prolongation and escalation of the conflict by facilitating the global expansion of drug markets in the 1980s – thus increasing sources of finance for the conflict back home. Yet, although some Colombians in the United States have engaged in lucrative drug-trafficking activities and drug-trafficking is funding armed actors in Colombia, we do not see from Colombians in the United States the kind of direct financing for the conflict itself – based on commitment to a cause, support for a particular party in the conflict, or a shared ideological vision of struggle – that has characterized other diaspora groups such as those supporting the Irish Republican Army, El Salvador's Frente Farabundo Martí para la Liberación Nacional (FMLN) or anti-Castro groups.[38] In part, this may be because armed groups in Colombia appear to have sufficient economic resources – albeit frequently gained from illicit activities including drug-trafficking, contraband, kidnappings and extortion – to sustain the conflict without need of outside support.[39]

On the other hand, an argument could be made that drug-trafficking – like migration – has provided an escape valve that has intermittently kept the conflict in Colombia from heating up even more. The participation of economically disadvantaged sectors in the drug economy, notwithstanding its criminalization by the state, has provided work and income to both rural farmers and unemployed urban professionals in times of economic crisis and, along with migration, has offered young Colombians survival options that constitute alternatives to joining the paramilitary or guerrillas forces.

In terms of political support by the diaspora for the war, Colombians living in the United States voted overwhelmingly in the 2002 presidential election for President Alvaro Uribe, who campaigned for a hard-line escalation of the war against the guerrillas. That said, the diaspora vote was in no way decisive. Uribe was elected with broad popular support at home and the diaspora vote was consistent with the vote within Colombia. The strong support for Uribe, coming on the heels of prolonged and ultimately unsuccessful peace talks between the government and FARC, reflected the tremendous frustration over the lack of movement toward peace, economic downturn and heightened security concerns.

Although Colombia is clearly in the throes of active conflict, it can also be considered to share some of the characteristics of a post-conflict environment since, for more than 25 years, Colombian governments have been involved in numerous peace processes, many of which have successfully demobilized and reintegrated some armed individuals and groups. Colombians in the United States appear not to have been active in either promoting or blocking these processes; nor have they taken an active role in contributing to subsequent reconciliation efforts.

Despite the long-standing nature of the Colombian conflict and the large size of the diaspora it has generated, Colombians in the United States, with some notable exceptions that will be addressed later, have predominantly been reluctant or inadvertent participants in the various phases of conflict back home. There are many possible explanations for this reticence.

For example, Colombians abroad have lacked a sense of shared identity as a diaspora community. In comparison with immigrants from other countries in Central America, Colombian immigrants, sometimes called the "invisible community", seem to have a less developed sense of themselves as an immigrant community.[40] Colombians abroad are marked by cleavages in class, regionalism, generation, education, ideology, ethnicity, gender and a host of other factors that exist inside the home country and that are sometimes exacerbated when they migrate to the United States. Such divisions have made the formation of a coherent group identity somewhat problematic, and have precluded the development of strong, inclusive, representative Colombian organizations abroad that might contribute to the formation of such an identity.[41]

The Colombian diaspora is characterized by a multiplicity of unique communities that have little in common. Where history itself is contested and the cultural milieus of the homeland vary dramatically, this "historical and cultural connection" may be a further source of tension in the Colombian case. Many Colombian-American service organizations limit their membership to upper- and upper-middle-class Colombians.[42] The same attitudes of superiority held by Colombia's Spanish-descent élites toward Afro-Colombians and indigenous groups within Colombia pervade the Colombian communities overseas. New divisions may also emerge between Colombians who settle in different parts of the United States.

Although relationships appear to have been forged within small subsets of the Colombian diaspora – such as the academic and scientific communities, and to an exceptional degree among Colombian participants in illegal drug and money-laundering activities – these horizontal networks among Colombians abroad are far less developed at this stage than the links between Colombians and their home country or Colombians and their host countries. In the Colombian case, the ability of particular groups of migrants to return to Colombia varies widely within the diaspora across time and space. Colombians in the United States, unlike their ex-guerrilla compatriots in Europe, have not experienced a collective expulsion on political grounds that might unite them, nor do they share a prohibition on their return.

Nor does the aspiration to return appear to be a unifying bond for Colombians living in the United States. Rather, the decision to return, like the decision to leave, is largely an individual or a family decision, and frequently the source of tension between Colombian migrants – particularly within the same family. Outside of the national territory, differences emerge between the aspirations of the young and the old, between men and women, between earlier migrants and more recent arrivals, between those who left Colombia and those who stayed behind, and between those who migrated to the big cities and those who did not.

Gender, for example, may have a larger role in determining aspirations to return than has heretofore been recognized. Migration can either reinforce or challenge traditional cultural and religious patriarchal structures, as it simultaneously creates new opportunities and places new pressures on gender and family relations.[43] There are more female than male immigrants from Colombia to the United States, and women are "increasingly migrating from Latin America independently or quasi-independently of men".[44] We do not yet know how and if shifts in family relationships and work patterns empower women, and whether these shifts will exert any indirect influence on the conflict back home. What we do know is that, in the United States, Latin American male immigrants tend to experience downward mobility, whereas Latin American women often are entering the paid workforce for the first time.[45] Furthermore, Latin American male immigrants have been found to be more likely than females to engage in transnational political activities. Men sometimes form and participate in ethnic organizations oriented toward their home countries as a way to compensate for their loss of status. In these organizations, furthermore, men tend to dominate the leadership positions, reproducing the prevalent gender inequities from their countries of origin. Women, on the other hand, appear more likely to shift their orientation toward the United States and let go of earlier aspirations to return.[46] A recent study found that Colombian immigrant women in New York City are more likely than men to become US citizens, and that they interact more than their male counterparts with US government agencies.[47] Whereas in and of themselves such activities (interacting with schools, clinics, government offices, etc.) might be considered merely an extension of women's home activities, in the context of adaptation to a new cultural positioning such activities may lead to a renegotiation of roles that will create spaces for dialogue on issues of inclusion and power inequities within the family and may have ripple effects in the body politic back home.

Colombia's diaspora community abroad is marked by other factors that militate against an active role in the conflict (though these same divisions, theoretically and in practice, could lead to a partial kind of involvement). First, Colombian immigrants are sharply divided according to their legal status. The restrictions on legal migration combined with fears for physical security upon their return have meant that a large number of Colombians – an estimated half-million in the United States alone – remain abroad illegally. This status makes it more difficult to advocate or organize as a community.

Secondly, the complex nature of the Colombian conflict and the behaviour of the armed actors have limited the diaspora's ability to agree upon and articulate a plan for action; this, in turn, affects the capacity of the host country to act. Where the causes or injustices of the conflict are relatively clear and it is easy to assign blame or responsibility to a single actor or set of actors, there is greater room for engagement on the part of a diaspora community. Such conditions facilitated the development of international opposition to the Pinochet dictatorship in Chile, international support for the Sandinistas to oust Nicaragua's Somoza dynasty, military intervention in Haiti following the overthrow of Aristide, and the development of a powerful anti-Castro lobby in the United States.

Colombia's status as a democracy, with executive, legislative and judiciary institutions and no clear tyrant who has overturned them, makes it difficult to know how to respond from abroad. Impunity and lawlessness reign in Colombia, and those at the forefront of defending freedom of expression and association – union workers, journalists and human rights workers – are among the most persecuted in the world. However, with a dizzying maze of institutional sites within the government to petition and multiple bureaucratic sites charged with addressing human rights claims, the path for international pressures is far from clear.[48]

Furthermore, the involvement of insurgents, paramilitaries and government forces alike in brutal violence, human rights violations and corruption in Colombia has alienated potential allies abroad. The FARC killing in 1999 of three North American indigenous rights activists on Colombian soil deepened this break and stands in marked contrast to the efforts of other Latin American insurgent groups – such as the Zapatista movement in Mexico, the Sandinistas in Nicaragua, or the FMLN in El Salvador – that actively courted world public opinion for their cause. Such clarity is absent in the Colombian case.

A third reason Colombians living in the United States may be reluctant to engage in the conflict at home is related to the circumstances of the migrants' departure from Colombia. Because Colombians often fled the violence at home or left under threat of kidnapping or persecution, many simply want to leave behind the conflict and begin a new life abroad. However, although the Colombian "diaspora" is largely a conflict-generated diaspora, the conflict has not been a defining common element of a diasporan consciousness. As Gimena Sanchez-Garzoli, founder of the Refugee Policy Group at the Brookings Institute, explained, "Those who come legally are often so persecuted that they don't want links to other Colombians, as they intend to go back. Those without papers don't want to be known. Others simply want to forget."[49]

Furthermore, the decision to leave Colombia is largely shaped by economic status and the existence of global networks of family and friends. Because many middle-class Colombians arrive in their host countries via personal contacts or as students coming to study in American universities, their integration into the new society has tended to be highly individualistic. The refugees from Central America in the 1980s, in contrast, came to the United States overland, often in family or community-based groups. They tended to be poor and uneducated and to share common experiences. Once in the United States, they turned to each other for support and were marked by strong group cohesion. The engagement of some Colombians in international drug-trafficking and dominant stereotypes of Colombians as drug-traffickers have also precluded the development of strong community identities among Colombians abroad and have sown discord within the diaspora community. Colombians abroad share a "distrust rooted in the stigma of drugs, or the fear of unwittingly involving oneself with people connected to the armed actors in the conflict or delinquents".[50] An unknown percentage of the Colombians who emigrate are involved in drug-trafficking and related criminal activity, but the stigma associated with Colombian drug-traffickers affects most Colombian emigrants, both abroad and upon their return to Colombia.[51] (In fact, the term "diaspora", rarely used by Colombians to refer to Colombians living outside the national territory, is sometimes equated with the Colombian drug-traffickers who go abroad and return sporting items of conspicuous consumption.) This stigma contributes to high levels of distrust within the Colombian diaspora, affects the capacity of Colombians abroad to be effective advocates, and has diminished the credibility of Colombian migrant groups within policy-making circles abroad.[52] Ironically, those Colombians involved in the international narcotics trade are highly organized and share "extremely high levels of social trust and cooperation inside their criminal organizations".[53]

Finally, political apathy and distrust of Colombian political and economic institutions at home appear to translate into low involvement in such institutions abroad. Colombians generally lack confidence in the political and economic institutions of the country, and their loyalties to Colombia's traditional political parties (Conservative and Liberal) and the "greater" Colombian nation are relatively weak.[54] Political parties in

Colombia and their overseas affiliates, which might ordinarily be conduits for diaspora engagement, are not seen as adequate interlocutors for the vast majority of Colombians. Based on their study of Colombians in New York City, Guarnizo, Portes and Haller found that most Colombians "show little inclination to engage in home country politics of any kind" and "want little to do with their country's politics, having escaped a situation of profound instability, official corruption, and widespread violence".[55]

Incipient signs of change?

If the conflict in Colombia is rooted in poverty, skewed incomes, socio-economic segregation and a long history of discrimination and political exclusion, diaspora activities that address these inequities may directly or indirectly contribute to the conflict's resolution, and those that exacerbate inequities may contribute to its perpetuation. In this regard, at least four key (and overlapping) areas – economics, politics, education and social relations – show incipient and potential signs of change that could affect the diaspora's relationship to the conflict.

Economic role of the diaspora

In the economic sphere, migrant remittances, trade, investment and development assistance have the capacity either to ease some of the economic difficulties that catalysed the Colombian conflict and have allowed it to flourish or to exacerbate the conflict. To the extent that these contributions cushion deepening socio-economic inequities, they may contribute to national development and macroeconomic stability and prevent a worsening of the conflict. The sums of money being sent back home are substantial and growing. Remittances rose from US$538 million in 1999 to US$3 billion (some 2.5 per cent of Colombia's GDP) in 2003. By 2003, these remittances for the first time constituted Colombia's largest source of foreign exchange, surpassing the income brought in by oil, foreign investment and aid, and public and private loans; and they represented income 3 times greater than that earned by coffee sales, and 2.5 times the amount brought in by coal.[56] Remittances were expected to increase in 2004 to US$4.46 billion, with some US$2.5 billion of that total coming from Colombians in the United States.[57]

Some of these remittances have been shown to come from drug-trafficking and related money-laundering activities. US Treasury officials reported that more than US$1.5 billion in remittances to Colombia from New York in 1995 – not coincidentally the year of a widespread crackdown on major Colombian drug cartels – were laundered drug profits.[58] Geographic Targeting Orders and threshold reporting requirements for transmittals of more than US$750 on wire transfers to Colombia and the Dominican Republic led immediately to a reduced volume of remittances and put 900 money transmittal centres out of business.[59] A decade later, nonetheless, the US National Drug Intelligence Center estimated that some US$3–6 billion (most likely US$5 billion) is laundered through the Black Market Peso Exchange (BMPE) annually by Colombian drug-trafficking organizations and criminal groups based in cities such as Miami and New York.[60] (On the BMPE, US currency is exchanged for pesos on Colombia's black market.)

Illegal and legal remittances alike have clearly grown in the past decade and have become increasingly important to the Colombian economy and to the broader society. First, the number of families and communities affected is considerable. In 2003, 70 per cent of Colombians living abroad sent an average US$250 per transaction seven times a year to some 3 million Colombian families.[61] Second, the flow of these remittances has been remarkably stable over time.[62] Third, although families of all economic sectors send these remittances, they are especially critical to the survival of the region's poorest families, represent an innovative coping strategy for indigent families, and may help reduce the huge income disparities within Colombia.[63] Most of the remittances are used to supplement expenditures for daily survival needs, followed by investments in education.[64] Fourth, the remittances are protected from the conditionality or repayment obligations that come with loans from commercial or international financial institutions.[65] Finally, in terms of their impact on the Colombian conflict, remittances may well contribute to a decline in the economic desperation that entices Colombia's displaced or poor to join the ranks of illegal armed forces.

Beyond remittances, Colombian migrants also support the Colombian economy by generating a demand abroad for Colombian-produced goods and services, and they support local development through associations as well as through social, educational and philanthropic organizations.[66] The Colombian weekly *Semana* launched a web-based programme, "Conexión Colombia", sponsored by large businesses, government entities and the media in Colombia to facilitate collaboration in humanitarian ventures, such as clinics, with Colombians living abroad.[67] Such initiatives suggest a potential role for the diaspora communities to generate income for the victims of the conflict in their regions of origin. To the extent that such programmes might also support local grassroots organizations for peace, human rights and development that are working to address the root causes of the conflict (which these programmes do not currently do), the initiatives could also have an impact on the conflict itself.

Given the growing economic import of diaspora contributions to Colombia's economy, it is perhaps no surprise that the government has shifted its view of and policies concerning migration.[68] The Colombian government now recognizes the diaspora community as a "vital part of the nation" with "great potential to contribute to the social and economic development of the country".[69] The government's taxation, immigration, electoral and regulatory policies have increasingly encouraged rather than penalized migration, enabling migrants to become political and social "agents of change" both abroad and at home.[70]

Political role of the diaspora

The political realm is another arena that holds some potential for new contributions on the part of the Colombian diaspora. Colombians abroad can hold dual citizenship and are able to vote in elections overseas and at home. Electoral reform laws passed in 1997 allow nationals abroad to elect and be elected to the National Congress as representatives of any of the 25 Colombian departments.[71] Article 176 of the 1991 Constitution called for the creation of a special electoral district abroad, and subsequent reforms now enable Colombians within and outside Colombia to elect a representative of the Colombian diaspora to the Colombian National Congress. These positions are creating new venues for participation by diaspora members in policies in Colombia, but thus far appear unlikely to become a vehicle for promoting further engagement of the diaspora in relation to the conflict because they respond more to voters within Colombia than to those outside the country.

There may nonetheless be emerging opportunities for political engagement abroad as the Colombian government actively looks toward Colombians living in the United States to leverage resources and influence.[72] In 2000, the Colombian government established a coordinator in the US Embassy in Washington to organize Colombians in the United States. This move responded largely to the growing presence in the United States of highly educated Colombians who want to have greater visibility on the US political scene.

Colombian diaspora communities in the United States have not enjoyed the same success as their Cuban-American counterparts in becoming an identifiable pressure group. A 1997 public opinion poll conducted among US congressional staffers showed that just over half of the 150 staffers questioned felt that Colombians living in the United States were "politically irrelevant", and only 6 per cent felt they were a key constituency.[73]

Nonetheless, an additional 27 per cent of congressional staffers felt that, although not yet a powerful political constituency in 1997, Colombians in the United States were becoming better organized.[74] They are increasingly forming associations and linking themselves via the Internet, and they are participating more in the US political process than ever before.[75] Colombian-North Americans have now been elected to state assemblies and town councils in the Carolinas, Florida, Rhode Island, New York and New Jersey.[76] Carlos Manzano, the only elected Colombian official in New York, representing the 64th Assembly district of Manhattan, observed, "In the U.S., it's quite different from Colombia in the sense that if you do get involved, if you do organize people and you bring different issues to the forefront as a group, you can be very effective."[77] Recent findings that length of residence in the United States increases Colombians' "interest or involvement in home country politics" make it likely that we can anticipate greater engagement of the Colombian diaspora community in the future.[78]

There is, however, no indication yet that these engaged diaspora politicians will attempt to wield their resources or influence to affect the conflict back home or to bring pressure to bear on US policies towards their home country. Most probable is that the Colombian government will offer attractive terms to capture diasporan loyalties for whatever policies it is seeking to implement at home. The extent to which diaspora politicians might be called on to lobby on behalf of US foreign policy in Colombia remains to be seen, and their growing clout is as likely as not to be put at the service of a militarized US policy.

The role of an educated diaspora

A third realm of diaspora activities relates to the education sector. Although there have been concerns about the "brain drain" caused by the conflict, diaspora brain power is also seen as a potential resource for the home country that might be brought to bear on the conflict and its underlying sources. Colombian migrants have created a network of global academic contacts, especially among the scientific community. As early as 1956, Colombian graduate students in the sciences organized associations in Europe and the United States to improve conditions at home. In 1990, Coltext, an electronic list of Colombian academics abroad, gathered new steam as its members debated the option of returning; the debate found that most of the list members believed they could help the country more from outside Colombia than within.[79] Meetings ensued in Paris, Madrid, Mexico, and later New York, and in November 1991 Colciencias, the government agency responsible for national research management and funding, created Caldas, the Colombian Network of Scientists and Engineers Abroad, thus formally incorporating the scientific diaspora into national planning and institutionalizing an expatriate network.[80] In 1993,

Caldas created R-Caldas, an electronic list dedicated to academic exchanges. Caldas members formed a host of local associations, and initiated joint projects between Colombian scientists abroad and local communities inside Colombia.[81] By 1996, of the 2,000 or so scientists in the Colombian diaspora, about half of these highly educated Colombians were networked through this electronic list.[82] More recently, other sectors of Colombia's intelligentsia have organized themselves through mechanisms and institutions such as the International University of Florida's Colombian Studies Institute, the seven-university Academic Consortium for Colombian Migration Studies, and the Colombian section of the Latin American Studies Association. Such mechanisms could help to generate ideas, analysis and partnerships that could contribute to creative resolutions to the conflict at home.

The diaspora and social relations

Finally, perhaps the least explored and most promising arena in which Colombians abroad might contribute to the resolution of Colombia's conflict is social relations. Although groups overseas tend to replicate the power hierarchies and social relations that have blocked social equity at home, there may nonetheless be ways to change or challenge these traditional power relationships. The migrants' removal from the daily violence and tensions within Colombia to a new environment may present opportunities for forging new alliances. For groups that are disempowered at home, in particular, relationships with international partners can provide opportunities for empowerment that re-frame "majority–minority" power relations at home.[83] This appears to be the case with ethnic minorities and women in particular.

The work of displaced Afro-Colombians living in the United States to educate US policy-makers about the impact of US policies on the conflict and on Afro-Colombian communities is a case in point. The migration of these experienced social and political leaders to the United States, particularly from the Afro-Colombian-dominated department of Chocó, has fed the advocacy of churches, human rights organizations, universities and African-American communities in the United States, and has helped to raise the visibility of the ethnic and humanitarian dimensions of the Colombian conflict. These individuals, notably, have not sought to mobilize primarily members of the Colombian diaspora per se, but have worked in tandem with a well-developed network of non-governmental organizations (NGOs), which includes religious and seasoned human rights groups, some 30 of which coordinate their efforts through the Washington-based Colombia Steering Committee (which includes a few Colombians). Their activities, aimed at coordinating grassroots educational campaigns beyond the Washington Beltway with targeted lobbying and educational efforts in Washington aimed at ending the violent conflict at home, are also building contacts between Afro-Colombians in Colombia on the one hand, and Afro-Colombians and Afro-Americans living in Chicago, New York, the Carolinas, Detroit, Oakland and other parts of the United States.[84]

Such efforts are bolstered by a changing international climate that is more receptive to ethnicity-based claims. The international community, particularly in the wake of the World Conference against Racism in Durban, South Africa, in 2001, has become more receptive and shown greater awareness of Afro-descendant issues in general. Multilateral organizations such as the World Bank have begun programmes of Junior Professionals to integrate Afro-descendants into the banks. The United States Agency for International Development (USAID) has sponsored a series of conferences to help strengthen Afro-Colombian institutions, each attended by hundreds of Afro-Colombian public officials and civic leaders, and has made resources available to NGOs dedicated to Afro-Colombian issues.[85] Recently, Howard University and Georgetown University signed an agreement, supported by a grant from USAID, to strengthen Afro-Colombian studies and communities through exchange programmes, technical assistance, and the reactivation of a Center of Documentation, Study and Promotion of Afro-Colombian Cultural Expression in the University of Chocó.[86]

Afro-Colombians living in the United States and in Colombia have been working with human rights organizations and religious groups to educate and cultivate relations with the Congressional Black Caucus (CBC) in Washington, and they have encouraged the CBC to send delegations of members and staffers to Colombia to meet with Afro-Colombian communities there.[87] As a result of such initiatives, US legislative discussions on Colombia have begun to consider how US policies affect Afro-descendant communities in Colombia. Marino Córdoba, the international coordinator for the Association of Displaced Afro-Colombians and head of the Regional Peasant Association, underscored the shift he has seen in recent years. He noted that, "in their internal debates, African American Congress people now speak about statistics relating to the Afro-Colombian population. This was unheard of before."[88]

On 13 February 2003, Representative Charles Rangel (D-NY) and 53 co-sponsors (including strong support from the Congressional Black Caucus) sponsored House Concurrent Resolution 47, a "sense-of-the-Congress" resolution (i.e. a non-binding resolution) that called on the international community and US policy-makers to "work to improve the situation of Afro-descendant communities in Latin America and the Caribbean". Although the resolution languished without action when the 108th Congress adjourned, two years later the same resolution (now numbered H. Con. Res. 175) was introduced and, in July 2005, was passed by the full House of Representatives.

There is nonetheless a long way to go, given the devastating impact that the war and displacement are having on Colombia's Afro-descent communities, the continued socio-economic disparities that these communities endure, and the spotty implementation of existing laws that favour the protection of Afro-Colombian communities and their land and resources. Still, the focus on these issues and the increasingly receptive international climate also appear to be opening new space for dialogue within Colombia and to be giving the issue newfound visibility among Colombian government authorities. Afro-Colombian leaders cite as indicators of this change increasing contact between the Afro-descent communities of the hemisphere, the presence of Colombian President Alvaro Uribe at the first-ever national Afro-Colombian conference, the inclusion on the Colombian census for May 2005 of a question that allows Colombians to self-identify as Afro-Colombians, the appointment of an Afro-Colombian to a cabinet-level position, and greater access to job opportunities for Afro-Colombians.[89] Such steps may mark the beginnings of confidence-building measures that may lay the groundwork for reforms and improvements that could contribute to the resolution of the conflict in at least some regions of Colombia.

Conclusion

Colombian migrants abroad – part of a conflict-generated diaspora in the making – have heretofore not engaged in "typical" diaspora behaviour in openly perpetuating or supporting conflict at home, and for the most part they have been relatively invisible actors with regard to promoting conflict-related policies at home and abroad. The generalized reticence of Colombians living in the United States to become involved in the conflict back home is in part owing to characteristics of the diaspora itself. Colombian immigrants are a heterogeneous migrant community marked by high levels of distrust of political and economic institutions; drug-trafficking and stereotypes associated with drug-trafficking; severe fragmentation by class, region, ethnicity, immigrant status, ideology, education and gender; the illegal status of a significant portion of its members; historically low levels of organization and political participation; and the lack of common aspirations to return or of a common vision for the future.

Nonetheless, there are some indications that the Colombian diaspora in the United States is playing a substantial and increasing economic role at home that may contribute to conflict prevention or mitigation. This role is likely to increase in a post-conflict phase, when economic development will be essential to forging a sustainable peace. There are also incipient signs of political organizing at home and abroad as Colombian migrants enter politics and forge new global alliances. These alliances are beginning to challenge traditional power dynamics and patterns of social inequities that simmer at the surface of the conflict at home. Finally, the new common geography shared by the Colombians in the United States – despite their many divisions – and the removal of these migrants from the intense conflict within Colombia provide as yet unexplored opportunities for opening dialogues abroad that could contribute to new models for inclusion, understanding, equity and, ultimately, reconciliation at home.

Notes

1. Alexandra Guáqueta, "The Colombian Conflict: Political and Economic Dimensions", in Karen Ballentine and Jake Sherman, eds, *The Political Economy of Armed Conflict: Beyond Greed and Grievance*, International Peace Academy Economic Agendas in Civil Wars Program, Boulder, CO: Lynne Rienner Publishers, 2003, p. 73.
2. See International Crisis Group, "Colombia and Its Neighbours: The Tentacles of Instability", ICG Latin America Report No. 3, 8 April 2003.
3. US Senate, *Foreign Operations, Export Financing, and Related Programs Appropriation Bill, 2001*, Report 106-291, p. 53.
4. US Department of State, *International Narcotics Control Strategy Report-2005*, Bureau for International Narcotics and Law Enforcement Affairs, March 2005; available at ⟨http://www.state.gov/p/inl/rls/nrcrpt/2005/vol1/html/42363.htm⟩ (accessed 25 October 2006).
5. Guáqueta, "The Colombian Conflict", p. 82; Connie Veillette, "Colombia: Issues for Congress", *CRS Report for Congress*, updated 19 January 2005, ⟨http://fpc.state.gov/documents/organization/44015.pdf⟩ (accessed 26 October 2006), p. 5.
6. Center for International Policy, "Information about the Combatants", at ⟨http://www.ciponline.org/colombia/infocombat.htm⟩ (accessed 25 October 2006); Guáqueta, "The Colombian Conflict", p. 81.
7. International Crisis Group, "War and Drugs in Colombia", Latin America Report No. 11, 27 January 2005, p. 18.
8. United Nations Office on Drugs and Crime and Government of Colombia, *Colombia: Coca Cultivation Survey*, June 2004; available at ⟨http://www.unodc.org/pdf/colombia/colombia_coca_survey_2003.pdf⟩ (accessed 25 October 2006).
9. Statistics on Colombian migration to the United States are unavailable prior to 1936, and there is some disagreement about the beginning and end of each wave of migration. Lack of statistics on undocumented Colombians makes this exercise somewhat problematic, although the Colombian government has come up with estimates of illegal migration flows by subtracting the number of those who return to Colombia from the number who do not. Cruz and Castaño divide the migration flows as follows: 1926–1935, 1936–

1945, 1945–1965, 1965–1976. See Carmen Inés Cruz and Juanita Castaño, "Colombian Migration to the United States (Part 1)", in *The Dynamics of Migration: International Migration. Interdisciplinary Communications Program*, Occasional Monograph Series 5.2, Washington, DC: Smithsonian Institution, 1976, pp. 49–50. Others suggest alternative chronologies, although they tend to be rather vague and without precise statistical documentation. Gamarra posits three waves: one from the decade of "La Violencia" (roughly 1948–1958) to the 1970s, one from the 1970s to the mid-1990s, and a third from the mid-1990s to the present. See Luis Eduardo Guarnizo, "La migración transnacional colombiana: Implicaciones teóricas y prácticas", and Eduardo A. Gamarra, "La diáspora colombiana en el sur de la Florida", in Ministerio de Relaciones Exteriores de Colombia (MREC), *Colombia Nos Une: Memorias: Seminario sobre Migración Internacional Colombiana y la Conformación de Comunidades Transnacionales, Junio 18 y 19 de 2003*, Bogotá, Colombia, March 2004, pp. 30–31 and 47; José Itzigsohn and Silvia Giorguli Saucedo, "Immigrant Incorporation and Sociocultural Transnationalism", *International Migration Review*, 2002, 36(3). These schema are all rather unsatisfying however, because they fail to specify the data on which they base their periodization, and they give a sense not of clear waves but of a scale of ever-increasing ripples.

10. Cruz and Castaño, "Colombian Migration to the United States", p. 49.
11. Ibid., p. 50.
12. Itzigsohn and Giorguli Saucedo, "Immigrant Incorporation and Sociocultural Transnationalism"; Guarnizo, "La migración transnacional colombiana", p. 30.
13. Gamarra, "La diáspora colombiana en el sur de la Florida", p. 47; Cruz and Castaño, "Colombian Migration to the United States", pp. 50–51.
14. Cruz and Castaño, "Colombian Migration to the United States", pp. 46–50.
15. MREC, *Colombia Nos Une*.
16. Gamarra, "La diáspora colombiana en el sur de la Florida", p. 47.
17. Francisco Echeverri, interview with the author, 2 August 2004; Luis Eduardo Guarnizo and Luz Marina Díaz, "Transnational Migration: A View from Colombia", *Ethnic and Racial Studies*, 1999, 22(2); Clifford Krauss, "The Cali Cartel and the Globalization of Crime in New York City", in Margaret E. Crahan and Alberto Vourvoulias-Bush, eds, *The City and the World: New York's Global Future*, New York: Council on Foreign Relations, 1997.
18. Krauss, "The Cali Cartel", p. 72.
19. Phil Williams, "Transnational Criminal Enterprises, Conflict, and Instability", in Chester A. Crocker, Fen Osler Hampson and Pamela Aall, eds, *Turbulent Peace: The Challenges of Managing International Conflict*, Washington, DC: United States Institute of Peace Press, 2001, p. 102.
20. Guarnizo and Díaz, "Transnational Migration".
21. Ibid.
22. Guarnizo, "La migración transnacional colombiana", p. 31.
23. Guarnizo and Díaz, "Transnational Migration", p. 400.
24. Gamarra, "La diáspora colombiana en el sur de la Florida", p. 56.
25. According to the Departamento Administrativo de Seguridad. MREC, *Colombia Nos Une*, p. 186.
26. MREC, *Colombia Nos Une*. The foreign relations ministry also estimated that, by December 2003, 4,243,208 Colombians, of whom 768,722 had registered, were living abroad – suggesting that large numbers of Colombians are also returning home to Colombia ("Los colombianos en el exterior", at ⟨http://portal.minrelext.gov.co/portal/webdriver.exe?MIval=cnu_colombianos_exterior.html⟩ (accessed 24 October 2006).
27. MREC, *Colombia Nos Une*, pp. 186–197.

28. Gamarra, "La diáspora colombiana en el sur de la Florida", p. 45.
29. Echeverri, interview with the author, 2 August 2004.
30. Milena Gómez Kopp, "Políticas para promover un mayor acercamiento con la diáspora: Las voces de los colombianos en Nueva York", in MREC, *Colombia Nos Une*, pp. 63–64.
31. Gómez Kopp, "Políticas para promover un mayor acercamiento con la diáspora", p. 54.
32. MREC, *Colombia Nos Une*, pp. 32, 46, 48; Gómez Kopp, "Políticas para promover un mayor acercamiento con la diáspora", p. 73.
33. Guarnizo, "La migración transnacional colombiana", p. 33.
34. Gamarra, "La diáspora colombiana en el sur de la Florida", p. 45.
35. Christopher Mitchell, "Una comparación de los esfuerzos de los grupos de migrantes del hemisferio occidental para influenciar la política estadounidense hacia sus países de origen", in Juan Gabriel Tokatlian, ed., *Colombia y Estados Unidos: problemas y perspectivas*, Bogotá: Tercer Mundo S.A., 1998.
36. Michael Lund, *Preventing Violent Conflicts: A Strategy for Preventive Diplomacy*, Washington, DC: United States Institute of Peace Press, 1996, p. 38.
37. Catalina Rojas with Sanam Naraghi Anderlini and Caille Pampell Conaway, *In the Midst of War: Women's Contributions to Peace in Colombia*, Women Waging Peace, Policy Commission, Washington, DC: Hunt Alternatives Fund, 2004, ⟨http://www.huntalternatives.org/download/16_in_the_midst_of_war_women_s_contributions_to_peace_in_colombia.pdf⟩ (accessed 26 October 2006); Women Waging Peace, *Preparing for Peace: The Critical Role of Women in Colombia. Conference Report, May 9–14, 2004*, Washington, DC: Hunt Alternatives Fund, ⟨http://www.huntalternatives.org/download/17_preparing_for_peace_the_critical_rose_of_women_in_colombia.pdf⟩ (accessed 26 October 2006); Virginia M. Bouvier, *Special Report: Civil Society under Siege in Colombia*, Washington, DC: United States Institute of Peace, February 2004; Virginia M. Bouvier, *Special Report: Peace Initiatives in Colombia*, Washington, DC: United States Institute of Peace, forthcoming.
38. See Daniel L. Byman, Peter Chalk, Bruce Hoffman, William Rosenau and David Brannan, *Trends in Outside Support for Insurgent Movements*, Santa Monica, CA: RAND, 2001.
39. Echeverri, interview with the author, 2 August 2004.
40. Gimena Sánchez-Garzoli, interview with the author, 20 July 2004; Paola Iuspa, "FIU Hopes to Analyze Colombian Influx into South Florida", *Miami Today*, week of 30 November 2000, at ⟨http://www.miamitodaynews.com/news/001130/story3.shtml⟩ (accessed 26 October 2006); Michael W. Collier and Eduardo A. Gamarra, "The Colombian Diaspora in South Florida", *Report of the Colombian Studies Institute's Colombian Diaspora Project*, Working Paper Series No. 1, Miami: Latin American and Caribbean Center, Florida International University, May 2001.
41. Guarnizo, "La migración transnacional colombiana", pp. 25–43.
42. Gamarra, "La diáspora colombiana en el sur de la Florida", pp. 45–62; Saskia Sassen-Koob, "Formal and Informal Associations: Dominicans and Colombians in New York", *International Migration Review*, 1979, Special Issue: International Migration in Latin America, 13(2): 314–332.
43. James Clifford, "Diasporas", *Cultural Anthropology*, 1994, 9; Patricia Fernández-Kelly and Ana García, "Power Surrendered, Power Restored: The Politics of Home and Work among Hispanic Women in Southern California and Southern Florida", in Louise A. Tilly and Patricia Guerin, eds, *Women and Politics in America*, New York: Russell Sage Foundation, 1990, pp. 215–228; Luin Goldring, "Gendered Memory: Constructions of Rurality among Mexican Transnational Migrants", in E. M. DuPuis and Peter Vendergeest, eds, *Creating the Countryside: The Politics of Rural and*

Environmental Discourse, Philadelphia: Temple University Press, 1996, pp. 303–329; Pierette Hondagneu-Sotelo, *Gendered Transitions: Mexican Experiences of Immigration*, Berkeley: University of California Press, 1994; Sarah Mahler and Patricia Pessar, "Gendered Geographies of Power: Analyzing Gender across Transnational Spaces", *Identities: Global Studies in Culture and Power*, 2001, 7: 441–459; Michael Jones-Correa, "Different Paths: Gender, Immigration and Political Participation", *International Migration Review*, 1998, 32(2): 326–349.

44. Clifford, "Diasporas", p. 314.
45. Luis Eduardo Guarnizo, Alejandro Portes and William Haller, "Assimilation and Transnationalism: Determinants of Transnational Political Action among Contemporary Migrants", *American Journal of Sociology*, 2003, 108(6); Jones-Correa, "Different Paths".
46. Jones-Correa, "Different Paths".
47. Ibid.
48. See Winifred Tate, "Counting the Dead: Human Rights Claims and Counter-Claims in Colombia", PhD dissertation, Department of Anthropology, New York University, January 2005.
49. Sánchez-Garzoli, interview with the author, 20 July 2004.
50. Guarnizo, "La migración transnacional colombiana", pp. 25–43.
51. Ibid., p. 32.
52. Juan Gabriel Tokatlian, ed., *Colombia y Estados Unidos: Problemas y perspectivas*, Bogotá: Tercer Mundo S.A., 1998, p. 405.
53. Gamarra, "La diáspora colombiana en el sur de la Florida", p. 60.
54. Ibid., p. 59; Gómez Kopp, "Políticas para promover un mayor acercamiento con la diáspora", p. 64; Alejandro Portes, Luis E. Guarnizo and Patricia Landolt, "The Study of Transnationalism: Pitfalls and Promise of an Emergent Research Field", *Ethnic and Racial Studies*, 1999, 22(2).
55. Guarnizo, Portes and Haller, "Assimilation and Transnationalism", pp. 1211–1248.
56. Guarnizo, "La migración transnacional colombiana", pp. 25–43; Inter-American Dialogue, "All in the Family: Latin America's Most Important International Financial Flow", *Report of the Inter-American Dialogue Task Force on Remittances*, Washington, DC: Inter-American Dialogue, January 2004, p. 7.
57. Fondo Multilateral de Inversiones, Banco Interamericano de Desarrollo, "Receptores de remesas en América Latina: El caso colombiano", Cartagena, Colombia, September 2004, p. 7.
58. US Department of the Treasury, Financial Crimes Enforcement Network News Release, "Treasury Acts Against Flow of Dirty Money to Colombia", 23 December 1996, at ⟨http://www.fincen.gov/gtortr.html⟩ (accessed 25 October 2006).
59. National Drug Intelligence Center, *National Drug Threat Assessment 2003: Money Laundering*, January 2003, at ⟨http://www.usdoj.gov/ndic/pubs3/3300/money.htm⟩ (accessed 25 October 2006).
60. National Drug Intelligence Center, *National Drug Threat Assessment 2006, Drug Money Laundering*, January 2006, at ⟨http://www.usdoj.gov/ndic/pubs11/18862/money.htm#6text⟩ (accessed 25 October 2006).
61. Carolina Barco, "Prefacio", in MREC, *Colombia Nos Une*, p. 9.
62. Inter-American Dialogue, "All in the Family", p. 7.
63. Gamarra, "La diáspora colombiana en el sur de la Florida", p. 57.
64. Fondo Multilateral de Inversiones, "Receptores de remesas en América Latina", p. 7.
65. Inter-American Dialogue, "All in the Family", p. 3.
66. Guarnizo, "La migración transnacional colombiana", p. 36; Guarnizo, Portes and Haller, "Assimilation and Transnationalism".

67. Echeverri, interview with the author, 2 August 2004.
68. Oscar Sandoval, "Vinculación de Nacionales en el Exterior: Una Prioridad de la Conferencia Sudamericana sobre Migraciones", in MREC, *Colombia Nos Une*, p. 14.
69. Barco, "Prefacio", p. 9.
70. Guarnizo, Portes and Haller, "Assimilation and Transnationalism"; Jean-Baptiste Meyer, D. Bernal, J. Charum, J. Gaillard, J. Granés, J. León, A. Montenegro, A. Morales, C. Murcía, N. Narváez-Berthelemot, L.-S. Parrado and B. Schlemmer, "Turning Brain Drain into Brain Gain: The Colombian Experience of the Diaspora Option", *Science, Technology and Society*, 1997, 2(2).
71. Guarnizo and Díaz, "Transnational Migration".
72. Gamarra, "La diáspora colombiana en el sur de la Florida", p. 58.
73. Tokatlian, *Colombia y Estados Unidos*, p. 405.
74. Ibid.
75. Echeverri, interview with the author, 2 August 2004.
76. Ibid.
77. Tanya Pérez-Brennan, "Colombian Immigration", *ReVista*, Spring 2003, at ⟨http://drclas.fas.harvard.edu/revista/?issue_id=14&article_id=265⟩ (accessed 25 October 2006).
78. Guarnizo, Portes and Haller, "Assimilation and Transnationalism".
79. Meyer et al., "Turning Brain Drain into Brain Gain".
80. See Jorge Charum and Jean-Baptiste Meyer, eds, *Hacer ciencia en un mundo globalizado: La diaspora científica colombiana en perspectiva*, Bogotá: Colciencias, Universidad National de Colombia, Tercer Mundo Editores, 1998.
81. Ibid.
82. Institut de recherche pour le développement, "Brain Drain: How to Benefit from Expatriates Skills?", *Scientific Bulletin*, No. 27, November 1996, at ⟨http://www.ird.fr/us/actualites/fiches/1996/27.htm⟩ (accessed 25 October 2006).
83. Clifford, "Diasporas"; Kim D. Butler, "Defining Diaspora, Refining a Discourse", *Diaspora*, 2001, 10(2).
84. Luis Gilberto Murillo, presentation to the US Congress, 23 July 2004.
85. United States Agency for International Development, "USAID Lends Lifeline to Many Afro-Colombians Caught in the Country's Violent Crossfire", ⟨http://www.usaid.gov/locations/latin_america_caribbean/country/colombia/afrocolombians.html⟩ (accessed 13 October 2006).
86. Interview with Luis Gilberto Murillo, Washington, DC, 19 October 2006; "Agreement of Cooperation between the University of Howard and the Technological University of Choco", no date.
87. In 2002, Democratic members and staff of the CBC – including Representatives William Jefferson (LA), Donald Payne (NJ), John Conyers, Jr (MICH) and James Clyburne (SC), and Mischa Thompson, a staffer for Representative Gregory Meeks (NY) – visited Bogotá and Cali.
88. Marino Córdoba, interview with the author, 22 July 2004.
89. Ibid.; Luis Gilberto Murillo, presentation to the US Congress, 23 July 2004.

8

The Cuban diaspora

Jean Grugel and Henry Kippin

The revolutionary government headed by Fidel Castro has generated an interwoven pattern of internal and external conflict since its inception in 1959. One consequence has been periodic waves of emigration out of the island. Most of the leavers have settled in Florida on the US mainland, although there are also smaller Cuban communities in Venezuela and elsewhere in Latin America and in Spain. More than anything else, the unique place that Cuba has occupied for over 45 years within US foreign policy has conditioned the complex evolution of the diaspora. Cuba became the target of a US boycott, and successive US governments have expressed deep hostility towards the Castro government.[1] That the revolutionary regime has survived, especially after the collapse of its closest international ally, the Soviet Union, in 1991, is undoubtedly a remarkable feat in an extremely hostile international environment. But its survival has also contributed to freezing US–Cuban relations – and by implication relations between the Cuban state and the diaspora – in an outmoded Cold War mould. Contemporary US concerns around security, democracy and human rights issues have simply been grafted onto the Cuba embargo policy, which, in essence, retains the hallmarks of the containment period of US policy in the late 1950s. More than in any other diaspora conflict, the nuances of politics within the United States have shaped diaspora identity and behaviour.

We argue in this chapter that a resolution of the schism that opened up between Cubans after 1959 is impossible without a settlement between the United States and Cuba. Equally, however, a resolution of the US–

Diasporas in conflict: Peace-makers or peace-wreckers?, Smith and Stares
(eds), United Nations University Press, 2007, ISBN 978-92-808-1140-7

Cuba conflict is now difficult to imagine without the cooperation of the Cuban diaspora. Its size, the capacity of its political leadership for organization and institutional penetration and its geographical concentration in Miami, a crucial state in US presidential elections, all contribute to making it a force impossible to ignore. The diaspora leadership retains the capacity to disrupt any (presently unlikely) settlement between the United States and Cuba and to endanger its resolution after Castro's death. Moreover, the leadership shows little willingness to accept a brokered deal unless the political order in Cuba is radically altered. A settlement of land and property claims, for example, may simply not go far enough. In the terms of this book, then, the diaspora is, potentially, a peace-wrecker. Nevertheless, we also aim to demonstrate that elements of a more diverse and tolerant culture, more in tune with the post–Cold War system, are discernible within the diaspora community. This opens up the possibility that, if a negotiated transition to democracy is achieved after the end of the Castro regime, the diaspora could over the longer term play an important bridging role between the island and the United States.

The chapter begins by outlining the creation and composition of the Cuban diaspora. We then look at the ways in which diaspora politics has both contributed to and benefited from the political stalemate of US–Cuban relations. This is followed by a discussion of the political organizations of the diaspora and the contemporary components of conflict between the diaspora and the regime in Havana, focusing in particular on the Elian Gonzalez episode in 2000. Finally, we turn directly to the conflict and assess the potential role of the diaspora in facilitating or blocking any long-overdue settlement of the Cuban saga.

Making the diaspora

By far the majority of Cuban exiles are to be found in the United States, mainly in the state of Florida. This community does not easily conform to dominant images of contemporary diasporas.[2] It has not been created through internal warfare; nor can it be considered as a distinct ethnic group; nor is it the result of geopolitical change consequent on the end of bipolarity. The Cuban diaspora dates back to the 1960s and is mainly made up of voluntary émigrés. In marked contrast to other Caribbean and Latin communities in the United States, Cubans were positively encouraged to leave for many years by the US state and received preferential access to residency and citizenship. Furthermore, Cuban-Americans possess considerable economic and political resources. This relatively privileged status inside the United States has contributed to a powerful sense of what it means to be "Cuban" in the United States and a belief in the central importance of the Cuban issue outside of Cuba.

The seminal "event" that explains Cuban diasporization[3] is the revolution of 1959 and the radical social and political upheaval that followed. Prominent amongst the first wave of émigrés were individuals with a good deal to lose from state appropriation of property and personal fortunes. This meant that the original diaspora was largely (though not uniformly) used to wealth and status. The fact that those affiliated to or sympathizing with the outgoing regime – *Batisteros*, civil servants, political cadres and ideological opponents of the revolution – also left provided the diaspora with its overtly political impetus. This first wave of Cuban exiles found support from a US government that saw in Castro not only a threat to its own dominance of the Caribbean Basin but a representative of international communism. The US government and the initial Cuban exile community thus found common ground in seeking to overthrow Castro and return to the "*Cuba de ayer*" (the Cuba of yesterday).

These first émigrés sought overwhelmingly to remove Castro through violence, a task in which they were supported openly and covertly by the US state. In the escalating Cold War context, the US government and the Central Intelligence Agency (CIA) were quick to mobilize the new community into a force that could be used to restore US influence on the island. Significant amounts of CIA money were given to anti-Castro Cuban groups such as the Democratic Revolutionary Resistance and the Counter-revolutionary Invasion Brigade 2506. These would also participate in the Bay of Pigs counter-invasion of 1961, the failure of which would leave a lingering sense of resentment amongst Cuban-Americans for what they felt was a betrayal by the Kennedy administration in shrinking from airstrikes as they invaded the island.

After the initial wave of 1959, and in view of the failure to unseat Castro, the diaspora community continued to grow. According to Lievesley, there have been five major diasporas in total: "the immediate post-1959 departure of regime officials and the privileged; the 'freedom flights' of 1959–1962 and 1963–1973; the 1980s Mariel boatlift; and the *balseros* crisis of 1994".[4] The period from 1960 to 1973 brought over 600,000 Cubans to the United States,[5] with over half of these arriving on the twice-daily flights that had been agreed by the two governments in Havana and Washington. These simultaneously served to rid Cuba of internal opposition and to provide the United States with apparent evidence of Castro's deep unpopularity. This new group, considerably less wealthy than the first wave, was regarded with some suspicion by the earlier arrivals even though it brought skills, trade and investment that contributed hugely towards the regeneration of Miami, which was gradually turning into an alternative Havana. For Croucher, the mixed reactions to the new arrivals meant that they were simultaneously seen as "as an economic miracle bestowed upon a city in decline [and] ... an unwelcome invasion, and the cause of great social, political and economic disruption."[6] Politically, these second and third waves did little to shake off perceptions of the diaspora as rabidly anti-Castro. By the 1970s, the notion of the Cuban diaspora as militantly anti-Castro dominated external perceptions of the community, not surprisingly since it continued to endorse "commando raids" on the island and undertook violent campaigns against US politicians who advocated rapprochement with Havana.[7] The image of the diaspora was thus set: at once a "*bona fide* paragon ... for all other immigrant groups ... to emulate"[8] in terms of its strong cohesiveness and sense of identity and, at the same time, something altogether more sinister, a community whose leaders endorsed violence, sought to suppress dialogue and rejected compromise.

The next significant wave of migration occurred in 1980, when 125,000 individuals were forcibly expelled from Cuba after a purge of "undesirables" by Castro.[9] During one month alone, 88,817 "*Marielitos*", as they came to be known after the name of the ship that carried them to Florida, were sent across the straits, more than the number of Cuban émigrés that had arrived in any one year previously. The *Marielitos* were a new breed of Cuban exiles, many too young to remember pre-communist Cuba, certainly less privileged in terms of social class and status, unwanted by the island authorities and stigmatized by perceived criminality. As a consequence, their arrival was treated with a good deal of suspicion by the established community – including the locally dominant *Miami Herald* newspaper.[10] Ultimately, though, this new influx of exiles was to lead to community leaders taking the view that new and more effective forms of community organization were required. As a result, the Cuban American National Foundation (CANF) was formed under the leadership of Jorge Más Canosa, a prominent anti-Castro Cuban-American. CANF went on to become a political machine, able to deliver a substantial vote in elections and willing to provide funds for US politicians prepared to support the Cuban cause.

The most recent wave of emigrants began to leave Cuba in the 1990s. The end of the Cold War signalled sweeping changes for Cuba and made visible its economic fragility, forcing austerity and economic reform on the island. A return to the early rhetoric of nationalism meant that the regime was able to shore up some support in difficult times,[11] but this did not prevent a wave of internal repression as Castro sought to assert his control. Cuba's economic isolation was made worse by the US decision to increase pressure on the island via the introduction of tougher new legislation (the Torricelli and Helms–Burton Acts), providing Cubans with evidence that the United States was unwilling to make peace with Cuba until Castro was forced out. The fact that the end of the Cold War signalled deepening difficulties for Cuba rather than the end of US hostility created a climate on the island in which rising numbers of young Cubans, weary of the long-running dispute with the United States and Cuba's isolation, wanted to abandon the island, hoping for a better life outside. This culminated in the so-called *"Balseros* crisis", as considerable numbers of young Cubans attempted to leave the island on small boats to seek their fortune in the United States, encouraged by the triumphalist tone of Cuban community leaders in Florida. How far the young people who set sail to cross the straits to Miami were allowed to do so by Havana in order to provoke fears on the US mainland of "another *Mariel"* and to force the United States to moderate its tone, as Greenhill claims, is a matter of dispute.[12] It should be noted, though, that the *Balseros* crisis culminated in the first migratory agreement between the United States and Cuba in 1995, which set limits for the first time on the number of Cubans who can enter the United States. That the United States has strictly enforced the agreement is indicative of a policy change on Cuban immigration and brought to a close the earlier open door policy.

The agreements put an end to the crisis; but not before considerable numbers of young Cubans had entered the United States. In contrast to earlier groups, these emigrants are mainly individuals who have left in search of jobs, dollars and a better life. They are less interested in regime politics on the island; they have left to escape the weight of being "Cuban", the ways in which Cuban identity is constructed on the island and the costs that international geopolitics has imposed upon them. Most do not wish to take on the equally burdensome task of being actively "Cuban" in the United States and to spend their lives in seeking to rewrite the past 40 years of Cuban history. As Molyneux points out, then, the *Balseros* represented "a more purely economic diaspora, somewhat at odds with the existing militant anti-communism of the (political) extremists".[13]

The picture of the Cuban diaspora is, in sum, complex. Normally identified through its most vocal members, the intransigent, sometimes violent, anti-Castroites, in fact the diaspora is now far from being a sociologically and politically homogeneous community. It is no longer made up of individuals whose entire *raison d'être* seems to be to overthrow the regime. Each migratory wave has contributed to making the Cuban diaspora a more eclectic mix. There are political opponents of Castro and communism of course. But others seeking greater cultural or sexual freedom have also left, as well as considerable numbers of "ordinary" Cubans for whom the motivations for exile have been the search for work and a desire to escape from isolation. This inevitably changes what it means to be Cuban-American and the relationship with the host country and, as a result, generates tensions within contemporary Cuban Miami. These tensions are becoming more visible within the community and they are reflected in the mix of nostalgia, resentment and dependence that now characterizes Cuban-American relations with the homeland. In a recent exploration of contemporary Cuban-American identity, Abreau writes:

> Travelling to Cuba – returning – is loaded with symbolic meaning ... Although for some it symbolises reunification, for others it symbolises an acceptance of communism and Fidel, and acceptance is a tribute that many see as incompatible with the repudiation that prompted exile in the first place.[14]

Shaping the diaspora: US–Cuban relations

Understanding the politics of the Cuban diaspora is not possible without a discussion of US policy and US–Cuban relations. Being "Cuban", in fact, is barely possible, on the island or off it, without reference to the United States. Cuban history has been indelibly shaped since the War of Independence in 1898 by US strategies for hegemony in the Caribbean Basin. It is perhaps not surprising, then, that the diaspora leadership – the pre-1959 élites – looked to the US state to restore "their" Cuba to them. Even after this proved impossible, diaspora leaders have continued to seek to influence policy in Washington. Their aim is to keep the Cuban issue on the agenda of US politics and to persuade US leaders to act on their behalf. In short, the US state has constituted a fixed point for diaspora politics, and the aspirations, expectations and culture of the diaspora are shaped by US policy. As a result, the diaspora leadership has struggled to come to terms with the shifts in US policy concerns away from the Caribbean.

The phases of conflict between the United States and Cuba have been well documented.[15] Following the failed counter-revolution at the Bay of Pigs, involving the newly formed Miami "oppositionists"[16] alongside the CIA, the Cuban Missile Crisis in 1962 marked Cuba out as an issue capable of generating a genuinely global crisis. Cuba was then categorized as a pariah state in Washington. Sanctions were imposed against a regime that the United States saw as a de facto arm of Soviet power. Regime change thus became the principal objective of US policy and the United States periodically supported attempts to remove Castro. That regime change – rather than a gradual transition – remains the principal aim of policy towards Cuba, so many years after the close of the Cold War, is in some ways surprising. Certainly, Cuba can no longer be constructed as a proxy for an alternative communist world order; nor can it be seen any more as an exporter of revolution, although Cuba's endorsement of Latin American nationalism, evident in Castro's open support for Hugo Chavez in Venezuela and Evo Morales in Bolivia, certainly unsettles Washington. Cuba's pariah status stands in sharp contrast to how the United States has chosen to deal with a number of other post-Marxist states, such as China. Even the visit by Pope John Paul II to Cuba in 1998, marking Cuba's gradual incorporation into the international order and Europe's rapprochement with the island, did nothing to change the US point of view. For Dominguez, the reasons behind the United States' implacable hostility after 1989 are difficult to understand.[17] Proximity is certainly a factor: Cuba is situated just 90 miles from Florida. Moreover, the years of hostility have left deep roots in the foreign policy establishment in Washington, which means that a softer line would seem to signal a climb-down. Antagonism between Castro and the US establishment is another contributing factor; Robinson even wonders whether "childish as it seems, the US–Cuban contest comes down [simply] to a battle of wills".[18] Perez Jr also notes that the conflict is now embedded in a deeply personal confrontation between Castro and leading US politicians, and US antagonism is, he argues, "very much conditioned by its deepening antipathy towards Castro".[19]

The continuance of US hostility can also be explained by institutional biases within the US political system. Key politicians in Congress have taken upon themselves the fight to unseat Castro and are unwilling to change. In this they have been supported by the diaspora leadership. This culminated in two pieces of new legislation in the 1990s. The Cuban Democracy Act (the Torricelli Act) in 1992 was designed to increase the effectiveness of already existing sanctions by preventing Cuba from trading with third countries – including European Union member states – and push the Cuban economy, already devastated by the end of Soviet preferences, towards collapse.[20] Crucially, however, this was now expressed as support for the democratization of Cuba, reflecting the endorsement of liberal democracy that had begun to colour US policy towards Latin America in the 1980s.[21]

Once it became clear that the Cuban Democracy Act had failed in its attempt to isolate the revolutionary regime to the point of disintegration, further measures were considered. Tensions rose between the authorities on the island and the US administration as elements of the diaspora community adopted increasingly aggressive strategies in their efforts to overthrow Castro. One of the direct action groups, Brothers to the Rescue, created in 1991, began patrolling the Florida straits with the aim of alerting the US Coastguard and thus providing Cubans crossing to the United States with safer passage. Later, they adopted a more explicitly political agenda, which involved dropping anti-Castro propaganda leaflets over Havana.[22] Tensions came to a head when two planes belonging to the Brothers were shot down by the Cuban air-force over international waters. The event allowed Castro to defuse domestic discontent with a good dose of anti-American posturing, as Leogrande commented: "By shooting down the Brothers' planes, Castro was certain to provoke a confrontation with Washington. He chose to sacrifice the gradually (albeit glacially) warming climate of US–Cuban relations for a quick fix of domestic patriotism."[23]

But the cost was that there was relatively little domestic opposition inside the United States to the Cuban Liberty and Solidarity Act (the Helms–Burton Act), which was quickly signed into law shortly after. The logic of Helms–Burton was to ensure that Cuba did not become a target of European or Asian investment and was thereby excluded from the opening up of global trade. The Act thus enshrined both existing sanctions and pressure for regime change and attempted to prevent other states from deepening economic relations with Cuba until the Cuban state endorsed both liberal economics and liberal democracy.[24]

The paradox of US policy is that tightening the boycott has actually allowed Castro to entrench his authority on the island. Rather than being able to seize the opportunity presented by the collapse of the Soviet Union to push for gradual reform, US hostility has turned Cuba into a victim and has made it possible for the revolutionary élite to appeal to nationalism and turn US hostility into a convenient and effective justification for increasing its surveillance over society. Moreover, the legislation failed to isolate Cuba as it intended to do. The Helms–Burton law provoked outrage in Europe. Cuba had become an important destination for European tourists in the 1990s; European aid and investment soon followed. Having supported US policy on Cuba through the 1970s and 1980s, Europe increasingly distanced itself from the United States' hard line by the end of the 1990s. The result was that US policy, although acceptable and responsive to the needs of the diaspora leadership, was in fact based on an unrealistic assessment of the threat Cuba presented to the international order and exaggerated the United States' own capacity to shape perceptions outside the United States on how Cuba should be treated.

Organizing the diaspora

The diaspora has been dominated organizationally by representatives from the early wave of exiles – those who identified with the overthrown Batista dictatorship and whose values are implacably hostile to the revolution. When early attempts at insurrection failed, the diaspora leadership turned to politics, although political organization has never fully replaced direct action and activist groups continue to seek to overthrow Castro.

The Cuban American National Foundation (CANF), which was formed initially to counter the negative publicity that the *Mariel* boat-lifts attracted, became the principal vehicle through which the diaspora was represented and organized. It also served to police its political loyalty and established near-hegemonic control over Cuban-American politics during the 1980s. According to its founder, Jorge Más Canosa, its aim was to "take the fight out of Calle Ocho [in downtown Miami, the centre of the Cuban community] and Miami Stadium and into the center of power".[25] Although CANF openly supported the commando raids on the island and direct action, the leadership also sought respectability as a political organization. Its aim was to win support from Washington. Unlike in the early 1960s, this time the diaspora leadership was able to offer something concrete in return: money and votes. The fact that Cuban-Americans have enjoyed preferential access to citizenship, in contrast to other migrant groups from Latin America and the Caribbean, coupled with their geographical concentration in Miami, meant that Cubans could be mobilized into an electoral force.[26] The Cuban vote is numerically significant in Miami; additionally, the Cuban-American leadership is sufficiently well-to-do to be able to offer electoral funding to prospective allies. As a result, a two-pronged approach emerged, namely working with key anti-communist politicians across the United States to keep the Cuban issue on the national agenda, alongside organizing within Florida so that the Cuban vote mattered.

The Cuban-American leadership was assisted by the context of the 1980s. The incoming administration of Ronald Reagan was heavily committed to stamping US authority across Latin America and the Caribbean and countering what it perceived as the spread of communism and anti-Americanism across Central and South America. Reagan saw CANF as an ally in the anti-communist struggle and ended the timid attempts at rapprochement that had begun under President Carter, which the diaspora had largely opposed. In the process, CANF came to be presented as the legitimate pro-democracy voice of the Cuban opposition. This endorsement from Washington marked the highpoint of CANF's visibility in US politics. Nevertheless, how far the relationship with the Reagan administration translated into real influence over policy is unclear. For Wayne Smith, long-time Cuban "watcher" and head of the US Interests Section in Havana under the Carter presidency, CANF's capacity to shape policy was always less than it seemed because, rather than institutionalized access to policy-making, CANF depended on personal contacts: "the Cuban Americans have had and still have a lot of influence, but only when their interests can be coordinated with those of the various administrations".[27]

The strength of its organizational resources meant that CANF was able to survive the end of the Reagan period. By the time of the 1992 presidential elections, the Democrats also began to benefit from CANF support. As Smith recounts:

> Clinton made friends with the Cuban Americans, had dinner with Mas Canosa and adopted a hard line against Cuba. As a result, he got a lot of money for his electoral campaign. The same thing happened in 1996. . . . The President's attitude towards them [CANF] has nothing to do with US foreign policy or human rights or democracy: it's all a matter of electoral interests and money.[28]

Ultimately, the result of CANF's support for Clinton was his backing for Helms–Burton. Clinton had previously expressed opposition to the exclusion of Cuba from global trade on the grounds that "it would punish foreigners doing business with Cuba, and w[ould] therefore [be] bitterly resented by US allies and trade partners".[29] But he had been forced to endorse the Torricelli Act while courting Miami votes in 1992 and he signed Helms–Burton in 1996. Despite Clinton's generally moderate line on Latin America, then, the importance of the Cuban-American vote meant that Cuba had to be treated as a case apart.

CANF's was the community's only organized voice through the 1980s. In 1985 its influence extended to Cuba itself through the establishment of Radio Martí, offering what it claimed was "unbiased news and programming"[30] to Cubans living on the island, and a television station (TV Martí) was established in 1990 with US state support – although the Cuban government was able to prevent the signal reaching the island. CANF's apparent success meant that many Cuban-Americans supported it unquestioningly. Some were undoubtedly in agreement with its hard line. But CANF's dominance was also a result of a degree of covert repression of alternative voices in Miami. In 1992, for example, CANF launched a campaign against the *Miami Herald* after it questioned the logic of the Torricelli Act; death threats were received by editors and a public sticker campaign was launched in boycott of the paper.[31]

Despite its success in mobilizing Cuban-Americans and in gaining the ear of prominent US politicians, CANF has failed in its primary aim to unseat Castro. This failure eventually led to the emergence of other, more tentative voices. Less confident, perhaps, in what the solution to the Cuban problem should be, these new groups are nonetheless trying to grapple more realistically than CANF can with the complexity of being

Cuban in the contemporary world. Although CANF still insists that democracy can come about only after the collapse of the present regime – the "reign of terror" as it is described[32] – the newer voices in the community are considerably more varied and some are markedly softer in tone. Moreover, the politics of the diaspora no longer simply revolves around removing Castro. "High" politics is gradually giving way to humanitarian concerns, cultural presence and the issue of post-Castro Cuba. The result is the emergence of new groups that adopt a more conciliatory stance towards the Havana regime.[33]

One of CANF's underlying assumptions is that the duty of all patriotic Cuban-Americans is to deny their impulse to return: to visit the island is to recognize the legitimacy of the regime. Instead, they are obliged to remain in exile and to refuse to visit, even when permitted to do so. Moreover, CANF rejects the possibility of contact or collaboration with Cubans living on the island – unless they are openly anti-Castro, a position that is extremely difficult for them to adopt. As a result, CANF has boycotted even academic visits and educational exchanges between Cuba and the United States. In 1991, CANF founded a small group on the island called the Coalición Democrática Cubana (CDC), which has received funding from the US National Endowment for Democracy, the bi-partisan pro-democracy Washington-based organization. But the CDC is forbidden to enter into negotiations or contacts with the Castro regime and, because of this, its impact is minimal.

Despite a shift after 1995 and a rhetorical embrace of a more gradualist paradigm of change, then, CANF has remained resolute that dialogue of any sort with the Castro regime cannot be allowed. But, for newer generations of Cuban-Americans, the desire to witness the end of Castro's regime exists alongside a real hope of engagement with their homeland. Recent figures indicate that over half of Cuban-Americans now favour being able to visit the island. Moreover, this figure apparently includes 93 per cent of Cubans who arrived in Miami since 1994. In addition, second- and third-generation Cuban-Americans, who have never experienced life on the island or witnessed anything other than the stalemate of US–Cuban antagonism, no longer see the conflict in quite such stark terms of good and evil as do the first migrants. There is a degree of pragmatism in how they too understand the "Cuban question".

These changes have created some spaces for different voices and the new set of political figures that have emerged since the 1990s. Such movements have sought to offer a vision of constructive engagement with Castro's Cuba rather than an outright rejection of his rule.[34] For a range of reasons, however, they have been unable to challenge CANF for dominance. The Cuban Committee for Democracy (CCD) and Cambio Cubano, two of the main alternative organizations, offer a perspective on the homeland that goes beyond the anti-Castro agenda of the political mainstream, encouraging dialogue with and – to a limited degree – acceptance of the regime in Havana. For the CCD, the key issue relates to protecting the "sovereignty" of the Cuban nation, and with it the right of Cubans on the island to self-determination. One of its driving forces is the desire to see the Cuban-American community represented by more than its conservative élite, which it views as having contributed to the present impasse in US policy. Cambio Cubano is the only Miami-based group that has taken seriously the need to forge close relations with opposition groups on the island. Overall, the agendas of both CCD and Cambio Cubano still reflect a rejection of Havana, as much because they blame Havana for the hardship and privations suffered on the island as for reasons of ideological conviction. But both are more centred on preparing for post-Castro Cuba than is CANF.[35] For both organizations, the question is not so much how to remove Castro but what role the Miami Cuban community can play in effecting and embedding both democracy and the market after regime change. Moreover, their approach is echoed by cultural figures in the community who also call for an end to the ideological dogmatism.[36] Nevertheless, they remain minority movements. Interestingly, these movements are also headed by veterans of the pre-*Mariel* period,[37] giving all the official diaspora organizations the look of an old-style gerontocracy, which hardly helps the CCD or Cambio to present as viable alternatives to CANF.

Elian Gonzalez

The weaknesses in all the diaspora organizations were revealed in the Elian Gonzalez case in 2000. On the one hand, the case indicated that, sociological change within the diaspora and the emergence of moderate voices notwithstanding, intransigence remains its leitmotif. The CCD and Cambio Cubano were sidelined. But the hard-liners who spoke for the community were completely unrealistic in their assessments of what they could achieve and poured their energies into a fight that could not be won.

Six-year-old Elian Gonzalez was part of a group of Cubans who left the island for Miami on rafts. His mother lost her life in the attempt and Elian was rescued floating off the Florida coastline by US patrols. A custody dispute ensued, with the United States and the Cuban government on opposing sides, in which the diaspora community insisted that the boy remain in the United States and the Cuban government asserting that, as a minor, he should be returned to the custody of his father, who had remained on the island. The case soon moved beyond the courts into the media. Feelings ran high. For the diaspora, to return Elian to Cuba was to imply that they should have remained there themselves:

> To suggest that living in Cuba might be preferable to living in the United States was to impugn the sacrifice [the diaspora] made when they left Cuba to come to the United States. [It] represented more than a custody battle over a little boy. Only that understanding explains the vehemence of the feelings so graphically documented by the United States media.[38]

Equally, for Cubans on the island, to propose that Elian remain in Miami was to imply that life on the island was more terrible than they could possibly accept. It was taken as evidence that the diaspora leadership was prepared to put a political game above human feelings, the rights of the boy and natural law. Given the emotive nature of the dispute, the case quickly won world attention. International journalists converged on the community in Miami and residents gave vent to their anger. Few Cuban-Americans could be found, it seemed, who thought that Elian should return home – or those who did, opted not to speak to the press:

> "They would have to go over the bodies of all of us Cubans who are here," said Maria Gonzalez, 70, who is not related to [Elian]. "They would have to kill us all."[39]

The strength of feeling within the diaspora community and the fact that 2000 was an election year, with both candidates desperately wanting to win votes in Florida, meant that US politicians had to tread very carefully. The Democrat presidential candidate, Al Gore, for example, tried in vain to straddle the argument, embracing the humanitarian view that put the rights of Elian to parental care above all and, at the same time, appeasing the diaspora by arguing that it was all Castro's fault: it was the "oppressive regime" in Havana that had put Elian in the awful position of "having to choose between freedom and his own father".[40]

The dispute was destined to end in the federal courts. And, whereas the Cuban-American community could count on the sympathy of Florida institutions, federal institutions were somewhat more insulated from diaspora influence. As a result, it was resolved that Elian be returned to the custody of his father. Initially, elements within the diaspora sought to challenge the ruling by hiding the boy. President Clinton was forced to intervene and federal police were sent in without warning to take Elian away by force. He was then swiftly sent home, in compliance with the United States' legal obligations.

Castro turned the return of Elian from "seven months of suffering" into a triumph of Cuban humanism over the United States and the diaspora.[41] It marked something of a public relations coup for Castro. The fate of the motherless boy has struck a deep chord on the island, where there were few families for whom the drama of separation – some members on the island and some in Cuba – was not real. As a result, as Gibb observed, "the 'battle for Elian' has been a win–win situation [for Castro] from the start".[42]

If Castro felt he had won, the diaspora, which had pitched the case as a moral choice between life on the island and exile, was bound to feel that it had lost. Community leaders were quick to condemn the federal authorities, the Democrats and the federal police who carried out a night raid on community members. Cuban-American public opinion – in the shape of the *Miami Herald* – was largely behind them. According to Damian Fernandez of Florida University, the event may even have contributed to the Republican vote in Florida a year later:

> Cuban Americans felt badly and it backfired on Al Gore ... Democrats had worked hard on the Cuban American community and Elian undid all the inroads the Democrats had made in the last several years.[43]

In one sense, it is perhaps difficult to understand why the diaspora felt so strongly about Elian. Its position entailed ignoring the human needs of a very small child. But, from the perspective of the diaspora leadership, Elian's needs could never be best served in Cuba, even if that meant separating him from his father forever. For them, the decision by US authorities to send Elian back to his father was to return him to a regime where he was in danger – and to a father who had opted to stay in Cuba. Many had devoted a significant part of their lives to opposing the regime on the grounds of what they saw as its repressive, dictatorial nature. To now accept that life in Cuba was preferable from a "human" point of view was to violate all their principles. Did it suggest that the federal authorities thought that they too should return – or worse, should never have left? Moreover, it revealed how profoundly embedded anti-Castro sentiment remains within the diaspora, the growing pluralism of the community notwithstanding. Equally, however, the case revealed the limits of the diaspora's influence. Even though this incident took place in the period leading up to presidential elections, in which Cuban-American votes in Florida were significant, the leadership was unable to deploy its resources to any great effect. It was forced to accept that there were very real limits on the support the United States would offer – whatever the cost in terms of votes. As a result, the diaspora leadership painted the community as having been "betrayed" once again, this time by the US authorities.

Ending the conflict: A role for the diaspora?

So far, we have sketched a sociological and political picture of the diaspora community. But what does all this mean for our understanding of its role in peace-building and conflict resolution? To understand the role of the Cuban diaspora, we need first to remind ourselves of some crucial elements of the conflict. Unlike some other cases dealt with in this book, the Cuban diaspora is not really external to the conflict. Of course it is located geographically outside the island. But the Cuban conflict has never been played out principally – hardly at all, in fact – within the confines of the island. The diaspora does not see itself as a support to an internal opposition, faction or ethnic group. Instead, it has positioned itself as the chief political opposition to Castro; it is one of the central parties directly implicated in the conflict. Only the newer – and weaker – groups, such as Cambio Cubano have tried seriously to link up with internal groups. To some extent, this line has been made possible by the fact that civil society inside Cuba is weak, opposition groups still relatively small and the Cuban state able and willing to employ repression against dissidents.[44] But the diaspora's role has also been inflated because it has been able to find common cause with the US state. In sum, the Cuban diaspora cannot be understood simply as a "sub-group" within a more general conflict; without it, the dynamics and patterns of Cuban politics would be considerably different.

Conflict resolution means creating the conditions for a functioning peacetime society. In the case of Cuba, this requires that the diaspora accept as legitimate members of the same national community those Cubans who supported the revolution, who chose to stay or who felt that they had little option but to accept it. The diaspora must learn to acknowledge that staying on the island and working with the communist order can also be construed as an act of patriotism. CANF in particular shows little sign of being able to accept the legitimacy of ideological difference. To some degree, this can be attributed to the intolerance of the left and of mass politics that has characterized Latin American élites traditionally; democratization across Latin America has rarely been based on any profound process of social reconciliation.[45] In the Cuban case, however, this élite intransigence is also a result of the environment in which the conflict has been played out. The support the United States has offered the diaspora has shielded it – and CANF especially – from pressure to change and provided an ideological justification for avoiding reconciliation. The limits of US support were made starkly clear by the Elian Gonzalez case. Nevertheless, rather than forcing the diaspora to moderate its views, the community adopted a hardline policy.

After more than 45 years of dispute over the legitimacy of the Cuban revolution, the essential issues now at stake are two-fold. The first is, quite obviously, what happens after Castro: what kind of political and economic order will be erected on the island; how will Cuba reintegrate into the global order; how far will the new authorities seek external investors to modernize the economy and on what terms; and how will the legal claims on property nationalized by the revolution be resolved? For the first-wave émigrés especially, the last question is especially important because it is "their" property at stake. These policy questions are intrinsically linked to a second issue: how are the long years of the revolution, spanning so much of the Cold War, to be understood? Should they be seen as a dark period of communist dictatorship; or are there elements of the revolution that can be reinterpreted in a more positive light? Will the new authorities seek to acknowledge the importance of reconciliation between all Cubans; or will the post-Castro system attempt to wipe away all traces of Castroism? For CANF especially, it is centrally important that the system that replaces Castro break completely – in terms of rhetoric, institutions, economic integration, organization, culture – with the revolutionary past. But for Cubans on the island, even those who recognize that change must come after Castro's demise, to dismiss all aspects of the past 40 years as disastrous and regrettable is very difficult. And to attempt to force through a legal settlement of the claims for land and property by Cuban-Americans might well antagonize Cubans generally disposed to accept reform. Any peaceful and negotiated end to the conflict thus requires some considerable change on the part of the diaspora.

It is more imperative than ever, especially in view of Castro's advancing age and increasingly evident fragility, that Cubans find some way of making peace with each other. If not, the island will continue to be divided into those who stayed and those who left and into those who will benefit from the new system and those who will be positioned very badly within it. The conflict that now divides the two communities on the island and in Miami will simply become one played out on the island instead. CANF is at present unable to provide the kind of leadership that endorses reconciliation, despite the fact that the political interests of the diaspora community would be best served by a less intransigent approach. Yet alternative organizations – which take a more pragmatic line – do not count with sufficient legitimacy within the community at large. Despite this, all is not completely hopeless. The increasing diversity within the community and its growing heterogeneity point to the possibility that society-based forms of reconciliation will emerge over the longer term. This would undoubtedly be assisted if policy-makers in the United States were able to recognize the greater levels of complexity and divergence that now characterize the Cuban-American community and, at the same time, seek a negotiated end to its own conflict with Havana. Leadership must come from the US state – but this is unlikely to happen in Castro's lifetime.

Conclusion

The Cuban diaspora is, as we have outlined in this chapter, organization-ally strong and benefits from highly effective political and sociological networks. It is concentrated geographically and tightly knit and has pro-vided a "soft landing" for exiles. The US state has provided privileged resources for the diaspora community, enabling it to survive and thrive. Partly as a result, the degree of integration that Cubans enjoy in the United States is unimaginable for many other diaspora communities. Nevertheless, it is hard to escape the view that the community's long-term interests have been badly served by community organizations and its leadership in particular, which have contributed to freezing a conflict that might otherwise have been resolved. Moreover, the political influ-ence of the Cuban-American community in Miami has meant that its hard line has reinforced the hard line adopted in Washington. It is impos-sible, in fact, meaningfully to separate the individual strands of diaspora demands and US policy preferences, for the two are impossibly entangled.

The limits of support for "constructive engagement" with Havana within the diaspora and the fragility of the spirit of compromise should be noted. The Elian case, more perhaps than anything else, demon-strated graphically the limits of community tolerance for the Castro re-gime. Whether one likes it or not, any attempt at transition or reconcilia-tion must take these feelings into account, alongside the rights of Cubans on the island. All of this means that any transition is impossible while Castro remains alive, for the diaspora community simply cannot concep-tualize of change without this rupture with the past. The question is whether, once Castro has gone, the community can play a constructive role in engaging with the island population, recognizing that compromise, in terms of style and language as much as of content, will be important if there is to be a peaceful end to the conflict and a productive transition to democracy.

Notes

1. See, for example, J. I. Dominguez, "US–Cuban Relations: From the Cold War to the Colder War", *Journal of Interamerican Studies and World Affairs*, 1997, 39(3): 49–75; J. I. Dominguez, "US–Latin American Relations during the Cold War and Its After-

math", in V. Bulmer-Thomas and J. Dunkerley, eds, *The United States and Latin America: The New Agenda*, London and Cambridge, MA: Institute of Latin American Studies & David Rockefeller Center for Latin American Studies, 1999, pp. 33–50; and also G. Lievesley, *The Cuban Revolution: Past, Present and Future Perspectives*, London: Palgrave Macmillan, 2003.

2. See Bercovitch's chapter in this volume.
3. Robin Cohen, *Global Diasporas: An Introduction*, Seattle: University of Washington Press, 1997.
4. Lievesley, *The Cuban Revolution*, p. 34.
5. S. L. Croucher, *Imagining Miami: Ethnic Politics in a Postmodern World*, Charlottesville and London: University Press of Virginia, 1997.
6. Ibid., p. 32.
7. P. J. Haney and W. Vanderbush, "The Role of Ethnic Interest Groups in US Foreign Policy: The Case of the Cuban American National Foundation", *International Studies Quarterly*, 1999, 43: 341–361.
8. M. S. Kenzer, "Review: M. C. Garcia, *Havana USA: Cuban Exiles and Cuban Americans in South Florida 1959–1994* (Berkeley: University of California Press, 1997)", *Journal of Historical Geography*, 2000, 26(1): 152.
9. Maxine Molyneux, "The Politics of the Cuban Diaspora in the United States", in Bulmer-Thomas and Dunkerley, eds, *The United States and Latin America*, pp. 287–310.
10. Croucher, *Imagining Miami*, pp. 42–47.
11. K. M. Greenhill, "Engineered Migration and the Use of Refugees as Political Weapons: A Case Study of the 1994 Cuban Balseros Crisis", *International Migration*, 2002, 40(4): 39–47.
12. Ibid., p. 39.
13. Molyneux, "The Politics of the Cuban Diaspora in the United States", p. 291.
14. A. G. Abreau, "Cubans without Borders: The Possible Dream", *Florida Law Review*, 2004, 55(1): 206–207.
15. Dominguez, "US–Cuban Relations"; and Dominguez, "US–Latin American Relations".
16. H. Ackerman, "Strategic Calculation and Democratic Society: The Cuban Democratic Resistance in the 1960s and 1990s", paper prepared for the XXI International Congress of the Latin American Studies Association, Chicago, 24–26 September 1998.
17. Dominguez, "US–Cuban Relations".
18. L. Robinson, "Towards a Realistic Cuba Policy", *Survival*, 2000, 42: 117.
19. L. A. Perez Jr, "Fear and Loathing of Fidel Castro: Sources of US Policy towards Cuba", *Journal of Latin American Studies*, 2002, 34: 228–229.
20. V. Perez-Lopez, "The Cuban External Sector in the 1990s", in Bulmer-Thomas and Dunkerley, eds, *The United States and Latin America*, pp. 267–286.
21. T. Carothers, *In the Name of Democracy: US Policy towards Latin America in the Reagan Years*, Berkeley: University of California Press, 1991.
22. Dominguez, "US–Cuban Relations", p. 63.
23. W. M. Leogrande, "Enemies Evermore: US Policy towards Cuba after Helms-Burton", *Journal of Latin American Studies*, 1997, 29: 212.
24. J. T. Cordovi, "Cuba's Economic Transformation and Conflict with the United States", in Bulmer-Thomas and Dunkerley, eds, *The United States and Latin America*, pp. 247–266; Dominguez, "US–Cuban Relations", p. 57.
25. Haney and Vanderbush, "The Role of Ethnic Interest Groups", p. 347.
26. J. I. Dominguez, "Cooperating with the Enemy: US Immigration Policy towards Cuba", in Chris Mitchell, ed., *Western Hemispheric Immigration and US Policy*, University Park, PA: Penn State University, 1992.

27. Wayne Smith, interview in H. Calvo and K. Declerq, eds, *The Cuban Exile Movement*, New York: Ocean Press, 2000, p. 159.
28. Ibid.
29. Leogrande, "Enemies Evermore", pp. 211–212.
30. See ⟨http://www.canf.org/2004/principal-ingles.htm⟩.
31. Molyneux, "The Politics of the Cuban Diaspora in the United States".
32. See ⟨http://www.canf.org/2004/principal-ingles.htm⟩.
33. I. L. Horowitz, "The Cuba Lobby Then and Now", *Orbis*, 1998, 42(4): 553–563.
34. F. Valdes, "Diaspora and Deadlock, Miami and Havana: Coming to Terms with Dreams and Dogmas", *Florida Law Review*, 2004, 55(1): 284–317.
35. D. Briquets and J. Perez-Lopez, *The Role of the Cuban-American Community in the Cuban Transition*, Cuba Transition Project, Institute for Cuban and Cuban-American Studies, University of Miami, 2003.
36. Abreau, "Cubans without Borders".
37. Horowitz, "The Cuba Lobby Then and Now"; Molyneux, "The Politics of the Cuban Diaspora in the United States".
38. Abreau, "Cubans without Borders", pp. 207–208.
39. "Miami Relatives Ask for 3 Independent Psychologists to Evaluate Elian: Child's Cuban Family Could Arrive Tuesday", CNN.com, 3 April 2000, ⟨http://www.cnn.com/2000/US/04/03/cuba.boy.05⟩.
40. See "The Elian Case, A Year Later", CBS News, 22 November 2000, ⟨http://www.cbsnews.com/stories/2000/11/22/national/main251527.shtml⟩.
41. *Granma Internationa*, 27 June 2000.
42. See Tom Gibb, "Analysis: Castro's Victory?", BBC News, 28 June 2000, ⟨http://news.bbc.co.uk/1/hi/world/americas/711828.stm⟩.
43. CBS News, 22 September 2001.
44. I. Saney, *Cuba: A Revolution in Motion*, London: Fernwood Publishing, 2004.
45. Jean Grugel, *Democratization: A Critical Introduction*, London: Palgrave Macmillan, 2002.

9

The Sri Lankan Tamil diaspora: Sustaining conflict and pushing for peace

C. Christine Fair

South Asia has been home to numerous ethno-nationalist insurgencies since the region was de-colonized with the departure of the British in 1947. Many of these insurgent movements benefited tremendously from the activities of co-ethnics and co-religionists organized in transnational diasporas throughout the world. Among these conflicts, the civil war in Sri Lanka has been perhaps the most enduring and seemingly intractable – with the notable exception of the Kashmir conflict. Although no exact date is ascribed to the start of the conflict, most writers note that it began to militarize in the 1970s. During this period, numerous Tamil militant groups formed. By the early 1980s, one group had emerged as pre-eminent: the Jaffna-based Liberation Tigers of Tamil Eelam (LTTE) under the leadership of Velupillai Prabhakaran. In 1983, the LTTE conducted its first military operation – an ambush on a police patrol in Jaffna.[1] Since 1983, the conflict has claimed over 65,000 lives and displaced over 1 million people.[2]

The Sri Lankan government claims that the conflict has internally displaced one-third of the pre-war Tamil population, which numbered around 600,000–700,000. Most of these people live in refugee camps and receive assistance from the government. Another one-third of this pre-war population left Sri Lanka altogether. By the end of 1998, at least 110,000 Sri Lankan Tamils were living in the southern Indian state of Tamil Nadu. Between 1983 and 1998, nearly half a million Sri Lankan Tamils sought asylum in Europe or North America.[3]

Diasporas in conflict: Peace-makers or peace-wreckers?, Smith and Stares (eds), United Nations University Press, 2007, ISBN 978-92-808-1140-7

Despite several failed ceasefire efforts, Norway brokered a ceasefire agreement that was signed between the rebels and the government in February 2002. This ceasefire agreement also established the Sri Lanka Monitoring Mission (SLMM), which was tasked with monitoring the ceasefire and noting violations.[4] Between September 2002 and March 2003, the LTTE and the Sri Lankan government convened six rounds of peace talks to widespread international support. The talks fostered a sense of optimism about a possible end to the civil war. However, the LTTE soon dampened these hopes when it left the negotiations in April 2003 and then demanded, in October 2003, an interim administration arrangement for the north-east under which the LTTE would control the judiciary and police, as well as oversee land and revenue concerns.[5]

In response, President Chandrika Kumaratunga declared a state of emergency and seized control of the ministries of defence, finance, and state media, crippling Wickremesinghe's administration. After suspending the parliament and declaring elections in April 2004, a coalition government was cobbled together, which adopted a confrontational posture towards the peace talks and rejected LTTE demands for an interim administration. After the European Union banned the LTTE in May 2006, the LTTE demanded that all SLMM monitors from European Union countries depart by 1 September 2006. With a much diminished SLMM and ever-increasing ceasefire violations by both rebels and government forces, most observers now fear that once again Sri Lanka is sliding into all out – even if undeclared – war.[6]

There were several reasons for the breakdown of the agreement. First was the dismissal by President Kumaratunga in February 2004 of the Wickremesinghe government, which came to power in December 2001 on a peace platform. At elections in April 2004, Kumaratunga's party won easily, at least in part because of her hawkish stance towards the LTTE. Kumaratunga, herself a rare survivor of an LTTE suicide attack, was opposed to the accord and contended that the LTTE benefited tremendously from the peace process.[7]

Second, the LTTE suffered a serious rupture in leadership. In March 2004, the Eastern Commander "Colonel Karuna" broke away from Prabhakaran over long-simmering frustration with the LTTE's inequitable treatment of Sri Lanka's eastern Tamils. For instance, these eastern Tamils are denied proportionate representation in LTTE leadership commensurate with their role in the organization and the size of their population.[8]

Third, the January 2005 tsunami ravaged Sri Lanka. Rather than working together to cope with the disaster, the LTTE and the government squabbled over who would distribute aid and where and with what division of funds. The LTTE claims that the Tamil areas affected by the tsunami have received fewer resources than the areas dominated by ethnic Singhalese, a claim the government denies. The LTTE made efforts to exclude a government presence in Tamil areas and insisted that its allied organization, the (now banned) Tamil Relief Organization, take primary responsibility for aid in Tamil areas. Although post-tsunami aid disputes have pushed the two sides even further apart, the LTTE demonstrated its abilities to provide for Sri Lanka's Tamils.[9] The LTTE's resource channels were blocked when the Tamil diaspora reduced financial support in the aftermath of 9/11. In many respects this drove the LTTE leadership toward a political process. As a result of the tsunami, however, critical Tamil diaspora resources resumed flowing to the LTTE to help mitigate the humanitarian disaster.

The Sri Lankan Tamil diaspora has been a crucial component of the lethality and tenacity of this conflict.[10] The huge expansion and increasing affordability of information technologies that began in the 1990s greatly enhanced the ability of the insurgents to exploit the resources available in the diaspora. However, it should be noted that, *inter alia*, fax, telephone and affordable air travel were important resources that pre-dated the important changes that began to take place in the mid and late 1990s.

Preview of the argument

When one examines the political opportunity-set available to the Tamil insurgents, there is little to suggest that the insurgency should have been as enduring as it has been. First, the Tamils were virtually excluded from political processes from the inception of the independent Sri Lankan state. Second, the rival Sinhalese ethnic group comprised nearly three-quarters of the population and was firmly in grasp of all state power; Sinhalese élites were and remain unified in their support for a united state. Third, for most of the conflict, there has been no influential state support for the Tamils in Sri Lanka.[11] Fourth, the Sri Lankan state perpetrated frequent and large-scale acts of repression to put down the insurgency. This substantially raised the cost of Tamil participation in the insurgency. Finally, despite these widespread abuses of power, Colombo faced no outside pressure to moderate its excesses. Thus the important empirical question arises: how have the Tamil militants been able to sustain the insurgency for this long with such efficacy and lethality in such unfavourable circumstances?

To answer this query, I appropriate the argument advanced by Wayland and expand upon it.[12] Wayland notes that scholarship on contentious politics generally concurs that, to be successful, social movements – and their militarized forms – require changes in the broader political context *in addition to* their own organization and internal resources. These changes are referred to as the "political opportunity structure" and are needed both to activate latent grievance and to provide incentives for collective action – principally by conditioning participants' expectations for success or failure. These are "factors external to a movement that influenced the movement's emergence and chance of success".[13] These political opportunity structures arguably help to explain why a mobilization's success may vary over time and why similar mobilizations achieve different results.

In her analysis of the Tamil insurgency, Wayland widens the notion of the political opportunity-set to include transnational factors and argues that this expanded notion of political opportunity structures explains the success of the LTTE in Sri Lanka despite numerous structural impediments. She posits that diaspora actors can operate within several opportunity structures simultaneously. This may explain why some insurgencies, which face unfavourable circumstances in the home country, may exploit these multiple transnational political opportunity structures to protract an insurgency or even to escalate a latent conflict.

I agree with Wayland that the movement of migrants from a situation of persecution and absence of political rights to open societies with democratic governance, freedom of expression and anti-discrimination laws creates opportunities for such migrants to publish, organize, lobby and raise funds to an extent not previously possible in the homeland. Furthermore, in diaspora, Sri Lankan Tamils have been able more easily to express their cultural, linguistic and religious identity in ways that were not permitted in the homeland. Thus the process of migration has actually enabled the production of a highly stylized and politicized Tamil identity from abroad.

However, I would add here that the LTTE could exploit this transnational political opportunity structure only as long as the LTTE and important segments of the diaspora shared a political vision and aspirations. For much of the conflict this was the case, at least in part because the diasporan Sri Lankan Tamils were themselves produced by the conflict and thus tended to leave Sri Lanka as politicized persons. The institutions they built were in many cases specifically designed to contend with their situation in the homeland and the problems of being refugees and exiles. This distinguishes the Tamil diaspora from other South Asian diasporas. I argue here that, in the world after 11 September 2001, the objectives of the Tamil diaspora and the LTTE diverged. The Tamil diaspora, whose resources were invaluable to the LTTE, was able to leverage its power over the LTTE to alter the LTTE's posture in Sri Lanka.

Thus I accept Wayland's contention that the diaspora has created transnational political opportunity structures that have enabled the Tamil rebels to sustain their civil war tenaciously and with great lethality. In this chapter I seek to expand upon her thesis in the context of the conflict cycle described by Jacob Bercovitch in this volume by identifying where in this cycle the diaspora's role has been most apparent and in what ways. I argue that the diaspora's role has been most apparent in escalating and sustaining the conflict. However, I will mobilize the available evidence to suggest that, as a result of changes in the global environment following the events of 9/11, the political opportunity structure for the insurgents changed in part because the diaspora perceived very different options and preferred trajectories in the post-9/11 world. This was a necessary, if insufficient, factor that brought about the 2002 ceasefire.

The evidence employed in this chapter involves my fieldwork in 2002 when I travelled throughout Sri Lanka, including Jaffna. During this trip, I met a wide array of Sri Lankan political, military and intelligence officials as well as US analysts, think-tanks and non-governmental organizations (NGOs). Where appropriate, I rely upon various discussions with Indian analysts of the conflict as well.[14] This work has also been informed by my previous work for the United States Army on urban insurgent movements during which I spoke with numerous US military experts about the LTTE and the government's political, military and diplomatic efforts to counter the LTTE.[15] The chapter draws on a wide array of secondary sources spanning the diverse disciplines of, *inter alia*, history, political science, policy studies and anthropology.

The remainder of this chapter will be organized as follows. The next section will provide the reader with a basic background to the militancy. After unpacking the notion of a Tamil diaspora, its interests and its opportunities, I shall examine diaspora support at various points in the conflict continuum. I shall conclude the chapter with some thoughts on the implications of this analysis.

The Tamil militancy

The Tamil insurgency is overwhelmingly an ethno-nationalist conflict rooted in Sri Lanka's history of colonization and de-colonization. This substantially distinguishes the Tamil uprising from other internal security challenges in South Asia, where militancy has tended to be intertwined with communal (e.g. religious) and sectarian differences. Dating the origin of conflict is difficult. Both scholars of Sri Lankan history and Sri Lankans themselves tend to disagree on the nascence of the ethnic conflict. The current phase of the conflict, which dates back to the 1970s, is largely the result of state failure to manage both the island's ethnic differences and colonial legacies in ways that are both free of violence and consonant with democracy.[16]

The Sinhalese ethnic community has been the overwhelming majority group in Sri Lanka. Present estimates place them at 74 per cent of the population. The Sinhalese tend to reside in the central and southern parts of the island. They are overwhelmingly Theraveda Buddhists and speak the Sinhala language. The Tamils, who are a minority, comprise about 12 per cent at present and they tend to inhabit the north (Jaffna area) and the north-east. They are mostly Hindus and speak the Tamil language. Another group of "up-country" Tamils comprise about 7 per cent of the population. Their origins are in the low-caste tea estate workers who were brought to the island from India by the British. The Sri Lankan Tamils do not tend to share a sense of co-ethnicity with these Tamils. The remaining 7 per cent of Sri Lanka's population is Muslim.[17]

The Portuguese first colonized the island in 1505; the Dutch followed in 1658. Prior to becoming independent in 1948, the island spent some 150 years under British governance, which disproportionately provided educational and employment opportunities to the minority Tamils. This preference towards the Tamils laid the foundation for the post-independent antagonisms between the Tamils and the majority Sinhalese communities. Upon independence, Sri Lanka adopted a unitary constitutional structure. Many Tamil parties worried that this constitutional arrangement would not protect minority communities against dominance by the majoritarian Sinhalese. Indeed, successive governments sought to reverse the privileges that were bestowed upon the Tamil community under the British.[18]

In the decades following independence, Colombo continued to pursue policies that were aimed at bolstering the relative position and strength of the Sinhalese majority. One such initiative was the "Sinhala Only" law enacted in 1956. This law made the Sinhala language the official language of Sri Lanka, thereby replacing English. Sinhala is very different from the Tamil language, so this law in effect precluded Tamils from economic opportunities in the state bureaucracy. Colombo also added a provision in the 1972 constitution that recognized Buddhism as the only state religion. Sri Lanka's Tamils were greatly alarmed by these various measures to remove minority safeguards and to reverse Tamil privileges. As Gunaratna notes, "the majoritarian rule and exclusivist ethnic policies of the successive Sinhala majority governments in the aftermath of independence crystallized the development of a separatist ideology among Tamil leaders".[19]

Interest in greater Tamil autonomy and even independence began to develop in the 1950s and 1960s. For instance, after 1956, Tamil political leaders began demanding autonomy for the northern and eastern regions of the country – albeit within a federal framework.[20] As late as the 1970s there were still efforts to resolve the issue politically.[21] The militant aspects began to materialize during the late 1970s and early 1980s, when a coherent militarized Tamil insurgency took form.[22] These groups included the Tamil Eelam Liberation Organization (TELO), the People's Liberation Organization for Tamil Eelam (PLOTE), the Eelam People's Revolutionary Liberation Front (EPRLF) and the Liberation Tigers of Tamil Eelam (LTTE). (The LTTE's commander, Velupillai Prabhakaran, founded the Tamil New Tigers in the mid-1970s, which later became the LTTE.[23]) The LTTE secured dominance among these groups through massive violence and coercion. Although some groups still exist at various levels, the LTTE has established itself as the principal and most lethal voice of militant Tamil aspirations.[24] As I shall explain, the LTTE has relied heavily upon the diverse and large Sri Lankan Tamil diaspora for support. For this reason, this chapter will focus upon the LTTE and these diasporic connections.

The Sri Lankan Tamil diaspora

The Sri Lankan Tamil diaspora comprises between 600,000 and 800,000 persons worldwide, nearly half of whom reside in Canada and the United Kingdom. Other Western countries with a significant diaspora population include Germany, Switzerland, France and Australia.[25] The Sri Lankan Tamil diaspora has been the backbone of the LTTE's global operations and has been a financial lifeline for the Tamil insurgency. This section details what is known about the Sri Lankan Tamil diaspora empirically and the organizations that it has established.

Scholars tend to describe the Sri Lankan Tamil diaspora as a monolithic entity that largely exists owing to the ethno-nationalist conflicts and ensuing persecution in the homeland.[26] Although this is true to a great extent, there are important caveats. Historically, there have been several waves of migration out of Sri Lanka, each of which had its own reasons for leaving and each of which has had different inclinations towards the LTTE. Consequently, as Gunaratna has argued, the LTTE has sought to adopt specific strategies to deal with each of these waves in order to access their resources. Note that because migration groups were motivated by particular types of events – some of which were contemporaneous – there is temporal overlap in some of the groups.

During the British occupation, Sri Lankan Tamils out-migrated for economic opportunities. Because many of them knew English, they travelled to Burma and the Federated Malay States where they worked for the governments there. This wave was not politicized towards Tamil secessionism. A second wave of migration began in 1956 as a consequence of the independent government's preferential treatment of the Sinhalese. Only a few thousand English-educated Tamils left in this phase. They generally settled in the United Kingdom, Australia, Canada and the United States.[27]

A third wave of migration was precipitated by ethnic violence (there were riots in the 1950s, 1961, 1977, 1979, 1981 and 1983). The riots in 1983, for instance, left around 300,000 Tamil homeless. A fourth wave of migration was precipitated when state authorities began targeting Tamil nationalist groups in the mid-1970s. This wave also included some 20,000 members of rival groups to the LTTE who sought protection. The fifth wave resulted from the civil war fought by the LTTE and the Sri Lankan government. By 2002 (the year of the ceasefire) it was estimated that one-third of the Sri Lankan Tamil community of 3 million was living outside of Sri Lanka.[28]

Gunaratna contends that migrants from the first two waves differed from later groups in that they spoke English and tended to look askance at the post-1983 refugees. The third and successive waves were largely composed of refugees and exiles who were forced to leave their homes (rather than choosing to leave voluntarily to pursue new opportunities), the majority leaving within the past 15–20 years. Thus, they are members of an archetypal "victim diaspora" and this is the group that is usually referred to when discussing diaspora support for the LTTE.[29]

As is often the case with ethno-national expatriate communities, individuals can elect to participate in multiple diasporas. Thus Sri Lankan Tamils may see themselves as part of a more general Tamil diaspora that includes Tamils whose putative homeland is Tamil Nadu in the south of India as well as Tamils from Sri Lanka. This greater transnational Tamil identity is facilitated by numerous cultural organizations in the countries of settlement that host Tamil language, cultural and religious events. However, Sri Lankan Tamils also see themselves as belonging to a sub-set of Tamils whose histories are tied to Sri Lanka and the ongoing war there. For this reason, Sri Lankan Tamils have established organizations in their countries of settlement that cater to this specific diasporan identity. Some of these organizations include diasporan affiliates of the Sri Lanka-based Tamil Relief Organization; e.g. Tamils Rehabilitation Organisation USA; Ilankai Tamil Sangam (Association of Tamils from Eelam and Sri Lanka in the United States). Other organizations are based in cyberspace, for example Tamilnation.org, which seeks to forge a transnational Tamil nationalist identity and which emphasizes the troubles confronting Sri Lanka's Tamils. As the next section details, many Tamil diasporan organizations have explicitly been set up to facilitate LTTE activities.

It is important to note for this analysis that these later migrants were highly politicized *before* leaving Sri Lanka. The third wave formed the core of the organizations that raised funds to care for the ever-expanding refugee population and to provide financial support to the armed separatist movement. Once the LTTE captured control over the rival outfits, this support from the diaspora predominantly went to the LTTE.[30] Many of the organizations built by this diaspora were initially intended to support homeland causes.

Because the Sri Lankan Tamil diaspora is a victim diaspora, there have been consequences for the kind of support the insurgency has enjoyed. This stands in contrast to other important South Asia diasporas that have been involved in homeland conflicts. For instance, the Sikh diaspora was very active in supporting the Sikh insurgency in India's northern state of Punjab throughout the 1980s. However, the diaspora was produced by different processes from those of the Sri Lankan Tamils. The Sikh diaspora was much older than the Sri Lankan Tamil diaspora and was formed initially by British imperial practice (indentured labour, military service, educational opportunities and service in various security forces). It was not a diaspora produced by conflict, although many Sikhs did seek asylum when the government began targeting Sikhs in its counter-insurgency efforts. This diaspora politicized unevenly throughout this conflict. Diaspora support for the conflict peaked following the Indian army invasion of the most important Sikh temple in 1984. However, because only a thin base of diaspora institutions was mobilized to support the insurgents, this momentum was quickly lost.[31] Thus the task of the Sikh militancy was to appropriate and reorient extant Sikh diaspora institutions in addition to specific organizations founded to support conflict. The Tamil insurgents had a much easier task because many of the institutions they built were built because of the conflict.

The Sri Lankan Tamil diaspora in the conflict cycle

In Chapter 4 in this volume, Bercovitch identifies several ways in which diasporas contribute to a conflict. They may participate in conflict prevention, conflict escalation, conflict termination and post-conflict reconstruction. Bercovitch also identifies specific kinds of resources – political, military, economic and socio-cultural – through which diasporas influence the conflict cycle at each of these points. The impacts of these contributions could in principle be either negative or positive. Negative contributions would foster the emergence or sustenance of the conflict, while positive contributions would serve to mitigate the conflict and/or bring about de-escalation or even a resolution. In the case of the ongoing Sri Lankan Tamil conflict, it is fair to say that, following the ceasefire of 2002, there was a brief de-escalation phase even though, as of September 2006, the agreement is nearly obsolete, with a return to active, if undeclared, conflict.

With respect to this conflict, I could find no evidence that earlier Tamil migrants (the first and second waves) sought either to prevent the conflict or, conversely, to actualize a latent conflict. This does not mean that such activities did not occur; rather, that the historical record appears silent on this issue. Thus the conflict prevention phase is not discussed here. Similarly, this chapter does not address the post-conflict role, because the conflict has not formally terminated, although it has de-escalated.[32] A final resolution remains out of sight for the policy-relevant future.

Note that, whereas the Sri Lankan Tamil diaspora has attracted much attention, there have been no studies to date of the large Sri Lankan Sinhalese diaspora, with concentrations in Italy, Canada and the United Kingdom. In previous work, I found that the Sri Lankan government has made very little effort to reach out to this potential ally in its war against the rebels. The Sinhalese diaspora has not engaged in the kinds of activities for which the Sri Lankan Tamil diaspora has become famous. Thus the important question lingers beyond the scope of this analysis as to why Colombo did not seek to access the Sinhalese diaspora as a potential partner. Because there is no evidence to suggest that the Sinhalese diaspora was involved, its role and contributions to the conflict cycle cannot be assessed.[33]

Conflict escalation

Economic contributions

The Sri Lankan Tamil diaspora is widely recognized as the "economic backbone of the militant campaign" through both coerced and voluntary contributions.[34] Since the early 1980s, the LTTE has established a global network of offices and cells that spans at least 40 countries and is unrivalled by any other insurgent organization worldwide.[35] Funds come from the countries where there are large Tamil diasporan communities: Switzerland, Canada, Australia, the United Kingdom, the United States and the Scandinavian countries.[36] The LTTE is assessed to have an annual income between US$82 million and US$100 million, of which the diaspora has contributed at least US$60 million annually.[37] According to most estimates, this US$60 million covers about 90 per cent of the LTTE's international military procurement budget and the remainder is used to maintain LTTE offices and other worldwide activities.[38]

Sometimes these monies are given willingly in the belief that the efforts of the LTTE are the only way to achieve autonomy and security for the Sri Lankan Tamil diaspora. In other cases, "donations" are collected like a tax, by force, by the threat of force or through the exploitation of individuals who may be in a country illegally and are seeking protection or assistance from the LTTE. In countries where the LTTE is proscribed, it operates through organizations such as the United Tamil Organization, the World Tamil Movement and the Tamils Rehabilitation Organisation USA.[39]

The amounts that flow into the coffers of the LTTE from the diaspora fluctuate with military developments on the ground in Sri Lanka. After military setbacks and defeats, donations typically decline. Conversely, when the LTTE was militarily successful, voluntary donations increased. As I discuss later, after the events of 2001, the diaspora pulled back funding in an effort to motivate the LTTE to pursue peace with Colombo. The LTTE also generates income by acting as a "proxy lender": the LTTE puts up the initial investment in Tamil-run small businesses and the profits are split between the LTTE and the ostensible owner. If evidence from the mid to late 1990s is still valid, these revenue streams are impressive: in Switzerland they are thought to raise some US$650,000 per month; in Canada they are thought to bring in C$1,000,000; in the United Kingdom they raise an estimated US$385,000 monthly. The LTTE has other revenue sources as well, such as the gem trade, human trafficking and possibly narcotics.[40] Whether or not the LTTE funds itself through narcotics trafficking has been hotly debated in recent years. In March 2001, both the United States Department of State and the Narcotics Bureau of the Sri Lankan government denied that they had any evidence that the LTTE was funding its activities through narcotics.[41] The Intelligence Chief of the US Drug Enforcement Administration (DEA), Steven W. Casteel, contradicted this earlier assertion in May 2003. Casteel testified to the US Senate that, according to DEA intelligence, the LTTE does in fact finance its insurgent activities through drug-trafficking. He further elaborated that "[i]nformation obtained since the mid-1980s indicates that some Tamil Tiger communities in Europe are also involved in narcotics smuggling, having historically served as drug couriers moving narcotics into Europe".[42]

In addition to supporting the LTTE, the Tamil diasporans also remit funds that directly support their families and localities of origin. These funds may have been given with the aim of ensuring the well-being of family members left behind in the war-torn Tamil areas, but they have also prolonged the conflict. These remittances have enabled Sri Lankan

Tamils to remain in the conflict-affected Tamil-dominated areas. Without such financial support, these Tamils would have fled the country and joined the diaspora. Alternatively, they would have been compelled to seek employment in other parts of Sri Lanka, contributing to the thinning of Tamils from their historical lands. Gunaratna found that, because these remittances subsidized the Tamils who remained, they indirectly contributed to the ability of the LTTE to recruit cadres by keeping these people in the region. Gunaratna's fieldwork also found that individuals who remitted funds to their immediate and extended families did so with the explicit exhortation to support the LTTE and the greater cause of Tamil Eelam. These diasporans (no doubt because of their financial largess) have had considerable influence upon the affairs of their kin in Sri Lanka and did much to incline them positively towards the LTTE.[43]

The LTTE exploits non-profit organizations that allegedly provide social, medical and rehabilitation assistance in Sri Lanka. The LTTE can deftly siphon funds from such organizations – or even establish front organizations to raise funds – because of the difficulty in establishing proof that such improprieties are occurring.[44] In addition to illicit means of fund-raising, the LTTE leverages numerous legitimate economic activities among its extensive and sophisticated diaspora. For example, the LTTE invests in stocks, money markets and real estate. The LTTE also owns numerous restaurants and shops throughout the world and has invested in farms, finance companies and other ventures that have high profit margins.[45] Such financial manoeuvring is advantageous because it is difficult to track and prosecute.[46]

Political contributions

The LTTE uses its global infrastructure to develop and maintain political and diplomatic support within host countries. To do so, it has aptly exploited the ethos of the liberal democracies in which its allied diasporans reside. Before being proscribed as a terrorist organization in many countries, the LTTE was itself able to set up offices that openly espoused the LTTE cause. The LTTE assigned two important men (Anton Balasingham and Sivagnanam Gopalarathinam) to head the LTTE's propaganda and publicity efforts, which utilize numerous sympathetic pressure groups, media teams, charities and NGOs. Even though their activities take place in over 54 countries, they tend to focus their efforts on the Western states that have large numbers of Tamils (e.g. the United Kingdom, Canada, Australia, France and Switzerland).[47]

LTTE lobbying efforts were extremely successful in cultivating state support for its movements in state capitals throughout the world during the 1980s and 1990s. Up until about 2001, the LTTE was able to develop political sympathy for its cause by mobilizing media and "grassroots" and other political organizations over the issue of Tamil rights and the abuse of those rights by the Sri Lankan government. The LTTE effectively co-ordinates these efforts through a number of "umbrella organizations" established in key countries. These include groups such as the Australasian Federation of Tamil Associations, the Swiss Federation of Tamil Associations, the French Federation of Tamil Associations, the Federation of Associations of Canadian Tamils, the Ilankai Tamil Sangam (based in the United States), the Tamil Coordinating Committee in Norway, and the International Federation of Tamils (in the UK).[48]

Political support and lobbying comprise a major activity of Sri Lankan Tamil diasporic organizations and individuals. As their numbers increase and as they move from being refugees to citizen claimants or permanent residents, Sri Lankan Tamils and their descendants have become important political constituents. For instance, in Toronto in 2003, the Canadian Minister of Foreign Affairs had 6,000 eligible Tamil voters in his constituency. Cheran believes that this motivated – at least in part – his inclusion of the Sri Lankan civil war in Canada's foreign policy agenda. In Ontario in September 2003, the Tamil community elected 86 Liberal Party delegates to support Paul Martin's leadership bid, from a total of 1,434 delegates. These Tamil delegates mostly came from metropolitan Toronto and Markham areas.[49]

Tamil organizations in diaspora also aim to mobilize support among other Tamils and to sustain dedication both to the LTTE and to the cause of Tamil Eelam. In addition, they work to garner the support of non-Tamils. Some of the means by which they do this include the establishment of non-governmental agencies, the hosting of conferences, patronising academic programmes, and holding marches and rallies. Through the use of international media, these local activities contribute to generating similar support in other places throughout the world. For instance, the LTTE and pro-LTTE websites use media footage of Tamil activities worldwide to publicize their cause and to depict global support for their efforts.

One of the primary objectives of these diaspora-based efforts is to attack Colombo while advancing political support for the cause of the LTTE. This is done by consistently propagating a three-fold message: (1) that Tamils in Sri Lanka are innocent victims of military repression by Sri Lanka's security forces and of Sinhalese anti-Tamil discrimination; (2) that the LTTE is the only legitimate voice of the Tamils and is the only vehicle capable of defending and promoting Tamil interests in Sri Lanka; and (3) that there can be no peace until Tamils achieve their own independent state under the LTTE's leadership.[50]

The LTTE's political and diplomatic activities have two target audiences. On the one hand, they aim to win the support of the diasporan

Tamils (which has financial payoffs). Their second target is the host government, to encourage it to take stances that are friendly towards the LTTE and critical of Colombo. In the aftermath of 9/11, the LTTE has faced many challenges on both counts (as I discuss below). Key tools of these efforts include dissemination of propaganda through electronic mail, the World Wide Web, dedicated telephone hotlines and radio broadcasts. Political, cultural and social gatherings are also used to promote these messages. Many of these events are set to coincide with significant dates on the LTTE calendar, such as Heroes Day (also translated incorrectly as "Martyr's Day").[51]

The United States designated the LTTE as a Foreign Terrorist Organization (FTO) as early as 1997. Ottawa followed suit in 1999, and the United Kingdom and Australia in 2001. It is believed that, as a result of these designations, overseas Tamils have been discouraged from contributing to the LTTE. Interlocutors in Colombo also explained that diasporan Tamils who were coerced into giving donations were able to exploit the greater global enforcement and monitoring of anti-terrorism measures since 9/11 to avoid paying the LTTE-imposed taxes. It is believed that these collective efforts seriously reduced the ability of the LTTE to raise revenue from its large Tamil diaspora in North America, Europe and Asia until the ravages of the 2005 Asian tsunami again motivated an outpouring of diasporan financial resources to the LTTE. Moreover, the LTTE's ability to maintain its linkages with terrorist groups in the Middle East and elsewhere had also been seriously affected by these international efforts.[52]

Military contributions

Militarily, the diaspora has been an important source of funding for the LTTE and has provided important logistical channels through which the LTTE could obtain war materials. For instance, the diaspora expanded the LTTE's range of contacts for weapons procurement. The diaspora network has also facilitated contacts between the LTTE and other unrelated insurgent groups. For example, the LTTE has established ideological, financial and technological linkages with various Khalistani-oriented Sikhs, Kashmiri separatists and other militant organizations based in the Middle East.[53] According to Gunaratna, these different militant organizations exchange and purchase arms from diverse sources that allow them to circumvent various international arms control conventions.

This vast diasporan network has also allowed the LTTE and other groups to raise funds in one location, operate from another location and fight in an altogether different place. This enables groups such as the LTTE to exploit fissures between law enforcement authorities and the failure of government agencies to cooperate.[54] The Sri Lankan government has been helpless in the face of the expanding and increasingly effective LTTE diasporan network and has yet to develop means to vitiate the political and diplomatic strength of the organization's transnational backbone. Nor has it promulgated an effective media management strategy to counter that of the LTTE.[55]

There is no evidence that diasporans have gone home to fight in the struggle. Some would say that in some ways this is the most cynical of military support: diasporan Tamils have contributed to the bloodshed without actually putting themselves at risk. Others would discount this view by pointing out that virtually every Sri Lankan Tamil either has been directly harmed by the insurgency or has family members who have been. Moreover, most Sri Lankan Tamils still have family in Sri Lanka and are therefore not in a completely consequence-free environment.

Socio-cultural contributions

Members of the diaspora have done much to advance Sri Lankan Tamil socio-cultural concerns. They have established numerous Tamil cultural and social institutions, established Hindu temples catering to Sri Lankan Tamils, and founded Tamil language programmes in private ventures and at universities. These organizations are aimed at encouraging families to reproduce Tamil families in diaspora that share collective political goals regarding Tamil Eelam. For instance, children are encouraged to learn Tamil and to engage in Tamil cultural activities. Girls are often enrolled in traditional Tamil dance classes. There are also numerous institutions by which families can arrange matrimonial alliances among Sri Lankan Tamils, a key aspect of reproducing Sri Lankan Tamil communities abroad. Most fundamentally, the diaspora has "sustain[ed] a society under stress, strain and displacement" through the development of social, cultural and religious organizations.[56]

Conflict de-escalation and termination

Evidence on the role of the diaspora in de-escalating and possibly terminating the conflict is less readily available and is overly reliant upon interview data. Information gathered from discussions with officials in the United States government, the Sri Lankan government and representatives from multilateral organizations such as the World Bank and the Asian Development Bank suggests that the diaspora was important in bringing about the ceasefire agreement in 2002.[57] This argument has several strands, each of which will be explained below.

Following the terrorist attacks of 11 September 2001, the United States and other states began to view groups such as the LTTE in very different terms. Increasingly, states were inclined to view the LTTE as a terrorist organization rather than an insurgent organization representing the legitimate interests of an oppressed and politically disenfranchised group – the Sri Lankan Tamils. In many cases these states had already enacted proscriptions against the LTTE and supporting the LTTE. However, until 9/11, many states did not prioritize efforts to limit the activities of the LTTE and its supporters.[58]

According to officials interviewed at the United States Embassy in Colombo in late 2002, many overseas Tamils who supported the LTTE were dismayed at being cast as a terrorist group. They saw their struggle as an insurgency and were deeply concerned that the global community now viewed them as terrorists. In an effort to shed the label "terrorist", diasporan Tamils sought out LTTE representatives at home and abroad and encouraged them to abandon the military struggle, pursue a diplomatic solution and restore legitimacy to the cause of Sri Lanka's Tamil communities. Some analysts observed that, even before the events of 9/11, the diaspora had become increasingly "jittery" about the activities of the LTTE. For example, the forcible recruitment of children and the tactic of suicide-bombing compelled some supporters to question the LTTE's operations and whether the LTTE ultimately helped or hindered the Tamil cause.[59]

Concurrently, the global change in policy towards the LTTE gave the Sri Lankan Tamils in diaspora legitimate means by which they could cease "willing donations" or at least have a more credible reason for resisting extortion by the LTTE tax collectors. This is because either governments were willing to enforce their own extant legislation regarding the LTTE or governments crafted new legislation to target the Tamil Tigers. Tamils could credibly claim that they were forced to stop giving owing to the enhanced vigilance of the state and fear of reprisals. Interlocutors in the US government and elsewhere have suggested that the ability of the diaspora to choke off funds to the LTTE was a direct manifestation of the preferences of the Tamil diaspora for a peaceful solution.[60] In this way the Sri Lankan Tamil diaspora had a positive role to play in bringing the LTTE to the negotiating table with Colombo.

Because the LTTE relies so heavily upon the diaspora for political, economic, military and socio-cultural support, the views of the diaspora had to be taken seriously by the LTTE leadership. Interlocutors maintain that it was these efforts of the diaspora that ultimately motivated Prabhakaran to permit Anton Balasingham to pursue political and diplomatic options with Colombo. Notably, in the first round of talks between the Tigers and Colombo, two diasporan Tamils were included to discuss development and rehabilitation issues: Jay Maheswaran and V. Rudrakumaran.[61]

In other words, the changed global environment and perceptions about armed struggle provided incentives to the Sri Lankan Tamils in diaspora to encourage alternative routes to resolve their problems. This changed environment, in conjunction with questions over LTTE tactics, arguably distanced the diaspora from the LTTE.

Two other important contextual changes created an enabling environment for the Norway-facilitated ceasefire of 2002. First, the LTTE was militarily at an all-time high in power following its successful and devastating attack on Colombo's only international airport. This attack had wide-ranging and deep economic and political consequences for the government. That the LTTE was so well positioned militarily no doubt made it easier to accommodate diaspora pressure to find a political and diplomatic solution. A second factor was the outcome of the December 2001 elections. The United National Front won, led by Ranil Wickremesinghe, who ran on a platform of finding a resolution to the conflict and reaching out to the rebels. Thus it is difficult to say whether the diaspora would have had such a receptive audience in the LTTE leadership without these two other enabling factors.

Conclusions and policy implications

This chapter, following Wayland, has argued that the Tamil diaspora has been crucial to the efforts of the LTTE and to ensuring a sustained and lethal conflict despite a number of factors that should have precluded such success. The diaspora achieved this by making transnational political opportunity structures available to the rebels. However, this occurred only as long as diaspora interests remained largely aligned with those of the LTTE. This chapter has also argued that the LTTE was able to engage diaspora institutions because the Sri Lankan Tamil diaspora was produced by the conflict and many of its institutions were established with the explicit goal of engaging with homeland politics and the problems facing the refugee diaspora. This is in sharp distinction from other South Asian diaspora communities and the role they played in conflicts in the homeland.

In examining the role of the diaspora in the conflict cycle, this chapter has argued that the diaspora's most obvious and enduring contribution has been in escalating and sustaining the conflict. However, owing to changes in the global environment following the terrorist attacks of 9/11, Tamil diasporans had become increasingly dismayed that their struggle had come to be characterized as "terrorist". They therefore sought to encourage the LTTE to pursue a political and diplomatic solution. Because the Tamil diaspora has been so thoroughly integrated into the global LTTE strategy, the LTTE could not simply act with impunity and disregard their interests. The desire of the Sri Lankan Tamil diaspora in the post-9/11 world to have its struggle viewed not as a terrorist movement but as a just struggle against Colombo's oppression was an important factor in the LTTE's decision to pursue a political solution (however defunct that process is now). Although there were other enabling factors that permitted the LTTE to pursue this alternative path, diaspora pressure was surely a necessary if insufficient consideration.

The evidence for this contention may take several years to solidify, but it does suggest that international actors can significantly affect the opportunity-set available to the diaspora and in turn expand its ability to influence events and actors in the home state. First, it may be useful to retain meaningful distinctions between "insurgent" and "terrorist" movements and to be clear about these distinctions. Tamil diasporans seeking an independent state were motivated to pursue political strategies with Colombo to avoid being characterized normatively as "terrorist". This normative distinction clearly had (and has) value for Tamils that could be exploited by state and international actors. In other words, it may be worth considering the rules of engagement (not targeting civilians or civilian institutions) that distinguish terrorist from insurgent groups.

Another policy implication may be that enforcement of domestic and international laws on proscribed organizations is in fact a good idea. Although most key states (the United States, Canada and the United Kingdom) had laws that prohibited funding the LTTE, these rules were apparently not enforced. Only after 9/11 were resources dedicated to circumscribing the LTTE. This in turn gave diasporans the opportunity to avoid funding the LTTE when it was not in their interest to do so. This fact arguably gave the varied diaspora community the tools it needed to lean on the LTTE leadership in pursuit of its goal to reverse the appellation of "terrorist" movement and to regain its status as an "insurgent" movement.

The experience of the LTTE over recent decades of using various tools of public diplomacy and political movements as well as social and cultural institutions to mobilize support for its objectives in Sri Lanka should give policy-makers pause as to how these groups were able to affect national interest formation in host states in the service of sustaining their conflict (however just or unjust) in the home state. It is notable that Colombo was unable to mobilize Sinhalese diasporans in the same way in defence of the state and this issue has remained relatively unexplained and unexplored. Indeed, Colombo should take time to understand how and why the LTTE was able to dominate the information arena.[62]

The post-9/11 action of states against the LTTE demonstrates – perhaps once again – that states become aware that their social and political institutions have been utilized by diasporan groups in the service of diasporans' varied political concerns only after a significantly lengthy period, at which point it is difficult to reverse the course of public understanding about these issues.[63] This suggests that states that host significant diasporas need to develop a much more sophisticated under-standing of these complex social and cultural formations and should view them not only as constituents who compete for votes but also as social, cultural and ethnic assets that can be deployed strategically to ensure the preservation of state interest. Simultaneously, host states need to be keenly aware of the fissures within a diaspora and how entre-preneurs within diasporas seek to mobilize the state in the pursuit of their particular interests. The US reliance on Ahmad Chalabi's fictitious "intelligence" in the decision to prosecute military action against Iraq in 2003 demonstrates the importance of this suggestion.[64] A host state should also think about how it may engage its diaspora populations in public diplomacy and strategic communications and how it can mobilize diasporas in anticipation of a conflict or in the mitigation of a conflict and its post-conflict stability operations.[65]

In conclusion, it appears that many diasporan formations have a so-phisticated understanding of how national interests are formed within states. States should empower themselves by developing the same kind of understanding.

Notes

1. See C. Christine Fair, "Military Operations in Urban Areas: The Indian Experience", *India Review*, 2003, 2(1): 49–76.
2. See Sarah Wayland, "Ethnonationalist Networks and Transnational Opportunities: The Sri Lankan Tamil Diaspora", *Review of International Studies*, 2004, 30: 405–426; United Nations High Commissioner for Refugees, *Background Paper on Sri Lanka for the European Union High Level Working Group on Asylum and Migration*, 18 March 1999, p. 19, cited by Wayland, "Ethnonationalist Networks and Transnational Opportu-nities", p. 414. "The War the World Is Missing", *The Economist*, 7 October 2000, p. 28.
3. Wayland, "Ethnonationalist Networks and Transnational Opportunities", pp. 414–415.
4. See Alan Bullion. "Norway and the Peace Process in Sri Lanka", *Civil Wars*, 2001, 4(3): 70–73; John Stephen Moolakkattu, "Peace Facilitation by Small States: Norway in Sri Lanka", *Cooperation and Conflict: Journal of the Nordic International Studies Associa-tion*, 2005, 40(4); and Ann Kelleher and James Larry Taulbee, "Bridging the Gap: Building Peace Norwegian Style", *Peace & Change*, 2006, 31(4).
5. See C. Christine Fair, "Sri Lanka's Drift Back into War", *International Journal of Peace Operations*, 2006, 2(3).
6. See Fair, "Sri Lanka's Drift Back into War".
7. For details about the various military, political and diplomatic gains obtained by the LTTE, see C. Christine Fair, *Urban Battle Fields of South Asia: Lessons Learned from Sri Lanka, India and Pakistan*, Santa Monica: RAND, 2004.

8. See Neil DeVotta, "Sri Lanka in 2004: Enduring Political Decay and a Failing Peace Process", *Asian Survey*, 2005, 45(1): 98–104.

9. See Sanjoy Majumdar, "Sri Lanka's Tsunami Aid Politics", BBC News World Edition, 21 March 2005, available at ⟨http://news.bbc.co.uk/2/hi/south_asia/4367935.stm⟩ (accessed 3 October 2006).

10. This chapter departs from others in this volume in that the conflict's origins and continuation are exogenous to the dynamics of the Cold War and its demise.

11. There was one very notable exception: India provided substantial military and political support to various factions of the Tamil insurgents throughout the 1970s and 1980s. This policy was mostly an effort to mollify the demands of its own Tamil population. By the late 1980s, India had reversed this policy. It has been argued that the military support was the most significant military training that the Tamil insurgents received and did much to enhance their battle effectiveness. This would turn out to be ironic. By the late 1980s, New Delhi came to believe that supporting this conflict was no longer in its interests and took active steps to broker a peace agreement between the government and the rebels. In 1987, India signed the Sri Lankan Accord and sent a peace-keeping force to the island. Soon, India found itself at war with the LTTE. This Indian Peace Keeping Force remained in Sri Lanka until 1990. The conflict claimed the lives of many Indian troops and has caused numerous controversies within India. The armed forces have, for example, complained that, while they were fighting the LTTE, India's intelligence agencies were still training the LTTE. See Fair, "Military Operations in Urban Areas: The Indian Experience"; Depinder Singh, *IPKF in Sri Lanka*, 3rd printing, New Delhi: Trishul Publications, 2001; Alan J. Bullion, *India, Sri Lanka and the Tamil Crisis, 1976–1994: An International Perspective*, London: Pinter, 1995; Rohan Gunaratna, *Indian Interventions in Sri Lanka: The Role of India's Intelligence Agencies*, Colombo: South Asian Network on Conflict Research, 1993.

12. Wayland, "Ethnonationalist Networks and Transnational Opportunities".

13. Ibid., p. 415.

14. This fieldwork has been published in Fair, *Urban Battle Fields of South Asia*; Christine Fair, "Diaspora Involvement in Insurgencies: Insights from the Khalistan and Tamil Eelam Movements", *Nationalism and Ethnic Politics*, 2005, 11(1).

15. This work is not available to the public. Aspects of this research were published in Fair, "Military Operations in Urban Areas: the Indian Experience".

16. Note that there is no widely accepted year in which the conflict began. Thus discussions of the conflict refer to its origins in general terms (e.g. "the 1970s"). See Rohan Gunaratna, "Sri Lanka: Feeding the Tamil Tigers", in Karen Ballentine and Jake Sherman, eds, *Political Economy of Armed Conflict: Beyond Greed and Grievance*, Boulder, CO: Lynne Rienner, 2003.

17. These population statistics are problematic: owing to the militancy in the Tamil-dominated areas, the last census that completely enumerated Tamils was conducted in 1981. Although Sri Lanka conducted a census in 2001, the only Tamils that could be enumerated thoroughly were those living outside the regions of the north and northeast. No enumeration was done in the Jaffna, Mullaitivu and Kilinochchi districts. In Mannar, 1 division (out of 5) was partially enumerated. In Vavuniya District, 1 of 4 divisions was enumerated completely and 2 were partially enumerated. In Batticaloa District, 5 of 12 divisions were enumerated completely and 6 were partially enumerated. In Trincomalee District, 7 of 11 divisions were enumerated completely and 2 were partially enumerated. See Sri Lanka Department of Census and Statistics, 2001 Provisional Census Data, "Table D – Percentage Distribution of Ethnicity by Districts, 1981–2001", available at ⟨http://www.statistics.gov.lk/census2001/population/text_tabd.htm⟩. Also see Wayland, "Ethnonationalist Networks and Transnational Opportunities", pp. 411–412.

18. This history is in no way intended to be comprehensive. A multi-optic account is well beyond the scope of this analysis. For further details, the reader may consult a number of sources: for example, Gunaratna, "Sri Lanka: Feeding the Tamil Tigers"; Devanesan Nesiah, "The Claim to Self-Determination: A Sri Lankan Tamil Perspective", *South Asia*, 2001, 10(1): 55–71; Asia Foundation, "Focus on Sri Lanka", San Francisco, CA, 2001; Manik De Silva, "Sri Lanka's Civil War", *Current History*, 1999, 98(632): 428–432; Manoj Joshi, "On the Razor's Edge: The Liberation Tigers of Tamil Eelam", *Studies in Conflict and Terrorism*, January/March 1996, 19: 19–42; Sumantra Bose, *States, Nations, Sovereignty: Sri Lanka, India and the Tamil Eelam Movement*, New Delhi: Sage Publications, 1994; Kenneth Bush, "Ethnic Conflict in Sri Lanka", *Conflict Quarterly*, 1990, 10: 41–58; Robert N. Kearney, "Tension and Conflict in Sri Lanka", *Current History*, 1986, 85: 109–112. See also K. M. De Silva, *A History of Sri Lanka*, Berkeley: University of California Press, 1981; K. M. De Silva, *Managing Ethnic Tensions in Multi-Ethnic Societies: Sri Lanka, 1880–1985*, Lanham, MD: University Press of America, 1986; Gunaratna, "Sri Lanka: Feeding the Tamil Tigers"; also see Wayland, "Ethnonationalist Networks and Transnational Opportunities", pp. 411–412.
19. Gunaratna, "Sri Lanka: Feeding the Tamil Tigers", p. 198.
20. Sumanra Bose, "State Crisis and Nationalities Conflict in Sri Lanka and Yugoslavia", *Comparative Political Studies*, 1995, 28(1): 94–95; Wayland, "Ethnonationalist Networks and Transnational Opportunities", pp. 411–412.
21. Nesiah, "The Claim to Self-Determination"; Asia Foundation, "Focus on Sri Lanka"; De Silva, "Sri Lanka's Civil War"; Joshi, "On the Razor's Edge"; Bose, *States, Nations, Sovereignty*; Bush, "Ethnic Conflict in Sri Lanka"; Kearney, "Tension and Conflict in Sri Lanka".
22. For a discussion of the economic impacts of this conflict, see Lisa Morris Grobar and Shiranthi Gnanaselvam, "The Economic Effects of the Sri Lankan Civil War", *Economic Development and Cultural Change*, 1993, 41(2): 395–405.
23. See Joshi, "On the Razor's Edge".
24. Most analysts of the LTTE have described it as a largely secular, ethno-nationalist organization. For instance, see Peter Chalk, "Liberation Tigers of Tamil Eelam's Internal Organization and Operations: A Preliminary Analysis", A Canadian Security Intelligence Service Publication, 17 March 2000; available at ⟨http://www.fas.org/irp/world/para/docs/com77e.htm⟩; Daniel Byman, Peter Chalk, Bruce Hoffman, William Grey Rosenau and David Brannan, *Trends in Outside Support for Insurgent Movements*, Santa Monica, CA: RAND Corporation, 2001; Zahabia Adamaly, Ana Cutter and Shyama Venkateswar, "Lessons from Sri Lanka: Communities in Conflict", The Asia Society and Carnegie Council on Ethics and International Affairs, New York, 2000. However, Michael Roberts' assessment of the LTTE diverges from this conventional wisdom. He mobilizes a large body of anthropological literature on religious practice in Sri Lanka; e.g. the weight attached to propitiatory rituals in Tamil culture and how this informs the LTTE's burial of the dead and the establishment of a sacred topography centred on their "war heroes" (*mavirar*) – although he translates this term inappropriately as "martyr" when it merely means "hero". Roberts argues that, in the same way that "heroic humans were deified in southern India's past, regenerative divine power is conceivably invested in today's Tiger mavirar". He concludes that this aspect of LTTE practice "suggests that 'enchantment' can nestle amidst secularized rationality in the structures of a modern political movement" and concludes that this extra-secular dimension of the organization has accounted for its varied political, economic and military successes. See Michael Roberts, "Tamil Tiger 'Martyrs': Regenerating Divine Potency?", *Studies in Conflict and Terrorism*, 2005, 28(6): 493–514. Also see United States Institute of Peace, *Simulation on Sri Lanka: Setting the Agenda for Peace*, A United States

Institute of Peace educational exercise, 2001, available at ⟨http://www.usip.org/class/ simulations/srilanka.pdf⟩; Helena Whall, "Assessing the Sri Lanka Peace Process", paper for the Political Studies Association – UK 50th Conference, London, 10–13 April 2000; Helena Whall, "Ethnonationalism and Receding Cultural Mobilization in Sri Lanka", working paper presented at the 16th European Conference on Modern Southern Asian Studies, Edinburgh, 6–9 September 2000; Joshi, "On the Razor's Edge".

25. See Human Rights Watch, *Funding the "Final War": LTTE Intimidation and Extortion in the Tamil Diaspora*, New York: Human Rights Watch, 2006.

26. Wayland, "Ethnonationalist Networks and Transnational Opportunities".

27. Gunaratna, "Sri Lanka: Feeding the Tamil Tigers", pp. 200–201; see also "A World of Exiles", *The Economist*, 2 January 2003.

28. Gunaratna, "Sri Lanka: Feeding the Tamil Tigers", pp. 200–201; see also "A World of Exiles".

29. See R. Cheran, "Diaspora Circulation and Transnationalism as Agents for Change in the Post Conflict Zones of Sri Lanka", a policy paper submitted to the Berghof Foundation for Conflict Management, Berlin, Germany, 2003, available at ⟨http://www. berghof-foundation.lk/scripts/publications.htm⟩; Chalk, "Liberation Tigers of Tamil Eelam's Internal Organization and Operations"; Byman et al., *Trends in Outside Support for Insurgent Movements*; Adamaly, Cutter and Venkateswar, "Lessons from Sri Lanka: Communities in Conflict".

30. Gunaratna, "Sri Lanka: Feeding the Tamil Tigers", p. 201. Cheran also recognizes that historically there have been different types of diaspora associated with the movement of Sri Lankan Tamils from the island. He too argues that it is within the emergence of the civil war that the notion of a Sri Lankan Tamil diaspora should be studied. See Cheran, "Diaspora Circulation and Transnationalism as Agents for Change in the Post Conflict Zones of Sri Lanka".

31. For a more detailed argument, see Fair, "Diaspora Involvement in Insurgencies".

32. The role of the Sri Lankan Tamil diaspora in providing support to Tamils affected by the January 2005 tsunami has been important and may augur well for the role it could play in post-conflict reconstruction.

33. See Fair, *Urban Battle Fields of South Asia*.

34. See Joshi, "On the Razor's Edge"; Philippe Le Billon, Jake Sherman and Marcia Hardwell, "Controlling Resource Flows to Civil Wars: A Review and Analysis of Current Policies and Legal Instruments", Background Paper for the International Peace Academy "Economic Agendas in Civil Wars" Project Conference *Policies and Practices for Regulating Resource Flows to Armed Conflicts*, Rockefeller Foundation Study and Conference Center, Bellagio, Italy, 20–24 May 2002, available at ⟨http://www.ipacademy. org/PDF_Reports/controlling_resource_flows.pdf⟩.

35. Rohan Gunaratna, "International and Regional Implications of the Sri Lankan Tamil Insurgency", Institute for Counter-Terrorism, 2 December 1998; available at ⟨http:// www.ict.org.il/articles/articledet.cfm?articleid=57⟩; Chalk ("Liberation Tigers of Tamil Eelam's Internal Organization and Operations") claims that the LTTE had cells in at least 54 countries as of winter 1999.

36. Chalk, "Liberation Tigers of Tamil Eelam's Internal Organization and Operations"; Valpy Fitzgerald, "Global Financial Information, Compliance Incentives and Conflict Funding", paper presented to the International Conference on Globalization and Self-Determination Movements, hosted by Pomona College, 21–22 January 2003.

37. Note that these figures are old and almost certainly out of date. Even recently published estimates use these figures, which do not reflect changes – if any – that may have occurred in the post-9/11 environment. Unfortunately, no more up-to-date estimates are available. See Gunaratna, "Sri Lanka: Feeding the Tamil Tigers", p. 209.

38. Gunaratna interviews with Sri Lankan intelligence officials in October 2001. See Gunaratna, "Sri Lanka: Feeding the Tamil Tigers", p. 209.
39. Gunaratna, "Bankrupting the Terror Business," *Jane's Intelligence Review*, 1 August 2000, 12(8). There are several other such organizations, as noted by Byman et al., *Trends in Outside Support for Insurgent Movements*, and Le Billon et al., "Controlling Resource Flows to Civil Wars".
40. Anthony Davis, "Asia, Tamil Tiger International", *Jane's Intelligence Review*, 1 October 1996.
41. See "U.S. Denies any Information about LTTE Indulging in Drug Trafficking", *India Express*, 3 March 2001.
42. "International Law Enforcement Cooperation Fights Narcoterror: Drug Enforcement Agency Official Testifies before Senate Committee", Statements of DEA Intelligence Chief, Steven W. Casteel, 20 May 2003.
43. Gunaratna, "Sri Lanka: Feeding the Tamil Tigers", pp. 206–207.
44. Ibid.
45. Gunaratna, "International and Regional Implications of the Sri Lankan Tamil Insurgency".
46. Le Billon et al., "Controlling Resource Flows to Civil Wars".
47. Byman et al., *Trends in Outside Support for Insurgent Movements*, p. 44.
48. Chalk, "Liberation Tigers of Tamil Eelam's Internal Organization and Operations".
49. See Cheran, "Diaspora Circulation and Transnationalism as Agents for Change in the Post Conflict Zones of Sri Lanka", pp. 10–11.
50. Anthony Davis, "Tiger International", *Asiaweek*, 26 November 1996, cited by Byman et al., *Trends in Outside Support for Insurgent Movements*, pp. 43–44.
51. Byman et al., *Trends in Outside Support for Insurgent Movements*, p. 45; Gunaratna, "The LTTE and Suicide Terrorism", *Frontline*, 5–8 February 2000, 17(3), available at ⟨http://www.frontlineonnet.com/fl1703/17031060.htm⟩ (accessed 3 October 2006).
52. See Byman et al., *Trends in Outside Support for Insurgent Movements*; and Reyko Huang, "In the Spotlight: Liberation Tigers of Tamil Eelam (LTTE)", Washington, DC: Center for Defense Information, 19 April 2002, available at ⟨http://www.cdi.org/terrorism/ltte.cfm⟩ (accessed 3 October 2006).
53. Gunaratna, "The LTTE and Suicide Terrorism"; Gunaratna, "International and Regional Implications of the Sri Lankan Tamil Insurgency".
54. See Gunaratna, "International and Regional Implications of the Sri Lankan Tamil Insurgency" and Gunaratna, "Sri Lanka: Feeding the Tamil Tigers".
55. See, *inter alia*, Byman et al., *Trends in Outside Support for Insurgent Movements*; Gunaratna, "International and Regional Implications of the Sri Lankan Tamil Insurgency"; Chalk, "Liberation Tigers of Tamil Eelam's Internal Organization and Operations".
56. Cheran, "Diaspora Circulation and Transnationalism as Agents for Change in the Post Conflict Zones of Sri Lanka", p. 9.
57. This is based on interviews in Sri Lanka in 2002 and discussions with individuals within multilateral organizations in late 2004.
58. See Fair, *Urban Battlefields of South Asia*.
59. See comments by Neil DeVotta, Center for Strategic and International Studies, Washington, DC, 14 February 2003.
60. See Fair, *Urban Battle Fields of South Asia*.
61. See V. S. Sambandan, "From Guns to Roses", *Frontline*, 9–22 November 2002, 19(9), available at ⟨http://www.frontlineonnet.com/fl1923/stories/20021122000113000.htm⟩.
62. This issue is discussed at some length in Fair, *Urban Battle Fields of South Asia*.
63. Several South Asian diasporans have played an enormous role in the national interest formation of the host state and in turn have affected policy decisions taken by the host

state against the home state. Sikh nationalists based in the United States had notable success in lobbying US lawmakers against the Indian state throughout the late 1980s and the 1990s. See Fair, "Diaspora Involvement in Insurgencies". Similarly, the Indian diaspora in the United States has explicitly mobilized political structures that mimic those of the American Jewish diaspora. The evolving sophistication and political development of the Indian diaspora were seen in its mobilization against Pakistan in the limited conflict over the Kargil-Dras sectors in 1999. Indian-Americans flooded their political representatives in Congress with letters demanding action (which was indeed forthcoming). It is not clear how much this mobilization affected the ultimate course of US action. But it did demonstrate to all observers that this diaspora has come into maturity and political development. Since then, it has served as the ballast in the ongoing strategic relationship developing between the United States and India. See Robert Hathaway, "Unfinished Passage: India, Indian Americans, and the U.S. Congress", *Washington Quarterly*, 2001, 24(2); and Amit Gupta, "The Indian Diaspora's Political Efforts in the United States", ORF Occasional Paper Series, September 2004, available at ⟨http://www.orfonline.org/publications/OccasionalPapers/op040918.pdf⟩ (accessed 3 October 2006).

64. See Robert Dreyfuss, "More Missing Intelligence", *The Nation*, 7 July 2004; Seymour M. Hersh, "The Stovepipe: How Conflicts between the Bush Administration and the Intelligence Community Marred the Reporting on Iraq's Weapons", *New Yorker*, 27 October 2003; CBS News, "Iraqi Exile Denies Misleading U.S.", 7 March 2004, ⟨http://www.cbsnews.com/stories/2004/03/05/60minutes/main604285.shtml⟩ (accessed 3 October 2006).

65. Yossi Shain makes this case persuasively in *Marketing the American Creed Abroad: Diasporas in the U.S. and Their Homelands*, Cambridge: Cambridge University Press, 1999.

10

Kurdish interventions in the Iraq war

Denise Natali

Like other diasporic communities, the Kurdish diaspora has benefited from globalization processes by gaining greater influence in shaping homeland politics. Having access to legitimate forms of political expression that were denied in countries of origin, the diaspora has become the protector of the Kurdish nation at home and abroad. This role has become particularly salient during periods when Kurdish national interests are at stake, such as the US–UK intervention in Iraq in 2003, which overthrew Saddam Hussein in the effort to create a federal political system of which Kurdish autonomy is a part. Protecting Kurdish nationalism in Iraq, however, has not resulted in uniform interventions by the diasporic community. Rather, it has led to varying diasporic roles during different periods of the conflict cycle, some of which supported peace-making and some of which encouraged conflict. Understanding the spatial and temporal dimension of Kurdish interventions can help identify particular behaviours of diasporic communities within the parameters of the wartime period, and the conditions in which the Kurdish diaspora acted as peace-makers or peace-wreckers in the Iraq conflict.

This chapter examines Kurdish diasporic interventions during different phases of the Iraq war and their influences on mitigating or encouraging conflict.[1] It reveals that the form of participation in the diaspora is linked to the political opportunity structures (POS) available to different group members at home and abroad. Stateless diasporic communities linked to legitimized leaders and organizations are more likely to pursue strategies based on negotiation than are diasporas delegitimized in the interna-

Diasporas in conflict: Peace-makers or peace-wreckers?, Smith and Stares (eds), United Nations University Press, 2007, ISBN 978-92-808-1140-7

tional arena. Legitimate networks can serve the peaceful interests of their diasporas and homelands, whereas illegitimate ones can discourage peace-making. Second, diasporas are likely to act as peace-makers if engagement in homeland politics is perceived as identity reinforcing and legitimate. The more inclusive the political system or proposed system, the more are diasporic activities channelled into that system and shaped accordingly, rather than taking place outside the system in more confrontational forms. Third, the higher the stakes for achieving nationalist claims in the war's outcome (nationalism legalized, statehood or autonomy), the more likely it is that interventions will support conflict resolution. Similarly, the lower the stakes (continuation of the status quo, loss of territorial sovereignty), the more likely it is that diasporas will refrain from negotiation or will engage in hostility.

These claims are teased out in the following sections, which examine the Kurdish diasporic condition and the differentiated migration experiences that have simultaneously encouraged pan-Kurdish ethnonationalism and greater complexity in diasporic organizations and claims-making. Kurdish diasporic diversity is then situated alongside the POS during distinct phases of the Iraq war from late 1998 to summer 2004, which resulted in different and changing interventions by the two main communities from Iraq and Turkey. The last section examines the policy implications for external actors and the Kurdish diaspora.

The Kurdish diasporic condition

The Kurdish diaspora is a stateless, socio-political grouping of the same ethnic origin that emigrated from different states (Iraq, Turkey, Iran and Syria), which resulted in different politicization processes and nationalist trajectories among group members.[2] Opportunity structures linked to democratic host country systems, however, have helped break down distinct notions of Kurdish nationalism while creating new forms of identification as part of a pan-ethnic category. Pan-Kurdish nationalism has become an underlying component of diasporic participation and claims-making.

To be sure, the distinct historical trajectories that shaped Kurdish identity formation remain a salient component of the diasporic condition. Organizations and social networks are often formed according to homeland parties, regional-specific membership, and towns or villages in different parts of Kurdistan, which can diminish interaction with Kurds from outside these localities. Iraqi Kurds are generally tied to Massoud Barzani's Kurdistan Democratic Party (KDP) and Jelal Talabani's Patriotic Union of Kurdistan (PUK). Kurds from Turkey support the Partiye Karkaren

Kurdistane (PKK), renamed Kongra-Gel in 2003,[3] the Kurdish socialist party (KOMKAR) or Alevi organizations – non-orthodox Shi'a Turkish and Kurdish communities – or remain independent. In many cases Kurdish politics has been transferred to diasporic settings, reinforcing power structures and identities linked to homeland localities. One Iraqi Kurd living in Dusseldorf stated, "When Talabani and Barzani fight in Kurdistan, we fight here. If they unify there, we unify here."[4] Settlement patterns in host countries have further strengthened allegiances to different sections of the homeland. In London, for instance, Kurds from Turkey have moved into Haringey and Hackney in the north-east, Kurds from Iraq have relocated to the west in Ealing and Acton, and Kurds from Iran have settled in Hammersmith and Fulham to the south.

Still, transnational diasporic networks have helped break down political identities shaped in countries of origin and create new ones.[5] Host country policies that categorize and resettle Kurdish refugees according to country of origin (citizenship) make precise figures of the Kurdish diaspora difficult to extract. However, approximately 1 million Kurds live in Europe, with smaller scatterings in the United States, Canada, Australia, Israel and Greece. Of this number, Kurds from Turkey represent the largest community (700,000), with about 600,000 in Germany alone. Kurds from Iraq comprise 250,000; Iranian and Syrian Kurds have insignificant representations, with about 50,000 and 15,000, respectively.[6] Although some educated Kurds have attained professional positions in universities and businesses, the overwhelming majority of uneducated, low-skilled refugees have not integrated into host country labour forces. They have, instead, created their own niche economies, which reinforce their distinct group identity. Even after attaining citizenship or residency permits, most Kurds are not considered, and do not consider themselves, as Europeans; they are Kurds first, living as migrants, foreigners, *étrangers* and *ausländische Mitbürger* in different European countries.

From open political spaces in democratic host countries, Kurdish diasporic communities have had opportunities to unite at the ideological, institutional and political levels, creating a virtual Kurdistan in exile. Intellectuals and non-partisan diasporic community leaders have created Kurdish cultural centres, associations, educational exchanges and self-help organizations that reach out to the larger Kurdish diaspora. The Kurdish National Congress, the Confederation of Kurdish Organizations in Sweden, the NAVEND Zentrum für Kurdische Studien in Bonn, the Kurdish Cultural Centre in London, the Finnish Kurdish Committee, the Kurdish Initiative Group in Holland, the Norwegian Kurdish Committee, the British-Kurdish Friendship Society, the Washington Kurdish Institute, and L'Institut Kurde de Paris bring together various Kurdish communities whose members originate from all parts of greater Kurdistan, regardless of socio-economic status, political party, language or country of origin.[7]

Access to public forums has encouraged pan-Kurdish, non-partisan diasporic groups to change their political behaviour and work together as one pan-ethnic migrant community. A former member of the Kurdistan Regional Government, the political institution democratically elected in 1992 to administer and govern the Kurdistan region in Iraq, who took refuge in Europe, remarked, "Now the Kurds in Germany, when we see each other we know we are Kurds and the feeling is the same. It's like finding our brothers we have never seen before. We have the same problem of the nation and having one land."[8] European diasporas and the ongoing suppression of Kurds in Turkey have also brought increasing attention to Kurdish problems across borders. Another Iraqi Kurdish refugee noted, "We are not like we were one hundred years ago. We now organize among ourselves. We have a national consciousness (*hushiryari neteway*). But there is also destruction against Kurds from Turkey and we support them."[9]

Differentiated migration experiences

Scattered across Europe, the Kurdish diasporic community has accessed different host country opportunity structures – permanent or national dimensions of the political environment that encourage or discourage different communities from using collective action that could advance Kurdish national interests. These structures include host country strategies for managing ethnic diversity at the state-wide and local levels, such as resettlement policies, citizenship laws, educational programmes and external resources that can be taken advantage of even by weak and disorganized groups.[10] Diverse opportunity structures have led to new types of differentiation in diasporic leadership, organization and claims-making.

Part of the differentiation processes is diverse migration experiences that have been processed by Kurdish communities in various ways. Although the first Kurdish migrations out of Kurdistan can be traced to the twelfth century during the Babylonian exile, the emigration of Kurds to the West is relatively a new phenomenon that commenced during the mid-twentieth century following political repression and economic hardship in the modern states of Iraq, Turkey, Iran and Syria.

Small student circles of Iraqi Kurds emigrated to Europe and the United States during the 1960s; however, the more important migrations to Europe and Iran occurred during the 1970s and 1980s by highly politicized and well-educated groups and those fleeing the Iran–Iraq war. Their migration experiences were relatively positive, because they were well received and integrated into host country systems and legitimized as victims of Saddam Hussein and the Ba'athist regime. Many became active diasporic leaders representing Iraqi Kurdish centres, professional groups, non-governmental organizations (NGOs) and academic institutions with extensive legal transnational networks abroad.

The third wave, which commenced after the 1991 Persian Gulf war, involved uneducated village communities and economic refugees, who joined family members in Europe and the United States. Many were youth without direct memories of the atrocities of Saddam Hussein; rather, they had experienced intra-Kurdish fighting in autonomous Kurdistan. They were received less hospitably in host countries and subject to new resettlement policies that dispersed them outside city centres. Instead of becoming engaged nationalists or active political party representatives, members of this group remain apolitical or antagonistic to Kurdish politics and host countries' systems.[11]

Kurds from Turkey began their exodus to Europe during the 1960s, although these migrations were economically generated and largely voluntary. This proletariat community, most of whom migrated to Germany and worked among Turkish and foreign migrant communities as *Gastarbeiters*, affiliated with leftist and working-class groups, although they identified as Kurds and Turks and Alevis – non-orthodox Shi'a Kurdish and Turkish communities.[12] The second wave commenced involuntarily after the 1980 military coup d'état in Turkey and was marginalized, highly politicized and organized, prone to radicalism, and largely linked to the PKK. Given this radicalized ideology and the special relationship between the US and European governments and Turkey (a NATO member), Kurdish nationalists from Turkey have had a more difficult time gaining international support for their nationalist claims. Unlike Iraqi Kurds, most of whom have been legitimized and integrated into host country systems, Kurds from Turkey, especially PKK-affiliated representatives, organizations and communications networks, have been placed under discreet or open surveillance, with constraints on their activities or access to public funds, or their offices have been closed.[13] Moderate diasporic leaders and organizations from Turkey that gained legal status in host countries did so by adopting an anti-PKK agenda and placing Kurdish nationalist interests alongside European socialism or human rights issues.

In contrast to the politicized diasporic communities from Iraq and Turkey, Kurds from Iran have had a less dynamic migration experience. Only 50,000 fled to Europe after the 1978 Iranian revolution, and another 4,000 fled to the Kurdish regions in Iraq, where they reside in refugee camps managed by the United Nations High Commissioner for Refugees. The small size of the Iranian Kurdish community abroad, its more integrative form of Kurdish nationalism, and the absence of effective leadership and nationalist organizations have limited its mobilization potential. Since the late 1980s, Iranian Kurds have played a relatively insignificant role in the diaspora, remaining independent or affiliating with Iranian cultural associations.

Instead of merging the heterogeneous Kurdish migrant communities into one ethnic category, Europe's diverse political and social systems hinder pan-Kurdish nationalism, despite the democratic context in which diasporic politics unfolds. Government resettlement programmes and policies do not always officially recognize Kurds by their ethnic group identity but rather distinguish them by their state of origin (e.g. Iraq, Iran, Turkey), which separates Kurds from one another and groups them with non-Kurds. Kurdish diasporas also lack the institutional support required to organize and mobilize as a unified ethno-national group across the borders of multiple sovereign states. The Kurdish National Congress (KNC), the diaspora-elected parliament in exile that brings together Kurdish communities from all countries of origin, does not have the legal status or access to official support from foreign offices that might enable it to unite the different Kurdish groups in one coherent structure.

Bounded by distinct juridical and administrative systems, diasporic communities have reframed their nationalist claims in relation to the political opportunity structures in their host countries. A process of institutional channelling has taken place whereby the forms of Kurdish activism have adapted to their political institutional environment.[14] According to one Kurdish diasporic leader in Bonn, "The overriding issue for Kurds in Germany is their migration status, rights inside the country (language), and the diaspora situation. The German government puts up a lot of barriers before us, so we need to defend our rights for Kurds here."[15] A different dynamic has emerged in the United States, where Kurds (mainly from Iraq) are a smaller and younger diaspora (25,000–30,000), more isolated from the homeland and more dispersed and integrated into US society. They lack the ghetto mentality that pervades in European cities and the need to organize as ethnic cultural groups at local council levels. Most remain attached to homeland political parties (the KDP or PUK) or have become non-partisan diasporic leaders committed to resolving the larger Kurdish problem.[16]

Differentiated migration experiences and POS have also led to new hyphenated identities that have encouraged greater diversification in transnational social networks and organizations.[17] While becoming nationalists from afar, diasporic Kurds have also become German Kurds, Swedish Kurds, Kurds from Iraq in France and American Kurds, with new cross-cutting identities tied to countries of origin. In Germany, for instance, dozens of Sunni Islamic and Alevi associations have established influential and legal transnational networks for Kurdish *and* non-Kurdish migrants from Turkey, encouraging the saliency of religious identities alongside or instead of pan-Kurdish nationalism. These organizations explicitly or tacitly exclude Kurds from Iraq and Iran, whose diasporic national consciousness remains secular. At the Kurdish Cultural and Information Centre in Paris, previously known as the Kurdish Prayer Centre, only a handful of the approximately 250 members are from Iraq. Most activities, including Friday prayer services held in the Kurmanji language, are oriented to members from Turkey.[18] Alevi Kurds have, since the early 1990s, affiliated with Alevi networks that include Turkish communities, alongside or instead of Kurdish nationalist organizations.

Different pasts, and narratives about those pasts, have shaped identities and organizations in different settings, further constraining uniform diasporic participation toward a pan-Kurdistan. The representative of the Kurdish Association for Refugees (KAR) in the London borough of Hammersmith and Fulham, a refugee from Iraq, remarked:

> We have a strong sense of ethnicity and we all belong to the same land. The war in Iraq and the capture of [Abdullah] Ocalan have brought many of us together. However, due to the political situation over the past eighty years and the artificial boundaries [across greater Kurdistan], mixing and living together is difficult. This history has made it very difficult, even today, to come together as a national community, despite the opportunities available in the diaspora.[19]

Language differences remain. Even though the KAR constitution does not limit membership to Kurds from specific host states, the group in fact provides services only in Sorani Kurdish and Arabic. This practice has encouraged new relationships between Kurds from Iraq and Iran, but not with Kurds from Turkey, who have not contacted the association since its inception. Instead, they have turned to the Halkevi Turkish/ Kurdish Community Centre in Hackney, which includes Turkish-speaking Kurds but also members of the Turkish Cypriot community.

Wartime interventions

In addition to diverse POS in host country settings, the heterogeneous Kurdish diasporic community had access to asymmetrical opportunity structures during various cycles of the Iraq war that encouraged different forms of diasporic participation.

Wartime opportunity structures included the discourses, policies and programmes implemented by the United States, foreign governments, international organizations and the Kurdish nationalist élite, which either advanced or discouraged Kurdish autonomy in Iraq. Different conflict phases also caused short-term changes in the POS, including decreased access to participation, shifts in alliance structures and conflicts within and among élites, which, in turn, shaped the types of intervention by the two main communities from Iraq and Turkey.[20]

Latent conflict phase

Iraqi Kurds had a higher stake in the war's outcome than did Kurds from Turkey and larger opportunities to negotiate their nationalist claims legally as part of the proposed federal system in Iraq. From the outset of the latent conflict phase (1998–March 2003) and after most post-Gulf war humanitarian relief programmes funded by the US Office of Foreign Disaster Assistance in northern Iraq had terminated, the US government employed confidence-building measures toward the Kurdish homeland national élite. It conducted international meetings with Massoud Barzani and Jelal Talabani to encourage Kurdish unity and prevent the Saddamization of the Kurdish north. Part of this campaign involved strengthening the Iraqi opposition movement, an international grouping of various opposition parties that framed Iraqi Kurdish nationalism within the territorial boundaries of a federal, post-Saddam Iraq and alongside the political claims of Shi'a and Sunni Arab communities.

Having access to international forums and benefiting from the legitimacy linked to these alliances, the members of the Iraqi Kurdish nationalist élite and their representatives abroad acted as a political conduit for US interests and direct intervention in the country. In 1998, after seven years of cooperation under the US-protected no-fly zone in Iraqi Kurdistan, Barzani and Talabani commenced consultations with the US government for regime change in Iraq. Their political party representatives in Washington, DC, started lobbying US government institutions, including the Foreign Relations Committee, the Armed Services Committee and US congressional representatives, to support the war that would depose Saddam Hussein and help create a federal Iraq. Over time, US officials sought out Kurdish counsel more and more, although they did not finance or support non-partisan, pan-Kurdish diasporic organizations and their activities. By 2002, Kurdish offices in Washington, DC, now jointly representing the two administrations of the Kurdish Regional Government (KRG) responsible for governing the regions of Iraqi Kurdistan influenced by Barzani (KDP) and Talabani (PUK), had created a bilateral channel with the Bush administration.[21]

US–Kurdish complicity strengthened after the US Special Forces arrived in Iraqi Kurdistan in the summer of 2002, further legitimizing Iraqi

Kurdish nationalist claims. KRG representatives became heavily engaged in consulting with the Bush administration on the operational aspects of the war, particularly in preparing the Northern Front, composed of Kurdish *peshmerga* forces (local militia; "those who face death") and US paramilitaries. In December 2002, Barzani and Talabani, further encouraged by the Bush administration, jointly participated in the Iraqi opposition meeting in London and situated Kurdish nationalism within a democratic post-Saddam Iraq. The US government, in turn, became increasingly receptive to Iraqi Kurds, so that the KRG Washington offices became and remained the hub of Iraqi Kurdish wartime politics.

By cooperating with the US government and negotiating Kurdish autonomy within a federal Iraq, rather than insisting on an independent Iraqi Kurdistan, the nationalist élite believed it had the most realistic possibilities of advancing the nationalist interests, particularly in a region hostile to Kurdish nationalism. Non-partisan and pan-Kurdish diasporic leaders who were geographically removed from regional pressures, however, were less willing to negotiate away Kurdish nationalism. They acted as intermediaries between the homeland élite, political party representatives abroad and foreign governments, and they intervened when they thought Kurdish interests were not being protected. During the 2002 London conference, for instance, when the issue of a federal Iraq was proposed, diasporic leaders demanded from Barzani and Talabani more specific guarantees of federalism and its contents. The following year some community leaders held various meetings in London and Iraqi Kurdistan and published a series of open letters expressing the concerns of the diasporic community.

Some issues were non-negotiable and actually united the non-partisan, pan-Kurdish diasporic leaders with the homeland élite, increasing the significance and influence of Kurdish interventions. For instance, when the US government announced its plans to invite Turkish troops into Iraqi Kurdistan in February 2003, the diaspora joined the nationalist élite and populations inside Kurdistan and rapidly mobilized against the proposal. They also lobbied US government agencies and conducted demonstrations, media campaigns, television and radio interviews, rallies and conferences abroad and in Kurdistan. The Turkish government's refusal to participate in the war effort ended the crisis, cooled US–Turkish relations, and increased the Iraqi Kurds' confidence that their national claims would be respected in a post-Saddam Iraq.

The POS and the high stakes in the war's outcome that existed for Iraqi Kurds were not available for Kurds from Turkey. Whereas Iraqi Kurds were legitimized as victims of Saddam and had generous international aid to help develop their region, Kurds from Turkey were struggling for political and cultural rights in their part of the Kurdish homeland and remained in conflict with the Turkish government. Kurds from Turkey also had a fundamentally different relationship with the United States than did Iraqi Kurds. Whereas the US government conducted confidence-building measures with the Iraqi Kurdish élite, it participated in the arrest of PKK leader Abdullah Ocalan (Apo) in Nairobi in January 1999. The criminalized status of leftist-nationalist Kurds from Turkey, their antagonistic relationship with Iraqi Kurdish political parties, and the US lack of interest in the Kurdish problem in Turkey reinforced political dichotomies between "good Kurds" from Iraq and "bad Kurds" from Turkey.

Asymmetrical policies that legitimized Kurdish nationalism in Iraq while ignoring or delegitimizing the Kurdish problem in Turkey alienated a large majority of the diaspora from Turkey. The proscription of the PKK as a terrorist organization by the US and European governments in May 2001 further radicalized the PKK and its supporters. During this period, PKK cadres in Europe financed military interventions against Kurdish parties in Iraq and the Turkish government. Thousands of Kurds in London also demonstrated outside the UK Home Office and signed petitions demanding the legitimization of the PKK. The "I am the PKK" movement quickly spread through dozens of European towns and cities and increased the significance of the nationalist claims by Kurds from Turkey. It also heightened dichotomies between leftist-nationalist communities and moderate diasporic groups from Turkey, Iraqi Kurdish political parties and foreign governments.

It was in this antagonistic context that Kurdish diasporic communities from Turkey approached the Iraq war. Committed to both leftist ideology and Kurdish nationalism, most supported regime change and Kurdish autonomy in Iraq. However, they disagreed on the methods of conducting the war and implementing change. Instead of supporting outside military intervention or turning to pan-Kurdish or Iraqi Kurdish organizations, they demanded political negotiation that included regional actors. By late 2002, when it was clear that negotiation was not an option and the UK government had become a partner in the war effort, they became critical of US–UK military intervention. Many joined the European-wide anti-war movements, which gave them a legal channel to organize as an ethnic community. In conjunction with Greenpeace, leftist parties and movements to stop terrorism, they lobbied members of parliament from the Labour and Green parties, participated in the Peace in Kurdistan campaign,[22] and sponsored weekly meetings with trade unions and community organizations, which were used as a lobbying platform for the larger leftist community. On 15 February 2003, thousands of Kurdish leftist nationalists in London and Glasgow mobilized in the "Don't Attack Iraq" and "Stop the War" campaigns.

Nevertheless, radicalized Kurdish nationalists from Turkey did not become peace-wreckers. Although the POS favoured Iraqi Kurds and their nationalist claims, the parameters of the latent conflict phase were ambiguous enough to allow Kurds from Turkey to believe that they too, as part of the pan-Kurdish category, could benefit from the US–Iraqi Kurdish alliance and the US democracy mission in Iraq. Instead of sending arms to PKK guerrillas in the mountains of Iraqi Kurdistan, they maintained a policy of neutrality tied to the unilateral ceasefire that the PKK had declared with Turkey in 1999. In fact, as tensions heightened between the United States and Turkey in March 2003, the nationalist faction within the PKK chose to support the United States, hoping that similar opportunities for autonomy would be available for Kurds in Turkey and neighbouring states. Another smaller faction continued to follow a strict leftist ideology and remained antagonistic to the war. According to a representative of the Halkevi Turkish/Kurdish Community Centre in London, "We did not want to cause trouble so we sent out press releases and conducted demonstrations throughout Europe in support of Iraqi Kurdish political demands, as well as to end the war."[23] Similarly, when representatives of the pro-Kurdish party Demokratik Halk Partisi (DEHAP), currently known as the Demokratik Toplum Partisi (DTP), met with US officials at the US Embassy in Ankara, they too assured cooperation and not conflict with US objectives in Iraq.[24]

Escalation, de-escalation and reconstruction

The escalation phase, which commenced in April 2003 and fluctuated between de-escalation, re-escalation and reconstruction after the downfall of Saddam Hussein and the Ba'athist regime that same month, altered the POS for Kurdish communities. Kurdish autonomy, in particular the status of Kirkuk, the petroleum-rich, Kurdish-populated city in northern Iraq that was Arabized by successive Ba'athist regimes, was subsumed in the unstable political and security environment. As Kurdish national interests became increasingly threatened and as dichotomies heightened between Kurds from Iraq and Turkey, potential peace-wreckers emerged within the diasporic community.

To be sure, the parameters of the early escalation and hot-conflict phases remained relatively favourable to Iraqi Kurdish interests and assured positive interventions or a continued willingness to compromise Kurdish nationalism within a federal Iraq. Saddam and the Ba'athist regime were overthrown, Turkey was marginalized from the war, and essential Kurdish territories were protected. Kurds celebrated across Europe and the United States, hailing the US government for "liberating Kirkuk" and guaranteeing Iraqi Kurdish autonomy. These important leverage points continued in the immediate post-Saddam period. In the effort to consolidate power and gain popular support, the US Coalition Provisional Authority (CPA), which administered the country alongside an Iraqi transitional government, retained the Kurdistan region's autonomous status, promised Kurds key posts in the Governing Council, and offered economic incentives to Kurdistan. In November 2003, the CPA transferred unused funds from the UN oil-for-food programme, providing about US$1.5 billion to the two administrations of the KRG to complete unfinished UN projects in the Kurdistan region. Economic liberalization policies encouraged international investment and trade agreements between Iraqi Kurdistan and regional states that spurred growth and new forms of wealth in their autonomous region.

As long as the CPA and Iraqi officials maintained key leverage points, and as long as engagement in homeland politics was perceived as identity enforcing and legitimate, the diaspora was willing to compromise Kurdish interests in a federal Iraq. Instead of taking advantage of the unstable war period to separate from Iraq or conduct military interventions, Kurdish diasporas used the Iraq war as means of consulting, disseminating information and lobbying foreign governments to advance Kurdish identity-based interests. High-ranking KDP and PUK party representatives in Europe returned to Iraq and started calling themselves Iraqis as well as Kurds. Many brought their ideas and experience with democratic political systems to Baghdad and became leading officials in the central government. The former Kurdish minister of reconstruction and development, Nasreen Barwari, became Iraqi minister of public works. Hoshir Zibari, former KDP spokesman, became Iraqi foreign minister. Kurdish party representatives abroad also received ambassadorial posts in the central government, including Ahmed Bamarni, Iraqi ambassador to Sweden, and Mohammed Sabir, Iraqi ambassador to China.

One of the most important positive roles of the Kurdish diaspora during this phase was in addressing post-conflict peace-building, including human rights issues, educational initiatives and the development of civil society.[25] Some community leaders, such as Serbest Kirkuki at the Kurdish Cultural Centre (KCC) in London, worked directly with international NGOs in Kirkuk, talked to decision-makers and tried to teach local populations how to resolve conflicts between Kurds and Arabs over land claims. Kurdish intellectuals abroad, alongside Western scholars, worked with the Kurdish homeland élite to design the Transitional Administrative Law (TAL) for Iraq (approved on 8 March 2004) to provide essential principles of power-sharing and guarantees for Kurdish autonomy in a future federal Iraqi state. Other Iraqi Kurds returned home and became actively involved in post-war reconstruction activities in telecommunications, construction and tourism.[26] The London-based Kurdistan

Development Corporation (KDC) initiated business investment, sponsored trade fairs and supported construction and telecommunications projects to ensure economic growth and political stability inside the Kurdistan region.

The POS and diasporic interventions linked to these structures changed as Iraq turned into a complex crisis caused by the combination of civil and political conflict and complicated by the breakdown of state authority.[27] Increasing instability threatened Kurdish national identity and territory, heightened pan-Kurdish claims-making, and created new tensions between the homeland political élite, their party representatives and non-partisan, pan-Kurdish diasporic communities. Certainly, diasporic communities became confrontational after the terrorist bombing in February 2004 in Arbil, the capital city of Iraqi Kurdistan and headquarters of the KRG, in which over 100 Iraqi Kurds were killed, and attacks by radical Arab nationalists against Kurds in Kamishli, Syria, the following month. Pan-Kurdish organizations and KRG representatives abroad issued press releases and staged protests in host countries demanding compensation. By denouncing the terrorist acts and upholding their commitment to Kurdish autonomy, the CPA and the Kurdish nationalist élite gained support at home and abroad. The popular thinking in the diaspora was that the United States was still interested in protecting Iraqi Kurds as well as other Kurdish groups, and was able to do so.

However, large gaps emerged between political promises and reality in post-Saddam Iraq, which helped turn peace-makers into potential peace-wreckers. Essential issues such as the nature of the Iraqi constitution, power-sharing and the status of Kirkuk remained neglected. The CPA and the transitional government failed to assist dispossessed Kurdish families who wanted to return to their original homes in Kirkuk, which had been confiscated by the Ba'athists, and to ensure the representation of Kurds in certain Kurdish-populated districts.[28] Worse still, UN Resolution 1546, passed in June 2004, made no mention of the special status of Kurdistan, Kurdish autonomy or the Kurdish right to veto as proposed in the TAL. Attempts to pacify Arab communities in the south kept Kurds from attaining two key posts as president or vice-president in the Interim Government, further discrediting the CPA's policies for a federal Iraq in which Kurdish autonomy was an integral aspect.

Non-partisan and pan-Kurdish diasporic community leaders hoped the homeland élite would have taken a stand against the Bush administration on behalf Kurdish interests and the larger Kurdish nation. Instead, Barzani and Talabani adopted a strategy that attempted to work with the Iraqi government to reverse the injustices perpetrated against Kurds by Ba'athist Arabization policies, while continuing to negotiate Kurdish interests in a federated Iraq. They also made short-term compromises on

Kirkuk. Immediately after the liberation of Kirkuk, they withdrew Kurdish militia forces from the city and then started talking about its multinational character, alongside its Kurdish origins.

Diasporic communities and populations in Iraqi Kurdistan were far less willing to negotiate away Kirkuk and essential Kurdish territories and criticized the US government and the Kurdish homeland élite. Some sent letters to Barzani and Talabani, calling them "traitors" for negotiating with Arab Iraqis and "selling out" Kurdish national identity. In London, non-partisan diasporic community leaders wrote an open letter to the KRG and Kurdish party representatives, urging the resolution of the Kirkuk issue before the proposed elections of January 2005 and according to the "geographical facts that Kirkuk and its provinces are part of Kurdistan in Iraq".[29] No longer willing to compromise Kurdish nationalism and less interested in seeking ways to gain influence in Baghdad, Iraqi Kurds abroad joined the Kurdish referendum movement, which originated in Iraqi Kurdistan and called for an independent Kurdistan separate from the rest of Iraq.

Growing criticisms of Barzani and Talabani, in conjunction with those made by Kurds in the homeland, made compromises over Kirkuk and essential Kurdish territories increasingly difficult to sustain. Over time, Kurdish party representatives abroad found themselves with a deeper role of having to respond to negative interventions by the diaspora. One Kurdish party representative in Washington, DC, stated,

> Our brothers in the diaspora are a thorn in our side. They are so nationalistic that it hurts our cause rather than helps it. They are constantly demanding the Kurdish masses to work against the Kurdish leadership and are too frequently criticizing them, rather than trying to mobilize themselves through lobbying and activism, to alter their host government policies towards Kurdistan. Their strong statements, if followed by the Kurdish leadership, will only get us into more conflicts. This is not about so-called lack of nationalism, but rather, our leaders dealing with the lousy hand the Kurds have been dealt with and making the most of it.[30]

By July 2004, having become further alienated from the CPA's "negotiation processes" and prospects for real federalism in Iraq, the homeland élite also threatened to withdraw from the Baghdad government if parts of the TAL were not implemented.

As Iraqi Kurdish autonomy assumed increasing significance in post-Saddam Iraq, and the Bush administration continued to delegitimize or ignore the other Kurdish problems in the region, Kurdish leftist-nationalists from Turkey became less willing to maintain their policy of neutrality. Some developed ideological differences with the anti-war movement, which offered no viable solution to Saddam Hussein and no particular support to the Kurds. Yet, they did not turn to Iraqi Kurdish communities to express their nationalist claims. In fact, tensions increased with Iraqi Kurds at home and abroad after the Iraqi transitional government, including Barzani and Talabani, declared the PKK/Kongra-Gel a terrorist group in April 2004, while making concessions to the Turkish government. One Kurdish representative of the Halkevi Turkish/Kurdish Community Centre in London remarked:

> We all feel happy and positive for Kurds in Iraq; however, there is some resentment. We are larger and our problem is serious, yet there is no mention of us, nor the Kurds in Syria and Iran. Kurds in Iraq are supported, and their leaders are also supporting Turkey against Kurds in Turkey. Now, we no longer want to be part of the US. We were wrong. Kurds from Turkey are more excluded than before and during the war. Our position is worse now than before.[31]

Even then, the PKK/Kongra-Gel, which terminated its ceasefire with Turkey in 2004, maintained a policy of non-intervention in Iraq. Most nationalists turned their energies toward Europe, where Kurds from Turkey had a direct stake in Turkey's candidature for the European Union and the required reforms that could create democracy and peace in their own region of Kurdistan in Turkey.

Policy implications for external actors

Variations in Kurdish interventions in the Iraq war reveal the influence of externally created opportunity structures on diasporic group behaviour. Foreign governments were able to encourage positive interventions by giving diasporic leaders, the homeland nationalist élite and their organizations a direct stake in the war's outcome and involving them in policy dialogues. By promising to protect Kurdish autonomy in a democratic, federal Iraq, the Bush administration initially encouraged peace-makers within Kurdish communities at home and abroad. It legitimized Kurdish nationalist claims by integrating the Iraqi Kurdish homeland élite and KRG representatives abroad in US wartime planning and giving them a direct stake in post-war reconstruction programmes. These leverage points created a willingness among Iraqi Kurds to work with, and not against, international institutions and foreign governments.

The use of democratic discourse alongside a pro-Iraqi Kurdish position also discouraged negative interventions from the Kurdish leftist-nationalist diasporic community from Turkey. Radicalized Kurds from Turkey, normally troublemakers, did not become serious peace-wreckers because the potential outcome – a federal and democratic Iraq – served as a reference point for resolving their own nationalist claims in Turkey.

By temporarily cooling relations with the Turkish government and criticizing radical Arab nationalists in Syria, the US government gave the impression, at least in the eyes of Kurds at home and abroad, that it was serious about changing the status quo for Kurds in the region. European governments and non-governmental organizations, with their anti-war movements and proposal for integrating Turkey into the European Union, also discouraged radical Kurdish groups from engaging in violence by providing a legal anti-war forum in which leftist groups could channel their criticisms in a peaceful manner.

How, then, did peace-makers turn into potential peace-wreckers in Iraq? The huge discrepancies that emerged between pre-war promises and wartime realities altered the stakes in the war's outcome and the opportunity structures for Kurdish communities. By disengaging Iraqi Kurds from essential decision-making processes after June 2004, by abandoning the TAL and by conducting back-door negotiations without the consent of the Kurdistan homeland élite, the Bush administration altered or removed important leverage points while weakening its credibility among Kurdish communities. Kurds became less willing to negotiate autonomy within the territorial borders of Iraq because they were placed outside legitimate policy-making networks and political structures.

Also, although external actors talked about political autonomy for the Kurds and about democracy in Iraq, they failed to consider the impact of these opportunity structures on cross-border Kurdish groups and other diasporic communities. The Bush administration implemented ad hoc measures that promised Kurdish autonomy in a federal Iraq; however, at no point did US officials attempt to develop a sustainable Kurdish policy in Iraq or a long-term resolution of the larger Kurdish problem in the region. Indeed, the Iraq war directly concerned Kurds in and from Iraq. Certain alliance structures were therefore necessary to ensure military operational success. However, by treating Kurdish nationalism in Iraq as an isolated issue and remaining silent about the Kurdish problems in neighbouring states, the Bush administration, foreign governments and the United Nations ultimately discredited their claims to democracy and Kurdish autonomy. They also antagonized potential allies among Kurdish populations in the region and the diaspora.

Given the pan-ethnic component of Kurdish nationalism, conflict resolution in Iraq and the Kurdistan region cannot be considered a three-way process but, rather, is a multi-level game in which different Kurdish communities negotiate simultaneously with regional and host states, central governments, non-state actors and one another to secure shared and distinct political objectives. To encourage and sustain positive diasporic interventions, external actors need to develop a more nuanced and even-handed policy that addresses the larger Kurdish problem in the region, alongside a specific policy toward Iraqi Kurds. Policies that denounce radical groups and fight terrorism should coincide with recognition and support for moderate diasporic groups from all parts of Kurdistan that support democratic principles. Failure to differentiate between the two will only fuel resentment and turn potential peace-makers into peace-wreckers.

Policy implications for Kurdish diasporic groups

The interventionist role played by the diaspora in protecting Kurdish nationalism from afar, restraining the homeland élite and channelling claims through international human rights organizations, pan-Kurdish institutes and European anti-war networks assured legitimacy and significance for Kurdish claims-making at the international level. The diaspora's unwillingness to negotiate Kirkuk at any cost sent a strong message to the US government and the homeland élite about the limits to compromising Kurdish nationalism in Iraq. Some interventions, such as the mobilization against the deployment of Turkish troops, helped prevent the potentially destabilizing effects of the presence of Turkish military forces in Iraqi Kurdistan. Others, such as assisting in designing the law for the transition period, had more long-lasting effects by establishing a legal basis for Kurdish claims for a permanent constitution in a federal Iraq.

Nonetheless, although the diaspora was able to make a difference to the war's outcome, its role in shaping final policy decisions by the Bush administration and the Iraqi government was limited. Asymmetrical political opportunity structures made available for different groups within the territorially fragmented ethno-national Kurdish diasporic community impeded cohesive interventions by the larger diaspora as a whole. Different organizational structures, ideologies and political allegiances kept communities from Iraq and Turkey apart and prevented the development of a unified policy that could have effectively mobilized the larger diasporic community and influenced foreign governments. For instance, although the Kurdish diaspora from Turkey represents about 75 per cent of the total Kurdish diaspora and maintains a highly organized and mobilizable community, its resources were not positively channelled toward the Iraqi Kurdish élite or Iraqi Kurdish diasporic activities. The vast majority of Kurds from Turkey did not participate in the reconstruction programmes in post-Saddam Iraq. Most focused on the Kurdish problem in Turkey.

Nor were the homeland nationalist élite and their party representatives very receptive to non-partisan and pan-Kurdish diasporic organizations.

The relatively simple organizational structure in Iraqi Kurdish politics allowed decision-making to remain tied to the two main Kurdish leaders and their political parties. Instead of capitalizing on diasporic experience and resources by turning to international Kurdish organizations and their pan-Kurdish community leaders, the Iraqi Kurdish élite relied on its political party representatives at home and abroad to influence US policy. "Outside Kurds" had less credibility than "inside Kurds", which prevented a formal and continuous relationship from being established between the two communities. Policies implemented by the United States, foreign governments and the Iraqi government reinforced these dichotomies by channelling demands to Barzani and Talabani and their party representatives instead of to non-partisan diasporic leaders, human rights groups or pan-Kurdish organizations.

For example, the Kurdish Human Rights Project (KHRP) is a highly influential organization that consults with foreign governments and the European Parliament. During the war the KHRP conducted research inside Iraqi Kurdistan as well as Chatham House-type talks about establishing operations in Iraq. Yet at no point did the Iraqi Kurdish homeland élite attempt to coordinate with the KHRP.[32] Rather, it put more effort into working with non-Kurdish NGOs outside the region or with newly hired American lobbying firms that represented Iraqi Kurdish interests in Washington, DC.

The central role of the homeland nationalist élite and its party representatives and the limited role of non-partisan, pan-Kurdish communities have further implications for Kurdish diasporic politics. If the larger Kurdish diaspora wants to play a more serious role in international, regional and national politics outside its victim status, it needs to attain greater clout that could increase its influence, as have mature diasporas such as the Jews, Greeks and Armenians. Strengthening diasporic influence requires developing professional, educated cadres at home and abroad that can effectively lobby foreign governments, financial institutions and the global media. It also requires non-partisan diasporic leaders and organizations to maintain a realistic view of the geographical, political and economic constraints on the homeland élite in different parts of Kurdistan. Those groups that engage in political extremism or refuse to compromise Kurdish interests for the larger objective of economic growth and political stability are likely to impede, rather than advance, Kurdish national interests in the long term. A more effective Kurdish diaspora also requires formal linkages, ongoing dialogue and a clear, cohesive policy shared by the homeland and key diasporic community leaders. Visionary leadership is needed to unite Kurdish diasporic communities and integrate the diverse Kurdish resources into the homeland political economy.

Conclusions

Kurdish diasporic interventions during different phases of the Iraq war were a function of changing political opportunity structures at home and abroad. Open political spaces in democratic host countries and different migration experiences strengthened the sense of pan-Kurdish nationalism while creating greater diversity in diasporic organizations and claims-making. Instead of building upon pan-Kurdish ethnicity, the POS linked to the Iraq war reinforced the dichotomies between politicized Kurds from different countries of origin and prevented cohesive interventions by the diasporic community.

Some political opportunity structures supported peace-makers and others encouraged potential peace-wreckers. Iraqi Kurds had a direct and vested interest in the war's outcome and greater incentives to nego-tiate their nationalist claims peacefully than did the Kurdish communities from Turkey, which remained peripheral to the war planning, delegiti-mized by the American government and indirectly affected by the war's consequences. Iraqi Kurdish diasporas mitigated conflict by compromis-ing their quasi-independent status to help construct and participate in a more inclusive federal democratic political system for all Iraqis. By actively engaging in post-conflict peace-building with the US government and international organizations, Iraqi Kurds helped assure human rights and democratic principles in Kurdish and Iraqi institutions. Radicalized Kurds from Turkey played an indirect role in preventing conflict in Iraq. Their policy of neutrality prevented the type of intra-Kurdish conflicts that marked the pre-war period and allowed economic and political development while the rest of the country was embroiled in civil war. However, as the parameters of the war changed and US guarantees of Kurdish autonomy lost credibility, non-partisan and pan-Kurdish com-munities became increasingly critical of the homeland élite and less will-ing to negotiate Kurdish autonomy within the territorial boundaries of a federal Iraq.

Fluctuations in Kurdish interventions reveal that there is nothing pre-determined about Kurdish nationalism or diasporic roles in homeland politics. Preventing Kurdish peace-makers from becoming future peace-wreckers requires credible foreign and domestic policies that maintain high leverage points for Kurdish nationalist communities. These points should include guarantees of Kurdish autonomy as stated in the Transi-tional Administrative Law of Iraq and the creation of a long-term agenda that addresses the other Kurdish problems as part of the democratization processes in the region. External policies should weaken the blatant divi-sions that have emerged between Kurdish nationalist claims in Iraq and those made by Kurds in Turkey and other regional states. The Kurdish case reveals that legitimized diasporic networks have a greater chance of encouraging peace-making activities than do those that are delegitimized or ignored in the international arena.

Acknowledgements

I would like to thank the United States Institute of Peace for financial support from its solicited grant program (SG-054-02S), Metin Achard for his research assistance, and the Washington Kurdish Institute, NA-VEND Zentrum für Kurdische Studien in Bonn and L'Institut Kurde de Paris for their resources and administrative support while I was in the United States, Germany, England, France and Iraqi Kurdistan. All findings and conclusions are my own and do not represent the views of supporting agencies or individuals.

Notes

1. The issue of whether peace can be achieved through violence or negotiation is a normative one. One can argue that peace was in effect achieved for Iraqi Kurds by overthrowing Saddam Hussein and protecting Kurdish rights in the state. In this analysis, however, peace-making (mitigating conflict) is regarded as the efforts by diasporic leaders to compromise with post-Saddam governments by negotiating Kurdish claims inside a federal Iraq. Similarly, peace-wrecking (encouraging conflict) refers to the refusal to negotiate Kurdish nationalist claims by resorting to political extremism and violence. This approach assumes that failure to compromise Kurdish nationalism during the sensitive pre- and post-war period would have a greater chance of instigating civil war than keeping the country territorially intact through political negotiation.
2. Denise Natali, *The Kurds and the State: Evolving National Identity in Iraq, Turkey, and Iran*, Syracuse: Syracuse University Press, 2005.
3. In 2005, Kongra-Gel reassumed its original name, the PKK.
4. Interview with Salar Bassireh, member of the Green Party, Dusseldorf, Germany, 13 July 2003.
5. Nina Glick Schiller, Linda Basch and Cristina Szanton Blanc, "From Immigrant to Transmigrant: Theorizing Transmigration", in Ludger Pries, ed., *Migration and Transnational Social Spaces*, Aldershot: Ashgate, 1999, p. 82; Stanley J. Tambiah, "Transnational Movements, Diaspora, and Multiple Modernities", *Daedalus*, 2000, 129(1): 179; Thomas Faist, *The Volume and Dynamics of International Migration and Transnational Social Spaces*, London: Oxford University Press, 2000, p. 15; Yossi Shain, "The Role of Diasporas in Conflict Perpetuation or Resolution", *SAIS Review*, 2002, 22(2): 116; and Gabriel Sheffer, *Diaspora Politics: At Home Abroad*, Cambridge: Cambridge University Press, 2003, p. 52.
6. NAVEND, *Rechtliche Situation und Integrationsperspektiven von Kurdischen Migrant-Innen*, Bonn: NAVEND, 2002, p. 17.
7. Birgit Ammann, "KurdInnen in der Bundesrepublik Deutschland", in Markus Ottersbach and Felix Weiland, eds, *KurdInnen in der Bundesrepublik Deutschland*, Bonn: NA-VEND, 1999, pp. 39–40.

8. Interview with Haji Namik, former representative in the KRG, Bonn, 14 July 2003.

9. Interview with Salar Bassireh, Dusseldorf, 13 July 2003.

10. Beth Schaefer Caniglia, "Elite Alliances and Transnational Environment Movement Organizations" in Jackie Smith and Hank Johnston, eds, *Globalization and Resistance: Transnational Dimensions of Social Movements*, Lanham, MD: Rowman & Littlefield, 2002, p. 155; Gregory M. Maney, "Transnational Structures and Protests: Linking Theories and Assessing Evidence" in Jackie Smith and Hank Johnston, eds, *Globalization and Resistance*, pp. 32–37; and Sidney Tarrow, *Power in Movement: Social Movements, Collective Action and Politics*, Cambridge: Cambridge University Press, 1994, p. 18.

11. For further historical sources on the Kurdish diaspora, see Osten Wahlbeck, *Kurdish Diasporas*, Basingstoke: Palgrave, 1999; David Griffiths, *Somali and Kurdish Refugees in London: New Identities in the Diaspora*, Aldershot: Ashgate, 2002; and Omar Sheikhmous, "The Kurds in Exile", Yearbook of the Kurdish Academy, Ratingen, 1990.

12. Bernard Falga, Catherine Wihtol de Wenden and Claus Leggewie, *De l'immigration à l'intégration en France et en Allemagne*, Paris: Les Editions du Cerf, 1994, pp. 112–113.

13. Desmond Fernandes, "The Targeting and Criminalisation of Kurdish Asylum Seekers and Refugee Communities in the UK and Germany", Peace in Kurdistan Campaign and The Ahmed Foundation for Kurdish Studies, London, 2001, and Isabelle Rigoni, "Les mobilisations des Kurdes en Europe", *Revue Européene des Migrations Internationals*, 1998, 14(3): 203–223.

14. For discussions of Kurds and other diasporas facing analogous situations, see Eva Ostergaard-Nielsen, *Transnational Politics: Turks and Kurds in Germany*, London: Routledge, 2003, p. 83; Ruud Koopmans and Paul Statham, "Migration and Ethnic Relations as a Field of Political Contention: An Opportunity Structure Approach", in Ruud Koopmans and Paul Statham, eds, *Challenging Immigration and Ethnic Relations Politics*, Oxford: Oxford University Press, 2000, p. 39; and Hanspeter Kriesi, et al., *New Social Movements in Western Europe: A Comparative Analysis*, London: University College, 1995, p. 18.

15. Interview with Metin Incesu, NAVEND Zentrum, Bonn, 9 July 2003.

16. Interview with Omar Sheikhmous, Voice of America, Washington, DC, 30 July 2004.

17. Tambiah, "Transnational Movements, Diaspora, and Multiple Modernities", p. 163.

18. Interview with Mullah Showkat, Centre Culturel et Information Kurde de France, Paris, 6 February 2003.

19. Interview with Salar Hussein, Kurdish Association for Refugees, London Borough of Hammersmith and Fulham, London, 31 March 2003.

20. Caniglia, "Elite Alliances and Transnational Environment Movement Organizations", p. 155; and Maney, "Transnational Structures and Protests", pp. 31–50.

21. Interview with Qubad Talabani, KRG Suleymaniya representative, Washington, DC, 31 July 2004.

22. Interview with Estella Schmidt, Peace in Kurdistan Campaign, London, 15 July 2004.

23. Interview with Ibrahim Doğuş, Halkevi Kurdish/Turkish Community Centre, London, 14 July 2004.

24. Interview with Faiq Yagizay, DEHAP representative in Europe, London, 15 July 2004.

25. Nomi Bar-Yaacov, "Diplomacy and Human Rights: The Role of Human Rights in Conflict Resolution in El Salvador and Haiti", *Fletcher Forum of World Affairs*, 1995, 19(2): 48.

26. Interview with Shaykh Mohammed Sargalo, Suleymaniya, Iraqi Kurdistan, 13 December 2003.

27. Gil Loescher, "Protection and Humanitarian Action in the Post-Cold War Era", in Aristide R. Zolberg and Peter M. Benda, eds, *Global Migrants, Global Refugees*, New York: Berghahn Books, 2001, pp. 171–204.

28. For instance, the Turkmen districts of Yaichi and the Kurdish districts of Karahenjir, Shwan and Sergarani were all destroyed by Saddam Hussein. The CPA decided to include representatives of Yaichi on the council for the province, but not the other three Kurdish districts. Interview with Serbest Kirkuki, Kurdish Cultural Centre (KCC), London, 14 July 2004.

29. In a letter dated 3 July 2004, Kurdish community leaders in London urged Barzani and Talabani to resolve the following points or refuse to participate in the proposed January 2005 elections: (1) recognition of Kirkuk province as a historical and geographical part of Kurdistan in Iraq as a whole province including Kifri, Doz, Chamchemal and Kalar; (2) further unity and assistance between the two main political parties; and (3) removal of every aspect of Arabization in Kirkuk city and permission for more than 200,000 Kurdish Kirkukis to return to their original homes. Interview with Serbest Kirkuki, KCC, London, 15 July 2004.

30. Interview with Qubad Talabani, KRG Suleymaniya representative, Washington, DC, 31 July 2004.

31. Interview with Ibrahim Doğuş, Halkevi Turkish/Kurdish Community Centre, London, 13 July 2004.

32. Interview with Karim Yildiz, Kurdish Human Rights Project, London, 14 July 2004.

11

The mobilized Croatian diaspora: Its role in homeland politics and war

Zlatko Skrbiš

In the final decade of the twentieth century, Croatia was involved in one of the most brutal military conflicts in post–World War II Europe.[1] When the Yugoslav Republics of Croatia and Slovenia proclaimed independence from Yugoslavia on 25 June 1991, these acts also marked a decisive shift towards the disintegration of the former Yugoslav state and the emergence of a hot conflict in some parts of the former Yugoslavia, particularly Croatia, Bosnia and Herzegovina and, towards the end of the 1990s, Kosovo. Through material and symbolic mobilization, the Croatian diaspora played an integral and decisive, yet mostly indirect, role in these processes.[2]

This chapter draws on the Croatian diaspora experience and interrogates the key dilemma raised in this volume: did the diaspora perform the role of peace-wrecker or peace-maker? If the results of the ethnographic research conducted among the Croatian diaspora during the conflict period are taken into account,[3] then the answer to this question is fairly clear. The research shows that during the conflict, in addition to identity issues that such circumstances bring to the fore, the diaspora population was overwhelmingly preoccupied with three interdependent goals: the protection of a newly independent homeland, the cessation of hostilities once the war broke out, and, ultimately, peace. Clearly, the members of the Croatian diaspora were overwhelmingly interested in pursuing each of these goals. However, linking these three issues opens up a number of additional questions that help us answer the question about what role the diaspora played in the conflict. First, in this constellation of factors, what

Diasporas in conflict: Peace-makers or peace-wreckers?, Smith and Stares (eds), United Nations University Press, 2007, ISBN 978-92-808-1140-7

is the relative value of peace vis-à-vis the cessation of hostilities and protection of the independent status of the homeland? Second, who defines the parameters of "peace"? Finally, could there be a discrepancy between the peace-directed intentions of a diaspora population and the possibility of their involvement prolonging a conflict on the ground? In this chapter, I argue that these questions can be answered only if the diaspora–homeland interactions are put in historical context. The question of diaspora involvement in the conflict is but one critical stage in the long-term constitution of the diaspora, which stretches over decades. The diaspora's contribution to conflict and peace can be understood only through such a historically sensitized lens.

The argument in this chapter will proceed as follows. The next section will discuss some aspects of the contested term "diaspora" that are particularly relevant to this case study, and then discuss the origins of the post–World War II Croatian diaspora. This historical outline is crucial for the argument of this chapter – without it, one cannot understand why the Croatian diaspora was so easily and effectively mobilized in this conflict. The rest of the chapter will proceed through an examination of four stages of the conflict cycle. These stages are linked in important ways to Bercovitch's model outlined in Chapter 2, yet they accommodate the distinct characteristics of the Croatian diaspora–homeland nexus. The stages are as follows:

(a) pre-conflict (before the mid-1980s)
(b) escalatory (mid-1987 to 1991)
(c) hot conflict (1991–1995)
(d) post-conflict and peace-building (after the 1995 Dayton Peace Accord).

Dimensions of diaspora politics

This section explores several broad theoretical themes that underline the contemporary scholarship on diasporas, which have direct relevance to the involvement of the Croatian diaspora in the homeland conflict. The first dimension is conceptual and definitional, and addresses the contestable nature of the term "diaspora". The second is historical and relates to the emergence of diasporas as key players in global politics since World War II, and particularly in the post–Cold War period. The third dimension concerns diasporas' inherent capacity to act as a mobilizable resource in transnational politics. Finally, such transnational involvement of diasporas raises new and complex ethical questions that require attention and analysis.

Definitional dilemmas

The existing literature understands diaspora as a contestable term.[4] Even though diaspora is an analytical category with no clear boundaries, I suggest that there are some key characteristics that members of diasporas have in common:

1. a sense of group identity based on ethnic self- and other ascriptions;
2. a sense of banishment from the homeland (real or imaginary) and an accompanying perception of alienation from the homeland;
3. a belief in collective and individual mission, which may include nostalgic yearnings for the homeland and the myth of return;
4. a continuing interaction with the homeland that can be either physical (through visits or telephone calls) or imaginary.

Two essential aspects of diasporas are captured in these characteristics. First, they indicate that diasporic identity is necessarily forged with reference to a group or community. And, second, they recognize what tends to be rendered invisible in most existing definitions of diasporas: the important role that subjective, imaginative and emotional elements play in shaping diasporic identities. It is often these subjective and emotional factors that enable the effective mobilization of members of diasporas and transform them from dormant to mobilized entities.[5] The case of the Croatian diaspora, and many other diasporas that have intervened decisively in homeland conflicts, can be used to illustrate this point.

Historical dimension

Although diasporas have been known for their capacity to intervene effectively in homeland affairs for more than a century, the number of diasporas has grown substantially and most have been increasing in size since the end of World War II. They have also become better organized and more involved in homeland politics and/or conflicts. The Jewish case is paradigmatic of this new role. More recently, in the post–Cold War era, a number of previously dormant diasporas have become actively involved in homeland politics. Two key reasons are behind this: global restructuring and the realignment of ethno-national units in the post–Cold War era; and the increased capacity of individual actors and social groups to respond rapidly, and effectively, to homeland crises on a transnational scale. This means that contemporary diasporas have the capacity to play an increasingly influential role in host-land and homeland politics and to do so on a scale that was unimaginable even a few decades ago.[6] Examples of this abound in as distant and different places as Israel, Ireland, Haiti, Iraq, Iran, Greece, Kosovo, Lithuania and Somalia.

Mobilizational capacity

The capacity of diasporas to be mobilized and co-opted into conflicts in the homeland is often thematized as one of the central dimensions of diaspora politics. In his classic account, Armstrong discusses the role that mobilized diasporas played in the politics of old empires.[7] Given the capacity of individuals efficiently and inexpensively to breach the previously formidable barriers of time and space, the question of transnational mobilization of diasporas is more pertinent today than ever before. Sheffer also emphasizes that diasporas have often been unjustly portrayed as "predisposed to disruption and conflict" rather than to the facilitation of "peaceful cultural, political, trade, and commercial exchanges".[8] Such concerns can effectively be dismissed if diasporas are examined in their individual specificities, taking into account historical and political circumstances that shape and influence them. The Croatian diaspora, along with the Jewish and many others, has displayed both tendencies quite strongly.

Ethical dilemmas

The increased ability of migrants to act transnationally epitomizes the new complexities of contemporary diaspora politics, including the fear among members of the host society of divided political and ethnic loyalties. These concerns are by no means new. For example, in the 1860s in the United States, a group of American Irish Fenians decided to liberate Ireland by invading Canada – few, not even the Archbishop, were impressed.[9] Campbell asserts that the Irish-Americans appeared to be "more concerned with the plight of their ancestral home than with their new country".[10] Eight decades later, during World War II, the concerns over disjuncture between the ethnic and host country loyalties of diaspora populations were behind the internment of Japanese-Americans and Italian-Australians.[11] Today, in the era of the "War on Terror", UK-, US- and Australian-based Arab diasporas confront a similarly suspicious reception because of their supposedly divided loyalties.

In his work on long-distance nationalism, Anderson makes a pertinent comment about the ethics of diaspora populations' participating in homeland politics.[12] For him, diaspora involvement is inevitably irresponsible. Diasporas, or "long-distance nationalists" as Anderson calls them, tend to "play identity politics" by participating in the politics of their "imagined *Heimat*" but without paying the price for the actions they undertake and being an easy prey for "shrewd political manipulators".[13]

Although one can disagree with Anderson's assertion about the inevitably irresponsible nature of diaspora politics, there is no doubt that any intervention of diasporas in a homeland conflict opens up a series of previously unknown ethical questions about contemporary political affairs. Perhaps the most common aspect of diaspora participation that gives rise to such ethical questions is the diaspora population's participation in fund-raising activities, which are commonly enveloped in secrecy.[14] Although the details of these transactions are notoriously difficult to obtain, they are an integral element of any diasporic mobilization. Fund-raising has played an integral role in the process of Croatian diaspora mobilization and will be addressed later in this chapter.

Pre-conflict stage

The possibility of successful mobilization of a diaspora group correlates with its organizational, symbolic and ideological homogeneity. The level of homogeneity is, in turn, associated with a sense of shared historical destiny, the experience of exile and persecution, a sense of banishment from the homeland, and a desire to return – in short, the factors identified in the previous section as defining elements of a diaspora existence. This chapter argues that any analysis of diaspora involvement in conflict must understand diaspora as a category located on a historical continuum. It is the historical factors that shape a diaspora that are predictive of its members' capacity to be mobilized.

In this section, the argument begins with a brief overview of the early phases of the Croatian diaspora but focuses on the pre-conflict period, encompassing the time between the end of World War II and the mid-1980s. This period may appear unusually long, but it was during this period that the Croatian diaspora, mobilized in the recent conflict, was constituted through various waves of migration. These migration waves were in no sense politically homogeneous. What they had in common, however, was a negative disposition toward the communist political establishment in the homeland, a belief in the systematic marginalization of everything Croatian in Yugoslavia, and a hope for (and propagation of) the eventual independence of Croatia.

The origin of the Croatian diaspora

Pre-World War II period and the emergence of ustaša

For Croatia, as a coastal country, emigration has been an integral part of its history.[15] According to Prpić, around 1.2 million Croatians emigrated before World War II, mostly to North America (620,000), South America (170,000), the East (275,000) and the rest of Europe (70,000).[16] Few of these migrants had a strong sense of being Croatian. Most of them have identified, typically for the era, with the region of origin (e.g. Dalmatia, Slavonia) rather than with Croatian nationality.[17] The migrants in this period were also strongly influenced by the ideology of Yugoslavism and had leftist political leanings.[18]

After World War I, Croatia became an integral part of the new Kingdom of Serbs, Croats and Slovenes, later re-named Yugoslavia, under the Serb dynasty of Aleksandar Karadjordjević. In 1928, when Radić, a Croatian parliamentarian, was assassinated in Belgrade, the tensions between the Serbs and Croats escalated. The Croats insisted on recognition of their cultural and national distinctiveness as an antidote to the Serb domination of key institutions in the new state.[19] In direct response to these tensions, Croatian militant groups were formed outside Yugoslavia.[20] These diasporic groups were led by Ante Pavelić and formed the *ustaša* (Ustasha) movement, whose members trained in camps from Italy to Argentina, and sought to liberate their homeland from Serb domination.

Mussolini's sponsorship and German backing propelled Pavelić's Ustasha back into the homeland in April 1941 and allowed it to establish the puppet state of the Independent State of Croatia (1941–1945). Although Croatian people initially welcomed the new state, seeing it as the culmination of their historical aspirations, many became disillusioned with the brutality of the new Ustasha regime and its killing of thousands of Serbs, communists, Jews and Roma. It was the sizeable Serb minority in Croatia that was the focus of this brutal extermination policy.[21] Even though Pavelić's Ustasha regime and the Independent State of Croatia collapsed in 1945, the remaining members of the movement and their dreams for an independent state exerted considerable influence over the post–World War II Croatian diaspora.

Reconstitution of the politicized Croatian diaspora in the post–World War II period

After the collapse of the Independent State of Croatia, Croatia became a republic within the new socialist Yugoslav state led by Josip Broz Tito and the Communist Party.[22] At the end of the war, Pavelić, his forces and his sympathizers, fearing the reprisals of Tito's new communist regime, became part of a massive flow of refugees across Europe involving more than 25 million individuals. The statistics on how many of these refugees were Croatian is unavailable but the numbers were in tens of thousands.[23] Immediately after the communist takeover in Yugoslavia, Tito's regime feared the formation of political and ideological opposition outside Yugoslavia's borders and orchestrated the execution of the fleeing refugees, predominantly the Ustasha soldiers.[24] The key Ustasha figure, Pavelić, and his circle escaped and sought refuge in Spain and Argentina.

This post-war victimization of Croatians had two important implications for the constitution of a Croatian diasporic identity. First, the massacres of Croatian refugees, and the associated trauma of those who survived and sympathized, provided a fertile source for diaspora anti-communism. Second, the surviving refugees, including many suspected war criminals, were transferred (predominantly legally) to Canada, South Africa, Australia, the United States and South America. Upon settlement in the host countries, these individuals became pivotal in the process of setting up Croatian diaspora communities. These communities have been intensely politicized and founded upon the experience of collective trauma and nostalgic memories of the independent state. Importantly, these post–World War II refugee settlers made no effort to establish a connection with the existing, pre–World War II communities, which were suspected of harbouring pro-communist and pro-Yugoslav tendencies and, hence, treated with suspicion.[25]

Many who joined the ranks of the Croatian diaspora after the initial post–World War II wave were economic migrants. Because the Yugoslav borders were closed until the early 1960s, when the Yugoslav communist regime embarked on a series of economic reforms, these economic migrants had to leave the country illegally.[26] This forced them to seek political asylum to achieve repatriation to a third country, usually an overseas one. Their refugee experience, however, made them forge links with the existing nationalist and anti-Yugoslav clubs and associations. By the time that emigration from Yugoslavia was legalized, these associations were clearly dominant and attracting an ever-growing number of migrant members. Although most migrants were economic, some political migrants also joined the diaspora around 1971 when the Croatian communist leadership, quite independently from the central government, spearheaded the process of political liberalization, which it mixed with a nationalist agenda. This process became known as the "Mass Movement" or "the Croatian Spring".[27] The suppression of the Croatian Spring by Tito's communist leadership resulted in the emigration of a number of people who had joined the movement. Many of these migrants, disillusioned with the socialist regime, found solace in the radical anti-communism and nationalist politics of the Croatian diaspora.

In this pre-conflict period, Croatian diaspora organizations were often fiercely vocal on the topic of opposition to the homeland political regime, but were, for the most part, safely non-interventionist. However, there are three exceptions worth mentioning. The first was an exile-led assault on socialist Yugoslavia by several small groups of exiles directed by Pavelić and his followers in 1946–1947. They expected to incite insurrection among the remaining sympathizers in Yugoslavia, but miscalculated the ability of the new Tito government effectively to suppress any such attempt. In fact, Tito's government used these incidents for showcase trials and executions as a way of asserting its grip on power and suppressing any desire for revolt among the population. The second case involved a group of about 20 commandos from primarily pro-Ustasha groups in Australia who decided to liberate the homeland from communism in 1972 by igniting popular revolt. They held out for a few weeks, but were later killed by the Yugoslav army.[28] The third case was in 1972 when members of the Croatian diaspora hijacked a Scandinavian Air DC-9,[29] and in 1976 a group of Croatian émigrés hijacked a Trans World Airlines flight out of New York City.[30]

These militant actions were celebrated amongst some sectors of the Croatian diaspora but, from the perspective of their impact on the homeland political regime, they were either counterproductive, or non-consequential, or both. If anything, these examples reveal the fundamental failure of the diaspora to understand the situation in the homeland, as well as a mistaken belief in its own capacity to influence events there. The Yugoslav regime under Tito was more cohesive and stable than the diaspora was willing to accept. Clearly, the end of communism in Yugoslavia could not be achieved by external intervention by the diaspora; rather, it would require changes in the political circumstances within the homeland. The first signs of these changes started to appear following the death of Tito in 1980.

By the time of Tito's death, the Croatian diaspora was, despite its internal diversity, already constituted as pro-independence, which also implied an anti-Yugoslavist and anti-communist platform. It was, however, isolated and lacked a corresponding movement in the homeland. Forced to wait for changes in the homeland, the diaspora worked in the meantime to preserve a traditionalist and folkloric expression of Croatianism in an attempt to protect it from the polluting influences of Yugoslavism and communist ideology. It was hoped that eventually a return to Croatia would be possible.[31]

The death of Tito and the destabilization of Yugoslavia – Implications for diaspora–homeland relations

Tito's death left a vacuum in the political leadership. As Ramet puts it: "He bequeathed to his country a system without a king, without even a president; it was a system without a center, a ship without a captain."[32] Most importantly, the political system, which had been so heavily dependent upon Tito's charisma, had lost its capacity to mend any social and political differences through his cult of personality. The collective presidency, a forum of leaders from different republics and autonomous provinces, that replaced Tito's leadership faced an increasingly impossible task of balancing various political and ethnic particularisms. With an indebted economy, it was incapable of enforcing policies and progressive reforms.

These tensions were exacerbated with Slobodan Milošević's ascension to power in Serbia in 1987 on a wave of Serb nationalist uprising in Kosovo.[33] Among the Yugoslav political leaders, Milošević was the first clearly and openly to challenge what had previously been firmly established boundaries of acceptable political conduct in Yugoslavia. In particular, Milošević's political strategy broke the ultimate Yugoslav taboo: the use of nationalist rhetoric and slogans to animate and manipulate ethnic constituencies.

All of this had profound consequences, not only for the way in which politics was conducted in Yugoslavia, but also for the relationship between the Croatian homeland and the diaspora. The emerging Croatian dissident élites began to exploit the growing tension between the ethnic/nationalist and Yugoslav/"brotherhood and unity" politics. They began, at first slowly but then increasingly publicly, to promote the ideas of democratic pluralism and the end of the communist-dominated one-party system.

This brought the emerging dissident élites in the homeland ever closer to the position advocated by the Croatian diaspora. For members of the diaspora, the relatively rapid shift in homeland politics was rather surprising, and was initially greeted with mistrust and scepticism. What had previously appeared as an unresponsive and invisible communist opposition in the homeland was now an increasingly public and vocal agent of political change. The once unimaginable convergence between the homeland and the diasporic vision of the future of Croatia was now suddenly a realistic possibility. The way in which this possibility could be turned into reality was the key preoccupation of the escalatory stage of the conflict (1987–1991), as discussed in the next section.

Escalatory stage (1987–1991)

Tudjman and the meeting of the homeland and diaspora paradigms

The person who best represented the aspirations of the new dissident élites in the Croatia of the late 1980s was the historian Franjo Tudjman. A retired general in Tito's army, Tudjman was, perhaps, best known for his revisionist approach to historical claims regarding the number of victims of the Croatian Ustasha regime imprisoned in the Jesenovac concentration camp during World War II. In comparison with official statistics on the Serb, Jewish, communist and other victims of Ustasha brutalities, he downgraded their number several-fold.[34] His interest in this question was driven as much by his historical interest as by his nationalist ambition to minimize Croatian responsibility for these killings. In 1972, following the suppression of the Croatian Spring movement, he was imprisoned for two years as one of the protagonists of that movement. He was again imprisoned in 1982 for a series of interviews he gave to the foreign media. This dissident profile made him one of the most visible Croatian opposition figures in the second half of the 1980s.

Aware of the increasing synergies between the diaspora and the newly emerging democratization movement in Croatia, Tudjman embarked on a visit to the North American Croatian diaspora in mid-1987. This was the first meeting between a respected Croatian dissident, and protagonist of political change, and the Croatian diaspora. The purpose of the visit was to foster ties between the opposition movement in Croatia and the diaspora, and to open up the possibilities for receiving financial support for the opposition's political programme. Tudjman chose Toronto and Ottawa because they were two key sites of Croatian diaspora radicalism. Not surprisingly, as a former Tito general, his very presence proved so alarming that during his first visit "only 10 percent of Croat émigrés came to hear him speak, while the other 90 percent condemned ... the organiser for bringing him over".[35] During his visit to Canada, Tudjman confronted some important differences in perspective between the emerging democratic movement in Croatia and the views that were widely held amongst the diaspora. First, even in late 1987, Tudjman could not clearly "foresee the imminent collapse of socialist Yugoslavia, something the rightwing émigrés had assumed since 1946".[36] Second, although the more radical elements of the diaspora shared Tudjman's view that Bosnia was an artificial creation and denied the existence of Muslim identity (subscribing instead to the idea that Muslims are Croats who have forgotten their true origin), they differed on how to resolve the issue. The diaspora radicals advocated that Bosnia and Herzegovina should be conquered militarily. Tudjman, on the other hand, was in favour of a peaceful solution.[37] What this suggests is that, at this stage, the question of military conflict in the push towards an independent Croatian homeland was not clearly contemplated by Tudjman, although it became acute only a short time later. These first tentative contacts between the diaspora and the homeland took place against a background of a rapidly deteriorating economic situation and escalating ethnic tension in Yugoslavia.

Despite the differences, Tudjman's 1987 visit to Croatian diaspora organizations had far-reaching consequences for the development of homeland–diaspora relations, not least because it indicated to the diaspora that the changes in the homeland were rapid and real. At the same time, it allowed the diaspora to enter into a dialogue with a representative of the opposition in the homeland.

The homeland–diaspora contacts had a single purpose: ousting the communist government and taking concrete steps towards independence. The emerging dissident nationalist élite in the homeland was incapable of making much progress on either of these two fronts unless it could involve the diaspora in this struggle. Tudjman's visit to the diaspora was the first of what was to become a series of hundreds of meetings between diaspora organizations around the globe and representatives of the homeland opposition movement.

Within a year of Tudjman's visit, the diaspora was effectively mobilized and co-opted into the homeland's efforts to bring down the communist government. Tudjman and the party that he later came to personify – the Croatian Democratic Union (HDZ) – opened up a range of new possibilities for communication and exchange, which were directed towards enabling independence and ousting the communist government. Fundraising, discussed in the next section, was an essential element in this, and it was through this process that the diaspora began actively, although indirectly, to influence the events in the homeland, and this eventually led to its involvement in the conflict.

Fund-raising, national reconciliation and the rhetoric of return to the homeland

This section addresses three interconnected issues: fund-raising, the programme of national reconciliation, and the idea of return to the homeland. What binds these issues together is that they are symptoms of the co-dependent relationship that was gradually established between the homeland and the diaspora. Fund-raising was an act of goodwill on the part of the diaspora but was underpinned by an expectation that the new anti-communist opposition would pursue specific actions to accommodate diasporic needs and goals.

Fund-raising

Diaspora fund-raising for political causes in the homeland is inherently connected with the notion of patriotic duty, often mixed with a strong sense of nationalist sentiment.[38] There are many examples of successful and systematic fund-raising campaigns by communities and individuals. Perhaps the best-known example of financial transfers from diaspora to homeland, and indeed financial dependency on the diaspora, is the state of Israel. Sheffer reports that, in the late 1980s, one of the principal Jewish fund-raising organizations in the United States transferred US$500 million in a single year to Israel.[39] Yallop and Rabinovich similarly show how one of Australia's richest men, Joe Gutnick, decisively intervened in Israeli affairs through his donations, which were aimed at mobilizing the ultra-orthodox Jewish vote.[40] Examples in relation to other ethnic groups abound, including Fuglerud's insightful analysis into the various ways through which diaspora Tamils in Norway and elsewhere channel financial resources through complex global financial networks to the Tamil Liberation Tigers on the Jaffna peninsula.[41]

Fund-raising activities within diasporas are commonly enveloped in secrecy. Sheffer observes, for example, that accurate data on diaspora financial donations are difficult to obtain, with the notable exception of the Jewish Diaspora.[42] Reports of the amounts transferred to the Croatian homeland from various diaspora communities are highly unreliable and the figures vary widely, although very substantial financial assistance was sent to the homeland from 1988 onwards (see below). In the period before the hot conflict, most diaspora funds were used to finance the political activities of the anti-communist opposition – specifically the HDZ election campaign following the official launch of HDZ in 1989. Indeed, after the initial contact between the diaspora and the homeland, the specific purpose of the frequent visits of Croatian opposition representatives was to rally moral and political support and to translate this support into financial contributions. The point to emphasize is that, at this stage, contact between the diaspora and the homeland was designed not to work towards the prevention of the conflict, particularly with the Serbs, but to work towards Croatian independence. Such a project, however, required a high level of ideological and political homogenization, which was achievable only through the process of national reconciliation.

National reconciliation

A great deal of reciprocity was built into these arrangements. Diaspora contributions were based upon the expectation that the homeland anti-communist opposition would deliver on some key diaspora aspirations, the main one of which was independence. Equally importantly, the financial mobilization of the diaspora was predicated on the expectation of national reconciliation – that is, reconciliation between all Croatians, regardless of their past or present political orientations. This demand was primarily aimed at allowing members of the former Ustasha and their families to return to the homeland safely and without harassment, although it also safeguarded the communists. This promise of reconciliation made it possible to see a new independent Croatia as a universal home for all Croatians, much as Israel is considered a national home for Jews regardless of their origin and political aspirations. National reconciliation was also an important strategy of the homeland opposition movement aimed at political homogenization, which was needed successfully to overthrow the communist regime.

After its official launch as a political party, HDZ developed into a movement and a broad coalition. HDZ, led by Tudjman, presented reconciliation as its key party ambition but its aim was to secure an *en bloc* diaspora vote and effectively position HDZ as a united front for all Croatian people. The translation of this ambition into outcomes was achieved at a large gathering of diaspora representatives in Zagreb a few months before the first multi-party democratic election in Croatia in the spring of 1990. The event was organized by Tudjman and his HDZ, and the delegates arrived from the United States, Canada, Australia, South Africa, Germany, Norway, Sweden and Switzerland.[43] The key purpose of this gathering was to demonstrate HDZ's credentials as a unifying force for the Croatian people. The gathering clearly achieved that aim. But there were some other political benefits as well, including the building of closer ties between the diaspora and the homeland and the mobilization of a broad spectrum of diaspora Croatians (including the representatives of radical diaspora groups as well as the previously politically ambivalent Croatian guest workers who had dispersed in the countries of Western Europe).

Return to the homeland

This harmonization of relations between the homeland and the diaspora tapped into one of the key desires of the diaspora population: a return to the homeland. From my research work in Australia,[44] nostalgia for home and the possibility of returning is one of the most pervasive topics among the diaspora population, and Winland reported similar findings from her research among Canadian-Croatians.[45] The aspiration among migrants to return, and the promise by the Croatian anti-communist opposition to create a welcoming homeland for all Croatians, were frequently evoked during the fund-raising actions of diaspora. The possibility of return to the homeland was also an important element of rhetoric from the anti-communist opposition. It was a promise predicated on the success of the anti-communist opposition at the ballot box, and the diaspora eagerly contributed towards the realization of this dream.

The international circumstances, including perestroika and the fall of the Berlin Wall, were promising signs that a radical change was possible. The following section discusses the first direct involvement of the diaspora in homeland politics: its participation in the first democratic elections in 1990.

First democratic elections in Croatia in 1990

The election requires specific consideration in the context of this discussion. It was as much a logical consequence of political developments in

Yugoslavia at the time, as an act of defiance against the federal Yugoslav government and the rise of Serb nationalism under Milošević. It was also a step towards the declaration of independence that followed a year later, and a step closer to the disintegration of Yugoslavia. It was an act in which the diaspora played a key role and it benefited from the election result.

Through a donation of US$4 million, the diaspora funded most of the election campaign, particularly through its support for HDZ.[46] A vast majority of Croatians in diaspora were "natural" allies of the HDZ anti-communist and pro-independence agenda. The diaspora population embraced the opportunity to participate in the election, although there were suggestions that voting rights had been granted to the diaspora too readily.[47] Not surprisingly, the HDZ and Tudjman overwhelmingly won the election, which delivered HDZ a mandate to steer the country towards independence. Not only did the election laws allow Croatians within the diaspora to vote, but the distribution of seats in the parliament ensured that seats were reserved for diaspora representatives. The election result delivered the diaspora 12 out of 127 seats – all these seats were unsurprisingly won by the HDZ diaspora representatives.[48]

To demonstrate its commitment to national reconciliation, and to facilitate the inclusion of the diaspora in its national project, it was essential for the new Croatian government to express this symbolically by elevating diaspora individuals to positions of significance in the government. Three ministries in the first Croatian government were given to diaspora individuals, and Tudjman – exercising his constitutional right to appoint up to five members of the Sabor (parliament) – appointed a former employee of the Ustasha education ministry.

No other diaspora representative played such a decisive role in the new Croatian state as Gojko Šušak, a Croatian migrant to Canada who was behind the most effective fund-raising efforts in the diaspora. Šušak left Yugoslavia in 1968 and became heavily involved in Canadian-Croatian affairs, including some smear campaigns against the communist regime in Yugoslavia. After conducting a series of successful fund-raising campaigns to help the election victory of the HDZ, he returned to Croatia to become a minister in the Croatian government, in a newly established ministry for return and immigration. In 1991 he became minister of defence and in 1993 vice-president of the governing HDZ. He remained in the position of defence minister until his death in May 1998. Šušak was often considered to be the Croatian president's "right-hand man", with enormous influence among Croatians in Herzegovina, the province that is currently a constituent part of the Bosnia and Herzegovina federation but is predominantly populated by Croats. He was celebrated as a hero and patriot by the government press, but was also one of the most nationalist ministers in the government, having authorized various military interventions that led to the displacement of thousands of non-ethnically Croat citizens from Croatia.

The election result was a step towards the disintegration of Yugoslavia, and the possibility of military conflict increased radically as a result. However, until the declaration of the independence of Croatia in June 1991, the question of war and peace was not prominently on the agenda (although the former was feared and the latter desired). Up to that point in the conflict cycle, the diaspora was preoccupied instead with the political victory of the anti-communist HDZ and the facilitation of Croatian independence, which was implicit in the HDZ victory.

Almost paradoxically, Croatia entered the hot conflict without any constructive attempts at conflict prevention. The nationalist aspirations of the political élites and the Yugoslav army obstructed the political processes and sectarian and nationalist interests prevented a move beyond the continuing political stalemate. Similarly, the international community, with its denial that Slovenia and Croatia were inevitably on the road to independence and its support for the political integrity of the Yugoslav state, rendered itself incapable of actively and meaningfully intervening in the process.

Hot conflict stage (1991–1995)

The declaration of Croatian independence in June 1991, along with that of Slovenia, was a key step towards the break-up of Yugoslavia. By this time, the relationship between the diaspora and the homeland was consolidated and the lines of communication and assistance were firmly established. Diaspora members strongly and uncritically supported the HDZ government and were content with the general direction of change: the government had declared independence, pushed communists into the opposition and begun the process of national reconciliation.

After the proclamation of independence, the focus shifted decisively towards questions of war and the country's defence. Even before the proclamation of Croatian independence, Croatian police units were fighting Serb paramilitary units in the Serb-dominated areas of Croatia. After the proclamation of independence, however, Croatia also became fully engaged with the Serb-dominated Yugoslav army forces.

Diaspora support was now firmly focused on fund-raising and funds were transferred both legally and illegally. Hockenos reports that, early in 1991, almost six months before the proclamation of independence, the Croatian government had opened a Swiss bank account in the name of "Aid for the Economic Renewal and Sovereignty of the Republic of

Croatia".[49] Diaspora institutions around the world were given details of the account and donations started to flow in almost immediately, eventually amounting to more than US$50 million. The diaspora population did not question the use of these funds, although a large proportion was clearly used for purchasing arms on the illegal market.

After re-taking the Serb-controlled Croatian territory in 1995, and when money was no longer needed for direct military activities, the Croatian government transferred the remaining funds (approximately US$1.4 million) into an HDZ-held account. This controversial move sparked allegations of corruption in Tudjman's regime.[50] More broadly, it also raises a host of ethical dilemmas about the practice of fund-raising by diaspora populations, as outlined at the beginning of this chapter. Importantly, however, in the circumstances of war, the diaspora was overwhelmingly and almost exclusively preoccupied with the question of defeating what it perceived as the enemy.

Behind these fund-raising schemes, both legal and illegal, were large numbers of Croatian migrants and their children who donated their savings, and even took out bank loans, in order to assist the homeland.[51] Financial support for the homeland was almost mandatory within diaspora organizations. Indeed, it was considered a betrayal of Croatian interests for migrants, including children, not to make as large a financial contribution as possible.[52] By the mid-1990s, the various fund-raising campaigns had slowly turned into a routine quest for money fuelled by a high emotional sensitivity among the diaspora population that the Croatian government worked to maintain. To this end, the Croatian homeland media provided diaspora members with special reports written by journalists who understood the significance of emotionalized narratives for the continuation of the fund-raising effort.

Fund-raising was one of the key contributions by the diaspora during the hot phase of the conflict. But there were also other large-scale projects involving collections for humanitarian aid, medicine, clothing or food. These contributions were significant and regular throughout the conflict in Croatia and Bosnia and Herzegovina. Additionally, and particularly at the beginning of the hot phase of the conflict, many diaspora resources were utilized for public relations campaigns to inform host society governments about the plight of Croatian people and the need for recognition of the new state. Protest marches were held in cities around the globe such as Berlin, Sydney and Washington. In one single march in Washington in 1991, more than 40,000 people gathered to express "their faithfulness and love towards the homeland".[53]

During the hot stage of the conflict, the diaspora trusted the homeland government to make decisions about where donated funds should be channelled. This obviously raises the question of the ethics of the diaspora's long-distance involvement in homeland politics – a dilemma raised earlier in this chapter. However, it also shows that the Croatian diaspora actively and decisively, yet mostly indirectly, influenced the course of events in the homeland. Strictly speaking, in the name of patriotic responsibility and the right to defend one's own country, it co-funded the maintenance of the conflict.

Post-conflict and peace-building stage (post-1995)

In December 1995, after re-taking the territories occupied by the Serb militia, Croatia became a signatory of the Dayton Peace Accord. This agreement committed Croatia to permanently end all hostilities and return any refugees, but it also coincided with a de-intensification of the diaspora–homeland relationship and its relatively rapid transformation.

The Croatian diaspora greeted the news about the victory of the Croatian military forces and the signing of the Dayton Peace Accord with enthusiasm. Diaspora members could now identify the Croatian homeland as a place of return and "homecoming": the homeland was free and independent, and its stability in the region was relatively secure. Whereas the diaspora had played an important role in assisting military and humanitarian efforts in the earlier stages of the conflict, it found itself without a specific task once the hostilities were over. As such, it did little to contribute to peace-making and peace-building.

The termination of conflict has brought an end to what appears to have been a symbiotic relationship between the diaspora and the homeland, which emerged during the pre-conflict and conflict periods. In the post-Dayton period, the Croatian diaspora remains visible in homeland politics through its elected representatives in the Croatian parliament, through the Croatian government's maintenance of an open-door policy for Croatian returnees from diaspora communities, and through big incentives offered by Croatian government-sponsored organizations to foster economic exchange with diaspora business and capital. Apart from that, the agendas in the diaspora have reverted to less heavily politicized topics, including the maintenance of ethnic identity, the cross-generational transmission of culture, and the establishment and maintenance of economic ties between business communities in the diaspora and the homeland.

Conclusion

There is no simple and direct answer to the question that this chapter set out to address: did the Croatian diaspora play the role of peace-maker or peace-wrecker in the conflict associated with the break-up of Yugoslavia?

To set the tone for the answer, the chapter began with an assertion that, during the conflict, the Croatian diaspora was preoccupied with a three-dimensional goal: the protection of a newly independent homeland, the cessation of hostilities once the war broke out, and, ultimately, peace.

The issue of an "independent homeland" should be seen as a defining element in any understanding of the diaspora's role in the conflict surrounding Croatian independence ambitions. It was the diaspora's historically conditioned interest in the independent homeland that prompted its mobilization in the conflict. The quest for an independent homeland was, as demonstrated in this chapter, clearly linked with negative attitudes towards the ideas of communism and Yugoslavism. The diaspora's role in the conflict was primarily defined and driven by these parameters.

The Croatian diaspora certainly played an active role in all stages of the conflict cycle. It clearly assisted in the military and humanitarian efforts of the war, but this was, first and foremost, in the service of asserting and maintaining independence. Independence, however, was achievable only through military victory; hence the diaspora was interested in victory that would bring peace rather than in peace per se. An imposed peace that entailed the loss of parts of the territory was not the kind of peace it was willing to accept and recognize. It is likely that the diaspora would have continued to support military engagement had the peace on its own terms – i.e. peace obtained through (military) victory – not been achieved. Peace here becomes a relative rather than an absolute category and it is deprived of its popular association with something normatively positive.

None of this is to dilute the significance of the Croatian diaspora's genuine hopes for peace throughout the conflict. But one must not lose sight of the historical lens through which the diaspora constructed and experienced the conflict. This lens predisposed the diaspora to view the opportunities associated with the conflict in terms of the one-dimensional ambition of the pursuit of independence – a pursuit to which everything else was subjugated.

What the Croatian case study shows is that there is no one-size-fits-all model that can help us understand the ways in which diasporas intervene in homeland conflicts. Although there are examples of diasporic communities taking measures to reduce the risk of conflict in the ancestral homelands (for example, the role played by the Irish diaspora in the recent peace process in Northern Ireland), the likelihood of the opposite scenario, in which diasporas more or less unintentionally contribute to the maintenance of conflict, is just as real. The only way to be able to differentiate between the peace-making and peace-wrecking ambitions of diasporas is to have a clear understanding of the historical and political context of their existence.

Notes

1. Marcus Tanner, *Croatia: A Nation Forged in War*, New Haven, CT: Yale University Press, 1997.
2. In this chapter, the term "diaspora" designates a diverse group of social, religious and political organizations set up and/or influenced by the post–World War II Croatian refugee settlers. The intensity of their adherence to nationalist ideology, anti-communism, anti-Yugoslavism and pro-independence aspirations varied considerably. Furthermore, the Croatian diaspora was internally fragmented. There were many sources of tension, including the symbolic prestige associated with educational differences, English-language ability and level of contact with the homeland. See Daphne N. Winland, "'We Are Now an Actual Nation': The Impact of National Independence on the Croatian Diaspora in Canada", *Diaspora*, 1995, 4(1): 3–29; Val Colic-Peisker, "Croatians in Western Australia: Migration, Language and Class", *Journal of Sociology*, 2002, 38(2): 149–166; Maja Povrzanović Frykman, "Homeland Lost and Gained: Croatian Diaspora and Refugees in Sweden", in Nadje Al-Ali and Khalid Koser, eds, *New Approaches to Migration?: Transnational Communities and the Transformation of Home*, London: Routledge, 2002, pp. 118–137.
3. Winland, "'We Are Now an Actual Nation'"; Zlatko Skrbiš, *Long-Distance Nationalism: Diasporas, Homelands and Identities*, Aldershot: Ashgate Publishing, 1999.
4. William Safran, "Diasporas in Modern Societies: Myths of Homeland and Return", *Diaspora*, 1991, 1(1): 83–99; S. Z. Klauser, "Diaspora in Comparative Research", in More Menachen, ed., *Eretz Israel, Israel and the Jewish Diaspora Mutual Relations*, Lanham, MD: Craighton University, 1991, pp. 194–221; Gabriel Sheffer, *Diaspora Politics: At Home Abroad*, Cambridge: Cambridge University Press, 2003.
5. Sheffer, *Diaspora Politics*, p. 21.
6. Benedict Anderson, *Long-Distance Nationalism: World Capitalism and the Rise of Identity Politics. The Werthem Lecture*, Amsterdam: Center for South Asian Studies, University of Amsterdam, 1992; Michael Brown, ed., *Ethnic Conflict and International Security*, Princeton, NJ: Princeton University Press, 1993.
7. John Armstrong, "Mobilized and Proletarian Diasporas", *American Political Science Review*, 1976, 70(2): 393–408.
8. Sheffer, *Diaspora Politics*, p. 257.
9. Nathan Glazer and Daniel P. Moynihan, *Beyond the Melting Pot: The Negroes, Puerto Ricans, Jews, Italians, and Irish of New York City*, Cambridge, MA: MIT Press, 1965, p. 242.
10. Charles Campbell, *The Transformation of American Foreign Relations, 1865–1900*, New York: Harper & Row, 1976, p. 8.
11. Greg Robinson, *By Order of the President: FDR and the Internment of Japanese Americans*, Cambridge, MA: Harvard University Press, 2001; Richard Bosworth and Romano Ugolini, eds, *War, Internment and Mass Migration: The Italo-Australian Experience 1940–1990*, Rome: Gruppo Editoriale Internazionale, 1992.
12. Anderson, *Long-Distance Nationalism*, p. 13.
13. Ibid.
14. Sheffer, *Diaspora Politics*, p. 187.
15. Zvonimir Šeparović, *Od Sydneya do San Franciska*, Čakovec: Zrinski, 1982; Ljubomir Antić, *Hrvati i Amerika*, Zagreb: Hrvatska Sveučilištna naklada, 1992.
16. Jure Prpić, *Hrvati u Americi*, Zagreb: Hrvatska matica iseljenika, 1997, p. 18.
17. Walker Connor, "When Is a Nation?", *Ethnic and Racial Studies*, 1990, 13(1): 92–103, p. 94.

18. Mato Tkalčević, *Hrvati u Australiji*, Zagreb: Nakladni zavod Matice hrvatske, 1992; Winland, "'We Are Now an Actual Nation'", p. 8.

19. Ivo Banac, *The National Question in Yugoslavia: Origins, History, Politics*, Ithaca, NY: Cornell University Press, 1984.

20. Tihomir Cipek, "The Croats and Yugoslavism", in Dejan Djokić, ed., *Yugoslavism: Histories of a Failed Idea 1918–1992*, London: Hurst, 2003, p. 76; Bogdan Krizman, *Pavelić and Ustaše*, Zagreb: Globus, 1978.

21. Aleksa Djilas, *The Contested Country: Yugoslav Unity and Communist Revolution: 1919–53*, Cambridge, MA: Harvard University Press, 1991, pp. 125–127.

22. Tito (1892–1980) was a defining figure of the post–World War II Yugoslavia who personified the Yugoslav path to socialism. He was the architect of the policies of "brotherhood and unity" and self-management. Internationally, he was one of the founders of the Non-Aligned Movement. Tito and his regime were also responsible for repressive actions against the so-called anti-socialist elements within Yugoslav society. See Milovan Djilas, *Tito: The Story from Inside*, New York: Harcourt Brace Jovanovich, 1980.

23. Skrbiš, *Long-Distance Nationalism*, pp. 29–32.

24. Nikolai Tolstoy, *Victims of Yalta*, London: Corgi Books, 1986; Tanner, *Croatia: A Nation Forged in War*.

25. These pro-Yugoslav communities are of marginal importance for this analysis because they did not contribute towards the nurturing of a politicized Croatian diaspora identity. They were nevertheless mobilized during the escalation of the recent conflict, particularly through the fund-raising efforts. The majority of pro-Yugoslav Croatian communities were located in European countries, although they were present in overseas countries as well. See Paul Hockenos, *Homeland Calling: Exile Patriotism and the Balkan Wars*, Ithaca, NY: Cornell University Press, 2003. Those Croatians who were members of the pro-Yugoslav communities were often humiliated and publicly labelled when they expressed interest in supporting the Croatian quest for independence. See Skrbiš, *Long-Distance Nationalism*, pp. 129–136.

26. Carl-Ulrik Schierup, *Immigration, Socialism and the International Division of Labour: The Yugoslav Experience*, Avebury: Aldershot, 1990, pp. 76–79; Susan L. Woodward, *Socialist Unemployment: The Political Economy of Yugoslavia 1945–1990*, Princeton, NJ: Princeton University Press, 1995.

27. Tanner, *Croatia: A Nation Forged in War*.

28. Hockenos, *Homeland Calling*.

29. Ibid.

30. Julienne Eden Bušić, *Lovers and Madmen: A True Story of Passion, Politics and Air Piracy*, New York: Writers Club Press, 2000.

31. Skrbiš, *Long-Distance Nationalism*.

32. Sabrina P. Ramet, *Balkan Babel: The Disintegration of Yugoslavia from the Death of Tito to the Fall of Milošević*, 4th edn, Cambridge, MA: Westview Press, 2002, p. 8.

33. Laura Silber and Allan Little, *The Death of Yugoslavia*, New York: Penguin, 1995; Lenard J. Cohen, *Serpent in the Bosom: The Rise and Fall of Slobodan Milošević*, Boulder, CO: Westview, 2002; Ramet, *Balkan Babel*.

34. Franjo Tudjman, *Bespuća povjestne zbiljnosti*, Zagreb: Nakladni zavod Matice Hrvatske, 1989.

35. Šušak, quoted in Hockenos, *Homeland Calling*, p. 47.

36. Hockenos, *Homeland Calling*, p. 44.

37. Ibid, p. 45.

38. Anderson, *Long-Distance Nationalism*; Sheffer, *Diaspora Politics*.

39. Sheffer, *Diaspora Politics*, pp. 187–188.
40. Richard Yallop and Abraham Rabinovich, "Gutnick's West Bank Gamble", *The Australian*, 18 February 1997, p. 11.
41. Oivind Fuglerud, *Life on the Outside: The Tamil Diaspora and Long-Distance Nationalism*, London: Pluto Press, 1999.
42. Sheffer, *Diaspora Politics*, p. 187.
43. Hockenos, *Homeland Calling*, pp. 50–53.
44. Skrbiš, *Long-Distance Nationalism*, Chapter 2.
45. Winland, "'We Are Now an Actual Nation'", p. 16.
46. Misha Glenny, *The Fall of Yugoslavia: The Third Balkan War*, London: Penguin Books, 1992, p. 63.
47. Robert M. Hayden, "Constitutional Nationalism in the Formerly Yugoslav Republics", *Slavic Review*, 1992, 51(4): 654–673.
48. According to the election law, Croatians from Bosnia and Herzegovina counted as diaspora representatives. Tudjman's government moved quickly to give Croatians in Bosnia and Herzegovina dual citizenship, benefiting from this move in the 1995 election. See Hockenos, *Homeland Calling*, p. 79.
49. Ibid., p. 85.
50. Ibid., p. 89. Some of the funds collected in the diaspora were transferred to the homeland in a non-transparent fashion. I obtained a glimpse into these shadowy activities and networks during my fieldwork in Australia. I learned through my informants that some funds collected in the diaspora did not go into the Croatian government accounts. For example, right-wing Croatian political parties in diaspora such as the Croatian Liberation Movement were sending funds directly to Croatian militias in Bosnia and Herzegovina.
51. Prpić, *Hrvati u Americi*, p. 368.
52. One young Croatian woman who participated in my Australian study stated that her mother donated some money on her behalf and published her name on the radio in the family's desperate attempt to protect its reputation. See Skrbiš, *Long-Distance Nationalism*, p. 70.
53. Prpić, *Hrvati u Americi*, p. 368.

12

African diasporas and post-conflict reconstruction: An Eritrean case study

Khalid Koser

Three principal arguments are developed in this chapter. First, and in contrast to most other chapters in this volume, the focus here is on contributions of diasporas towards peace and reconstruction in the post-conflict period. This is not to deny that diasporas are often also involved in conflict. The point is to provide a counterweight to the negative discourse that has dominated recent literature on the relationship between diasporas and conflict. Diasporas – and often a single diaspora – can be both "peace-wreckers" and "peace-makers". A particular concern expressed here about unduly emphasizing the former rather than the latter is that it can further fuel anti-immigrant and anti-immigration agendas in migrant destination countries.

The second argument is that it is impossible to generalize about African diasporas, let alone their roles in conflict. Instead, the focus here is just one case study – the Eritrean diaspora. This is not to claim that the Eritrean diaspora is somehow emblematic, or necessarily representative of African diasporas as a whole; indeed, a number of its characteristics make it quite unusual. It does, nevertheless, provide a useful case study from which to begin to draw out wider lessons, given its more or less continuous involvement in conflict and post-conflict reconstruction in the post–Cold War era.

The final argument put forward here is that policy interventions can make a difference to the role played by diasporas in conflict. It is shown how targeted policies can enhance the more constructive contributions of diasporas and reduce their negative impacts.

Diasporas in conflict: Peace-makers or peace-wreckers?, Smith and Stares (eds), United Nations University Press, 2007, ISBN 978-92-808-1140-7

The chapter is structured around these three arguments. First, I briefly review recent evidence on the relationship between diasporas and conflict and argue for a more balanced perspective that considers the positive as well as the negative impacts of diasporas. I then demonstrate that it is as impossible to generalize about Africans and African diasporas as it is about Africa, and provide background to the Eritrean diaspora. In the remainder of the chapter, I focus on the contribution of the Eritrean diaspora to post-conflict reconstruction. I categorize and discuss its interventions and expand on the policy implications. Finally, I consider the implications of this particular case study for understanding the dynamic relationship between African diasporas and conflict more generally.

This chapter largely draws on primary research conducted between 1998 and 2001, focusing on the contributions of the Eritrean diaspora first in the aftermath of the struggle for independence and then during and after the Ethio-Eritrean conflict.[1] Interviews were conducted with Eritrean government representatives both inside and outside Eritrea, and within the Eritrean diaspora in the United Kingdom, Germany and the United States.

Diasporas and conflict

In the recent spate of literature on the links between diasporas and conflict, the overwhelming discourse has been fundamentally negative. The most important work has emanated from Paul Collier and his colleagues at the World Bank, whose extensive study of the economics of conflict draws two main conclusions about the role of diasporas. The first is that external resources provided by diasporas can spark conflict, and the second is that diasporas represent a significant risk factor in the re-ignition of conflicts once they have abated.[2]

Using specific case studies, other authors have identified the precise mechanisms that explain the correlation that Collier has identified through macro-scale analysis. Focusing on the Ethiopian diaspora, for example, Terrence Lyons explains that diaspora communities have distinctive attitudes towards the "homeland", and characteristically develop networks based on solidarity that emphasize identity and work to keep nationalist hopes alive from abroad; for many, homeland conflict is a touchstone of identity. His conclusions concur with those of Collier: "Diaspora organizations thereby often become a factor that complicates processes of conflict resolution and may make homeland conflicts more protracted."[3]

The breadth and depth, respectively, of research by Collier and Lyons lend it a credibility that is undeniable. There is no doubt that diasporas can and do fuel conflict in their home countries. But it has proved difficult to advance this conclusion to concrete policy recommendations. Where the effort has been made, the recommendations are rather idealistic – one recommendation from the Institute of Contemporary Studies in the United States, for example, is to develop "education, religious and traditional authority organizations to imbue society with values of pluralism, diversity, tolerance and compromise".[4] This idealism is, of course, one way to avoid more hard-line policy recommendations that might be implied, such as reducing migration, limiting remittances and even encouraging the return of migrant diasporas.

A keenness to avoid any convergence with anti-immigrant and anti-immigration agendas is one reason for the decision to focus in this chapter on the more constructive role of diasporas in post-conflict reconstruction. Particularly where the implications of research that focuses only on diasporas' role in conflict might potentially be very damaging for the communities concerned, it is important to adopt an alternative outlook and thus try to work towards a more balanced perspective. This is probably particularly true in the African context. As O'Connor puts it, "[t]o think of Africa is to think of conflict, poverty and corruption" and what is needed is a counterweight to such misperceptions.[5] Diasporas can fuel conflict, and conflict is widespread in Africa. But diasporas can also make positive contributions towards resolving conflict and building peace, and these processes are just as important and significant as conflict in contemporary Africa.

African diasporas

The vast majority of literature on the African diaspora – also sometimes described as the "black diaspora" – considers it to have arisen from the dispersal of Africans as a result of the slave trade.[6] Some authors also extend the concept to include the descendants of slaves who continue to live away form their "homeland", and their focus in particular has been communities in the United States.[7] Another characteristic of most African diaspora studies is their insistence on a single diaspora. Clearly the suggestion is not that slaves were transported from a single origin to a single destination, or that there was a single slave experience. Although fully acknowledging difference within the African diaspora, much of the literature nevertheless focuses on its unifying characteristics. These are suggested to include a pan-African political movement, a shared cultural heritage, a common experience of ambiguous identities, and outright racism and exclusion from host societies.

Given the focus of this volume, such a conceptualization of the African diaspora needs updating in at least two significant ways.[8] First, it is usually more recent African migrants, and not the descendants of early African migrants, who are actively involved in the politics of their home countries. Without underestimating the significance of slavery, including even for new African migrants, a preoccupation with slavery and its descendants has probably diverted attention from striking new patterns and processes associated with recent migrations. There are, for example, over 200,000 Somalis outside Africa, representing one-third of their total population. There are 30,000 Senegalese in Italy alone, and over 15,000 people from the Democratic Republic of Congo just in London.[9] These Africans have arrived variously as students, professionals, asylum seekers and "irregular migrants". A second way that the African diaspora concept thus needs updating is to recognize a plurality of African diasporas rather than a single African diaspora.

Particularly given that the concept of "diaspora" has come to be used so widely that it is in danger of losing any explanatory or even descriptive value, it is worth asking whether the term should be used at all to describe recent African migrants. In an edited volume on *New African Diasporas*, the various contributors identified three main reasons the concept might still be useful.[10] Some authors saw in certain recent African migrations reflections of the original African diaspora. There are some similarities, for example, between slaves forced to leave their homes and refugees. There are arguably even closer parallels between slavery and the contemporary trafficking of women and children out of Africa.[11] Another reason the concept is argued still to be relevant is that it has recently entered policy circles and the vocabulary of migrant groups too. An increasing number of African countries, for example, are recognizing the futility of trying to encourage the permanent return of migrants – particularly the highly skilled – and are now attempting to harness the potential of their diasporas.

Perhaps the most interesting reason that emerges from the edited volume is that the term "diaspora" is gaining currency within a number of African communities themselves – including Eritrean communities. Arguably, self-definition is as legitimate a reason to describe a group as a diaspora as any other. At least three reasons emerge. One concerns relations with the host society, and arises from the perception on the part of some communities that the term "diaspora" currently has fewer negative connotations than the terms "immigrant", "refugee" or "asylum seeker". Perhaps as a result of its longstanding association with the dispersal of Jews and African slaves, the term has yet to be adopted in a derogatory manner by the media. Secondly, for at least some communities, the term appears to be "self-motivational". "Diaspora" is becoming a buzzword rather like globalization, and for some communities it appears to have connotations with which they are keen to be associated. Finally, for at least some communities, there is a sense that their experiences in some way compare with those of the original Diaspora – they too are victims, just as were dispersed Jews and African slaves. It is possible that association with these groups might promote a more widespread sympathy within host societies.

The Eritrean diaspora

The focus of the rest of this chapter is on refugees who fled during Eritrea's struggle for independence (1961–1991) and sought asylum in industrialized countries (interviews for this research took place in the United Kingdom, Germany and the United States). Many refugees were also displaced to neighbouring countries, especially Sudan.[12] In contrast, relatively few Eritrean (or Ethiopian) refugees were generated by the Ethio-Eritrean conflict (1998–2000), although large numbers of expulsions did take place in both directions across the border.

There are no accurate data on the size of the Eritrean diaspora in Europe or North America. The main reason is that Eritreans were registered upon arrival in most host countries as Ethiopians (until 1991 the territory of Eritrea was formally a province of Ethiopia), and very few censuses have yet disaggregated Eritrean from Ethiopian refugees. One indicator is the voting figures for the 1993 referendum for independence, according to which a total of 84,370 votes were cast by Eritreans outside Africa.[13] The figures indicate that the most significant host countries for Eritreans were Saudi Arabia (37,785), the United States and Canada (14,941) and Germany (6,994).

Most sources do not dispute assertions by the Eritrean Constitutional Commission that the turnout for the referendum was over 98 per cent.[14] Nevertheless, these data almost certainly significantly underestimate the true size of the Eritrean diaspora because they cover only Eritreans eligible to vote, that is, over the age of 18. In addition, the data are by now over 10 years out of date, and the vast majority of Eritreans outside the African continent have remained abroad. Eritrean community leaders in the United Kingdom, for example, suggest that between 20,000 and 25,000 Eritreans are currently living there.

In Europe, there were broadly three main waves of arrivals of Eritrean refugees during the struggle for independence. The first was in the mid-1970s, and coincided with the deposing of Haile Selassie and the accession of the Derg (military committee) in Ethiopia in 1974. Respondents report that the Derg transformed intermittent harassment of Eritreans into systematic imprisonment and persecution. Many Eritreans fled initially to Sudan, from where resettlement programmes brought them to various countries, including the United States, Canada, Germany, the United Kingdom and Sweden. The second wave occurred in the year after the so-called "Red Star Campaign", which launched the largest attack by Ethiopia and involved some 90,000 Ethiopian soldiers.[15] The final major wave arrived at the end of the 1980s, as the Eritrean People's Liberation Front launched a sustained series of attacks that were to culminate in victory in 1991. Many Eritreans who arrived at this time were "unaccompanied minors".

Diaspora interventions

The purpose of this section is to elaborate the positive interventions that have been made by the Eritrean diaspora in rebuilding its homeland, not once but twice. In Table 12.1, a simple empirical typology of its activities is presented, distinguishing economic, political, social and cultural activities. A distinction is also made between activities focused on the home country and those focused on the host country. Perhaps the most obvious activities that can contribute towards reconstruction at home

Table 12.1 Categorization of individual and community activities by type and geographical focus

	Geographical focus	
Type of activity	Home country	Host country
Economic	• Financial remittances • Other remittances • Investments • Charitable donations • Taxes • Purchase of government bonds	• Charitable donations • Donations to community organizations
Political	• Participation in elections • Constitutional roles	• Political rallies and demonstrations • Mobilization of political contacts in host country
Social	• Social contacts • "Social remittances"	• Attendance at social gatherings • Participation in discussion groups
Cultural	• Cultural events including visiting performers from the home country	• Education • Language training

Source: Field data, 1998–2001.

are those with a direct impact there, for example investments by the diaspora in land or businesses. At the same time, activities that sustain the homeland society and culture within the diaspora were considered by respondents to be equally important in shaping the future of Eritrea. There is, for example, a strong conviction within the diaspora that children born in the host country should learn their mother tongue and share a national consciousness.

The table combines activities that took place at individual, family and community levels. The main reason is that these distinctions are often blurred – many Eritreans, for example, made donations to relief efforts in Eritrea on an individual basis and via collections centred on the local community, as well as via collections focused more widely on the entire Eritrean population in host countries. What is also clear from the table is that there is a wide range of activities, which is another indication of the multiple opportunities there were for individuals to contribute towards reconstruction.

Economic activities

The main example of economic activities found amongst the study communities was remittances. Of a total of 44 respondents, 35 reported sending back money to relatives still living in Eritrea. Only 3 respondents said they had family in Eritrea but had not sent home remittances, and in each case the reason was a lack of surplus money. Besides responding to specific family needs, remittances also had a wider impact in Eritrea. First, in the absence of a social welfare system, they provided a crucial "safety net" during periods of shortfall. Many young men and women, for example, were absent from their families during the conflict, in effect withdrawing a source of income. Remittances were one way to fill the gap. Second, in the immediate aftermath of both conflicts, local communities in Eritrea were often required to contribute towards the costs of community projects (rebuilding schools, for example), and money from relatives abroad was often directed towards these contributions.

A peculiarity of the Eritrean case study is that all Eritreans in the diaspora are asked to pay 2 per cent of their monthly income directly to the Eritrean government. This system has been in place since the end of the struggle for independence in 1991, and has applied across all social categories including the unemployed. Although the payment is not compulsory, most respondents considered it a "duty" as Eritreans to meet the payments. During and in the aftermath of the Ethio-Eritrean conflict, Eritreans in the diaspora were asked to increase their contributions. In the United Kingdom, for example, Eritreans were asked to pay an additional contribution of £1 per day, plus a one-off annual payment of £500.

In Germany, the monthly payment rate was increased and there were additional one-off requests for contributions.

In addition to direct requests for payments, the Eritrean government also devised a number of more innovative ways of raising money from the diaspora. In 1999, for example, government bonds were issued for the first time in Eritrea. The Economic Advisor to the President estimated in August 1999 that expenditure on bonds already amounted to some US$30 million in the United States, US$20 million in Europe and US$15–20 million in the Middle East.

The burgeoning presence of Eritrea on the Internet provides an interesting additional channel for members of the diaspora to contribute towards reconstruction in their home country. One web page, for example, makes a request for donations to plant trees in the National Martyrs' Park outside the capital Asmara, which includes a monument, a museum and forest trails and commemorates martyrs from the independence struggle; 15 nakfa (about US$3) pays for one tree to be planted. White, silver or gold certificates are issued to contributors depending on how many trees they sponsor.

Political activities

Every Eritrean respondent who was eligible to vote at the time reported having voted in the April 1993 referendum for independence. A further political process that incorporated the diaspora was the drafting of the constitution of Eritrea. The diaspora was involved in three main ways. First, elected representatives of the diaspora served on the executive assembly of the Constitutional Commission. Second, extensive consultation took place at each stage of the drafting of the constitution. Finally, the diaspora was represented during the ratification of the constitution in 1997. One of the requirements of the constitution is the holding of constitutional elections on Eritrea. These have not yet taken place, but the diaspora is guaranteed voting rights when they do.

Another way in which other diasporas have been found to influence the politics of their home countries is by bringing pressure to bear on the government of their host country.[16] Little evidence for such activities was found among the Eritrean respondents during either post-conflict phase. Several key informants expressed the view that, although the Eritrean community is well organized internally, it is not organized in terms of external affairs. In March 1999, peace demonstrations were held in the German cities of Bonn, Stuttgart, Frankfurt and Mannheim, one aim of which was to raise the profile of the conflict against Ethiopia. They were, however, reported to have been poorly organized and attended.

Social activities

It is not only people and money that move between countries, but also ideas, values and cultural artefacts. The latter have been described as "social remittances".[17] Although they are hard to identify and quantify, the greatest potential for social remittances among the Eritrean diaspora is through the website DEHAI, the Eritrean Community Online Network. It provides current news on Eritrea, links to other relevant websites and a bulletin board for discussion. During and after the Ethio-Eritrean conflict, it provided a venue for critical discussion of the conduct of the Eritrean government. Limited Internet access in Eritrea restricted (and continues to restrict) the extent to which discussions affected that country directly, but they certainly shaped the ideas of the diaspora, which both formally – for example, through elections – and informally – through contacts with friends and family – has a role to play in determining the future of the country.

Cultural activities

Cultural activities often overlap with social activities, but it is possible to identify several trends that characterize cultural exchanges and activities. At the core of most cultural activities, for example, lies an attempt to maintain cultural links between the diaspora and its home country. The sorts of activities listed in Table 12.1 often simultaneously have a home and a host country focus. This is because many events organized by the Eritrean diaspora also invited musicians, artists and writers from Eritrea to perform in the host country. The best example is probably the festival organized each year in Frankfurt.

In addition, the Eritrean diaspora maintains an active cultural calendar. A good example of how the diaspora maintains a cultural link with Eritrea is through the celebration of public holidays marking significant historical events. The three most important are Independence Day on 24 May, National Martyrs' Day on 20 June and the Start of the Armed Struggle on 1 September.

A final example of cultural activities revolves around language. Many Eritreans fear their children will lose their mother tongue. Largely in response to demands from parents, several Eritrean communities therefore organize "cultural" lessons, which focus mainly on language training but also include lessons on Eritrean history and culture. In London there at least two "schools", associated with the Orthodox Church and the Catholic Church, that also include a religious element. The language for these lessons is Tigrinya, and several Muslim Eritreans have complained that Arabic is not also taught within the community. Language can be a divisive issue.

Enhancing the positive contributions of diasporas

The purpose of this final substantive section of the chapter is to identify policy interventions that might enhance the positive contributions of diasporas. These interventions can take place in both origin and destination countries.

In understanding what encouraged Eritreans in the diaspora to contribute, it is important to distinguish between individuals' capacity – or ability – to contribute and their desire – or willingness.[18] On the one hand, it is clear that, where an individual is unemployed or earns only a low salary, he or she will often have no surplus money to contribute. In this case, the individual's capacity to contribute is inhibited. On the other hand, if an individual is in opposition to the government in the home country, and therefore does not want to support national reconstruction under that government, he or she may choose not to contribute despite being able to afford to. In this case, political opposition to the government in the home country influences the desire of the individual to contribute. The crucial implication is that the capability of any one individual to contribute to the home country is influenced by a combination of both capacity and desire.

Building upon this distinction between capacity and desire, Table 12.2 combines two types of information. At one level it indicates the main factors that influence both capacity and desire – distinguishing broadly between economic, political and social factors. At the same time these factors are qualified, to indicate the particular circumstances in which the capabilities of individuals were found to be increased. Thus, for example, access to savings and a secure legal status in the host country were found to increase the capacity of individuals to contribute.

One advantage of presenting the factors in this qualified way is to stress their dynamism. The factors listed relate to the personal circumstances of individuals (such as their contacts with friends and family in the home country), as well as to more contextual circumstances in both the host country (such as the policy of the host government towards refugees) and the home country (such as economic or political stability). Changes can occur in each of these categories.

In turn, an advantage of emphasizing that the factors influencing capabilities to contribute are dynamic is that it highlights the role that policy interventions can play in increasing capabilities. Importantly, the table demonstrates that it is not only host governments but also home governments that might usefully intervene. In host countries, removing obstacles to integration can increase capabilities to contribute; as can, equally, removing economic disincentives to remittances in home countries. Finally, there are also implications for community organizations

Table 12.2 Factors increasing individual capabilities to contribute to reconstruction in the home country

| Type of factor | Factors influencing capability to contribute | |
	Capacity	Desire
Economic	• Employment • Savings • Access to welfare and pensions from home country • Access to information • Access to banking facilities	• Financial stability in host country • Economic incentives for remittances and investments in home country • Economic stability in home country
Political	• Secure legal status • Positive attitude of host government and population towards diasporas • Political integration of diaspora by home government	• Secure legal status • Political stability in home country • Lack of ethnic/religious discrimination in home country
Social	• Freedom of movement within host country • Gender equality • Social integration in host country	• Links with family and friends in home country • Integration within the diaspora in host country • Desire to maintain "national consciousness"

Source: Field data, 1998–2001.

and non-governmental organizations in host countries, relating for example to factors such as social integration and gender equality within the diaspora.

Capacity to contribute

As described above, a significant number of the Eritreans surveyed sent home financial remittances. Unsurprisingly, employment, which provides a regular salary and the possibility of savings, was the single most important factor to increase the capacity of the respondents financially to assist their relatives. Chances of employment, in turn, were found to be related to factors such as language skills, education, professional background and experience, the transferability of qualifications, access to training, discrimination and specific labour market conditions in the host country. A concrete example of the correlation between employment and capacity to contribute comes from a comparison of employed and unemployed Eritrean respondents. Although all reported regularly paying 2 per cent of their monthly income to the government of Eritrea, the unemployed consistently simply could not afford to make the extra payments requested during and after the Ethio-Eritrean conflict.

There also tended to be a close correlation within the Eritrean diaspora between legal status and the employment and level of wages. The respondents had a variety of legal statuses, none of which prohibited them legally from working. The insecurity of some statuses, nevertheless, meant that some respondents could only take on short-term jobs, and limitations on movement associated with certain statuses in Germany geographically delimited the job market for others.

Desire to contribute

Political factors proved particularly important influences on the desire of the Eritrean diaspora to contribute. In particular, after the Ethio-Eritrean conflict, a strong distinction emerged between supporters and opponents of the government of Eritrea. This is more complex than it first appears, because opposition has traditionally been spread across a range of groups who base their position variously on religion, regionalism and politics. Besides political divisions based on attitudes towards the government in Eritrea, there were also indications of other divisions within Eritrean communities that were more influenced by the politics of the diaspora. In particular, many Muslim respondents perceived the Eritrean community structure in the United Kingdom as being dominated by Christians. Their feeling of exclusion limited their desire to participate in community-level activities, ranging from charitable collections to festivals.

Information was another significant factor enhancing the desire to contribute. Ever since independence the Eritrean government has made substantial efforts to publicize its fund-raising exercises and to provide a range of economic incentives for remittances. The flexibility associated with the government bonds is a good example. The bonds are redeemable in either US dollars or nakfa; they can be transferred between individuals as long as the transfer is registered with the issuing office; and, in Eritrea, bonds can be used at the central bank as credit notes for investment loans.

A complex range of other political and social variables were found to influence the desire of Eritrean respondents to contribute. Legal status in the host country appeared to be a significant variable, as was the distinction between those born in the host country and the home country. The correlations are not straightforward, because these factors tended to combine with others to influence the overall desire of respondents to contribute.

A good example of the complexity of these correlations is provided by a focus on the influence of age on the desire to contribute. Many elderly

Eritreans maintained a general view that youngsters were not engaged in developments in Eritrea and had little interest in playing an active part in the future of the country. In particular, they rued what they perceived as a lack of national consciousness amongst youngsters. This was certainly true for some, who seemed to have decided to focus their attention on life in the host country. It was equally clear during the research, however, that other Eritrean youngsters were amongst the most active members of the diaspora. Most of the main Eritrean websites, for example, have been started by and are maintained by students.

Conclusions

A deliberately narrow perspective has been adopted in this chapter. First, as a means of providing a counterweight to the negative discourse that has dominated recent literature on the relationship between diasporas and conflict, the focus has been on the positive contributions of diasporas in the post-conflict period. Second, it has been impossible to generalize about a single African diaspora, and instead just one case study – the Eritrean diaspora – has formed the focus. Third, in some ways at least the Eritrean diaspora is particularly unusual even in the variegated African context: it comprises mainly forced (as opposed to voluntary) migrants, it demonstrates a striking unity over many issues, and it has consistently been generally supportive of the government in Eritrea. It is also true that the conflicts under study are unusual, because the vast majority of contemporary African conflicts take place within, and not between, countries.

What nevertheless makes the Eritrean diaspora a useful case study from which to begin to draw out wider lessons is its involvement in conflict and post-conflict reconstruction more or less continuously since 1961. Few other African diasporas have been so consistently involved and actively engaged with their home country over so long a period. The types of contribution identified in the Eritrean diaspora apply in equal measure to most other diasporas – although for the Eritreans they may be better developed given the time over which they have evolved. They provide one blueprint for the types of contribution diasporas might make to post-conflict reconstruction. And the factors that are described as enhancing the capabilities of the diaspora to contribute are equally more widely applicable – not just across other African diasporas but across diasporas more generally.

Just as this chapter began by criticizing some authors for generalizing about the contribution of diasporas to conflict, however, it is worth concluding by warning equally against generalizations about diasporas' interventions after conflict. A range of factors has been alluded to in this chapter that make some members of the diaspora unwilling or unable to contribute, and the stance of individuals changes over time as these factors do. Diasporas should not automatically be associated with war, but neither should they automatically be associated with peace.

Notes

1. Nadje Al-Ali, Richard Black and Khalid Koser, "Refugees and Transnationalism: The Experience of Bosnians and Eritreans in Europe", *Journal of Ethnic and Migration Studies*, 2001, 27(4).
2. Paul Collier and Anke Hoeffler, *Greed and Grievance in Civil War*, Washington, DC: World Bank, 2000.
3. Terrence Lyons, "Globalization, Diasporas and Conflict", unpublished paper presented at the Institute for International, Comparative and Area Studies, San Diego, January 2004.
4. Ted Morse, "How Do We Change the Way We Use Foreign Assistance to Help Prevent Deadly Conflicts?", paper presented at a USAID conference on The Role of Foreign Assistance in Conflict Prevention, January 2001, p. 6.
5. Anthony O'Connor, *Poverty in Africa*, London: Berghahn, 1992.
6. Henry Louis Gates, ed., *The Classic Slave Narratives*, New York: New American Library, 1987; V. B. Thompson, *The Making of the African Diaspora in the Americas, 1441–1900*, London: Longman, 1998.
7. Oliver Lake, "Towards a Pan-African Identity: Diaspora African Repatriates in Ghana", *Anthropological Quarterly*, 1995, 68(1).
8. Khalid Koser, ed., *New African Diasporas*, London: Routledge, 2003.
9. Ibid.
10. Ibid.
11. Amy O'Neill Richard, *International Trafficking in Women to the United States: A Contemporary Manifestation of Slavery and Organized Crime*, DCI Exceptional Intelligence Analyst Program, Washington, DC: Center for the Study of Intelligence, November 1999.
12. Jonathan Bascom, *Losing Place: Refugee Populations and Rural Transformations in East Africa*, Oxford: Berghahn, 1998.
13. Referendum Commission of Eritrea, *Report on the Eritrean Referendum*, Asmara: Ministry of Information, 1993.
14. David Styan, "Eritrea 1993: The End of the Beginning", in Tim Allen, ed., *In Search of Cool Ground*, London: James Currey, 1993.
15. Dan Connell, *Against All Odds: A Chronicle of the Eritrean Revolution*, Trenton, NJ: Red Sea Press, 1997.
16. Chris McDowell, *A Tamil Asylum Diaspora*, Oxford: Berghahn, 1997.
17. Peggy Levitt, "Social Remittances: Migration-Driven Local-Level Forms of Cultural Diffusion", *International Migration Review*, 1998, 34(4).
18. Al-Ali et al., "Refugees and Transnationalism".

13

Political remittance: Cambodian diasporas in conflict and post conflict

Khatharya Um

War, revolution, genocide and exile have marked the political history of Cambodia over the past 30 years. The toppling of the Khmer Rouge regime in 1979 was followed by 10 years of foreign occupation and protracted insurgency, a period that came to be known as the Third Indochina War. During this period of turmoil, over 1 million Cambodians perished under the Khmer Rouge and another half a million sought refuge in third-country resettlement in the aftermath of the regime's collapse. As with other communities dislocated by conflict, politics shapes the vision and direction of Cambodian diasporan activities, which, in large part, were aimed at bringing an end to the exilic condition. Aided by the convergence of circumstances and complementarity of interests with regional and extra-regional powers, Cambodian diasporas,[1] scattered throughout refugee camps along the Thai–Cambodian border and in third-country resettlement, played integral roles in homeland developments that took various forms and dimensions during the different phases of conflict. Beginning with disparate and unorganized attempts to resist the Khmer Rouge from mid 1975 to late 1978, to the transnational mobilization against Viet Nam's occupation of Cambodia, which immediately followed the collapse of the Khmer Rouge regime, they helped provide the financial, moral and human resource support needed to sustain the military and political struggle. In the end, the resistance – waged and sustained as much from Long Beach, Seattle, Washington, DC, and Bangkok as it was from inside Cambodia – was an important catalyst compelling the negotiated settlement of 1991 that officially marked the end of the

Diasporas in conflict: Peace-makers or peace-wreckers?, Smith and Stares
(eds), United Nations University Press, 2007, ISBN 978-92-808-1140-7

Third Indochina War. From it emerged an internationally endorsed formula for multi-party governance of post-war Cambodia that included, in form and content, overseas Cambodians who had returned to participate in the political process. The peace accords and the political opening of Cambodia have since led to the expansion and deepening of diasporas' engagement in homeland developments across multiple arenas in ways that were not previously possible.

Though their participation has been contested, diasporas continue to be an important force in Cambodia's post-war political, economic and socio-cultural realities despite repeated derailment of the peace process. Return and reintegration, however, have not produced the hoped-for peace, nor has symbolic unification led to the inculcation of trust and abandonment of force as an instrument of conflict resolution. The culture of distrust, forged over decades of fratricidal war, has been reinforced by the continued primacy of force and by the prevailing power imbalance among coalition partners. The bloody confrontation of July 1997 and prevailing volatility in Cambodian politics attest to the persisting challenges of post-war (though not post-conflict) reconciliation.

Although Cambodian diasporas asserted themselves in the making of history, a process that has been made easier in the age of globalization, they were also, like other diasporan communities, fundamentally subjected to forces beyond their control, at both the national and the international levels. Thus, in analysing transnational political projects, it is important to recognize the multiple positionality that diasporas inhabit and that reflects both their agency and their subjectivity. Their desire for engagement notwithstanding, diasporas necessarily operate within prevailing situational constraints. Whether in border camps in Southeast Asia or in third-country resettlement, Cambodian diasporas had to navigate and negotiate the larger political contexts in which they found themselves. As asylum seekers, they were subjected to the politics of their host countries. They were especially vulnerable in the refugee camps where, as displaced people denied legal protection, they had to depend upon the political largess of the first asylum states. Their right to stay, move around, cross borders, arm themselves or receive external assistance in any form was strictly controlled by the host authorities, whose attitudes and policies toward them were driven by their own expedient national interests. In their countries of final resettlement, refugees continued to be subjected to various constraints, not the least of which is the conditional tolerance of the receiving state of the political activism of ethnic communities.

In all, the Cambodian experience underscores the fact that diasporan politics and transnational activism cannot be understood independently of the environment in which they are situated. The ability of diasporas to engage in homeland politics thus depends not only on their desire and intrinsic capabilities but also on the *opportunity* to do so. In this sense, it is contingent as much upon the resources and capacity of the diasporan community as on external facilitators. State and transnational actors and forces do play critical roles in defining possibilities and limits for the maintenance of transnational ties. In charting diasporas' involvement in homeland politics, it is necessary, therefore, to frame these dynamics within local, national, regional and global contexts, and to give due analytic attention to the forces that promote or deter both the interest and the prospect for engagement.

Focusing on the period of the late 1970s to the mid-1990s, this chapter explores the nature, scope and depth of Cambodian diasporas' engagement in homeland politics and the tension present in the quest for postwar reconciliation. Though I shall place the greater emphasis on the political activities of Cambodian-Americans, the flow of information, people, capital and coordination across Europe, Asia and the United States and into and through the refugee camps in Thailand necessarily situates the discourse and analysis of Cambodian diasporan intervention in a larger context than the United States. As such, the study will examine the networks that cut across and link the many nodes in diaspora. These connections and relations were and remain transnational in scope and nature.

In tracing the evolving roles of Cambodian diasporas in the politics of their ancestral homeland, I shall address three fundamental components of what has been referred to as "long-distance nationalism",[2] namely (1) the desire of diasporas to engage effectively in homeland politics, (2) their ability to do so, and (3) the scope and nature of that engagement. I fold into the analysis a critical examination of the forces and conditions that promote or undermine transnational political projects. The ability of diasporas to be effectively involved in the political developments of their homelands, I shall argue, is contingent to a large extent on factors and dynamics that are both internal *and* external to diasporan communities. It hinges as much on the inherent capacity of the community to mobilize, organize and advocate as it does on the larger national, international and transnational forces that deter or facilitate these processes. In the analysis of the Cambodian experience, I shall therefore also address dimensionalities that are integral to the transnational question, i.e. (1) the role of sending and receiving states and state policies in promoting or deterring the development of transnational links; (2) the triangulated relationships between the diasporan community, the sending state and the receiving state as they strengthen or undermine transnational relations; and (3) the importance of international and transnational forces in influencing transnational dynamics. In so doing, I investigate and interrogate the more overarching concerns regarding state sovereignty, trans-nationalism, citizenship and belonging that have been complicated and problematized by the increasing porosity of the economic, cultural and geopolitical borders.

The Cambodian transnational experience in analytical and conceptual frameworks

Though transnational studies continue to privilege the examination of economic relationships among communities and discussions of remit-tances largely confined to the transfer of economic resources back to the sending countries, the histories and experiences of many diasporas point to the importance of transnational political engagement. For refugee communities, the diaspora itself is a direct outcome of political strife. Hence, politics constitutes a principal preoccupation that informs the identity and much of the political activities of the diasporan community. It defines the contexts both of *dis*-connection and of *re*-connection. As one refugee survivor puts it, "it is because of politics that I ended up a refugee, and it is because of politics that I have returned".[3] Political re-mittance, like many other aspects of reconnection, is thus an important feature of transnationality. It is also in the political arena that the chal-lenges of transnational engagement are most registered.

The desire to re-engage notwithstanding, the ability of diasporan com-munities to advocate effectively for homeland causes depends, to a large extent, upon the tolerance of the country of resettlement and on the re-ceptivity of the country of origin. Through legislation and policies, send-ing and receiving governments define the parameters, terms and nature of diasporan involvement. In various historical instances, diasporas' polit-ical concerns have been advanced or deterred, depending upon the fol-lowing: (1) the degree to which influential segments of the receiving soci-ety identify with these causes, (2) the congruence between the concerns of the diasporas and the interests of both the receiving and sending re-gimes, and (3) the bilateral relationship between the sending and receiv-ing governments. Except for the few often-cited examples of the more politically connected and economically endowed diasporas such as the Jewish communities, diasporas are less than effective in influencing a rad-ical shift in the receiving government's political agendas unless there is an alignment of interests or unless the interests and commitment of the receiving government have been firmly established. Where the political agenda of diasporas contradicts the national interests of the receiving country, their *cause célèbre* is often paralysed by the political disregard of, or the active suppression by, their adoptive government. The vulnerability of diasporas is particularly acute when the community is without the means to influence politics in its country of resettlement through votes or campaign contributions, as is the case with Cambodians in the United States. Under those conditions, not only do diasporas find themselves subjected to what Ling-chi Wang has referred to as "dual domination",[4] i.e. subordinated to the politics of the ancestral country's government and to socio-economic marginalization in their places of re-settlement, they are additionally circumscribed, in many instances, by the self-interests of their adopted government's foreign policies.

Like receiving states, sending states can do much to facilitate or im-pede transnational relations. In formulating the course of the country's political and economic development, governments can choose to solicit or curtail diasporan contributions. Through policies that give priority to national reconciliation, governments can signal their openness towards overseas communities. A state's formulation of laws and policies govern-ing matters such as immigration and citizenship, property and investment rights further defines access and inclusivity for overseas communities. In particular, the formulation of critical laws regarding political and eco-nomic participation can fundamentally shape the form and substance of transnational involvement. Conversely, sending regimes manifest their wariness or disregard of diasporas through initiatives that restrict, limit or render ambiguous the role of overseas ethnic communities. In short, whether or not the social, economic and political capital that diasporas may possess is fungible across geopolitical domains additionally depends upon the receptivity and responsiveness of the receiving regime.

The Cambodian experience not only delineates critical features of transnationality but also contests some common assumptions in the exist-ing scholarship. Although the literature on transnationalism often refers to "host" and "home" governments,[5] there are limitations on the ability of these terms fully to capture the nuances and complexity of the transna-tional experience. For instance, both connote a defined linearity in refu-gee movement from the point of exit to the point of reincorporation. The fluidity of transnational movement and attachment, further complicated by the generational shift that is evident in many diasporan communities, however, makes it difficult to locate "home" in a fixed, singular place. In fundamental ways, the complex movement of Cambodian diasporas, in-volving long-term return and multi-directional flow of political, cultural and financial remittances, challenges the unequivocal location of an orig-inary point. References to "home" are necessarily punctuated with no-tions of temporality, with constantly shifting power relations and with the multiplicity and simultaneity of identities that diasporas deploy. Equally limiting, the concept of "host" conveys a sense of transitoriness, and is therefore misleading given the permanency of third-country refugee resettlement. In the Cambodian-American experience, except for a small community of deportable residents numbering fewer than 2,000, the majority of Cambodian refugees have made the United States their adopted "home" over the past 30 years.

The Cambodia conflict and diasporan politics in historical context

Diasporas in emerging conflict: Anti-Khmer Rouge resistance (1975–1978) and evolving security imperatives on mainland Southeast Asia

Prior to the formal organization of the resistance movement in the late 1970s, political mobilization among externally displaced Cambodian communities was hindered by a host of factors. From 1975 to 1979, Cambodia, under the Khmer Rouge, was kept virtually sealed from the outside world. Little news filtered out and little influence was allowed into the country. Outside Cambodia, the refugee community that emerged in the aftermath of the communist seizure of power in 1975 was essentially without the ability or the means to mobilize effectively. Scattered in various countries, the number of resettled refugees was relatively small. In the United States, the initial Cambodian community numbered some 5,000 in 1975,[6] with most of the refugees overwhelmed by the challenges of starting again in a foreign land.

Whatever small attempts were made by Cambodian diasporas to call attention to the sanguinary developments in Democratic Kampuchea[7] were further undermined by the reticence in the West in the aftermath of the Viet Nam war. Reflecting on the silence regarding Khmer Rouge atrocities, Ed Lazar of the American Friends Committee wrote:

> The long Vietnam War had just ended and many in the peace movement, including myself, were weary from that struggle … In reactive response, peace movement people for the most part had dismissed the bloodbath scenario as well as the falling domino concept. When reports started coming in about what could be described as a bloodbath, they were dismissed as yet one more example of government and media duplicity.[8]

In Asia, regional and extra-regional powers were still assessing the strategic implications of the United States' exit from the region. Expedient national interests worked to suppress whatever concerns regional states may have had about Democratic Kampuchea. Thailand, for one, was attempting to cultivate amicable relations with the new regime in Phnom Penh. As a result, much of the anti-Khmer Rouge mobilization and resistance that took place in 1975–1978, waged largely from the borderland between Cambodia and Thailand,[9] went unnoticed.

Rather than engendering peace and stability, the collapse of the Khmer Rouge regime plunged Cambodia into renewed political strife, which included a decade-long occupation by Viet Nam, an imperfect peace agreement, the deployment of a United Nations peace-keeping mission of a scale that was historically unprecedented though with mixed results, and an ensuing decade of post-settlement instability. Like most conflict situations, the "Cambodia conflict" that spanned the decade 1979–1991 must be analysed in the complex multidimensionality that it commands. In critical aspects, the war did not simply involve Cambodians of different ideological persuasion, nor was it just about Cambodia. It reflected, rather, the broader regional and international geopolitical dynamics. Though the epicentre of the war rested in Cambodia and in the contest for power between the People's Republic of Kampuchea (PRK), installed by Viet Nam, and the exiled Coalition Government of Democratic Kampuchea (CGDK), the implications and reverberations of the conflict extended throughout and beyond the region.

At the regional level, the conflict can be understood as an extension of the scramble after the Viet Nam war for control and influence on mainland Southeast Asia, with Viet Nam, China and Thailand as the principal contenders. It was a process in which regional actors, namely member states of the Association of Southeast Asian Nations (ASEAN), and extra-regional powers, namely the United States and the Soviet Union, had a great deal of strategic interest. Viet Nam's consolidation of control over Cambodia and Laos after 1979, in effect, altered the balance of power on mainland Southeast Asia, a development that proved disconcerting to China, which regarded the sub-region as its critical southern periphery, and to Thailand, which feared the loss of traditional buffers. Viet Nam's defence treaty with the Soviet Union, compelled by Hanoi's expedient need for military support for the war in Cambodia, further fuelled China's strategic concern and prompted US re-engagement in former Indochina, albeit in a tentative and measured way. The positions that the regional and extra-regional powers adopted through the various phases of the Cambodia conflict, in particular the support of the United States, China and ASEAN of the Khmer Rouge-fortified resistance movement and government-in-exile, thus must be read in the context of these overarching geopolitical concerns.

Diasporas in conflict escalation: Occupation and resistance (1979–1991)

The preceding discussion underscores the complex set of forces and factors that both advance and delimit Cambodian diasporas' ability effec-

tively to shape the course and dynamics of conflict in the ancestral homeland. It further emphasizes the political nature of displacement and makes
comprehensible the political roles that diasporas came to embrace.[10] Although the genocidal encounter had fractured the Khmer nation, literally
and metaphysically, the Vietnamese occupation and subsequent installation of a pro-Vietnamese regime in Phnom Penh created an ideological
common ground for overseas Cambodians and provided a new catalyst
for diasporan mobilization. The loss of self-determination pricked the
deeply rooted anxiety about national survival and provided the fulcrum
for political mobilization inside Cambodia, in the border camps and in
diaspora.

The party history of the Khmer People's National Liberation Front
(KPNLF), one of the members of the coalition government-in-exile that
was subsequently formed, spoke of that historical moment as a "national
awakening", proclaiming that "the liberation of the country ... is the affair of all Khmers, wherever they may be".[11] In diaspora, nostalgia became fortified with a moralizing purpose as overseas Cambodians came
to view themselves, and to be viewed by their external supporters, as the
vestigial voice of the Cambodian nation, which had been silenced by a
colonized and oppressive state. Urging overseas Cambodians to embark
on this transnationalist project, a Cambodian refugee pointed out that
"each of us can contribute according to his capabilities. Even if we decide
not to go back home, our conscience will not be serene when learning
about the extinction of the Khmer race. Do something for our children.
Let survive the Khmer people."[12]

Along the Thai–Cambodian border, various armed factions, including
that of the Khmer Rouge, sprouted under the mantle of national liberation.[13] Though many were motivated by sheer opportunism, some had
tangible political agendas. Among them were groups that saw themselves
as fighting for an independent *and* a non-communist Cambodia, and as
an alternative to the "impossible choice" between the "pestilence of
imperialist Vietnam" and the "cholera" of the Khmer Rouge that confronted the Cambodian people.[14] With the growth of the refugee population along the border and infusion of leadership, structure and organization from the diaspora, the resistance movement grew.

The politics of representation

Mobilization also took on an ideological and partisan feature. With the
institutionalization of the resistance, the question of representation became critical. Consensus among diasporas faltered over two fundamental
issues: Prince Sihanouk and the Khmer Rouge. For some, the greatest

hope for the restoration of a peaceful and independent Cambodia rested upon the Prince, who appeared to command the greatest legitimacy, particularly in the international arena. In August 1979, a convention of royalist supporters was held in Los Angeles to endorse the Prince's leadership. Outside the United States, organizations such as the Confederation of Khmer Nationalists, based in France and presided over by Sihanouk himself, provided a transnational venue for political mobilization.

Republican elements among Cambodian diasporas, on the other hand, saw the monarchy not as the solution to but as the cause of the country's political ills. Their vision of the nation's future thus included not only an independent and non-communist Cambodia but one that was also a republic. Others positioned themselves as a viable "fifth force", an alternative to the tripartite coalition government-in-exile and to the communist regime of the Cambodian People's Party (CPP) in Phnom Penh.[15] In a letter addressed to US Senator Pell on the eve of the peace agreement in 1990, the Federation of Khmer Serei (Free Khmers), based in San Jose, California, presented itself as "a grassroots movement to promote an alternative path to the continued Cambodian crisis" that sought to prevent "the return of any form of dictatorship, including *the restoration of the monarchy*".[16]

Initially composed of various competing military factions, the movement, conceived in the West and given birth to in the borderland, was subsequently organized into a loosely structured front. On 5 March 1979, less than two months after Viet Nam's occupation of Cambodia, the Khmer People's National Liberation Armed Forces, presided over by Son Sann, former prime minister during the Sihanouk regime who had been living in France, was formed to unify the disparate non-communist resistance groups. The aim was to reduce conflicts among the various armed factions and to create a unified stance necessary to confront Viet Nam's better-equipped and more seasoned fighting forces. It was strengthened by a political arm, the Khmer People's National Liberation Front (KPNLF), which was officially proclaimed on 9 October 1979. Royalist supporters, in turn, coalesced under the mantle of the Sihanoukist National Army (Armée Nationale Sihanoukienne, ANS) and its political wing, the United National Front for an Independent, Neutral, Peaceful, and Cooperative Cambodia (Front Uni National pour un Cambodge Indépendant, Neutre, Pacifique, et Coopératif, FUNCINPEC), led by Prince Sihanouk, then in exile in North Korea, with his son Prince Norodom Ranaridh, a law professor from Aix-en-Provence, as his deputy. The remainder of the non-communist forces continued to conduct military campaigns as independent splinter groups, many without any real political base outside the refugee population under their control or any genuine political agenda. In 1982, compelled by mounting exigencies, the

KPNLF and FUNCINPEC came together with the Khmer Rouge to form a multi-party government-in-exile, formally known as the Coalition Government of Democratic Kampuchea (CGDK).

The creation of CGDK was prompted by two prevailing realities. First, the multiplicity of arenas in which the struggle had to be fought, together with the unviability of unilateral engagement by any one of the factions, was the overriding factor in the decision to form a coalition with the Khmer Rouge. Although the non-communist groups may have possessed political cachet, they lacked the military assets of the Khmer communists. At the onset of the war in 1979, the Khmer Rouge, according to one estimate, commanded a force of 25,000–50,000 guerrillas and "camp followers" whereas the non-communist groups numbered around 5,000–10,000.[17] Moreover, in contrast to the non-communist groups, which were described by one journalist as little more than "a grouping of dirt poor Khmers who … are now being called on to resist with all that is left to them",[18] the Khmer Rouge could count on sustained military assistance from China. That Democratic Kampuchea featured prominently in the name of the government-in-exile despite its sanguinary record attested to the preponderance of Khmer Rouge military power within the united front and to the primacy of realpolitik. It was an expedient decision that was to have some political costs in the years to follow.

Secondly, the CGDK was born out of the recognition that the contest was as much over political legitimacy as it was over territory and people, and that it was to be waged as much in the diplomatic arenas of Bangkok, Jakarta, Paris, New York and Washington as in Cambodia. In his public statement, Prince Sihanouk emphasized the imperative of a political resolution to the conflict: "My people are in agony and I am not crazy enough to believe that it can win an armed struggle."[19] Similarly, republican forces acknowledged that, "since its creation, [the KPNLF] never pretended to be able to throw the Vietnamese Communists out of Cambodia with our military forces. Our Front was always in favor of a political solution."[20] Towards this aim, establishing political credentials as a unified group of home-grown nationalists with a reach and a presence deep inside Cambodia was imperative for the resistance movement with its support base in cross-border refugee camps and in diaspora. The issue of legitimacy became integrally linked to the question of representation at the United Nations.

As such, the political legitimacy and appearance of a unified organizational structure that CGDK imparted were necessary for the extension of diplomatic recognition and of vital material support to the resistance groups. An open letter urging speedy consensus among Cambodian diasporas with regard to the united front pointed to that political imperative: "don't forget that numerous countries are waiting to aid us but we need to take the first step by forming a union in which the leader has the support of all Khmers living abroad."[21] The flow of material and diplomatic assistance that stemmed from this political formation was indispensable to the sustainability of the movement. In addition to financing the military struggle, aggressive support by external powers and active lobbying by Cambodian diasporas of their host governments made it possible for the government-in-exile to retain control over the representational seat at the United Nations despite the morally problematic and politically stigmatizing presence of the Khmer Rouge in the coalition.

With the war being waged on multiple fronts, the movement acquired a transnational feature. The resistance movement recruited its fighting forces from among the refugees in cross-border sanctuary, as diasporan élites came out of exile in Europe, the United States, Canada and Australia to assume prominent positions in the various political factions. Drawing upon the support network in the diaspora, the leadership of the movement moved fluidly between the camps along both sides of the Thai–Cambodian border and Bangkok, Beijing and other major capitals in Asia and the West. It was within and among the multiple nodes of these transnational networks that money, human resources and other forms of support also flowed. In refugee camps and in cities in the West, Cambodian diasporas mobilized and channelled much-needed financial resources to help sustain the struggle. Throughout the United States, in cities with a concentrated Cambodian-American presence, political meetings and fund-raising activities were frequent and numerous as the different parties made their national tours in search of support; even local Buddhist temples were not immune to political mobilization. Through these measures, the resistance grew in size and in political significance, reaching an estimated combined force of 50,000–60,000, and acquiring sufficient political clout to insist upon its representation not only at the United Nations but eventually in the peace process that gained momentum towards the end of the Cold War.[22]

Despite the advantages that it proffered, the united front was beset with internal challenges. What was created was, in fact, a fragile coalition of various political factions with different ideological platforms and leadership styles. Although member factions may have harboured a common desire for national independence, they differed on the ways to achieve it and were polarized by personality and partisan politics. They were split between communist and non-communist groups, which, in turn, were divided between royalist and republican forces. The latter group was further splintered into a faction loyal to Son Sann and one aligned with General Sak Sutsakhan. Throughout the conflict period and persisting into the present, these internecine fissures gnawed at the collective strength of the non-communists.

The issue of Khmer Rouge membership also plagued the government-in-exile. During Viet Nam's occupation, the CGDK was able to deflect the problem posed by Khmer Rouge membership in the coalition by framing the issue in terms of the morally problematic choice between genocide and colonialism. Vietnamese occupation, it was argued, threatened the very survival of the Khmer nation, and as such presented a more immediate and pressing crisis than the possible return of the Khmer Rouge, which was deemed less likely because of post-genocide international scrutiny. Prince Sihanouk's articulation of his position spoke of that moral predicament: "the Khmer Rouge are tigers ... But I would rather be eaten by a Khmer Rouge tiger than by a Vietnamese crocodile ... Oh, they [the Khmer Rouge] are vicious, they are cruel, they are murderers. But they are not traitors like Hun Sen."[23] The withdrawal of Vietnamese forces from Cambodia in 1988 eventually came to undermine that argument and to destabilize the base of support for the government-in-exile.

External actors in and responses to the "Cambodia" conflict

With ASEAN unclear about its long-term interests and the United States still recoiling from the Viet Nam debacle, the initial response of the international community to Viet Nam's invasion and occupation of Cambodia in 1979 was rather muted. The United Nations merely registered its concern with a resolution calling for the immediate withdrawal of Vietnamese troops from Cambodia that went unheeded. Of his early US campaign to get support for the burgeoning resistance movement, Prince Sihanouk commented. "I got much sympathy but little concrete help", and concluded that "no one is interested" in his proposal for the resolution of the Cambodia conflict.[24] Thomas Reston, a US State Department spokesman, articulated Washington's position as follows: "we have no United States blueprint in Cambodia, nor do we believe it would be appropriate to impose one."[25] This position was to contrast sharply with the administration's appeal to Congress a decade later to increase its assistance budget to the non-communist factions as a counterweight to the Khmer Rouge.

As Hanoi continued to insist on the "irreversibility" of the situation in Cambodia, however, the United States, Thailand and, along with it, ASEAN were compelled to reassess their positions. The United States rested its Viet Nam policy on the principle of "no trade, no aid, no normalization of relations" and made its reversal conditional upon the removal of Vietnamese troops from Cambodia. It also pursued a dual-track policy of providing covert and overt assistance to the Cambodian resistance and extending diplomatic recognition to the coalition government-in-exile. As the United States' strategic interests became more enmeshed with developments on mainland Southeast Asia, the commitment of the United States also increased. Militarily, US aid, though not large (amounting to less than US$20 million annually), was nonetheless critical to the Cambodian resistance, especially the non-communist factions, which unlike the Khmer Rouge could not count on sustained support from China.[26] Politically, the diplomatic recognition extended by Western democracies and ASEAN was particularly invaluable to the government-in-exile in its bid for international legitimacy.

In light of the United States' post–Viet Nam reluctance to re-engage openly in a land war in former Indochina, ASEAN and its leading member states (Thailand, Singapore, Indonesia and Malaysia) emerged as instrumental intermediaries in the conflict. Having shared borders with Cambodia and Laos, Thailand's security concerns were heightened not only by the presence of Viet Nam's 200,000-strong occupation force in Cambodia but, additionally, by the presence of over a quarter of a million Cambodian refugees on Thai soil, among them camp followers and armed recruits of the Cambodian resistance. As a result, Thailand became the front-line state and, along with Singapore, an important conduit for the Cambodian resistance, providing vital support in the form of training, assistance and sanctuaries for "refugee-warriors". With most refugees denied the prospect of third-country resettlement, the cross-border camps in Thailand in fact served as a sheltered reservoir of potential recruits for the Cambodian resistance movement. Without Bangkok's active collaboration, the resistance forces and the concomitant government-in-exile would have been left without the necessary access, means and support to achieve their objectives.

Collectively, ASEAN was the regional mechanism for exerting political pressure on Viet Nam. It subsequently positioned itself as an important interlocutor in the peace dialogue that became possible with the thawing of the Cold War. Shepherded by Indonesia, the Jakarta Informal Meetings (JIM 1 and 2) paved the way for the internationally guaranteed peace accords that eventually brought the war to an official end in 1991.

De-escalation of the Cold War and denouement of regional conflict: Diasporas and peace-building

The de-escalation and subsequent resolution of the multidimensional Cambodia conflict rested, as had its escalation, upon changing geopolitical dynamics that trickled down from the global arena to the regional level and on to local contexts. Just as external sponsorship contributed to the escalation of the conflict in mainland Southeast Asia, it was the alteration in the global balance of power brought on by the end of the Cold War that produced the necessary conditions for the termination of regional conflict. Without that sea change, it is likely that the conflict situation in Cambodia would have persisted, despite the concerted efforts of the diasporan community to compel a resolution.

As it was, the economic decline and eventual collapse of the Soviet Union meant loss of subsidies for Viet Nam's occupation forces. Vietnamese troop withdrawal from Cambodia fundamentally altered the geopolitical terrain on mainland Southeast Asia by removing the strategic threat to Thailand and, in so doing, eliminated the security imperative that had kept Cambodian diasporan politics aligned with that of regional supporters. In the aftermath, Thailand's volte-face diplomacy was redirected towards "turning the battlefield into a market place".[27] This signalled a reversal of position by other regional powers from previously unconditional support for the CGDK.

With the taint of foreign occupation lifted from the regime in Phnom Penh, the onus of proving legitimacy now shifted onto the government-in-exile. The Hun Sen regime could now articulate, with increasing resonance, that "to assist the non-communist resistance is to open the door for the return of Pol Pot ... that if one tries to weaken the PRK, it just helps Pol Pot".[28] In 1988, ASEAN sponsored an addendum to the UN resolution on Cambodia to include, for the first time, "the non-return to the universally condemned policies and practices of [the] recent past".[29] The resolution passed by 122 votes. In the West, the efforts of the Coalition Against the Return of the Khmer Rouge gained a new momentum, with directed efforts aimed at divesting the Khmer Rouge of its international support. Some 2,300 Cambodian survivors in the diaspora joined in the appeal to international conscience: "we cannot believe that the international community will acquiesce in allowing those responsible for genocide to remain active in Cambodian and international life, or tolerate the return by such criminals to positions of state power."[30] By the time the peace accords were implemented, the Khmer Rouge was no longer part of the equation except as a potential spoiler of peace.

With China, the United States and ASEAN tactically distancing themselves from the Khmer Rouge in the diplomatic arena, and the Soviet Union exerting pressure on Viet Nam to seek a political resolution on Cambodia, the roadblock to peace was progressively dismantled. Proclaiming that "a solution must be reached by the Cambodian people themselves", Hun Sen touted the joint communiqué of 4 December 1987 as "a call to all other Cambodian factions to come sit at the negotiating table".[31] Implicit recognition of the government-in-exile, unprecedented reference to a future "independent, neutral and democratic Cambodia" and an emphasis on the political rather than a military route to this eventuality were part of the conciliatory language. From the initial thaw augured by the meeting between Hun Sen and Sihanouk in 1987, a series of informal "cocktail" parties (the JIM 1 and 2 meetings) brought together two of the three Cambodian parties of the government-in-exile, the People's Republic of Kampuchea in Phnom Penh,[32] Viet Nam and other "interested parties" to negotiate the terms of peace. These meetings paved the way for the formulation of a "road map" towards an international accord and the cessation of war. In October 1991, a multilateral agreement was reached, resulting in the signing of the Agreements on a Comprehensive Political Settlement of the Cambodia Conflict (or Paris Agreements), which established the framework for a political resolution to the protracted war and for moving the country towards pluralistic democracy through multi-party elections.

Shored up by the deployment of a large-scale UN peace-keeping operation to oversee the transition to peace, the internationally endorsed Paris Agreements in essence brought exile politics in from the margins by creating a framework for the structural reintegration of the government-in-exile (minus the Khmer Rouge) into the country's political processes. By encoding the principle of national reconciliation into the peace plan, the international community sanctified the return and re-engagement of Cambodian diasporas in the country's politics and post-war national reconstruction. As a result, the critical roles that Cambodian diasporas had assumed earlier during the conflict period took on different and expanded dimensions in the aftermath of the brokered settlement. Though the power-sharing formula that emerged from the UN-endorsed elections of 1994 did not reflect the electoral will, it nonetheless provided a structured opportunity for the political participation of overseas Cambodians in the country's politics. With the longed-for opportunity for peaceful re-engagement in the homeland, Cambodian-Americans advocated, and won, the right to run for office and vote in the elections. The decision to allow Cambodian-Americans also to cast their ballots at a polling station at the UN headquarters in New York symbolized the concessions made by all the parties concerned, including the international guarantors, to the political centrality of Cambodian diasporas in the process of national reconciliation and reconstruction. Some returning Cambodians hitched their political future to the new multi-party framework of the UN-sanctioned peace plan. Of the 20 political parties represented on the ballot in 1993, 8 were led by returning Cambodian-Americans. Others worked from the diaspora to create mechanisms for ensuring accountability. With bases in France and the United States, the Opinion of the Khmer People was formed in April 1989 with a veiled mission as "an organ for contact, networking, consultation and exchange of information of all sorts with individuals, groups or associations, cultural, political and economic, inside [Cambodia] and abroad".[33] Elsewhere, loyalties shifted as returning diasporas reassessed their options against new power realities on the ground. On the eve of the 1994 elections, some members of the non-communist parties, particularly FUNCINPEC, defected to the opposition.

The nature, scope and nuances of transnational engagement that have emerged since the early 1990s reflect both the complexity of the diasporan community and the changing characteristics of the transnational relations that now span the political, economic and socio-cultural arenas. These ties, forged through individual, family, community and institutional initiatives, are both formal and informal. Given the new structure of governance, overseas Cambodians have returned to occupy prominent positions at the national and local levels, some as elected officials, others on short-term employment contracts with the government or with international agencies.

Though greater emphasis has been placed on the politically motivated return, many Cambodian diasporas have also capitalized on the growing vitality of the private and non-government sectors, which have proliferated since the political liberalization of the early 1990s. Whereas the official status of non-governmental organizations (NGOs) has yet to be recognized in Viet Nam and Laos, the extensive reliance of the Phnom Penh government on NGOs for the provision of fundamental services, even pre-dating the political opening of the country, had given these extra-governmental entities a certain pre-eminence and legitimacy. Their presence and importance in post-war reconstruction increased with the inflow of foreign assistance that followed the internationally endorsed elections in 1994. The opportunities created drew in returning Cambodians, many of whom had amassed tremendous expertise and leadership skills in the non-profit sectors in the West. It is noteworthy that many prominent social advocates in Cambodia are women who had returned from the diaspora. The former minister for women's and veterans' affairs and the directors of the country's two leading advocacy organizations – the Center for Social Development and the Cambodian League for the Promotion and Defense of Human Rights (LICADHO) – were among the many prominent women who returned to participate in the country's post-war reconstruction.[34] In a country in desperate need and with a post-genocide gender imbalance, they are well positioned to make a significant contribution to the peace- and nation-building process.

The politics of return and the challenges of reconciliation

Despite the commitment to the termination of conflict, the Comprehensive Political Settlement failed to establish a viable foundation for a durable peace. In fact, the internationally crafted and endorsed plan was based on an unfounded premise. Whereas the UN blueprint rested on a presumption that peace would prevail in Cambodia, what the Paris Agreements were able to produce was, at best, a negotiated postponement of violence. Though the brokered settlement did provide the framework for the coming together of the various contending parties and for articulating the principles of national reconciliation, it was unable, at the operational level, to do away with the inequity inherent in the structure and relations of power. The bureaucratic apparatus and most aspects of governance were inherited almost *in toto* from the socialist regime. Far from being "comprehensive", the plan, with its externally construed ideals and expectations not rooted in local realities, was compromised from the start. In the end, the formula and structure of power-sharing imposed on the members of the new coalition government in Phnom Penh did not reflect popular will, but represented a desperate compromise extracted in the face of violence and renewed threats of war. It was a tragic statement on the hollowness of the internationally endorsed agreements.

Above all, the negotiated resolution could not undo the legacy of distrust. Despite the implementation of the Paris Agreements, progress towards national reconciliation has been slow and tentative, thwarted largely by endemic conflict between and within the ruling parties. In essential aspects, the process has been largely symbolic, with the veneer of structural integration largely masking the power asymmetry that continues to prevail within the coalition government. Thus, although returning Cambodians have been allowed to participate in the government, and even hold positions of responsibility, they are, for the most part, divested of any real power.

As a result, though the contributions of diasporas to Cambodia's postwar reconstruction were widely anticipated, especially in overseas communities, the actuality fell short of expectations. Despite the continued preoccupation of Cambodian diasporas with homeland politics, it remains true that long-term or permanent repatriation has been the privilege of only a few. In fact, the prevailing constraints may actually reinforce transnational mobility because most overseas Cambodians have not been able to relocate permanently and instead travel back and forth, largely engaged in various cultural or entrepreneurial activities. Yet others simply remit money and other resources without embarking on a physical return.

The limited scope and duration of return are a function of both constraint and restraint, and are rooted in both sending and receiving contexts. At a very basic level, economic concerns such as home mortgages, college tuition, job and other financial responsibilities undermine the possibility of return for many Cambodian diasporas. The difficulty in attracting established professionals for long-term relocation has dampened the initial euphoria regarding the transnational remittance of skills. For instance, despite its potential, the Cambodian American National Development Organization (CANDO) programme, also referred to as the "Cambodian peace corps", fell far short of the vision of helping transfer skills and talents from the diaspora, largely because of problems recruiting highly skilled professionals. Most of the programme participants were young Cambodian-Americans, who were full of enthusiasm and commitment but had few of the professional, linguistic and cultural skills needed to make vital contributions.

In most instances, active engagement and return require not only economic but also political capital. Access to positions and power remains confined to those with dedicated party standing – measured in many instances less by political or professional credentials than by monetary contributions to the party coffers – and to those with family pedigree and connections. These are assets that are not readily available to many refugees. In the same vein, factors such as corruption, the volatility of Cambodian politics, political paralysis, an absence of genuine reconciliation and overall distrust in the system act as additional deterrents to return. As a result, the country, especially the non-communist parties, has been unable to turn to diasporas to fill the critical shortage of highly skilled human resources. This has posed a grave challenge, especially for pro-democracy groups, and has reinforced the perception that the integration of non-communist elements within the governing structure has been largely symbolic.

For those able to return, reintegration and reconciliation have not been without challenges. Given the acute scarcity of human capital in post-genocide Cambodia, the talent re-imported from the diaspora has been both significant and needed. It has nevertheless been met with resistance. Rhetoric of national reconciliation aside, intentions are still questioned. In essence, regimes in transition, such as those of Cambodia and Viet Nam, are typically ambivalent about overseas communities. As one Cambodian-American candidate in the recent elections noted, "they want our money, they don't want us; they want our money but not our influence".[35] At a symposium in Long Beach, California, a Cambodian-American panellist, who was asked to comment on the role of diasporan Cambodians in the country's post-war reconstruction, spoke vociferously about the need for the Cambodian government to "open its arms to the overseas Cambodians", emphasizing that "it's a two way street".[36]

The regime's distrust of returning diasporas and uneasiness about the forced reconciliation are evident in the controversy surrounding the issue of dual citizenship, which surfaces at strategic intervals, especially at times of heightened political tension. At present, many in the non-communist leadership – including Cambodia's newly crowned king, Norodom Siha-moni, his half-brother, former prime minister Prince Ranaridh, members of parliament, and other government officials and advisers – currently hold dual citizenship. Given this reality, any measure that invalidates this status would fundamentally alter the power structure and dynamics of Cambodian politics. The frequent recurrence of this debate reflects the tremendous political investment that opposing parties have in this issue. Though it pertains principally to government officials and politicians, this issue is nonetheless a focal point of general discussion among overseas Cambodians, attesting to the perception of their own vulnerability as members of that diasporan community.

The politics of differentiation in post-war discourse

The fissures, however, were not just the result of historical experiences. They have also been deliberately cultivated by the contending parties. Oppositional images and contesting interpretations of history have been central features of the political discourse of the past two decades, both in Cambodia and in the diaspora. From the vantage point of the diaspora, Cambodia under the Hun Sen regime was and, many would argue, remains a captured nation-state, its body politic compromised by Vietnamese occupation, its economy and security dependent on external support, and its society and culture subjugated by neo-colonialism. The Phnom Penh regime was thus seen as devoid of inherent legitimacy.

Hun Sen's Cambodian People's Party (CPP), on the other hand, argued that regime legitimacy should be judged by actual governance, specifically by control over the population, the territory and the state's coercive apparatus. It is largely on the basis of this claim that the formula for power-sharing in Cambodia adopted in the aftermath of the 1994 elections ended up reflecting not the electoral will but the prevailing power realities. Additionally, legitimacy was argued on moral grounds. In contrast to the opposition, and its unholy alliance with the Khmer Rouge, the CPP presents itself as the "true" nationalist party that fought to topple the genocidal Khmer Rouge. Contrary to the opposition's depiction of Cambodia as a colonized state, the government in Phnom Penh argued that it had always been self-reliant and self-determined, as demonstrated by the regime's ability to survive the decade-long embargo by the West. In fact, Hun Sen had repeatedly dismissed threats of a renewed embargo with claims that Cambodia had survived past isolation and could do so again if necessary. This myth of self-reliance, inscribed in official ideology, is deployed in poignant rebuttal, though it denies the years of dependence on Eastern bloc assistance. Furthermore, unlike the

returning diasporas from the West, who are compromised by their royalist and capitalistic tendencies, the CPP contends that it alone represents
the populist interests of Cambodia.

In essence, what are being contested are not only the *possibility* but
also the *right* of return. The discourse of nationalism extends beyond the
political question of legal rights and entitlements to become an essential-
ist one. Legitimacy is measured not only by political actions and citizenship but by the degree of "Khmer-ness". To the diaspora's charge that
the Phnom Penh regime has been essentially tainted by Viet Nam's colonization, the CPP posits that Cambodians who remained in Cambodia
are "purer", because they have not experienced the physical, meta-
physical and cultural disconnect of exile. Hence, they are more "authen-
tically" Khmer. To the insistence of overseas Cambodians on an inalienable place in the imagined community of "Khmer Angkor", Phnom Penh
counters that such membership is compromised by their status as diasporas, as *"Khmer chaol nokor"* (Khmers who abandoned the country).
From the political and ideological position of Phnom Penh, flight, rather
than being seen as compelled by forces beyond the individual's control, is
imbued with an element of agency; overseas Cambodians "chose" to escape while more patriotic individuals elected to stay. Nationalism and
cultural authenticity, thus, are made coterminous with territorial bound-
edness. To diasporas' contestation that exit is "not an alternative for
voice but a necessary condition for the exercise of voice",[37] the counter-
claim is that, because of exit, there can be no voice. In short, by "opting"
for flight and external refuge, diasporic Cambodians have forfeited their
right to belong. The highly politicized discourse over essential "Khmer-
ness" and "cultural authenticity" points to the saliency of Clifford's observation that "self–other relations are matters of power and rhetoric
rather than of essence".[38]

Despite concerted attempts, the CPP was unable to do away with the
political participation of the non-communist parties in the government.
Though only temporarily, the non-communist factions were able, despite
their entrenched internal differences, to unite and effectively thwart what
they deemed to be an "unconstitutional" attempt by the CPP to form
a one-party government following the 2003 elections. The retention of
multi-party representation, at least in form if not in substance, underscores the continued viability of diasporan participation in the country's
politics despite the flawed nature of power-sharing. While the juggling
for primacy among and within the various political parties continues to
undermine the prospects for stability and progress in Cambodia, the in-
ability of the non-communist forces to maintain solidarity, in particular,
has compromised the hope for democratization. Over a decade after the
signing of the externally compelled agreements, peace remains elusive,

with the shifts and movements in Cambodian politics not always indicative of positive change.

Conflict after the "peace"

The schisms that surfaced in the post-settlement period do not situate neatly within the oppositional binary between Cambodia and the diaspora. They are also evident *within* the diasporan community. Despite the increasing de-politicization of the issues of engagement and return, homeland politics continues to fractionalize and, to some extent, even intensify intrinsic cleavages among overseas Cambodians. As hopes for durable peace and reconciliation dim with post-settlement disillusionment, a line is increasingly drawn between regime-opposing and regime-accommodating forces in the diaspora, each proclaiming a nationalistic stance. Those advocating constructive engagement deem it the "patriotic duty" of all Cambodians, at home and abroad, to participate in national reconstruction. Diasporas, they argue, have a moral obligation to contribute to the process of nation rebuilding. After all, "if the international community, if even strangers, have been moved towards intervention, it would be unconscionable for Cambodians to stand aside".[39] The hyphen in "nation-state" is seen as a literal divide, denoting the necessity of keeping the *nation* separate from the *state*. Hence, objection to the regime and resistance to the state, it is argued, should not translate into a callous disregard for the nation.

For others, the ultimate expression of nationalism is to withstand the temptation towards regime accommodation. Genuine reform in Cambodia, they argue, can be achieved only through unrelenting pressure from the outside. Conciliatory politics, even the peace agreements, they point out, have produced little positive change, and return and engagement have in many respects only evoked the sense of opportunism among diasporas. In a system where access to power and opportunity is largely tied to party allegiance, and where patronage permeates all aspects of life, a politically well-connected Cambodian-American reflected on the necessity of being pragmatic: "it can be very cold out there, so people seek refuge under other (powerful) people's wings."[40] Nationalist concern, as a result, risks becoming subordinated to individual self-interest and co-opted by the realpolitik of both the sending and the receiving states.

The political tension simmering beneath the rhetoric of reconciliation both in Cambodia and in the diaspora was brought to the fore by the eruption of violence and brief return to war in July 1997. The developments of that summer highlighted the fragility of the peace accords and the seemingly intractable impediments to post-settlement reconciliation.

In the wake of summary executions and custodial deaths, unlawful mass arrests, and repression of political opposition,[41] the halting steps taken towards national reconciliation and democratic pluralism were reversed. The multi-party coalition government, as it was conceived in 1994, was destroyed. The CPP-led coup against its non-communist coalition partners did away with the system of dual prime ministership that previously had included Prince Norodom Ranaridh as head of the royalist party. Intimidation and co-optation of the leadership, combined with the extensive damage inflicted upon their political infrastructure, further crippled the non-communist parties. Many of the leaders, including Prince Ranaridh, were forced back into temporary exile, while, paradoxically in Phnom Penh, trials in absentia were held not for the Khmer Rouge, who were now viewed as Phnom Penh's vital allies, but for the non-communist, former coalition partners.

Faced with the prospect of renewed war in 1997, anti-regime Cambodians in diaspora were once again mobilized in a campaign to sanction the Hun Sen regime diplomatically and economically for violating both the spirit and the structured agreements of the Paris Agreements. Almost immediately, eyewitness accounts and graphic pictures of attacks on pro-democracy ralliers, along with reports and images of the coup-induced pandemonium, blanketed websites and listserves frequented by Cambodia watchers. Discussion forums, such as *Camdisc*, were enlivened with political debates. Together, they constituted an effective incubator of "internet nationalism". Protests from government and non-government sources further drew international attention to the political violence. While Cambodians in the West lobbied their governments for active intervention, the non-communist leadership formed the Union of Democrats from their temporary asylum in Bangkok and fought for their right to return and share power.

Although the call for accountability that emanated from the diasporan communities and from government and non-government supporters was instrumental in forcing regime concession, it was by no means uncontested. With its investment in the presumed success of the brokered agreements, the international community, including the signatories of the Paris Agreements, was torn between the expedient desire for stability and the hope for systemic change. Diasporan activism, rather than being seen as an important intervention against the derailment of peace, was viewed in some corners as a spoiler of peace. Along with state-sanctioned violence, the perceived absence of any real mechanism of accountability or of genuine interest by external powers in Cambodia's political liberalization fortified the culture of impunity, and correspondingly of fear, and eroded popular belief in the possibility of change in the near future. The malaise that accompanied the 2003 elections reflected that prevailing sense of political fatalism. In this sense, Cambodia is possibly in a worse state today than during the inaugural elections of 1994.

The 1997 coup and its impact on oppositional politics were a decisive blow to the hope for national reconciliation, and a serious setback to the democracy-building project. Pressured by the international community, the contours of power-sharing are retained, but the spirit of the coalition has, to all intents and purposes, been destroyed. Though the non-communist parties continue to be represented in the government, power has since been firmly consolidated in the hands of the Cambodian People's Party.

Leveraging for accountability: The importance of international and transnational connections

Although protestation from Cambodian diasporas against the renewed violence of 1997 was critical, its efficacy was greatly amplified by the transnational networks. The pressure exerted on the Hun Sen regime by the international community did, in effect, prevent the complete collapse of the peace agreement. The concession made by Phnom Penh to allow pro-democracy members to return to Cambodia to participate in the 1998 elections attested to its recognition of the importance of international goodwill.[42]

These outcomes, however measured, point to the leverage that international and transnational entities do possess to influence positive change. Though international intervention is necessarily constrained by state sovereignty, in transitional systems such as Cambodia where international assistance constitutes over 40 per cent of the national budget, accountability is not simply to the contractual relationship between state and society but also to the larger donor community and to transnational civil society. Given the central roles that external actors have assumed in Cambodia during the conflict and post-conflict periods, culminating in the surrender of Cambodian national sovereignty to the United Nations Transitional Authority in Cambodia (UNTAC), it is arguable that the process of nation-state-building is as much an international project as it is Cambodian. In a political context in which violence emanates from the source traditionally assumed to be the guarantor of security – i.e. the state – and in which civil society remains incipient, dissenting voices need to harness the weight and influence of transnational civil society. In those instances, the only safeguard against wanton abuse of power is international conscience. Although international intervention in Cambodia has had mixed consequences, it remains one, if not the only, hopeful vehicle for post-war conflict mediation.

Conclusion

With the full implications of the transnational dynamics still to be un-veiled, the Cambodian experience points to the significant and varied roles that diasporas assume in conflict and post-war situations. Like any other entities, diasporan communities are complex, with diverse and at times conflicting interests. These features are reflected in the nature and extent of their engagement with the ancestral homeland. Over the past three decades, Cambodians in diaspora have asserted themselves in the political processes of their adopted countries and in the transnational spaces of social and political advocacy. Where the impasse appeared in-surmountable, some have channelled their nationalist sentiments into so-cial justice and peace-building projects in the limited space outside the political arenas. Others, such as the Cambodian Freedom Fighters, con-tinue to opt for a more militant stance that seeks nothing less than the complete, forcible dismantling of the Hun Sen regime, however improb-able the prospect may be.

Differing strategies and visions notwithstanding, these varied forms of transnational political engagement all point to the heightened presence of non-state actors in contemporary politics as an incontrovertible fea-ture of the age of globalization. In the expanded political space for trans-local intervention, there are greater prospects for diasporas to engage in the politics of their ancestral homeland. At times, varied groups and indi-viduals have looked upon the cessation of war as the key to peace; at other times, continued conflict is seen as necessary to compel genuine resolution.

Where their capacity to influence is intrinsically weak, where politics remains entrenched and domestic civil society in an infantile state, dia-sporas' contribution to the peace- and democracy-building project rests on their ability to harness the structure and influence of transnational social forces. Given that international organizations such as the United Nations have yet to evolve into a supranational mechanism for account-ability, transnational civil society may be the sole counterweight to authoritarian regimes. With the proliferation of rights groups, most of which are based in Western democracies, which are also the principal donor countries, there is an opportunity for a partnership to be forged within these translocal political spaces between diasporan communities and international and transnational actors around their shared interest in fostering durable peace. For that eventuality to be possible, both the means and the opportunities must additionally be created for diasporas to systematically and effectively contribute to the peace-building process outside of partisan politics or the confined realm of small-scale, social development projects. Through constructive dialogue and meaningful participation, Cambodian diasporas can assist the governments of their adopted countries and the international community to realign their national and collective agendas to the *spirit* of the peace accords and not just to the compromised structure of the settlement, and to re-envision successful nation-state-building as resting not just on stability – the "silence of the graves" – but on measurable progress towards a more transparent and accountable system.

Notes

1. I am using the term "diasporas" to refer to Cambodians who had been forcibly dispersed and who are living outside the country in cross-border refugee camps and third-country resettlement. Though the camps are now closed and asylum-seekers were repatriated to Cambodia in 1993, over 1 million Cambodians have permanently resettled outside the country, mostly in the West, with the largest concentration being in the United States, Canada, France, Australia and the Scandinavian countries.
2. See Nina Glick Schiller and George Fouron, *When George Woke up Laughing*, Durham, NC: Duke University Press, 2001.
3. "Back to Help Rebuild Cambodia", *Cambodia Times*, July 1996.
4. Ling-chi Wang cited in Ron Takaki, *Strangers from a Different Shore*, Boston: Little, Brown, 1998.
5. See, for instance, Yossi Shain, *Marketing the American Creed Abroad*, Cambridge: Cambridge University Press, 1999.
6. See the Southeast Asia Resource Action Center, *Southeast Asian Admissions FY 1952–2001*, available at ⟨http://www.searac.org⟩.
7. Scholars, journalists and activists such as Gareth Porter, Malcolm Caldwell, Ben Kiernan and W. Burchett, among others, had written favourably about the Khmer Rouge. In diaspora, the insipid efforts to draw attention to the news of death and deprivation in Cambodia such as during a rally in San Diego, California, in 1978 were condemned by regime supporters as reactionary attempts to subvert the revolution.
8. Ed Lazar, "The Peace Movement and Cambodia", *Humanitas*, 1988, 4: 1.
9. For more details on the anti-Khmer Rouge resistance, see Justin Corfield, "A History of the Cambodian Non-Communist Resistance 1975–1983", Working Papers Series, Monash University, Australia, 1991.
10. Lazar, "The Peace Movement and Cambodia".
11. KPNLF Memorandum, 5 March 1979, Hann So Collection, University of California, Berkeley (archival files).
12. Khong Hann So, "The Turning Point", 28 August 1979, Hann So Collection, University of California, Berkeley (archival files).
13. The Khmer Serei (Free Khmers) group, at an estimated 5,000, was splintered under various leaders, each with control over specific refugee camps.
14. "How to Combat the Pestilence and the Cholera", internal communiqué of the Resistance for the Liberation of Cambodia (RLC), n.d., Hann So Collection, University of California, Berkeley (archival files).
15. The four Cambodian groups that were featured in the peace negotiations were Phnom Penh's Cambodian People's Party (CPP) and the three member parties of the coalition government-in-exile, namely the royalist FUNCINPEC, the republican KPNLF and the Khmer Rouge.

16. Letter by Mour Ley, Secretary of the Federation of Khmer Serei, to Senator Pell, 11 March 1990, Hann So Collection, University of California, Berkeley (archival files).
17. Dan Southerland, "The Struggle for Cambodia", *Christian Science Monitor*, 28 November 1979.
18. Quoted in Southerland, "The Struggle for Cambodia".
19. *Southeast Asian Record*, 2–9 November 1979, p. 9.
20. KPNLF Aide-Memoire, March 1982, Hann So Collection, University of California, Berkeley (archival files).
21. Khong Hann So, "Stop the Quarrels", 30 August 1979, Hann So Collection, University of California, Berkeley (archival files).
22. See Khatharya Um, "Cambodia in 1993: Year Zero Plus One", *Asian Survey*, 1994, "Cambodia 1989: Still Talking but No Settlement", *Asian Survey*, 1990, and "The Curved Road to Settlement: Cambodia 1988", *Asian Survey*, 1989.
23. T. D. Allman, "Sihanouk Sideshow", *Vanity Fair*, April 1990, p. 58.
24. Bernard Gwertzman, "Sihanouk Fails to Get US Support", *New York Times*, 23 February 1980.
25. Ibid.
26. In 1982, Congress approved an annual budget of US$3.5 million; it was paired with covert assistance that purportedly grew from an estimated US$5 million to approximately US$12 million. By the late 1980s, the United States, in anticipation of the peace negotiations, moved to strengthen its support of the non-communist factions. A congressional plan to triple its appropriation to the Cambodian resistance ran aground on a corruption scandal involving high-ranking Thai officials.
27. See Khatharya Um, "Thailand and the Regional Divide: Future Regional Power Configurations in Asia-Pacific", *Contemporary Southeast Asia*, 1990.
28. Interview with Hun Sen by the Federation of American Scientists, 27 February 1989.
29. Foreign Broadcast Information Service, Daily Report/East Asia, 26 September 1988. For more on the Cambodia conflict in 1988, see Khatharya Um, "The Curved Road to Settlement: Cambodia 1988", *Asian Survey*, 1989, p. 73.
30. Letter of appeal from the diaspora cited in *Humanitas*, 1988, 4: 1; Hann So Collection, University of California, Berkeley (archival files).
31. Nayan Chanda, "Cambodia in 1987", *Asian Survey*, January 1988, p. 114.
32. In the period 1989–1993, the People's Republic of Kampuchea was renamed the State of Cambodia in an effort to distance itself from its political history as a communist government installed by Viet Nam.
33. Protocol of Agreement signed at Torcy, 14 April 1989, Hann So Collection, Berkeley, California (archival files).
34. The head of LICADHO, one of the leading organizations working with vulnerable populations, is a French Cambodian woman. At the helm of the Center for Social Development is a Cambodian-American woman who had held a leadership position in a community-based organization in the United States.
35. Um, personal communication, California, 1998.
36. Asia Society Symposium, Long Beach, California, 21 March 1997.
37. Yossi Shain, *The Frontier of Loyalty*, Connecticut: Wesleyan University Press, 1989, p. 24.
38. Linda Basch, Nina Glick Schiller and Cristina Szanton Blanc, *Nations Unbound: Transnational Projects, Post-Colonial Predicaments and Deterritorialized Nation-States*, Amsterdam: Gordon & Breach, 1994, p. 32.
39. Um, personal interview, Washington, DC, 1996.
40. Um, personal interview, Long Beach, California, March 1997.
41. Various international human rights organizations, including Amnesty International,

Asia Watch and Human Rights Watch, have reported on the July 1997 coup and the post-coup implications for human rights in Cambodia.

42. Then-minister of commerce, Cham Prasidh, acknowledged that progress on trade talks centring on the extension of the US Generalized System of Preferences had stalled as a result of US concerns over the resurgence of violence in Cambodia. See "Cambodia Says US Worry Holds up Trade", Reuters, May 1997, Hann So Collection, Berkeley, California (archival files).

Bibliography

Abreau, A. G., "Cubans without Borders: The Possible Dream", *Florida Law Review*, 2004, 55(1): 206–207.

Abu Sitta, Salman, *The Atlas of Palestine 1948*, London: Palestine Land Society, 2005.

Ackerman, H., "Strategic Calculation and Democratic Society: The Cuban Democratic Resistance in the 1960s and 1990s", paper prepared for the XXI International Congress of the Latin American Studies Association, Chicago, 24–26 September 1998.

Adamaly, Zahabia, Ana Cutter and Shyama Venkateswar, "Lessons from Sri Lanka: Communities in Conflict", The Asia Society and Carnegie Council on Ethics and International Affairs, New York, 2000.

"Adel Mana", *A'lam Filastin fin Awakher al-'Ahd al-'Uthmani (1800–1918)* [Notable Palestinians during the Late Ottoman Period 1800–1918], Beirut: Institute of Palestine Studies, 1997.

Al-Abbasi, Mustapha, *Safad fi 'Ahd al-Intitab al-Baritani* [Safad under the British Mandate], Beirut: Institute of Palestine Studies, 2005.

Al-Ali, Nadje, "Transnational or A-National: Bosnian Refugees in the UK and the Netherlands", in Nadje Al-Ali and Khalid Koser, eds, *New Approaches to Migration: Transnational Communities and the Transformation of Home*, London: Routledge, 2002.

Al-Ali, Nadje, "Losses in Status or New Opportunities? Gender Relations and Transnational Ties among Bosnian Refugees", in Deborah Fahy Bryceson and Ulla Vuorel, eds, *Forging New European Frontiers: Transnational Families and Their Global Networks*, Oxford: Berg Publisher, 2003.

Al-Ali, Nadje and Khalid Koser, eds, *New Approaches to Migration: Transnational Communities and the Transformation of Home*, London: Routledge, 2002.

Al-Ali, Nadje, Richard Black and Khalid Koser, "Refugees and Transnationalism: The Experience of Bosnians and Eritreans in Europe", *Journal of Ethnic and Migration Studies*, 2001, 27(4).

Allman, T. D., "Sihanouk Sideshow", *Vanity Fair*, April 1990.

Ammann, Birgit, "KurdInnen in der Bundesrepublik Deutschland", in Markus Ottersbach and Felix Weiland, eds, *KurdInnen in der Bundesrepublik Deutschland*, Bonn: NAVEND, 1999.

Anderson, Benedict, *Long-Distance Nationalism: World Capitalism and the Rise of Identity Politics. The Werthem Lecture*, Amsterdam: Center for South Asian Studies, University of Amsterdam, 1992.

Angoustures, Aline and Valerie Pascal, "Diasporas et Financement des Conflits", in Francois Jean Rufin and Jean-Christophe Rufin, eds, *Economie des Guerres Civiles*, Paris: Hachette, 1996.

Antić, Ljubomir, *Hrvati i Amerika*, Zagreb: Hrvatska Sveučilištna naklada, 1992.

Armstrong, John, "Mobilized and Proletarian Diasporas", *American Political Science Review*, 1976, 70(2).

Asia Foundation, "Focus on Sri Lanka", San Francisco, CA, 2001.

Babadji, Ramadane, Monique Chemillier and Géraud de La Pradelle, *Haq al-'Awdah lil-Sha'b al-Filastini wa Mabadi' Tatbiqihi*, Beirut: Institute of Palestine Studies, 1996.

Baechler, Gunther, "Civilian Conflict Resolution in the Context of International Peace Promotion in the 1990s", in Gunther Baechler, ed., *Promoting Peace. The Role of Civilian Conflict Resolution*, Berne: Staempfli Publishers, 2002, pp. 8–19.

Bamyeh, Mohammed A., "Palestine: Listening to the Inaudible", *South Atlantic Quarterly*, Fall 2003.

Banac, Ivo, *The National Question in Yugoslavia: Origins, History, Politics*, Ithaca, NY: Cornell University Press, 1984.

Barco, Carolina, "Prefacio", in Ministerio de Relaciones Exteriores de Colombia (MREC), *Colombia Nos Une: Memorias: Seminario sobre Migración Internacional Colombiana y la Conformación de Comunidades Transnacionales, Junio 18 y 19 de 2003*, Bogotá, Colombia, March 2004.

Bar-Yaacov, Nomi, "Diplomacy and Human Rights: The Role of Human Rights in Conflict Resolution in El Salvador and Haiti", *Fletcher Forum of World Affairs*, 1995, 19(2).

Basch, Linda, Nina Glick Schiller and Cristina Szanton Blanc, *Nations Unbound: Transnational Projects, Postcolonial Predicaments, and Deterritorialized Nation-States*, Langhorne, PA: Gordon & Breach, 1994.

Bascom, Jonathan, *Losing Place: Refugee Populations and Rural Transformations in East Africa*, Oxford: Berghahn, 1998.

Bercovitch, Jacob, *Social Conflicts and Third Parties*, Boulder, CO: Westview Press, 1984.

Bercovitch, Jacob, "Managing Ethnic Conflicts: The Role and Relevance of Mediation", *World Affairs*, 2003, 166(3): 56–69.

Bose, Sumantra, *States, Nations, Sovereignty: Sri Lanka, India and the Tamil Eelam Movement*, New Delhi: Sage Publications, 1994.

Bose, Sumantra, "State Crisis and Nationalities Conflict in Sri Lanka and Yugoslavia", *Comparative Political Studies*, 1995, 28(1): 94–95.

Bosworth, Richard and Romano Ugolini, eds, *War, Internment and Mass Migration: The Italo-Australian Experience 1940–1990*, Rome: Gruppo Editoriale Internazionale, 1992.

Boutros-Ghali, Boutros, *An Agenda for Peace*, New York: United Nations, 1992.

Bouvier, Virginia M., *Special Report: Civil Society under Siege in Colombia*, Washington, DC: United States Institute of Peace, February 2004.

Bouvier, Virginia M., *Special Report: Peace Initiatives in Colombia*, Washington, DC: United States Institute of Peace, forthcoming.

Brah, Avtar, *Cartographies of Diaspora, Contesting Identities*, London and New York: Routledge, 1996.

Briquets, D. and J. Perez-Lopez, *The Role of the Cuban-American Community in the Cuban Transition*, Cuba Transition Project, Institute for Cuban and Cuban-American Studies, University of Miami, 2003.

Brown, Michael, ed., *Ethnic Conflict and International Security*, Princeton, NJ: Princeton University Press, 1993.

Buijs, Gina, "Introduction", in Gina Buijs, ed., *Migrant Women: Crossing Boundaries and Changing Identities*, Cross-Cultural Perspectives on Women Vol. 7, Oxford: Berg, 1993.

Bullion, Alan J., *India, Sri Lanka and the Tamil Crisis, 1976–1994: An International Perspective*, London: Pinter, 1995.

Bullion, Alan, "Norway and the Peace Process in Sri Lanka", *Civil Wars*, 2001, 4(3): 70–73.

Bush, Kenneth, "Ethnic Conflict in Sri Lanka", *Conflict Quarterly*, 1990, 10: 41–58.

Bušić, Julienne Eden, *Lovers and Madmen: A True Story of Passion, Politics and Air Piracy*, New York: Writers Club Press, 2000.

Butler, Kim D., "Defining Diaspora, Refining a Discourse", *Diaspora*, 2001, 10(2).

Byman, Daniel L., Peter Chalk, Bruce Hoffman, William Rosenau and David Brannan, *Trends in Outside Support for Insurgent Movements*, Santa Monica, CA: RAND, 2001.

Calvo, H. and K. Declerq, eds, *The Cuban Exile Movement*, New York: Ocean Press, 2000, p. 159.

Campbell, Charles, *The Transformation of American Foreign Relations, 1865–1900*, New York: Harper & Row, 1976.

Caniglia, Beth Schaefer, "Elite Alliances and Transnational Environment Movement Organizations", in Jackie Smith and Hank Johnston, eds, *Globalization and Resistance: Transnational Dimensions of Social Movements*, Lanham, MD: Rowman & Littlefield, 2002.

Carothers, T., *In the Name of Democracy: US Policy towards Latin America in the Reagan Years*, Berkeley: University of California Press, 1991.

Casteel, Steven W., "International Law Enforcement Cooperation Fights Narcoterror: Drug Enforcement Agency Official Testifies before Senate Committee", Statements of DEA Intelligence Chief, Steven W. Casteel, 20 May 2003.

Center for International Policy, Colombia Program, "Information about the

Combatants", 2004, ⟨http://www.ciponline.org/colombia/infocombat.htm⟩ (accessed 25 October 2006).

Chalk, Peter, "Liberation Tigers of Tamil Eelam's Internal Organization and Operations: A Preliminary Analysis", A Canadian Security Intelligence Service Publication, 17 March 2000, available at ⟨http://www.fas.org/irp/world/para/docs/com77e.htm⟩.

Chanda, Nayan, "Cambodia in 1987", *Asian Survey*, January 1988.

Charum, Jorge and Jean-Baptiste Meyer, eds, *Hacer ciencia en un mundo globalizado: La diaspora científica colombiana en perspectiva*, Bogotá: Colciencias, Universidad National de Colombia, Tercer Mundo Editores, 1998.

Cheran, R., "Diaspora Circulation and Transnationalism as Agents for Change in the Post Conflict Zones of Sri Lanka", a policy paper submitted to the Berghof Foundation for Conflict Management, Berlin, Germany, 2003, available at ⟨http://www.berghof-foundation.lk/scripts/DiasporaCirc.pdf⟩.

Cipek, Tihomir, "The Croats and Yugoslavism", in Dejan Djokić, ed., *Yugoslavism: Histories of a Failed Idea 1918–1992*, London: Hurst, 2003.

Clifford, James, "Diasporas", *Cultural Anthropology*, 1994, 9(3).

Cockburn, Cynthia, "Background Paper: Gender, Armed Conflict and Political Violence", World Bank Conference on Gender, Armed Conflict and Political Development, Washington, DC, 1999, p. 8.

Cockburn, Cynthia and Dubravka Zarkov, "Introduction", in Cynthia Cockburn and Dubravka Zarkov, eds, *The Postwar Moment: Militaries, Masculinities and International Peacekeeping*, London: Lawrence & Wishart, 2002.

Cohen, Lenard J., *Serpent in the Bosom: The Rise and Fall of Slobodan Milošević*, Boulder, CO: Westview, 2002.

Cohen, Michael, *Truman and Israel*, Berkeley: University of California Press, 1990.

Cohen, Robin, *Global Diasporas: An Introduction*, Seattle: University of Washington Press; London: UCL Press, 1997.

Colic-Peisker, Val, "Croatians in Western Australia: Migration, Language and Class", *Journal of Sociology*, 2002, 38(2): 149–166.

Collier, Michael W. and Eduardo A. Gamarra, "The Colombian Diaspora in South Florida", *Report of the Colombian Studies Institute's Colombian Diaspora Project*, Working Paper Series No. 1, Miami: Latin American and Caribbean Center, Florida International University, May 2001.

Collier, Paul and Anke Hoeffler, *Greed and Grievance in Civil War*, Washington, DC: World Bank, 2000.

Collier, Paul and Anke Hoeffler, "Aid, Policy and Peace: Reducing the Risks of Civil Conflict", *Journal of Defense Economics*, 2002, 13(6): 435–450.

Colson, Elizabeth, "Gendering Those Uprooted by 'Development'", in Doreen Indra, ed., *Engendering Forced Migration*, New York: Berghahn, 1999.

Connell, Dan, *Against All Odds: A Chronicle of the Eritrean Revolution*, Trenton, NJ: Red Sea Press, 1997.

Connell, Robert, *Gender and Power*, Cambridge: Polity Press, 1987.

Connell, Robert, *Masculinities*, Cambridge: Polity Press, 1995.

Connor, Walker, "When Is a Nation?", *Ethnic and Racial Studies*, 1990, 13(1): 92–103.

Cordovi, J. T., "Cuba's Economic Transformation and Conflict with the United States", in V. Bulmer-Thomas and J. Dunkerley, eds, *The United States and Latin America: The New Agenda*, London and Cambridge, MA: Institute of Latin American Studies & David Rockefeller Center for Latin American Studies, 1999, pp. 247–266.

Corfield, Justin, "A History of the Cambodian Non-Communist Resistance 1975–1983", Working Papers Series, Monash University, Australia, 1991.

Corrin, C., "Introduction", in C. Corrin, ed., *Women in a Violent World: Feminist Analyses and Resistance across "Europe"*, Edinburgh: Edinburgh University Press, 1996.

Crocker, Chester, Fen Hampson and Pamela Aall, *Taming Intractable Conflicts*, Washington, DC: United States Institute of Peace, 2004.

Croucher, S. L., *Imagining Miami: Ethnic Politics in a Postmodern World*, Charlottesville and London: University Press of Virginia, 1997.

Cruz, Carmen Inés and Juanita Castaño, "Colombian Migration to the United States (Part 1)", in *The Dynamics of Migration: International Migration. Interdisciplinary Communications Program*, Occasional Monograph Series 5.2, Washington, DC: Smithsonian Institution, 1976, pp. 49–50.

D'Amico, Francine, "Citizen-Soldier? Class, Gender, Sexuality and the US Military", in Susie Jacobs, Ruth Jacobson and Jennifer Marchbank, eds, *States of Conflict: Gender, Violence and Resistance*, London: Zed Books, 2000.

Danner, Mark, "The Killing Fields of Bosnia", *New York Review of Books*, 1998, 45(14): 63–77.

Davis, Anthony, "Asia, Tamil Tiger International", *Jane's Intelligence Review*, 1 October 1996.

Davis, Anthony, "Tiger International", *Asiaweek*, 26 November 1996.

Davis, David R., Keith Jaggers and Will H. Moore, "Ethnicity, Minorities, and International Conflict Patterns", in David W. Carment and Patrick James, eds, *Wars in the Midst of Peace: The International Politics of Ethnic Conflict*, Pittsburgh, PA: University of Pittsburgh Press, 1997.

De Silva, K. M., *A History of Sri Lanka*, Berkeley: University of California Press, 1981.

De Silva, K. M., *Managing Ethnic Tensions in Multi-Ethnic Societies: Sri Lanka, 1880–1985*, Lanham, MD: University Press of America, 1986.

De Silva, Manik, "Sri Lanka's Civil War", *Current History*, 1999, 98(632): 428–432.

De Waal, Thomas, *Black Garden: Armenia and Azerbaijan through Peace and War*, New York: New York University Press, 2003.

Deutsch, Morton, *The Resolution of Conflict*, Yale: Yale University Press, 1973.

DeVotta, Neil, "Sri Lanka in 2004: Enduring Political Decay and a Failing Peace Process", *Asian Survey*, 2005, 45(1): 98–104.

Djilas, Aleksa, *The Contested Country: Yugoslav Unity and Communist Revolution: 1919–53*, Cambridge, MA: Harvard University Press, 1991.

Djilas, Milovan, *Tito: The Story from Inside*, New York: Harcourt Brace Jovanovich, 1980.

Dominguez, J. I., "Cooperating with the Enemy: US Immigration Policy towards Cuba", in Chris Mitchell, ed., *Western Hemispheric Immigration and US Policy*, University Park, PA: Penn State University, 1992.

Dominguez, J. I., "US–Cuban Relations: From the Cold War to the Colder War", *Journal of Interamerican Studies and World Affairs*, 1997, 39(3): 49–75.

Dominguez, J. I., "US–Latin American Relations during the Cold War and Its Aftermath", in V. Bulmer-Thomas and J. Dunkerley, eds, *The United States and Latin America: The New Agenda*, London and Cambridge, MA: Institute of Latin American Studies & David Rockefeller Center for Latin American Studies, 1999, pp. 33–50.

Dotan, Shmuel, *The Debate about Partition during the Mandatory Period*, Jerusalem: Yad Ben Zvi, 1980 (in Hebrew).

Doumani, Beshara, *Rediscovering Palestine: Merchants and Peasants in Jabal Nablus, 1700–1900*, Berkeley: University of California Press, 1995.

Dreyfuss, Robert, "More Missing Intelligence", *The Nation*, 7 July 2004.

Elath, Eliyahu, *The Struggle for Statehood*, 3 vols, Tel Aviv: Am Oved, 1979–1982 (in Hebrew).

Enderlin, Charles, *Shattered Dreams: The Failure of the Peace Process in the Middle East 1995–2002*, New York: Other Press, 2003.

Enloe, Cynthia, "Feminist Thinking about War, Militarism and Peace", in B. Hess, ed., *Analysing Gender: A Handbook of Social Science Research*, Newbury Park. CA: Sage, 1987.

Enloe, Cynthia, *Maneuvers: The International Politics of Militarizing Women's Lives*, Berkeley: University of California Press, 2000.

Enloe, Cynthia, "Demilitarization – or More of the Same? Feminist Questions to Ask in the Postwar Moment", in Cynthia Cockburn and Dubravka Zarkov, eds, *The Postwar Moment: Militaries, Masculinities and International Peacekeeping*, London: Lawrence & Wishart, 2002, pp. 22–24.

Esman, Martin J. and Robert J. Herring, eds, *Carrots, Sticks and Ethnic Conflict*, Ann Arbor: University of Michigan Press, 2001.

Evron, Yair, *War and Intervention in Lebanon*, Baltimore, MD: Johns Hopkins University Press, 1987.

Fair, C. Christine, "Military Operations in Urban Areas: The Indian Experience", *India Review*, 2003, 2(1): 49–76.

Fair, C. Christine, *Urban Battle Fields of South Asia: Lessons Learned from Sri Lanka, India and Pakistan*, Santa Monica: RAND, 2004.

Fair, Christine, "Diaspora Involvement in Insurgencies: Insights from the Khalistan and Tamil Eelam Movements", *Nationalism and Ethnic Politics*, 2005, 11(1).

Fair, C. Christine, "Sri Lanka's Drift Back into War", *International Journal of Peace Operations*, 2006, 2(3).

Faist, Thomas, *The Volume and Dynamics of International Migration and Transnational Social Spaces*, London: Oxford University Press, 2000.

Falga, Bernard, Catherine Wihtol de Wenden and Claus Leggewie, *De l'immigration à l'intégration en France et en Allemagne*, Paris: Les Editions du Cerf, 1994.

Farsoun, Samih and Jean Landis, "The Sociology of an Uprising: The Roots of the Intifada", in Jamal Nassar and Roger Heacock, eds, *Intifada: Palestine at the Crossroads*, New York: Praeger, 1990.

Fearon, James, "Commitment Problems and the Spread of Ethnic Conflict", in

David A. Lake and Donald Rothchild, eds, *The International Spread of Ethnic Conflict: Fear, Diffusion and Escalation*, Princeton, NJ: Princeton University Press, 1998.

Fearon, James and David Leitin, "Ethnicity, Insurgency and Civil War", *American Political Science Review*, 1994, 79(1): 75–90.

Fernandes, Desmond, "The Targeting and Criminalisation of Kurdish Asylum Seekers and Refugee Communities in the UK and Germany", Peace in Kurdistan Campaign and The Ahmed Foundation for Kurdish Studies, London, 2001.

Fernández-Kelly, Patricia and Ana García, "Power Surrendered, Power Restored: The Politics of Home and Work among Hispanic Women in Southern California and Southern Florida", in Louise A. Tilly and Patricia Guerin, eds, *Women and Politics in America*, New York: Russell Sage Foundation, 1990, pp. 215–228.

Field, G. Lowell and John Higley, *Elitism*, London: Routledge & Kegan Paul, 1980.

Fitzgerald, Valpy, "Global Financial Information, Compliance Incentives and Conflict Funding", paper presented to the International Conference on Globalization and Self-Determination Movements, hosted by Pomona College, 21–22 January 2003.

Fondo Multilateral de Inversiones, Banco Interamericano de Desarrollo, "Receptores de remesas en América Latina: El caso colombiano", Cartagena, Colombia, September 2004.

Fortna, Virginia, *Peace Time: Cease-Fire Agreements and the Durability of Peace*, Princeton, NJ: Princeton University Press, 2004.

Fuglerud, Oivind, *Life on the Outside: The Tamil Diaspora and Long-Distance Nationalism*, London: Pluto Press, 1999.

Galtung, Johan, *Essays in Peace Research*, vols 1–5, Copenhagen: Christian Ejlers, 1975–1980.

Gamarra, Eduardo A., "La diáspora colombiana en el sur de la Florida", in Ministerio de Relaciones Exteriores de Colombia (MREC), *Colombia Nos Une: Memorias: Seminario sobre Migración Internacional Colombiana y la Conformación de Comunidades Transnacionales, Junio 18 y 19 de 2003*, Bogotá, Colombia, March 2004.

Ganin, Zvi, *Truman, American Jewry and Israel 1945–1948*, New York: Holmes & Meier, 1979.

Ganin, Zvi, *An Uneasy Relationship: American Jewish Leadership and Israel, 1948–1957*, Syracuse: Syracuse University Press, 2005.

Gates, Henry Louis, ed., *The Classic Slave Narratives*, New York: New American Library, 1987.

Gervais, Myriam, "Human Security and Reconstruction Efforts in Rwanda: Impact on the Lives of Women", in Haleh Afshar and Deborah Eade, eds, *Development, Women, and War: Feminist Perspectives*, Oxford: Oxfam, 2004, pp. 301–314.

Ghahayem, Zuhair, *Liwa' 'Akka fi 'Ahd al-Tanzimat al-'Uthmaniyyah 1864–1918* [Akka Province during the Ottoman Tanzimat 1864–1918], Beirut: Institute of Palestine Studies, 1999.

Gibb, Tom, "Analysis: Castro's Victory?", BBC News, 28 June 2000, ⟨http://news.bbc.co.uk/1/hi/world/americas/711828.stm⟩.

Glazer, Nathan and Daniel P. Moynihan, *Beyond the Melting Pot: The Negroes, Puerto Ricans, Jews, Italians, and Irish of New York City*, Cambridge, MA: MIT Press, 1965.

Glenny, Misha, *The Fall of Yugoslavia: The Third Balkan War*, London: Penguin Books, 1992.

Glick Schiller, Nina, "Transmigrants and Nation-States: Something Old and Something New in the U.S. Immigrant Experience", in C. Hirschmann, P. Kasinitz and J. DeWind, eds, *The Handbook of International Migration*, New York: Russell Sage Foundation, 1999, pp. 94–119.

Glick Schiller, Nina and George Fouron, *When George Woke up Laughing*, Durham, NC: Duke University Press, 2001.

Glick Schiller, Nina, Linda Basch and Cristina Szanton Blanc, "From Immigrant to Transmigrant: Theorizing Transmigration", in Ludger Pries, ed., *Migration and Transnational Social Spaces*, Aldershot: Ashgate, 1999.

Glubb, J. B., "Violence on the Jordan–Israel Border: A Jordanian View", *Foreign Affairs*, July 1954.

Goff, Patricia F. and Kevin C. Dunn, *Identity and Global Politics: Theoretical and Empirical Elaborations*, New York: Palgrave Macmillan, 2004.

Goldring, Luin, "Gendered Memory: Constructions of Rurality among Mexican Transnational Migrants", in E. M. DuPuis and Peter Vendergeest, eds, *Creating the Countryside: The Politics of Rural and Environmental Discourse*, Philadelphia: Temple University Press, 1996, pp. 303–329.

Gómez Kopp, Milena, "Políticas para promover un mayor acercamiento con la diáspora: Las voces de los colombianos en Nueva York", in Ministerio de Relaciones Exteriores de Colombia (MREC), *Colombia Nos Une: Memorias: Seminario sobre Migración Internacional Colombiana y la Conformación de Comunidades Transnacionales, Junio 18 y 19 de 2003*, Bogotá, Colombia, March 2004.

Greenhill, K. M., "Engineered Migration and the Use of Refugees as Political Weapons: A Case Study of the 1994 Cuban Balseros Crisis", *International Migration*, 2002, 40(4): 39–47.

Griffiths, David, *Somali and Kurdish Refugees in London: New Identities in the Diaspora*, Aldershot: Ashgate, 2002.

Grobar, Lisa Morris and Shiranthi Gnanaselvam, "The Economic Effects of the Sri Lankan Civil War", *Economic Development and Cultural Change*, 1993, 41(2): 395–405.

Grugel, Jean, *Democratization: A Critical Introduction*, London: Palgrave Macmillan, 2002.

Guáqueta, Alexandra, "The Colombian Conflict: Political and Economic Dimensions," in Karen Ballentine and Jake Sherman, eds, *The Political Economy of Armed Conflict: Beyond Greed and Grievance*, International Peace Academy Economic Agendas in Civil Wars Program, Boulder, CO: Lynne Rienner Publishers, 2003.

Guarnizo, Luis Eduardo, "La migración transnacional colombiana: Implicaciones teóricas y prácticas", in Ministerio de Relaciones Exteriores de Colombia (MREC), *Colombia Nos Une: Memorias: Seminario sobre Migración Internacional Colombiana y la Conformación de Comunidades Transnacionales, Junio 18 y 19 de 2003*, Bogotá, Colombia, March 2004.

Guarnizo, Luis Eduardo and Luz Marina Díaz, "Transnational Migration: A View from Colombia", *Ethnic and Racial Studies*, 1999, 22(2).

Guarnizo, Luis Eduardo, Alejandro Portes and William Haller, "Assimilation and Transnationalism: Determinants of Transnational Political Action among Contemporary Migrants", *American Journal of Sociology*, 2003, 108(6).

Gunaratna, Rohan, *Indian Interventions in Sri Lanka: The Role of India's Intelligence Agencies*, Colombo: South Asian Network on Conflict Research, 1993.

Gunaratna, Rohan, "International and Regional Implications of the Sri Lankan Tamil Insurgency", Institute for Counter-Terrorism, 2 December 1998, available at ⟨http://www.ict.org.il/articles/articledet.cfm?articleid=57⟩.

Gunaratna, Rohan, "Bankrupting the Terror Business," *Jane's Intelligence Review*, 1 August 2000, 12(8).

Gunaratna, Rohan, "The LTTE and Suicide Terrorism", *Frontline*, 5–8 February 2000, 17(3), available at ⟨http://www.frontlineonnet.com/fl1703/17031060.htm⟩ (accessed 3 October 2006).

Gunaratna, Rohan, "Sri Lanka: Feeding the Tamil Tigers", in Karen Ballentine and Jake Sherman, eds, *The Political Economy of Armed Conflict: Beyond Greed and Grievance*, Boulder, CO: Lynne Rienner, 2003.

Gupta, Amit, "The Indian Diaspora's Political Efforts in the United States", ORF Occasional Paper Series, September 2004, available at ⟨http://www.orfonline.org/publications/OccasionalPapers/op040918.pdf⟩ (accessed 3 October 2006).

Gurr, Ted R., *Peoples Versus States: Minorities at Risk in the New Century*, Washington, DC: USIP Press, 2003.

Gurr, Ted R. and Martin Marshall, *Peace and Conflict*, Maryland: CIDCM, 2005.

Guyatt, Nicholas, *The Absence of Peace: Understanding the Israeli–Palestinian Conflict*, New York: Zed Books, 1998.

Gwertzman, Bernard, "Sihanouk Fails to Get US Support", *New York Times*, 23 February 1980.

Hall, Stuart, "Cultural Identity and Diaspora", in Jonathan Rutherford, ed., *Identity: Community, Culture, Difference*, London: Lawrence & Wishart, 1990.

Hanafi, Sari, "Palestinian Diaspora Contribution to Investment and Philanthropy in Palestine", October 2000, at ⟨http://www.palesta.gov.ps/academic/publication/diaspora.htm⟩ (accessed 22 February 2006).

Hanafi, Sari, *Huna wa Hunak: Nahwa Tahlil lil-'Alaqah bayn al-Shatat al-Filastini wa al-Markaz* [Here and There: Towards an Analysis of the Relationship between the Palestinian Diaspora and the Centre], Ramallah: Muwatin (Palestinian Institute for the Study of Democracy), 2001.

Haney, P. J. and W. Vanderbush, "The Role of Ethnic Interest Groups in US Foreign Policy: The Case of the Cuban American National Foundation", *International Studies Quarterly*, 1999, 43: 341–361.

Hartmann, Heidi, "Capitalism, Patriarchy and Job Segregation by Sex", in Zillah Eisenstein, ed., *Capitalist Patriarchy and the Case for Socialist Feminism*, New York: Monthly Review Press, 1979.

Hathaway, Robert, "Unfinished Passage: India, Indian Americans, and the U.S. Congress", *Washington Quarterly*, 2001, 24(2).

Hayden, Robert M., "Constitutional Nationalism in the Formerly Yugoslav Republics", *Slavic Review*, 1992, 51(4): 654–673.

Hersh, Seymour M., "The Stovepipe: How Conflicts between the Bush Administration and the Intelligence Community Marred the Reporting on Iraq's Weapons", *New Yorker*, 27 October 2003.

Hijab, Nadia, "The Role of Palestinian Diaspora Institutions in Mobilizing the International Community", paper presented at the Economic and Social Commission for Western Asia (ESCWA), "Arab-International Forum on Rehabilitation and Development in the Occupied Palestinian Territory: Towards an Independent Palestinian State", Beirut, 11–14 October 2004.

Hilal, Jamil, *Al-Nizam al-Siyasi al-Filastini ba'd Oslo* [The Palestinian Political System after Oslo], Beirut: Institute for Palestine Studies, 1998.

Hockenos, Paul, *Homeland Calling: Exile Patriotism and the Balkan Wars*, Ithaca, NY: Cornell University Press, 2003.

Hondagneu-Sotelo, Pierette, *Gendered Transitions: Mexican Experiences of Immigration*, Berkeley: University of California Press, 1994.

Horowitz, I. L., "The Cuba Lobby Then and Now", *Orbis*, 1998, 42(4): 553–563.

Huang, Reyko, "In the Spotlight: Liberation Tigers of Tamil Eelam (LTTE)", Washington, DC: Center for Defense Information, 19 April 2002, available at ⟨http://www.cdi.org/terrorism/ltte.cfm⟩ (accessed 3 October 2006).

Human Rights Watch, *Funding the "Final War": LTTE Intimidation and Extortion in the Tamil Diaspora*, New York: Human Rights Watch, 2006.

India Express, "U.S. Denies any Information about LTTE Indulging in Drug Trafficking", 3 March 2001.

Indra, Doreen, ed., *Engendering Forced Migration*, New York: Berghahn, 1999.

Institut de recherche pour le développement, "Brain Drain: How to Benefit from Expatriates Skills?", *Scientific Bulletin*, No. 27, November 1996, at ⟨http://www.ird.fr/us/actualites/fiches/1996/27.htm⟩ (accessed 25 October 2006).

Inter-American Dialogue, "All in the Family: Latin America's Most Important International Financial Flow", *Report of the Inter-American Dialogue Task Force on Remittances*, Washington, DC: Inter-American Dialogue, January 2004.

International Crisis Group, "Colombia and Its Neighbours: The Tentacles of Instability", ICG Latin America Report No. 3, 8 April 2003.

International Crisis Group, "War and Drugs in Colombia", Latin America Report No. 11, 27 January 2005.

Isaac, Rael Jean, *Briera*, New York: Counsel for Judaism, 1977.

Itzigsohn, José and Silvia Giorguli Saucedo, "Immigrant Incorporation and Sociocultural Transnationalism", *International Migration Review*, 2002, 36(3).

Iuspa, Paola, "FIU Hopes to Analyze Colombian Influx into South Florida", *Miami Today*, week of 30 November 2000, at ⟨http://www.miamitodaynews.com/news/001130/story3.shtml⟩ (accessed 26 October 2006).

Johnson, Paul, *A History of the Jews*, New York: Harper & Row, 1987.

Jones-Correa, Michael, "Different Paths: Gender, Immigration and Political Participation", *International Migration Review*, 1998, 32(2): 326–349.

Joseph, Suad, "Patriarchy and Development in the Arab world", *Gender & Development*, 1996, 4(2): 14–19.

Joshi, Manoj, "On the Razor's Edge: The Liberation Tigers of Tamil Eelam", *Studies in Conflict and Terrorism*, January/March 1996, 19: 19–42.

Kaldor, Mary, *New and Old Wars: Organized Violence in a Global Era*, London: Polity Press, 1999.

Kasbarian, John Antranig, "We Are Our Mountains: Geographies of Nationalism in the Armenian Self-Determination Movement in Nagorno-Karabakh", unpublished dissertation, Rutgers University, Geography Department, 2004.

Kaufman, Menachem, *An Ambiguous Partnership*, Detroit: Wayne State University Press, 1991.

Kearney, Robert N., "Tension and Conflict in Sri Lanka", *Current History*, 1986, 85: 109–112.

Kellas, John, *The Politics of Nationalism and Ethnicity*, New York: St Martin's, 1991.

Kelleher, Ann and James Larry Taulbee, "Bridging the Gap: Building Peace Norwegian Style", *Peace & Change*, 2006, 31(4).

Kelly, Liz, "Wars against Women: Sexual Violence, Sexual Politics and the Militarized State", in Susie Jacobs, Ruth Jacobson and Jennifer Marchbank, eds, *States of Conflict: Gender, Violence and Resistance*, London: Zed Books, 2000.

Kelman, Herb, "Interactive Problem-Solving: Informal Mediation by the Scholar-Practitioner", in Jacob Bercovitch, ed., *Studies in International Mediation*, London and New York: Palgrave/Macmillan, 2002, pp. 165–192.

Kenzer, M. S., "Review: M. C. Garcia, *Havana USA: Cuban Exiles and Cuban Americans in South Florida 1959–1994* (Berkeley: University of California Press, 1997)", *Journal of Historical Geography*, 2000, 26(1): 152.

Khalidi, Walid, *Before Their Diaspora: A Photographic History of the Palestinians 1876–1948*, Washington, DC: Institute of Palestine Studies, 2004 [1984].

Khmer People's National Liberation Front Memorandum, 5 March 1979, Hann So Collection, University of California, Berkeley (archival files).

Khmer People's National Liberation Front, Aide-Memoire, March 1982, Hann So Collection, University of California, Berkeley (archival files).

Khong Hann So, "Stop the Quarrels", 30 August 1979, Hann So Collection, University of California, Berkeley (archival files).

Khong Hann So, "The Turning Point", 28 August 1979, Hann So Collection, University of California, Berkeley (archival files).

King, Charles, "The Benefits of Ethnic War: Understanding Eurasia's Unrecognized States", *World Politics*, 2001, 53: 524–552.

King, Charles and Neil J. Melvin, "Diaspora Politics: Ethnic Linkages, Foreign Policy, and Security in Eurasia", *International Security*, 1999/2000, 24(3).

Klauser, S. Z., "Diaspora in Comparative Research", in More Menachen, ed., *Eretz Israel, Israel and the Jewish Diaspora Mutual Relations*, Lanham, MD: Craighton University, 1991, pp. 194–221.

Koenig, D., "Women and Resettlement", in R. S. Gallin, A. Ferguson and J. Harper, eds, *The Women and International Development Annual*, No. 4, 1995, pp. 21–49.

Koopmans, Ruud and Paul Statham, "Migration and Ethnic Relations as a Field of Political Contention: An Opportunity Structure Approach", in Ruud Koopmans and Paul Statham, eds, *Challenging Immigration and Ethnic Relations Politics*, Oxford: Oxford University Press, 2000.

Korac, Maja, *Linking Arms: Women and War in Post-Yugoslav States*, Uppsala: Life and Peace Institute, 1998.

Koser, Khalid, ed., *New African Diasporas*, London: Routledge, 2003.

Krauss, Clifford, "The Cali Cartel and the Globalization of Crime in New York City", in Margaret E. Crahan and Alberto Vourvoulias-Bush, eds, *The City and the World: New York's Global Future*, New York: Council on Foreign Relations, 1997.

Kriesberg, Louis, *Constructive Conflicts*, Lanham, MD: Rowman & Littlefield, 1998.

Kriesi, Hanspeter, et al., *New Social Movements in Western Europe: A Comparative Analysis*, London: University College, 1995.

Krizman, Bogdan, *Pavelić and Ustaše*, Zagreb: Globus, 1978.

Lake, Oliver, "Towards a Pan-African Identity: Diaspora African Repatriates in Ghana", *Anthropological Quarterly*, 1995, 68(1).

Lazar, Ed, "The Peace Movement and Cambodia", *Humanitas*, 1988, 4.

Le Billon, Philippe, Jake Sherman and Marcia Hardwell, "Controlling Resource Flows to Civil Wars: A Review and Analysis of Current Policies and Legal Instruments", Background Paper for the International Peace Academy "Economic Agendas in Civil Wars" Project Conference *Policies and Practices for Regulating Resource Flows to Armed Conflicts*, Rockefeller Foundation Study and Conference Center, Bellagio, Italy, 20–24 May 2002, available at ⟨http://www.ipacademy.org/PDF_Reports/controlling_resource_flows.pdf⟩.

Lentin, Ronit, *Gender and Catastrophe*, London: Zed Books, 1997.

Leogrande, W. M., "Enemies Evermore: US Policy towards Cuba after Helms-Burton", *Journal of Latin American Studies*, 1997, 29: 212.

Levitt, Peggy, "Social Remittances: Migration-Driven Local-Level Forms of Cultural Diffusion", *International Migration Review*, 1998, 34(4).

Libaridian, Gerard J. G., ed., *The Karabagh File: Documents and Facts on the Question of Mountainous Karabagh, 1918–1988*, Cambridge, MA, and Toronto: Zoryan Institute for Contemporary Armenian Research and Documentation, 1988.

Lievesley, G., *The Cuban Revolution: Past, Present and Future Perspectives*, London: Palgrave Macmillan, 2003.

Loescher, Gil, "Protection and Humanitarian Action in the Post-Cold War Era", in Aristide R. Zolberg and Peter M. Benda, eds, *Global Migrants, Global Refugees*, New York: Berghahn Books, 2001, pp. 171–204.

Lund, Michael, *Preventing Violent Conflicts: A Strategy for Preventive Diplomacy*, Washington, DC: United States Institute of Peace Press, 1996.

Lynch, Dov, *Engaging Eurasia's Separatist States: Unresolved Conflicts and De Facto States*, Washington, DC: United States Institute of Peace Press, 2004.

Lyons, Terrence, "Globalization, Diasporas and Conflict", Institute for Conflict Analysis and Resolution, George Mason University, January 2004.

McDowal, David, *Modern History of the Kurds*, London: I. B. Tauris, 2004.

McDowell, Chris, *A Tamil Asylum Diaspora*, Oxford: Berghahn, 1997.

Mahler, Sarah and Patricia Pessar, "Gendered Geographies of Power: Analyzing Gender across Transnational Spaces", *Identities: Global Studies in Culture and Power*, 2001, 7: 441–459.

Majumdar, Sanjoy, "Sri Lanka's Tsunami Aid Politics", BBC News World Edition, 21 March 2005, available at ⟨http://news.bbc.co.uk/2/hi/south_asia/4367935.stm⟩ (accessed 3 October 2006).

Makovsky, David, *Engagement through Disengagement: Gaza and the Potential for Renewed Israeli–Palestinian Peacemaking*, Washington, DC: Washington Institute for Near East Policy, 2005.

Malmat, Avraham, et al., *History of the Jewish People*, 3 vols, Tel Aviv: Dvir, 1969 (in Hebrew).

Mandel, Neville, *The Arabs and Zionism before World War I*, Berkeley: University of California Press, 1976.

Mandelbaum, Michael, ed., *The New European Diasporas: National Minorities and Conflicts in Eastern Europe*, New York: Council on Foreign Relations, 2000.

Maney, Gregory M., "Transnational Structures and Protests: Linking Theories and Assessing Evidence", in Jackie Smith and Hank Johnston, eds, *Globalization and Resistance: Transnational Dimensions of Social Movements*, Lanham, MD: Rowman & Littlefield, 2002, pp. 32–37.

Mardam-Bey, Farouk and Elias Sanbar, eds, *Le Droit au Retour: Le Problème des Réfugiés Palestiniens*, Paris: Actes Sud, 2002.

Meyer, Jean-Baptiste, D. Bernal, J. Charum, J. Gaillard, J. Granés, J. León, A. Montenegro, A. Morales, C. Murcía, N. Narváez-Berthelemot, L.-S. Parrado and B. Schlemmer, "Turning Brain Drain into Brain Gain: The Colombian Experience of the Diaspora Option", *Science, Technology and Society*, 1997, 2(2).

Mezey, G., "Rape in War", *Journal of Forensic Psychiatry*, 1995, 5(3).

Meznaric, Silvia, "Gender as an Ethno-Marker: Rape, War and Identity Politics in the Former Yugoslavia", in Valentine Moghadam, ed., *Identity, Politics and Women: Cultural Reassertions and Feminisms in International Perspective*, Oxford: Westview Press, 1994.

Miall, Hugh, Oliver Ramsbotham and Tom Woodhouse, *Contemporary Conflict Resolution*, London: Polity Press, 1999.

Midlarsky, Manus I., ed., *The Internationalization of Communal Strife*, London: Routledge, 1992.

Miles, William and Gabriel Sheffer, "Francophonie and Zionism: A Comparative Study in Transnationalism and Trans-Statism", *Diaspora*, 1998, 7(2).

Ministerio de Relaciones Exteriores de la República de Colombia (MREC), "Los colombianos en el exterior", ⟨http://portal.minrelext.gov.co/portal/webdriver.exe?MIval=cnu_colombianos_exterior.html⟩ (accessed 24 October 2006).

Mitchell, Christopher, "Una comparación de los esfuerzos de los grupos de migrantes del hemisferio occidental para influenciar la política estadounidense hacia sus países de origen", in Juan Gabriel Tokatlian, ed., *Colombia y Estados Unidos: problemas y perspectivas*, Bogotá: Tercer Mundo S.A., 1998.

Molyneux, Maxine, "The Politics of the Cuban Diaspora in the United States", in V. Bulmer-Thomas and J. Dunkerley, eds, *The United States and Latin*

America: The New Agenda, London and Cambridge, MA: Institute of Latin American Studies & David Rockefeller Center for Latin American Studies, 1999, pp. 287–310.

Moolakkattu, John Stephen, "Peace Facilitation by Small States: Norway in Sri Lanka", Cooperation and Conflict: Journal of the Nordic International Studies Association, 2005, 40(4).

Morris, Benny, Righteous Victims: A History of the Zionist–Arab Conflict 1881–2001, New York: Vintage, 2001.

Morse, Ted, "How Do We Change the Way We Use Foreign Assistance to Help Prevent Deadly Conflicts?", paper presented at a USAID conference on The Role of Foreign Assistance in Conflict Prevention, January 2001.

Munir, Isbir, Al-Lid fi 'Ahdai al-Intitab wa al-Ihtilal [Lydda between Mandate and Occupation], Beirut: Institute of Palestine Studies, 2003.

Natali, Denise, Manufacturing Identity and Managing Kurds in Iraq, Turkey, and Iran, Syracuse: Syracuse University Press, 2005.

Natali, Denise, The Kurds and the State: Evolving National Identity in Iraq, Turkey, and Iran, Syracuse: Syracuse University Press, 2005.

National Drug Intelligence Center, National Drug Threat Assessment 2003: Money Laundering, January 2003, at ⟨http://www.usdoj.gov/ndic/pubs3/3300/money.htm⟩ (accessed 25 October 2006).

National Drug Intelligence Center, National Drug Threat Assessment 2006, Drug Money Laundering, January 2006, at ⟨http://www.usdoj.gov/ndic/pubs11/18862/money.htm⟩ (accessed 25 October 2006).

NAVEND, Rechtliche Situation und Integrationsperspektiven von Kurdischen MigrantInnen, Bonn: NAVEND, 2002.

Nesiah, Devanesan, "The Claim to Self-Determination: A Sri Lankan Tamil Perspective", South Asia, 2001, 10(1): 55–71.

O'Connor, Anthony, Poverty in Africa, London: Berghahn, 1992.

O'Neill Richard, Amy, International Trafficking in Women to the United States: A Contemporary Manifestation of Slavery and Organized Crime, DCI Exceptional Intelligence Analyst Program, Washington, DC: Center for the Study of Intelligence, November 1999.

Oren, Michael, Six Days of War: June 1967 and the Making of the Modern Middle East, Oxford: Oxford University Press, 2002.

Ostergaard-Nielsen, Eva, Transnational Politics: Turks and Kurds in Germany, London: Routledge, 2003.

Palestinian Center for Policy Survey and Research (PSR), "Results of PSR Refugees' Polls in the West Bank/Gaza Strip, Jordan and Lebanon on Refugees' Preferences and Behavior in a Palestinian-Israeli Permanent Refugee Agreement", Ramallah, 2003.

Pankhurst, Donna, "The 'Sex' War and Other Wars: Towards a Feminist Approach to Peace Building", in Haleh Afshar and Deborah Eade, eds, Development, Women, and War: Feminist Perspectives, Oxford: Oxfam, 2004.

Peretz, Don, Palestinians, Refugees, and the Middle East Peace Process, Washington, DC: United States Institute of Peace, 1993.

Perez, L. A., Jr, "Fear and Loathing of Fidel Castro: Sources of US Policy towards Cuba", Journal of Latin American Studies, 2002, 34: 228–229.

Pérez-Brennan, Tanya, "Colombian Immigration", *ReVista*, Spring 2003, at ⟨http://drclas.fas.harvard.edu/revista/?issue_id=14&article_id=265⟩ (accessed 25 October 2006).

Perez-Lopez, V., "The Cuban External Sector in the 1990s", in V. Bulmer-Thomas and J. Dunkerley, eds, *The United States and Latin America: The New Agenda*, London and Cambridge, MA: Institute of Latin American Studies & David Rockefeller Center for Latin American Studies, 1999, pp. 267–286.

Porath, Yehoshua, *The Emergence of the Palestinian Arab National Movement*, London: Frank Cass, 1974.

Portes, Alejandro, Luis E. Guarnizo and Patricia Landolt, "The Study of Transnationalism: Pitfalls and Promise of an Emergent Research Field", *Ethnic and Racial Studies*, 1999, 22(2).

Povrzanović Frykman, Maja, "Homeland Lost and Gained: Croatian Diaspora and Refugees in Sweden", in Nadje Al-Ali and Khalid Koser, eds, *New Approaches to Migration?: Transnational Communities and the Transformation of Home*, London: Routledge, 2002, pp. 118–137.

Prpić, Jure, *Hrvati u Americi*, Zagreb: Hrvatska matica iseljenika, 1997.

Quandt, William, *Peace Process: American Diplomacy and the Arab–Israeli Conflict since 1967*, Washington, DC: Brookings Institution Press, 2002.

Rabinovich, Itamar, *The War for Lebanon 1970–1983*, Ithaca, NY: Cornell University Press, 1984.

Radford, J. L. and M. Hester, "Introduction", in M. Hester et al., eds, *Women, Violence and Male Power*, Milton Keynes: Open University Press, 1996, p. 3.

Ramet, Sabrina P., *Balkan Babel: The Disintegration of Yugoslavia from the Death of Tito to the Fall of Milošević*, 4th edn, Cambridge, MA: Westview Press, 2002.

Referendum Commission of Eritrea, *Report on the Eritrean Referendum*, Asmara: Ministry of Information, 1993.

Resistance for the Liberation of Cambodia, "How to Combat the Pestilence and the Cholera", internal communiqué, n.d., Hann So Collection, University of California, Berkeley (archival files).

Rigby, Andrew, *Justice and Reconciliation: After the Violence*, Boulder, CO: Lynne Rienner, 2001.

Rigoni, Isabelle, "Les mobilisations des Kurdes en Europe", *Revue Européene des Migrations Internationals*, 1998, 14(3): 203–223.

Roberts, Michael, "Tamil Tiger 'Martyrs': Regenerating Divine Potency?", *Studies in Conflict and Terrorism*, 2005, 28(6): 493–514.

Robinson, Greg, *By Order of the President: FDR and the Internment of Japanese Americans*, Cambridge, MA: Harvard University Press, 2001.

Robinson, L., "Towards a Realistic Cuba Policy", *Survival*, 2000, 42: 117.

Rogan, Eugene L. and Avi Shlaim, *The War for Palestine: Rewriting the History of 1948*, Cambridge: Cambridge University Press, 2001.

Rojas, Catalina, with Sanam Naraghi Anderlini and Caille Pampell Conaway, *In the Midst of War: Women's Contributions to Peace in Colombia*, Women Waging Peace, Policy Commission, Washington, DC: Hunt Alternatives Fund, 2004, ⟨http://www.huntalternatives.org/download/16_in_the_midst_of_

war_women_s_contributions_to_peace_in_colombia.pdf⟩ (accessed 26 October 2006).

Rose, Norman, "The Debate on Partition", *Middle Eastern Studies*, 1970/1971 (6 and 7).

Rosenthal, Steven, *Irreconcilable Differences? The Waning of the American Jewish Love Affair with Israel*, Hanover and London: Brandeis University Press, 2003.

Ross, Dennis, *The Missing Peace: The Inside Story of the Fight for Middle Eastern Peace*, New York: Farrar Straus Giroux, 2004.

Rupesinghe, Kumar, *Civil Wars, Civil Peace*, London: Pluto Press, 1998.

Sachar, Howard Morley, *A History of Israel. From the Rise of Zionism to Our Time*, Tel Aviv: Steimatzky, 1976.

Sachar, Howard Morley, *A History of the Jews in America*, New York: Vintage, 1992.

Sachar, Howard Morley, *A History of the Jews in the Modern World*, New York: Knopf, 2005.

Safran, Nadav, *Israel the Embattled Ally*, Cambridge, MA: Harvard University Press, 1981.

Safran, William, "Diasporas in Modern Societies: Myths of Homeland and Return", *Diaspora*, 1991, 1(1): 83–99.

Safran, William, "Comparing Diasporas: A Review Essay", *Diaspora*, 1999, 8(3): 255–292.

Safran, William, "The Jewish Diaspora in a Comparative and Theoretical Perspective", *Israel Studies*, 2005, 10(1).

Saideman, Stephen, "Explaining the International Relations of Secessionist Conflicts", *International Organization*, 1997, 51(4).

Sambandan, V. S., "From Guns to Roses", *Frontline*, 9–22 November 2002, 19(9), available at ⟨http://www.frontlineonnet.com/fl1923/stories/20021122000113000.htm⟩.

Sandoval, Oscar, "Vinculación de Nacionales en el Exterior: Una Prioridad de la Conferencia Sudamericana sobre Migraciones", in Ministerio de Relaciones Exteriores de Colombia (MREC), *Colombia Nos Une: Memorias: Seminario sobre Migración Internacional Colombiana y la Conformación de Comunidades Transnacionales, Junio 18 y 19 de 2003*, Bogotá, Colombia, March 2004.

Saney, I., *Cuba: A Revolution in Motion*, London: Fernwood Publishing, 2004.

Sassen, Saskia, *Losing Control: Sovereignty in an Age of Globalisation*, New York: Columbia University Press, 1997.

Sassen-Koob, Saskia, "Formal and Informal Associations: Dominicans and Colombians in New York", *International Migration Review*, 1979, Special Issue: International Migration in Latin America, 13(2): 314–332.

Schierup, Carl-Ulrik, *Immigration, Socialism and the International Division of Labour: The Yugoslav Experience*, Avebury: Aldershot, 1990, pp. 76–79.

Seikaly, May, *Haifa: Transformations of an Arab Society 1918–1939*, London: I. B. Tauris, 2002.

Šeparović, Zvonimir, *Od Sydneya do San Franciska*, Čakovec: Zrinski, 1982.

Shain, Yossi, *The Frontier of Loyalty*, Connecticut: Wesleyan University Press, 1989.

Shain, Yossi, "Marketing the American Creed Abroad: Diasporas in the Age of

Multiculturalism", *Diaspora: A Journal of Transnational Studies*, 1994, 4(1): 85–111.

Shain, Yossi, *Marketing the American Creed Abroad: Diasporas in the U.S. and Their Homelands*, Cambridge: Cambridge University Press, 1999.

Shain, Yossi, "American Jews and the Construction of Israel's Jewish Identity", *Diaspora: A Journal of Transnational Studies*, 2000, 9(2): 163–202.

Shain, Yossi, "The Role of Diasporas in Conflict Perpetuation or Resolution", *SAIS Review*, 2002, 22(2): 115–143.

Shain, Yossi and Martin Sherman, "Dynamics of Disintegration: Diasporas, Succession, and the Politics of Nation States", *Nations and Nationalism*, 1998, 4(3).

Sheffer, Gabriel, ed., *Modern Diasporas in International Politics*, New York: St Martin's, 1986 and 2002.

Sheffer, Gabriel, "Ethnic Diasporas: A Threat to Their Hosts?", in Myron Weiner, ed., *International Migration and Security*, Boulder, CO: Westview Press, 1993.

Sheffer, Gabriel, "Ethno-National Diasporas and Security", *Survival*, 1994, 36(1).

Sheffer, Gabriel, "A Nation and Its Diaspora: A Re-Examination of Israeli–Jewish Diaspora Relations", *Diaspora*, 2002, 11(3).

Sheffer, Gabriel, "The Study of Ethnic Conflict Resolution", *Migration*, 2003, no. 42.

Sheffer, Gabriel, *Diaspora Politics: At Home Abroad*, Cambridge and New York: Cambridge University Press, 2003.

Sheffer, Gabriel, "Diasporas, Terrorism and WMD", *International Studies Review*, 2005, 7.

Sheffer, Gabriel, "Is the Jewish Diaspora Unique? Reflections on the Diaspora's Current Situation", *Israel Studies*, Special Issue, 2005, 10(1).

Sheikhmous, Omar, "The Kurds in Exile", Yearbook of the Kurdish Academy, Ratingen, 1990.

Shiff, Zeev and Ehud Yaari, *Israel's Lebanon War*, New York: Simon & Schuster, 1984.

Shipler, David, *Arab and Jew: Wounded Spirits in a Promised Land*, New York: Penguin Books, 2002.

Shlaim, Avi, *The Iron Wall, Israel and the Arab World*, London: Penguin Books, 2000.

Silber, Laura and Allan Little, *The Death of Yugoslavia*, New York: Penguin, 1995.

Singh, Depinder, *IPKF in Sri Lanka*, 3rd printing, New Delhi: Trishul Publications, 2001.

Singh, Gurharpal, "A Victim Diaspora? The Case of the Sikhs", *Diaspora*, 1999, 8(3): 204.

Skrbiš, Zlatko, *Long-Distance Nationalism: Diasporas, Homelands and Identities*, Aldershot: Ashgate Publishing, 1999.

Southeast Asia Resource Action Center, *Southeast Asian Admissions FY 1952–2001*, available at ⟨http://www.searac.org⟩.

Southerland, Dan, "The Struggle for Cambodia", *Christian Science Monitor*, 28 November 1979.

Sri Lanka Department of Census and Statistics, 2001 Provisional Census Data,

"Table D – Percentage Distribution of Ethnicity by Districts, 1981–2001", available at ⟨http://www.statistics.gov.lk/census2001/population/text_tabd.htm⟩.

Styan, David, "Eritrea 1993: The End of the Beginning", in Tim Allen, ed., *In Search of Cool Ground*, London: James Currey, 1993.

Takaki, Ron, *Strangers from a Different Shore*, Boston: Little, Brown, 1998.

Tambiah, Stanley J., "Transnational Movements, Diaspora, and Multiple Modernities", *Daedalus*, 2000, 129(1).

Tanner, Marcus, *Croatia: A Nation Forged in War*, New Haven, CT: Yale University Press, 1997.

Tarrow, Sidney, *Power in Movement: Social Movements, Collective Action and Politics*, Cambridge: Cambridge University Press, 1994.

Tate, Winifred, "Counting the Dead: Human Rights Claims and Counter-Claims in Colombia", PhD dissertation, Department of Anthropology, New York University, January 2005.

Tatla, Darshan Singh, *The Sikh Diaspora*, Seattle: University of Washington Press, 1999.

Tessler, Mark, *A History of the Israeli–Palestinian Conflict*, Bloomington: Indiana University Press, 1994.

The Economist, "The War the World Is Missing", 7 October 2000.

The Economist, "A World of Exiles", 2 January 2003.

The Jewish People Policy Planning Institute, *The Jewish People 2004, Between Thriving and Decline*, Jerusalem, 2005.

Thompson, V. B., *The Making of the African Diaspora in the Americas, 1441–1900*, London: Longman, 1998.

Tkalčević, Mato, *Hrvati u Australiji*, Zagreb: Nakladni zavod Matice hrvatske, 1992.

Tokatlian, Juan Gabriel, ed., *Colombia y Estados Unidos: Problemas y perspectivas*, Bogotá: Tercer Mundo S.A., 1998.

Tölölyan, Khachig, "Martyrdom as Legitimacy: Terrorism as Symbolic Appropriation in the Armenian Diaspora", in Paul Wilkinson and Alasdair Stewart, eds, *Contemporary Research on Terrorism*, Aberdeen: Aberdeen University Press, 1987, pp. 89–103.

Tölölyan, Khachig, "Cultural Narrative and the Motivation of the Terrorist", *Journal of Strategic Studies*, 1987, 10(4): 217–233.

Tölölyan, Khachig, "Exile Government in the Armenian Polity", in Yossi Shain, ed., *Governments-in-Exile in Contemporary World Politics*, New York: Routledge, 1991, pp. 166–187.

Tölölyan, Khachig, "Rethinking Diasporas: Stateless Power in the Transnational Moment", *Diaspora: A Journal of Transnational Studies*, 1996, 5(1): 3–36.

Tölölyan, Khachig, "Elites and Institutions in the Armenian Transnation", *Diaspora: A Journal of Transnational Studies*, 2000, 9(1): 107–136.

Tolstoy, Nikolai, *Victims of Yalta*, London: Corgi Books, 1986.

Totoricaguena, Gloria, "Basques around the World: Generic Immigrants or Diaspora?", *Euskonews & Media*, 2000, Issue 72.

Tudjman, Franjo, *Bespuća povjestne zbiljnosti*, Zagreb: Nakladni zavod Matice Hrvatske, 1989.

Turki, Fawaz, *The Disinherited: Journal of Palestinian Exile*, New York: Monthly Review Press, 1972.

Um, Khatharya, "The Curved Road to Settlement: Cambodia 1988", *Asian Survey*, 1989.

Um, Khatharya, "Thailand and the Regional Divide: Future Regional Power Configurations in Asia-Pacific", *Contemporary Southeast Asia*, 1990.

Um, Khatharya, "Cambodia 1989: Still Talking but No Settlement", *Asian Survey*, 1990.

Um, Khatharya, "Cambodia in 1993: Year Zero Plus One", *Asian Survey*, 1994.

United Nations High Commissioner for Refugees, *Background Paper on Sri Lanka for the European Union High Level Working Group on Asylum and Migration*, 18 March 1999.

United Nations Office on Drugs and Crime and Government of Colombia, *Colombia: Coca Cultivation Survey*, June 2004, ⟨http://www.unodc.org/pdf/colombia/colombia_coca_survey_2003.pdf⟩ (accessed 25 October 2006).

United States Agency for International Development (USAID), "USAID Lends Lifeline to Many Afro-Colombians Caught in the Country's Violent Crossfire", 31 March 2005, ⟨http://www.usaid.gov/locations/latin_america_caribbean/country/colombia/afrocolombians.html⟩ (accessed 13 October 2006).

United States Institute of Peace, *Simulation on Sri Lanka: Setting the Agenda for Peace*, A United States Institute of Peace educational exercise, 2001, available at ⟨http://www.usip.org/class/simulations/srilanka.pdf⟩.

Urofsky, Melvin, *We Are One*, New York: Anchor, 1978.

US Department of State, *International Narcotics Control Strategy Report-2005*, Bureau for International Narcotics and Law Enforcement Affairs, March 2005; available at ⟨http://www.state.gov/p/inl/rls/nrcrpt/2005/vol1/html/42363.htm⟩ (accessed 25 October 2006).

US Department of the Treasury, Financial Crimes Enforcement Network News Release, "Treasury Acts Against Flow of Dirty Money to Colombia", 23 December 1996, at ⟨http://www.fincen.gov/gtortr.html⟩ (accessed 25 October 2006).

US Senate, *Foreign Operations, Export Financing, and Related Programs Appropriation Bill, 2001*, Report 106-291.

Valdes, F., "Diaspora and Deadlock, Miami and Havana: Coming to Terms with Dreams and Dogmas", *Florida Law Review*, 2004, 55(1): 284–317.

Veillette, Connie, "Colombia: Issues for Congress", *CRS Report for Congress*, updated 19 January 2005, ⟨http://fpc.state.gov/documents/organization/44015.pdf⟩ (accessed 26 October 2006).

Vertovec, Steven, "Three Meanings of Diaspora", *Diaspora*, 1997, 6(3).

Vertovec, Steven, "Transnationalism and Identity", *Journal of Ethnic and Migration Studies*, 2001, 27(4): 573–582.

Wahlbeck, Osten, *Kurdish Diasporas*, Basingstoke: Palgrave, 1999.

Walker, Edward, "No Peace, No War in the Caucasus: Secessionist Conflicts in Chechnya, Abkhazia and Nagorno-Karabakh", Occasional Papers of the Strengthening Democratic Institutions Project, Harvard Center for Science and International Affairs, Cambridge, MA, 1998.

Wallensteen, Peter, *Understanding Conflict Resolution*, London: Sage Publications, 2002.

Wayland, Sarah, "Ethnonationalist Networks and Transnational Opportunities: The Sri Lankan Tamil Diaspora", *Review of International Studies*, 2004, 30: 405–426.

Weiner, Myron, ed., *International Migration and Security*, Boulder, CO: Westview, 1993.

Whall, Helena, "Assessing the Sri Lanka Peace Process", paper for the Political Studies Association – UK 50th Conference, London, 10–13 April 2000.

Whall, Helena, "Ethnonationalism and Receding Cultural Mobilization in Sri Lanka", working paper presented at the 16th European Conference on Modern Southern Asian Studies, Edinburgh, 6–9 September 2000.

Williams, Phil, "Transnational Criminal Enterprises, Conflict, and Instability", in Chester A. Crocker, Fen Osler Hampson and Pamela Aall, eds, *Turbulent Peace: The Challenges of Managing International Conflict*, Washington, DC: United States Institute of Peace Press, 2001.

Winland, Daphne N., "'We Are Now an Actual Nation': The Impact of National Independence on the Croatian Diaspora in Canada", *Diaspora*, 1995, 4(1): 3–29.

Women Waging Peace, *Preparing for Peace: The Critical Role of Women in Colombia. Conference Report, May 9–14, 2004*, Washington, DC: Hunt Alternatives Fund, ⟨http://www.huntalternatives.org/download/17_preparing_for_peace_the_critical_rose_of_women_in_colombia.pdf⟩ (accessed 26 October 2006).

Women's Commission for Refugee Women and Children at ⟨http://www.womenscommission.org⟩ (accessed 26 September 2006).

Woodward, Susan L., *Socialist Unemployment: The Political Economy of Yugoslavia 1945–1990*, Princeton, NJ: Princeton University Press, 1995.

World Bank, *Breaking the Conflict Trap: Civil War and Development Policy*, Washington, DC: Oxford University Press, 2003.

Yallop, Richard and Abraham Rabinovich, "Gutnick's West Bank Gamble", *The Australian*, 18 February 1997.

Yuval-Davis, Nira, *Gender and Nation*, London: Sage Publications, 1997.

Yuval-Davis, Nira and Floya Anthias, eds, *Woman, Nation, State*, London: Sage Publications, 1989.

Zartman, I. William, *Ripe for Resolution: Conflict and Intervention in Africa*, New York: Oxford University Press, 1996.

Zureik, Elia, *Palestinian Refugees: A Negotiations Primer*, Beirut: Institute of Palestine Studies, 1996.

Index

Note: *Italicized* page numbers indicate figures and tables.